Villa Borghese
Corso d'Itali
Via del
Via
compagni
Piazza
Augusto
Imperatore
P. Cavour
Via della Scrofa
Corso
Via Stamper
Viadel Tritone
Via XX Settembre
Via Ag. Depretis
V. Quirinale
Piazza
Rotonda
V. Seminario
Via Nazionale
Via Panisperna
Via Plebiscito
Via d. Botteghe Oscure
Via dei Fori Imperiali
Via Giovanni
Piazza
Venezia
Via Arrenula
Teatro Marcello
V. Consalazione
Lung. d. Ceci
Via S. Gregorio
Via Claudia
Via del Cerchi
Lung. Ripa
Aventino

D0591653

# ITALIAN at a Glance

## Phrase Book & Dictionary for Travelers

Fifth Edition

**BY MARIO COSTANTINO, M.A.**
Boston University
Università degli Studi di Roma, Italy

**Editorial Consultants**

GIOVANNA M. PIDOTO–REIZIS, M.A.
New York University
Istituto Magistrale, Taormina, Italy

HEYWOOD WALD, Ph.D.
New York University
Università per Stranieri, Perugia, Italy

BARRON'S

To Daniel Lawrence Costantino, the hope and joy of my life.

3162121096688

Ann Arbor
District Library
aadl.org

ANN ARBOR DISTRICT LIBRARY
31621210906688

**PREFACE** ix

**QUICK PRONUNCIATION GUIDE** 1

**THE BASICS FOR GETTING BY** 3
General Information 3
Most Frequently Used Expressions 6
Exclamations, Colloquialisms 11
Problems, Problems, Problems (Emergencies) 12
Numbers 16

**WHEN YOU ARRIVE** 20
Passport and Customs 20
Foreign Embassies 24
Baggage and Porters 23

**BANKING AND MONEY MATTERS** 26
Exchanging Money 28
Business Banking Terms 30

**AT THE HOTEL** 32
Getting to Your Hotel 38
Checking In 39
Travelers with Special Needs 44
Ordering Breakfast 47
Hotel Services 48
Checking Out 52
Tipping 52

**GETTING AROUND TOWN** 54
The Subway (Underground) 55
The Bus (Streetcar, Tram) 59
Taxis 61
Sightseeing and Tours 64
A Sightseeing Itinerary 67
Religious Services 71

**PLANNING A TRIP** **73**
Air Service Within Italy 73
Train Service 75
Shipboard Travel 82
Italy by Bus 84

**DRIVING A CAR** **85**
Traveling by Car 86
Car Rentals 87
Parking 90
On the Road 91
At the Service Station 92
Accidents and Repairs 96

**ENTERTAINMENTS AND DIVERSIONS** **103**
Movies, Theater, Concerts, Opera, Ballet 103
Nightclubs, Dancing 107
Sports and Leisure Activities 109
Spectator Sports 110
Active Sports 114
At the Beach/Pool 116
On the Slopes 118
On the Links 123
Camping 123
In the Countryside 125

**FOOD AND DRINK** **127**
Eating Out 130
Regional Italian Specialties 150
Selecting Italian Wines 160

**MEETING PEOPLE** **164**
Small Talk 164
Dating and Socializing 167
Saying Good-bye 169

**SHOPPING** **170**
Typical Arts and Crafts 170
Flea Markets 172
Going Shopping 173
Books 176
Clothing 177

Electrical Appliances 186
Foods and Household Items 187
Jewelry 190
Audiovisual Equipment 192
Photographic Equipment 194
Newspapers and Magazines 195
Souvenirs, Handicrafts 196
Stationery Items 197
Tobacco 198
Toiletries 199

**PERSONAL CARE AND SERVICES 202**
At the Barber 202
At the Beauty Parlor 204
Laundry and Dry Cleaning 207
Shoe Repairs 208
Camera Repairs 209

**MEDICAL CARE 210**
The Pharmacy (Chemist) 210
With the Doctor 214
At the Dentist 223
With the Optician 225
Pharmaceuticals—Minidictionary 227

**COMMUNICATIONS 230**
Post Office 230
Telephones 232
Faxes 240
Photocopies 241
Computers 242
Computer Terms—Minidictionary 244
Business Services 246

**GENERAL INFORMATION 250**
Telling Time 250
Days of the Week 253
Months of the Year 254
The Four Seasons 255
The Weather 256
National Holidays 258
Local Holidays 258

Important Signs 259
Common Abbreviations 260
Centimeters/Inches 261
Meters/Feet 262
When You Weigh Yourself 262
Liquid Measurements 263
Minidictionary for Business Travelers 263

**QUICK GRAMMAR GUIDE 268**
Nouns 268
Articles 269
Adjectives 271
Pronouns 274
Verbs 276
Prepositions 282
To Form Negative Expressions 282
To Form Questions 283

**ENGLISH-ITALIAN DICTIONARY 284**

**ITALIAN-ENGLISH DICTIONARY 315**

**INDEX 335**

**MAPS 339**

# PREFACE

So you're taking a trip to one of the many fascinating countries of the world. That's exciting! This phrase book, part of Barron's popular *At a Glance* series, will prove an invaluable companion.

In these books we present the phrases and words that a traveler most often needs for a brief visit to a foreign country, where the customs and language are often different. Each phrase book highlights the terms particular to that country, in situations that the tourist is most likely to encounter. This revision includes dialogues using words and expressions for each situation. Travel tips found throughout the book have been updated. With a specially developed key to pronunciation, this book will enable you to communicate quickly and confidently in colloquial terms. It is intended not only for beginners with no knowledge of the language, but also for those who have already studied it and have some familiarity with it.

Some of the unique features and highlights of the Barron's series are:

- Easy-to-follow *pronunciation keys* and complete phonetic transcriptions for all words and phrases in the book.
- Compact *dictionary* of commonly used words and phrases—built right into this phrase book so there's no need to carry a separate dictionary.
- Useful phrases for the *tourist*, grouped together by subject matter in a logical way so that the appropriate phrase is easy to locate when you need it.
- Special phrases for the *business traveler*, including banking terms, trade and contract negotiations, and secretarial services.
- Thorough section on *food and drink*, with comprehensive food terms you will find on menus.
- *Emergency phrases* and terms you hope you won't need: legal complications, medical problems, theft or loss of valuables, replacement or repair of watches, cameras, etc.
- *Sightseeing itineraries*, shopping tips, practical travel tips, and regional food specialties to help you get off the

beaten path and into the countryside, to the small towns and cities, and to the neighboring areas.

- A *reference section* providing: important signs, conversion tables, holidays, abbreviations, telling time, days of the week and months of the year.
- A brief *grammar section*, with the basic elements of the language quickly explained.

Enjoy your vacation and travel with confidence. You have a friend by your side.

# QUICK PRONUNCIATION GUIDE

Although all the phrases in this book are presented with an easy-to-use key to pronunciation, you will find speaking Italian quite a bit easier if you learn a few simple rules. Many vowels and consonants in Italian are pronounced as they would be in English. There are some exceptions, however, which are given below. Since these sounds don't usually vary, you can follow these guidelines in pronouncing all Italian words. Note: When pronouncing the words in the following examples, stress the vowels that appear in CAPITAL letters.

| Italian Letter(s) | Sound in English | Example |
|---|---|---|
| | **Vowels** | |
| **a** | ah (yacht) | **casa** (*kAH-sah*), house |
| **è** | eh (net) | **lèggere** (*lEH-jeh-reh*), to read |
| **e** | ay (hay) | **mela** (*mAY-lah*), apple |
| **i** | ee (feet) | **libri** (*lEE-bree*), books |
| **o** | oh (rope) | **boccone** (*boh-kOH-neh*), mouthful |
| **u** | oo (cool) | **tutto** (*tOOt-toh*), everything |
| | **Consonant Sounds** | |
| **ci** | chee (cheese) | **cinema** (*chEE-nay-mah*), movies |
| **ce** | chay (chair) | **piacere** (*pee-ah-chAY-reh*), pleasure |
| **ca** | kah (cot) | **casa** (*kAH-sah*), house |
| **co** | koh (cold) | **cotto** (*kOHt-toh*), cooked |
| **che** | kay (kent) | **perché** (*pehr-kAY*), because |
| **chi** | key (key) | **pochi** (*pOH-key*), few |
| **gi** | jee (jeep) | **giro** (*jEE-roh*), turn |

| Italian Letter(s) | Sound in English | Example |
|---|---|---|
| **ge** | jay (general) | **generale** (*jay-nay-rAH-leh*), general |
| **gh** | gh (spaghetti) | **spaghetti** (*spah-ghAYt-tee*) |
| **gli** | ll (million) | **egli** (*AY-ly-ee*), he<br>**bottiglia** (*boht-tEE-ly-ee-ah*), bottle |
| **gn** | ny (canyon) | **magnifico** (*mah-ny-EE-fee-koh*), magnificent |
| **qu** | koo (quiet) | **àquila** (*AH-koo-ee-lah*), eagle |
| **sce**<br>**sci** | sh (fish) | **pescc** (*pAY-sheh*), fish<br>**sciòpero** (*shee-OH-peh-roh*), strike |
| **z or zz** | ts (eats) | **pizza** (*pEE-tsah*), pizza<br>**zero** (*tsEH-roh*), zero |

**Travel Tips** There are many theories and much research on how to survive jet lag—the adjustment to a long trip into a different time zone. Some multinational corporations take jet lag so seriously they do not allow employees to make business decisions on the first day abroad. Most experts agree on several techniques: avoid alcohol but drink plenty of other fluids while flying to avoid dehydration; take frequent strolls around the plane to keep your blood circulating; if possible, get some rest on the flight; ear plugs, an eye mask, and an inflatable neck collar make sleep easier; if you arrive early in the morning, take an after-lunch nap, get up for some exercise and dinner, then go to bed at the regular new time; if you arrive at your destination in the afternoon or later, skip the nap and let yourself sleep late the next morning; in countries where massage or saunas are standard hotel service, indulge yourself on the evening of your arrival to help you sleep soundly that night.

# THE BASICS FOR GETTING BY

## GENERAL INFORMATION

### ITALY

**Population:** 61,020,000.

**Population Density:** 512 per sq. mile.

**Capital:** Rome (2,760,000 inhabitants).

**Ethnic Groups:** Italy includes clusters of German, French, and Slovene-Italians in the north, and Albanian-Italians and Greek-Italians in the south.

**Language:** Italian. French, German, Slovene, and Ladino are also spoken by minorities.

**Religions:** 90% Roman Catholic, 10% other including Protestant, Jewish, and Muslim communities.

**Climate:** Temperate.

**Winter:** Mild/warm in Sicily and on the Neapolitan and Ligurian coasts. Cold in the Alps, cold and foggy in the Po Valley and Central Apennines. Ideal for skiing in mountain areas.

**Summer:** Hot and dry. The coasts are mitigated by sea breezes. The Alps and Apennines are pleasantly cool. Ideal for camping, excursions, and hiking. Beaches and lake resorts are packed with tourists.

**Spring and Fall:** Temperatures are mild. It is an optimal time to visit the cities rich in artistic treasures.

**Currency:** The **euro** is now the official currency of Italy and of eleven other European Union members. Tourists have to declare any amount exceeding 10,000 euros imported into the country. A similar amount can be exported out of the country.

**Customs:** The following items are allowed duty free:

- 200 cigarettes or 100 cigarillos or 50 cigars or 250 grams of loose tobacco.
- 1 liter of alcohol over 22% or 2 liters of alcohol under 22%, 2 liters of wine, 500 grams of coffee, and 50 cc of perfume.
- Non-EU citizens are allowed to bring in reasonable amounts of jewelry, 2 cameras, 1 video camera, 1 radio, 1 television, 1 bicycle, 1 boat (with or without motor), 2 pairs of skis, 2 tennis rackets, 1 canoe, and 1 surfboard.

**Documents:** A visa is *not* required for citizens of the U.S. or Canada, Australia, and New Zealand holding valid passports. A **permesso di soggiorno** (*pehr-mAYs-soh dee soh-jee-Ohr-noh*) or permit to stay is required for stays after 90 days. You must go to the **Questura** (*koo-ehs-tOO rah*), the Main Police Station, to apply for either a **permesso di lavoro** (*payr-mAYs-soh dee lah-vOH-roh*), a permit to work, or a **permesso di studio** (*payr-mAYs-soh dee stOO-dee-oh*), a permit to study.

Vaccination certificates are *not* required to enter Italy or to reenter the United States.

Minors who do not have a personal identity document and are traveling with parents must be included in the passport of one of the parents.

Pets are allowed to enter Italy only if they are in good health and vaccinated against rabies. The pet should be identified with a microchip that meets ISO standards 11784/11785. If the pet does not have the ISO microchip insertion, the pet must be revaccinated after insertion, and the owners must provide their own scanners. See *www.pettravel.com/immigration/Italy.cfm*

**Electric Appliances:** The voltage is 220 volts and the cycle is 50. Tourists should carry a transformer. Usually, Italian plugs have two round-pronged plugs. An adapter is a must.

**Gasoline:** Fuel prices per liter are very high. The use of **la benzina verde** (*lah behn-tzEE-nah vAYr-deh*), the green fuel that contains less lead, is recommended for the protection of the environment. On the motorways, service stations are open 24 hours a day. Carrying fuel in gas containers is strictly prohibited.

**Hotels:** There are more than 38,000 hotels in Italy. Rates include air-conditioning, heating, service, and taxes. The current value-added tax (IVA) is 10%. In cities, towns, and resort centers, November to March, hotels offer low rates. At ski resorts, during April, May, and September through November, hotel rates are lower. Accommodations are also available in private homes, youth hostels, day hotels, and rural cottages and farmhouses (agriturism).

Motels along the roads are modern and comfortable. They offer parking facilities and delicious food. Gardens, small parks, swimming pools, private beaches, and tennis courts are also provided in many motels. **AGIP** is the main motel chain on **L'Autostrada del Sole** (*lah-oo-toh-strAH-dah dAYl sOH-leh*), the Italian superhighway network.

**Medical Insurance:** U.S. citizens traveling in Italy are not covered by Italian medical programs and should either buy insurance before visiting the country or check with their insurance provider/company for proper coverage before departing. Check *italy.angloinfo.com/healthcare/health-system/*

**Papal Audiences:** In Vatican City, Wednesday at 10:30 A.M. is usually the time for the general audiences with His Holiness either inside St. Peter's Basilica itself or in the Hall of the Papal Audiences, **Aula Paolo VI**, with a seating of 7,000.

In summer, they take place either in Saint Peter's Square or at Castel Gandolfo, the papal summer residence. Check *http://www.romanhomes.com/your_roman_vacation/papal_audiences.htm* or *www.santasusanna.org/popeVatican/tickets.html*

**Traffic Regulations:**

- Valid drivers licenses and other traffic documents from other countries are recognized in Italy.
- An International Drivers License issued by AAA is recommended for visitors from the U.S. and Canada.
- A green card or an equivalent international insurance certificate is required for citizens from non-EU countries.
- Seat belts front and rear are obligatory.
- Children under four must travel in the back and use a restraint system. Children between four and 12 can travel in the front but must use a restraint system.

- Obey the traffic laws to avoid getting tickets. In many cities, municipal police have been cracking down on unruly drivers.
- Speed limits

| | Motorways | Dual Carriageway | Open Road | Town |
|---|---|---|---|---|
| | 130 km/h | 110 km/h | 90 km/h | 50 km/h |
| When wet | 110 km/h | 90 km/h | 80 km/h | 50 km/h |

- Alcohol: 0.5 mg/ml

## MOST FREQUENTLY USED EXPRESSIONS

The following are expressions you'll use over and over—the fundamentals of polite conversation, the way to express what you want or need, and some simple question tags that you can use to construct all sorts of questions. We suggest you become very familiar with these phrases.

| | | |
|---|---|---|
| Yes | **Sì** | *see* |
| No | **No** | *noh* |
| Maybe | **Forse** | *fOHr-seh* |
| Please | **Per piacere** | *pehr pee-ah-chAY-reh* |
| Thank you (very much) | **(Mille) grazie** | *(mEEl-leh) grAH-tsee-eh* |
| You're welcome | **Prego** | *prEh-goh* |
| Excuse me | **Mi scusi** | *mee skOO-see* |
| I'm sorry | **Mi dispiace** | *mee dee-spee-AH-cheh* |
| Just a second | **Un momento** | *oon moh-mEHn-toh* |
| That's all right, okay | **Va bene** | *vah bEH-neh* |
| It doesn't matter | **Non importa** | *nohn eem-pOHr-tah* |

| | | |
|---|---|---|
| *Good morning (afternoon) | **Buon giorno** | *boo-Ohn jee-Ohr-noh* |
| *Good evening (night) | **Buona sera (notte)** | *boo-Oh-nah sAY-rah (nOHt-teh)* |
| Sir | **Signore** | *see-ny-OH-reh* |
| Madame | **Signora** | *see-ny-OH-rah* |
| Miss | **Signorina** | *see-ny-oh-rEE-nah* |
| Good-bye | **Arrivederci** | *ahr-ree-veh-dAYr-chee* |
| *See you later (so long) | **A più tardi (ciao)** | *ah pee-OO tAHr-dee (chee-AH-oh)* |
| See you tomorrow | **A domani** | *ah doh-mAH-nee* |

*NOTE: Generally, **buon giorno** is used throughout the day until about 4–6 P.M. The expression **buon pomeriggio** ("good afternoon") is generally not used in conversation but might be heard on the radio. **Buona sera** is used when meeting people in the late afternoon and throughout the evening. **Buona notte** is used when leaving at the end of the evening. The casual expression **ciao** ("Hello," "Bye," "So long") is used only with friends and family.

## COMMUNICATING

| | | |
|---|---|---|
| Do you speak English? | **Parla inglese?** | *pAHr-lah een-glAY-seh* |
| I don't speak Italian. | **Io non parlo italiano.** | *EE-oh nohn pAHr-loh ee-tah-lee-AH-noh* |
| Is there anyone here who speaks English? | **C'è qualcuno qui che parli inglese?** | *chEH koo-ahl-kOO-noh koo-EE kay pAHr-lee een-glAY-seh* |
| Do you understand? | **Capisce? (ha capito?)** | *kah-pEE-sheh (ah kah-pEE-toh)* |
| I understand. | **Capisco (ho capito).** | *kah-pEE-skoh (oh kah-pEE-toh)* |

| | |
|---|---|
| I don't understand. | **Non capisco (non ho capito).** *nohn kah-pEE-skoh (nohn oh kah-pEE-toh)* |
| What does that mean? | **Che cosa significa (quello)?** *kay kOH-sah see-ny-EE-fee-kah (koo-Ayl-loh)* |
| What? What did you say? | **Che? Che cosa ha detto?** *kAY kay KOH-sah ah dAYt-toh* |
| What do you call this (that) in Italian? | **Come si chiama questo (quello) in italiano?** *kOH-meh see key-AH-mah koo-AYs-toh (koo-Ayl-loh) een ee-tah-lee-AH-noh* |
| Please speak slowly. | **Per piacere parli lentamente.** *pehr pee-ah-chAY-reh pAHr-lee lehn-tah-mEHn-teh* |
| Please repeat that. | **Lo ripeta per favore.** *loh ree-pEH-tah pehr fah-vOH-reh* |
| What's your name? | **Lei, scusi, come si chiama?** *lEH-ee skOO-see kOH-meh see key-AH-mah* |
| My name is _____. | **Mi chiamo _____.** *mee kee-AH-moh* |
| How are you? | **Come sta?** *kOH-meh stAH* |
| How's everything? | **Come va?** *kOH-meh vAH* |
| Very well, thanks. And you? | **Molto bene, grazie. E lei?** *mOHl-toh bEH-neh grAH-tsee-eh Ay lEH-ee* |

## LOCATIONS

| | |
|---|---|
| Where is _____? | **Dove si trova _____?** *dOH-veh see trOH-vah* |
| ■ the bathroom | **un gabinetto (una toilette)** *oon gah-bee-nAYt-toh (OO-nah too-ah-lEHt)* |

- the dining room (restaurant) — **un ristorante** *oon rees-toh-rAHn-teh*
- the entrance — **l'ingresso** *leen-grEHs-soh*
- the exit — **l'uscita** *loo-shEE-tah*
- the telephone — **un telefono** *oon teh-lEH-phoh-noh*

I'm lost. — **Non so dove mi trovo.** *nohn sOH dOH-veh mee trOH-voh*

Where are _____? — **Dove sono _____?** *dOH-veh sOH-noh*

I am looking for _____. — **Sto cercando _____.** *stOH chehr-kAHn-doh*

Which way do I go? — **In che direzione devo andare?** *een-kAY dee-reh-tsee-OH-neh dAY-voh ahn-dAH-reh*

- to the left — **a sinistra** *ah see-nEE-strah*
- to the right — **a destra** *ah dEH-strah*
- straight ahead — **sempre diritto** *sehm-preh dee-rEEt-toh*

| | |
|---|---|
| around the corner | **all'angolo (della via)** *ahl-lAHn-goh-loh (dAYl-lah vEE-ah)* |
| the first street on the right | **la prima strada a destra** *lah prEE-mah strAH-dah ah dEH-strah* |
| after (before) the second traffic light | **dopo il (prima del) secondo semaforo** *dOH-poh eel (prEE-mah dAYl) say-kOHn-doh say-mAH-foh-roh* |

## SHOPPING

| | |
|---|---|
| How much is it? | **Quanto costa?** *koo-AHn-toh kOH-stah* |
| I'd like _____. | **Vorrei _____.** *vohr-rEH-ee* |
| Please bring me _____. | **Per piacere mi porti _____.** *pehr pee-ah-chAY-reh mee pOHr-tee* |
| Please show me (please let me see) ____. | **Per piacere mi mostri (per piacere mi fa vedere) _____.** *pehr pee-ah-chAY-reh mee mOH-stree (mee fah veh-dEH-reh)* |
| Here it is. | **Eccolo(a).** *EH-koh-loh(lah)* |

## MISCELLANEOUS

| | |
|---|---|
| I'm hungry. | **Ho fame.** *oh fAH-meh* |
| I'm thirsty. | **Vorrei bere (ho sete).** *vohr-rEH-ee bAY-reh (oh sAY-teh)* |
| I'm tired. | **Mi sento stanco(a).** *mee sEHn-toh stAHn-koh(ah)* |
| What's that? | **Che cos'è quello(a)?** *kay ko-sEH koo-AYl-loh (lah)* |
| What's up? | **(Che) cosa succede?** *(kay) kOH-sah soo-chEH-deh* |

## QUESTIONS

| | |
|---|---|
| Where is _____? | **Dov'è _____?** *doh-vEH* |
| When? | **Quando?** *koo-AHn-doh* |
| How? | **Come?** *kOH-meh* |
| How much? | **Quanto?** *koo-AHn-toh* |
| Who? | **Chi?** *key* |
| Why? | **Perchè?** *pehr-kAY* |
| Which? | **Quale?** *koo-AH-leh* |

## EXCLAMATIONS, COLLOQUIALISMS

| | |
|---|---|
| How beautiful! | **Che bellezza! (Che bello!)** *kay behl-lEH-tsah (kay bEHl-loh)* |
| That's awful! | **Non va! Non si fa così!** *nohn vAH nohn see fAH koh-sEE* |
| Great! Wonderful! | **Magnifico! Splendido!** *mah-ny-EE-fee-koh splEHn-dee-doh* |
| That's it! | **Proprio così!** *prOH-pree-oh ko-sEE* |
| Bottoms up! Cheers! | **(Alla) salute! Cin-cin!** *(Ahl-lah) sah-lOO-teh cheen-chEEn* |
| Quiet! | **Silenzio!** *see-lEHn-tsee-oh* |
| Stop it! | **Piàntala!** *pee-AHn-tah-lah* |
| That's enough! | **Basta!** *bAH-stah* |
| Never mind! | **Non importa!** *nohn eem-pOHr-tah* |
| Of course! | **Naturalmente!** *nah-too-rahl-mEHn-teh* |

| | |
|---|---|
| With pleasure! | **Con piacere!** *kohn pee-ah-chAY-reh* |
| Let's go! | **Andiamo!** *ahn-dee-AH-moh* |
| What a shame (pity)! | **Peccato!** *pehk-kAH-toh* |
| What a nuisance! (showing annoyance) | **Che seccatura!** *kay sayk-ah-tOO-rah* |
| Nonsense! No way! | **Ma che! Impossibile!** *mah kay eem-pohs-sEE-bee-leh* |
| Get out of the way! | **Cambia aria!** *kAHm-bee-ah AH-ree-ah* |
| Good luck. | **Buona fortuna. (In bocca al lupo!)** *boo-OH-nah fohr-tOO-nah (een bOHk-ah ahl lOO-poh)* |
| God bless you! | |
| ■ (sneeze) | **Salute!** *sah-lOO-teh* |
| ■ (congratulations) | **Dio ti (vi) benedica!** *dEE-oh tee(vee) beh-neh-dEE-cah* |

## PROBLEMS, PROBLEMS, PROBLEMS (EMERGENCIES)

| | |
|---|---|
| Watch out! Be careful! | **Attenzione! Stia attento(a)!** *ah-tehn-tsee-OH-neh stEE-ah aht-tEHn-toh(ah)* |
| Hurry up! | **Si sbrighi!** *see sbrEE-ghee* |
| Look! | **Guardi!** *goo-AHr-dee* |
| Wait! | **Aspetti un momento!** *ah-spEHt-tee oon moh-mEHn-toh* |
| Fire! | **Al fuoco!** *Ahl foo-OH-koh* |

## ANNOYANCES

| | |
|---|---|
| What's the matter with you? | **Ma che cosa ha?** *mah kay kOH-sah ah* |
| Stop bothering me! | **Non mi stia a seccare!** *nohn mee stEE-ah ah sayk-kAH-reh* |
| Go away! | **Se ne vada!** *say nay vAH-dah* |
| Leave me alone! | **Mi lasci in pace!** *mee lAH-shee een pAH-cheh* |
| I'm going to call a cop! | **Adesso chiamo un poliziotto!** *ah-dEHs-soh key-AH-moh oon poh-lee-tsee-OHt-toh* |
| Help, police! | **Aiuto, polizia!** *ah-ee-OO-toh poh-lee-tsEE-ah* |
| That (one) is a thief! | **Quello è un ladro!** *koo-AYl-loh EH oon lAH-droh* |
| He has snatched my bag! | **Mi ha scippato la borsa!** *mee ah sheep-pAH-toh lah bOHr-sah* |

| | |
|---|---|
| He has stolen _____. | **Mi ha rubato _____.** *mee ah roo-bAH-toh* |

| | |
|---|---|
| I have lost _____. | **Ho perduto _____.** *oh pehr-dOO-toh* |
| ■ my passport | **il (mio) passaporto** *eel (mEE-oh) pahs-sah-pOHr-toh* |
| ■ my purse | **la (mia) borsa** *lah (mEE-ah) bOHr-sah* |
| ■ my suitcase | **la (mia) valigia** *lah (mEE-ah) vah-lEE-jee-ah* |
| ■ my wallet | **il (mio) portafoglio** *eel (mEE-oh) pohr-tah-fOH-ly-ee-oh* |
| This young man is annoying me. | **Questo giovanotto mi sta disturbando.** *koo-AYs-toh jee-oh-vah-nOHt-toh mee stah dee-stoor-bAHn-doh* |
| He keeps following me. | **Sta continuando a seguirmi.** *stah kohn-tee-noo-AHn-doh ah say-goo-EEr-mee* |
| Stop that boy! | **Fermate quel ragazzo!** *fayr-mAH-teh koo-AYl ra-gAH-tsoh* |

## TROUBLE

| | |
|---|---|
| I haven't done anything. | **Non ho fatto niente.** *nohn oh fAHt-toh nee-AYn-teh* |
| It's not true. | **Non è vero.** *nohn EH vEH-roh* |
| I'm innocent. | **Sono innocente.** *sOH-noh een-noh-chEHn-teh* |
| I want a lawyer. | **Voglio un avvocato.** *vOH-ly-ee-oh oon ahv-voh-kAH-toh* |
| I want to go _____. | **Voglio andare ___.** *vOH-ly-ee-oh ahn-dAH-reh* |

| | |
|---|---|
| to the American (British) (Australian) (Canadian) Consulate. | **al Consolato Americano (Inglese) (Australiano) (Canadese).** *ahl kohn-soh-lAH-toh ah-meh-ree-kAH-noh (een-glAY-seh) (ah-oo-strah-lee-ah-noh) (kah-nah-dAY-seh)* |
| *to the police station. | **all'ufficio di polizia (al Commissariato)** *ahl-loof-fEE-chee-oh dee poh-lee-tsEE-ah (ahl kohm-mees-sah-ree-AH-toh)* |

*NOTE: In small towns and villages without a local police force, ask to go to **la caserma dei carabinieri**.

| | |
|---|---|
| I need help, quick! | **Ho bisogno d'aiuto, subito!** *oh bee-sOH-ny-oh dah-ee-OO-toh sOO-bee-toh* |
| Can you help me, please? | **Può aiutarmi, per favore?** *poo-OH ah-ee-oo-tAHr-mee pehr fah-vOH-reh* |
| Does anyone here speak English? | **Qui c'è qualcuno che parli inglese?** *koo-EE chEH koo-ahl-kOO-noh kay pAHr-lee een-glAY-seh* |
| I need an interpreter. | **Ho bisogno di un interprete.** *oh bee-sOH-ny-oh dee oon een-TEHR-preh-teh* |

# NUMBERS

## CARDINAL NUMBERS

| | |
|---|---|
| 0 | **zero** *tsEH-roh* |
| 1 | **uno** *OO-noh* |
| 2 | **due** *dOO-eh* |
| 3 | **tre** *trEH* |
| 4 | **quattro** *koo-AHt-troh* |
| 5 | **cinque** *chEEn-koo-eh* |
| 6 | **sei** *sEH-ee* |
| 7 | **sette** *sEHt-teh* |
| 8 | **otto** *OHt-toh* |
| 9 | **nove** *nOH-veh* |
| 10 | **dieci** *dee-EH-chee* |
| 11 | **undici** *OOn-dee-chee* |
| 12 | **dodici** *dOH-dee-chee* |
| 13 | **tredici** *trEH-dee-chee* |
| 14 | **quattordici** *koo-aht-tOHr-dee-chee* |
| 15 | **quindici** *koo-EEn-dee-chee* |
| 16 | **sedici** *sAY-dee-chee* |
| 17 | **diciassette** *dee-chee-ahs-sEHt-teh* |
| 18 | **diciotto** *dee-chee-OHt-toh* |
| 19 | **diciannove** *dee-chee-ahn-nOH-veh* |
| 20 | **venti** *vAYn-tee* |
| 21 | **ventuno** *vayn-tOO-noh* |
| 22 | **ventidue** *vayn-tee-dOO-eh* |
| 23 | **ventitrè** *vayn-tee-trEH* |
| 24 | **ventiquattro** *vayn-tee-koo-AHt-troh* |
| 25 | **venticinque** *vayn-tee-chEEn-koo-eh* |

| | |
|---|---|
| 26 | **ventisei** *vayn-tee-sEH-ee* |
| 27 | **ventisette** *vayn-tee-sEHt-teh* |
| 28 | **ventotto** *vayn-tOHt-toh* |
| 29 | **ventinove** *vayn-tee-nOH-veh* |
| 30 | **trenta** *trEHn-tah* |
| 40 | **quaranta** *koo-ah-rAHn-tah* |
| 50 | **cinquanta** *cheen-koo-AHn-tah* |
| 60 | **sessanta** *sehs-sAHn-tah* |
| 70 | **settanta** *seht-tAHn-tah* |
| 80 | **ottanta** *oht-tAHn-tah* |
| 90 | **novanta** *noh-vAHn-tah* |
| 100 | **cento** *chEHn-toh* |
| 101 | **centouno** *chEHn-toh OO-noh* |
| 102 | **centodue** *chEHn-toh dOO-eh* |
| 200 | **duecento** *doo-eh-chEHn-toh* |
| 300 | **trecento** *treh-chEHn-toh* |
| 400 | **quattrocento** *koo-aht-troh-chEHn-toh* |
| 500 | **cinquecento** *cheen-koo-eh-chEHn-toh* |
| 600 | **seicento** *seh-ee-chEHn-toh* |
| 700 | **settecento** *seht-teh-chENn-toh* |
| 800 | **ottocento** *oht-toh-chEHn-toh* |
| 900 | **novecento** *noh-veh-chEHn-toh* |
| 1.000 | **mille** *mEEl-leh* |
| 1.001 | **mille e uno** *mEEl-leh eh OO-noh* |
| 1.100 | **mille e cento** *mEEl-leh eh chEHn-toh* |
| 1.200 | **mille e duecento** *mEEl-leh eh doo-eh-chEHn-toh* |
| 1.350 | **mille trecento cinquanta** *mEE-leh treh-chEHn-toh cheen-koo-AHn-tah* |
| 2.000 | **duemila** *dOO-eh mEE-lah* |
| 5.000 | **cinque mila** *chEEn-koo-eh mEEl-lah* |

| | | |
|---|---|---|
| 10.000 | **dieci mila** | *dee-EH-chee mEEl-lah* |
| 100.000 | **cento mila** | *ch-EHn-toh mEEl-lah* |
| 1.000.000 | **un milione** | *oon mee-lee-OH-neh* |
| 2.000.000 | **due milioni** | *dOO-eh mee-lee-OH-nee* |
| 1991 | **mille novecento novantuno** | *mEEl-leh noh-veh-chEHn-toh noh-vAHn-tOOn-noh* |
| 1992 | **mille novecento novanta due** | *mEEl-leh noh-veh-chEHn-toh noh-vAHn-tah dOO-eh* |
| 2000 | **due mila** | *dOO-eh mEEl-lah* |

## ORDINAL NUMBERS

| | | |
|---|---|---|
| first | **primo** | *prEE-moh* |
| second | **secondo** | *seh-kOHn-doh* |
| third | **terzo** | *tEHr-tsoh* |
| fourth | **quarto** | *koo-AHr-toh* |
| fifth | **quinto** | *koo-EEn-toh* |
| sixth | **sesto** | *sEHs-toh* |
| seventh | **settimo** | *sEHt-tee-moh* |
| eighth | **ottavo** | *oht-tAH-voh* |
| ninth | **nono** | *nOH-noh* |
| tenth | **decimo** | *dEH-chee-moh* |
| the last one | **l'ultimo** | *lOOl-tee-moh* |
| once | **una volta** | *oo-nah vOHl-tah* |
| twice | **due volte** | *dOO-eh vOHl-teh* |
| three times | **tre volte** | *trEH vOHl-teh* |

## QUANTITIES AND FRACTIONS

| | | |
|---|---|---|
| a bag of | **un sacchetto di** | *oon sahk-kAYt-toh dee* |
| a bottle of | **una bottiglia di** | *OO-nah boht-tEE-ly-ee-ah dee* |
| a box (can) of | **una scatola (lattina) di** | *OO-nah skAH-toh-lah (laht-tEE-nah) dee* |
| a dozen of | **una dozzina di** | *OO-nah doh-tsEE-nah dee* |

| | | |
|---|---|---|
| a kilo of | **un chilo di** | *oon kEE-loh dee* |
| a liter of | **un litro di** | *oon lEE-troh dee* |
| a package of | **un pacchetto di** | *oon pahk-kAYt-toh dee* |
| a pair of | **un paio di** | *oon pAH-ee-oh dee* |
| a slice of | **una fetta di** | *OO-nah fAYt-tah dee* |
| a little of | **un po' di** | *oon pOH dee* |
| half a _____. | **mezzo** | *mEH-tsoh* |
| ■ half a kilo | **mezzo chilo** | *mEH-tsoh kEE-loh* |
| a fourth (quarter) | **un quarto** | *oon koo-AHr-toh* |
| a dozen | **una dozzina** | *OO-nah doh-tsEE-nah* |
| ■ a dozen oranges | **una dozzina d'arance** | *OO-nah doh-tsEE-nah dah-rAHn-cheh* |

# WHEN YOU ARRIVE

## PASSPORT AND CUSTOMS

Italian passport control is a very simple process. If the visitor's passport is in order (up to date), questions are hardly ever asked. In the event of difficulties, the following information will be useful.

| | |
|---|---|
| My name is _____. | **Mi chiamo _____.** *mee key-AH-moh* |
| I'm American (British) (Australian) (Canadian). | **Sono americano(a) (inglese) (australiano[a]) (canadese).** *sOH-noh ah-meh-ree kAH-noh(ah) (een-glAY-seh) (ah-oo-strah-lee-AH-noh[ah]) (kah-nah-dAY-seh)* |
| My address is _____. | **Il mio indirizzo è _____.** *eel mEE-oh een-dee-rEE-tsoh EH* |
| I'm staying at _____. | **Starò a _____.** *stah-rOH ah* |
| Here is (are) _____. | **Ecco _____.** *EHk-oh* |
| ■ my documents | **i (miei) documenti** *ee (mee-EH-ee) doh-koo-mEHn-tee* |
| ■ my passport | **il (mio) passaporto** *eel (mEE-oh) pahs-sah-pOHr-toh* |
| ■ my I.D. card | **la (mia) carta d'identità** *lah (mEE-ah) kAHr-tah dee-dehn-tee-tAH* |
| I'm _____. | **Sono _____.** *sOH-noh* |
| ■ on a business trip | **in viaggio d'affari** *een vee-AH-jee-oh dahf-fAH-ree* |
| ■ on vacation | **in vacanza** *een vah-kAHn-tsah* |
| ■ visiting relatives (friends) | **venuto(a) a trovare i parenti (gli amici)** *vay-nOO-toh(ah) ah troh-vAH-reh ee pah-rEHn-tee (ly-ee ah-mEE-chee)* |
| ■ just passing through | **solo di passaggio** *sOH-loh dee pahs-sAH-jee-oh* |

| | |
|---|---|
| I'll be staying here for _____. | **Resterò qui per _____.** *ray-steh-rOH koo-EE pehr* |
| ■ a few days | **alcuni giorni** *ahl-kOO-nee jee-OHr-nee* |
| ■ a week | **una settimana** *OO-nah seht-tee-mAH-nah* |
| ■ a few weeks | **alcune settimane** *ahl-kOO-neh seht-tee-mAH-neh* |
| ■ a month | **un mese** *oon mAY-seh* |
| I'm traveling _____. | **Sto viaggiando _____.** *stOH vee-ah-jee-AHn-doh* |
| ■ alone | **da solo(a)** *dah sOH-loh(ah)* |
| ■ with my husband | **con mio marito** *kohn mEE-oh mah-rEE-toh* |
| ■ with my wife | **con mia moglie** *kohn mEE-ah mOH-ly-ee-eh* |
| ■ with my family | **con la mia famiglia** *kohn lah mEE-ah fah-mEE-ly-ee-ah* |
| ■ with my friend | **con il mio amico (la mia amica)** *kohn eel mEE-oh ah-mEE-koh (lah mEE-ah ah-mEE-kah)* |

Customs (**la dogana**—*lah doh-gAH-nah*) in the major port-of-entry airports in Italy is divided into two sections: one, indicated by a red arrow, is for passengers with goods to declare (**merci da dichiarare**); another, marked with a green arrow, is for those with nothing to declare (**nulla da dichiarare**).

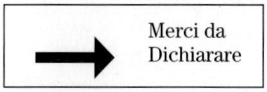


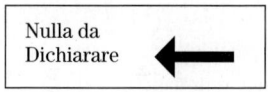


The following can be brought into Italy duty-free: Tobacco products (200 cigarettes or 100 cigarillos or 50 cigars or 250 grams of tobacco), alcohol (1 liter of spirits over 22% of volume or 2 liters of fortified wine or sparkling wine or 2 liters of still wine), perfume (50 cc), eau de toilette (250 ml). Generally, all items for personal use enter the country duty-free.

| | |
|---|---|
| These are my bags. | **Queste sono le mie valigie.** *koo-AYs-teh sOH-noh leh mEE-eh vah-lEE-jee-eh* |
| I have nothing to declare. | **Non ho nulla da dichiarare.** *nohn oh nOOl-lah dah dee-key-ah-rAH-reh* |
| I only have _____. | **Ho solo _____.** *oh sOH-loh* |
| ■ a carton of cigarettes | **una stecca di sigarette** *OO-nah stAYk-kah dee see-gah-rAYt-teh* |
| ■ a bottle of whisky | **una bottiglia di whisky** *OO-nah boht-tEE-ly-ee-ah dee oo-EE-skey* |
| They're gifts. | **Sono regali.** *sOH-noh reh-gAH-lee* |
| They're for my personal use. | **Sono cose di uso personale.** *sOH-noh kOH-seh dee OO-soh pehr-soh-nAH-leh* |
| Do I have to pay duty? | **Devo pagare dogana?** *dAY-voh pah-gAH-reh doh-gAH-nah* |
| May I close the bag now? | **Posso chiudere la valigia adesso?** *pOHs-soh key-OO-deh-reh lah vah-lEE-jee-ah ah-dEHs-soh* |

## IDENTITY CARD

Upon entering the country (or on your flight into the country), you will be required to complete an identity card, usually with the following information.

| | |
|---|---|
| **Cognome:** _____ | Last name: _____ |
| **Nome:** _____ | First name: _____ |
| **Nazionalità:** _____ | Nationality: _____ |
| **Data di nascita:** _____ | Date of birth: _____ |
| **Professione:** _____ | Profession: _____ |
| **Indirizzo:** _____ | Address: _____ |
| **Passaporto da:** _____ | Passport from: _____ |

## FOREIGN EMBASSIES

**United States Embassy in Rome**
- Palazzo Margherita – Via Vittorio Veneto, 119/a, 00187 Roma
- Office Hours: 8:30 A.M. to 5:30 P.M.
- Phone: +39 06 4674-1
  Fax: +39 06 4882-672 or +39 06 4674-221
- Website: *http://rome.usembassy.gov*

**Embassy of Canada in Rome**
- Via Zara 30 – 00198 Rome, Italy
- Office Hours: Monday to Friday: 8:30 to 4:30
- Phone: +39 (06) 85 444 2911 or +39 (06) 85 444 1
  Fax: 39 (06) 85 444 2912
- E-mail: *rome.citizenservices@international.gc.ca*
- Website: *http://www.Italy.gc.ca*

**United Kingdom Embassy in Rome**
- Via XX Settembre, 80/a, 00187 Roma
- Phone: +39 06 42200001
  Fax: +39 6 42202333
- E-mail: *RomePoliticalSection@fco.gov.uk*
- *InfoRome@fco.gov.uk - ConsularRome@fco.gov.uk*
- Website URL: *www.britain.it*

For other embassies (or consulates) in Italy, search *embassy.goabroad.com/embassies-in/italy*

## BAGGAGE AND PORTERS

Porters are scarce at European airports. You may be able to locate one, but you'll find it easier and faster to simply use the baggage carts provided at the baggage claim. You can usually wheel your bags right through customs out to the street.

Where can I find a baggage cart?

**Dove posso trovare un carrello portabagagli?** *dOH-veh pOHs-soh troh-vAH-reh oon kahr-rEHl-loh pohr-tah-bah-gAH-ly-ee*

I need a porter.

**Ho bisogno di un portabagagli.** *oh bee-sOH-ny-oh dee oon pohr-tah-bah-gAH-ly-ee*

Porter!

**Portabagagli! Facchino!** *pohr-tah-bah-gAH-ly-ee fahk-kEE-noh*

These are our (my) bags.

**Queste sono le nostre (mie) valigie.** *koo-AYs-teh sOH-noh leh nOH-streh (mEE-eh) van-lEE-jee-eh*

Put them here (there).

**Le metta qui (lì).** *leh mAYt-tah koo-EE (lEE)*

Be careful with that one!

**Stia attento a quella lì!** *stEE-ah aht-tEHn-toh ah koo-AYl-lah lEE*

I'll carry this one myself.

**Questa la porto io.** *koo-AYs-tah lah pOHr-toh ee-oh*

I'm missing a suitcase.

**Mi manca una valigia.** *mee mAHn-kah OO-nah vah-lEE-jee-ah*

| | |
|---|---|
| How much do I owe you? | **Quanto le devo?** *koo-AHn-toh leh dAY-voh* |
| Thank you (very much). This is for you. | **(Molte) grazie. Questo è per lei.** *(mOHl-teh) grAH-tsee-eh koo-AYs-toh EH pehr lEH-ee* |
| Where can I get a bus (taxi) to the city? | **Dove posso prendere l'autobus (il tassì) per andare in città?** *dOH-veh pOHs-soh prAYn-deh-reh lAH-oo-toh-boos (eel tahs-sEE) pehr ahn-dAH-reh een cheet-tAH* |

*Travel Tips* There was a time when buying an airline ticket was simple. Now travelers must either rely on scarce travel agents who sometimes seem to be overwhelmed by the ever-changing market or do the homework themselves and navigate hundreds of sites offering comparative options. Read the fine print in ads and ask questions when making reservations. Often, discount fare tickets cannot be exchanged for cash or another ticket if travel plans must be changed.

It is a sad fact that airlines become more miserly with each passing year. Unless you are one of the blessed ones who can afford to buy first-class tickets, you should shop around and see which company will feed you for free and not charge you extra for your second suitcase. Also, most airlines nowadays may lose your luggage and do little or nothing about compensation. Keep all your valuables in your hand luggage!

# BANKING AND MONEY MATTERS

Banks in Italy are open five days a week (Monday through Friday) from 8:35 A.M. to 1:35 P.M. and from 3:00 to 4:00 P.M. They are closed all day Saturday and Sunday and on national holidays (see page 258). In some cities banks are open for one hour in the afternoon. Exchange offices in major airports and railroad stations keep longer hours. A passport is required to exchange cash and checks at a bank. Many hotels will exchange money for you but you will get a better exchange at a bank.

Italian money, the **euro**, is issued in the following denominations: notes—5, 10, 20, 50, 100, 200, and 500; coins—1, 2, 5, 10, 20, 50 cent(s), 1 and 2 euros.

The ATMs in Italy are known as **bancomats**. They may be found in the large cities and in small towns. The machines are easy to operate. At the beginning of the transaction they prompt the user for the preferred language.

- Most Italian Bancomats impose a maximum daily withdrawal limit of 250 euros.
- A 4-digit PIN code is needed when making a transaction.
- We suggest using bancomats/ATMs during regular banking hours, from morning until 1 or 1:30 P.M. That way, if the machine malfunctions, a teller from inside the bank can assist you. Italian banks are closed on Saturday and Sunday; therefore, if there are problems with the machine, nobody will be able to help you.
- Watch for all messages written on the screen such as **Fuori servizio**, which means "Out of Service." Do not insert your card in such cases!
- Look into bank credit cards offered to overseas travelers with low to no conversion fees.

Look out!

- Notify your bank and your credit card companies before leaving for Italy.
- It is advisable to bring two working ATM cards with four digit numbers.
- Conceal important documents and cards under shirts or inside pants.

Check *http://goitaly.about.com/od/planningandinformation/qt/ATM-bancomat.htm*

Visa, MasterCard, and American Express cards are widely accepted, as well as Eurocheque cards. Travelers' checks are accepted almost everywhere.

If you lose your travelers' cheques, contact *www.thomascook.com* or *www.americanexpress.com*

If you need money wired to you, contact American Express Moneygram at *www.moneygram.com* or Western Union at *www.westernunion.com* or Thomas Cook at *www.thomascook.com*

## EXCHANGING MONEY

| | |
|---|---|
| Where is the currency exchange (bank)? | **Dov'è l'ufficio cambi (la banca)?** *doh-vEH loof-fEE-chee-oh kAHm-bee (lah bAHn-kah)* |
| I wish to change _____. | **Desidero cambiare _____.** *day-sEE-deh-roh kahm-bee-AH-reh* |
| ■ money | **il denaro** *eel deh-nAH-roh* |
| ■ dollars (pounds) | **i dollari (le sterline)** *ee-dOHl-lah-ree (le stehr-lEE-neh)* |
| ■ travelers' checks | **travelers' checks (assegni da viaggiatori)** *(ahs-sAY-ny dah vee-ah-jee-ah-tOH-ree)* |
| What time do they open (close)? | **A che ora aprono (chiudono)?** *ah kay OH-rah AH-proh-noh (key-OO-doh-noh)* |
| Where is the cashier's window? | **Dov'è lo sportello del cassiere?** *doh-vEH loh spohr-tEHl-loh dayl kahs-see-AY-reh* |

The current exchange rates are posted in banks that exchange money and are also published daily in the city newspapers. Since the rates fluctuate from day to day, it may be useful to convert the following euro amounts into their values in your own currency so that you can readily compare prices and determine values.

| EUROS | YOUR OWN CURRENCY | EUROS | YOUR OWN CURRENCY |
|---|---|---|---|
| 1 | _____ | 50 | _____ |
| 5 | _____ | 100 | _____ |
| 10 | _____ | 200 | _____ |
| 20 | _____ | 500 | _____ |

The euro is worth more than the dollar!

**L'euro vale più di un dollaro!** *lEH-oo-roh vAH-leh pee-OO dee oon dOHl-ah-roh.*

What's the current exchange rate for dollars (pounds)?

**Qual è il cambio corrente del dollaro (della sterlina)?** *koo-ahl EH eel kAHm-bee-oh kohr-rEHn-teh dayl dOHl-lah-roh (dAYl-lah stehr-lEE-nah)*

What commission do you charge?

**Quale percentuale vi fate pagare?** *koo-AH-leh pehr-chehn-too-AH-leh vee fAH-teh pah-gAH-reh*

Where do I sign?

**Dove debbo firmare?** *dOH-veh dAYb-boh feer-mAH-reh*

I'd like the money _____.

**Vorrei i soldi _____.** *vohr-rEH-ee ee sOHl-dee*

- in large (small) bills

**in grosse (piccole) banconote** *een grOHs-seh (pEEk-oh-leh) bahn-koh-nOH-teh*

- in small change

**in spiccioli** *een spee-chee-oh-lee*

Give me two twenty-euro bills.

**Mi dia due biglietti da venti euro.** *mee dEE-ah dOO-eh bee-ly-ee-AYt-tee dah vayn-tee EH-oo-roh*

- a 1-euro coin

**una moneta da un euro** *oo-nah moh-nAY-tah dah Oon EH-oo-roh*

- five hundred euros

**cinquecento euro** *cheen-koo-eh-chEHN-toh EH-oo-roh*

| | |
|---|---|
| one hundred twelve euros | **centododici euro** *chehn-toh-dOH-dee-chee EH-oo-roh* |
| Do you accept credit cards? | **Si accettano carte di credito?** *see ah-chEHt-tah-noh kAHr-teh dee krEH-dee-toh* |

## BUSINESS BANKING TERMS

| | |
|---|---|
| amount | **ammontare** *ahm-mohn-tAH-reh* |
| bad check | **assegno scoperto** *ahs-sAY-ny-oh skoh-pEHr-toh* |
| banker | **banchiere** *bahn-key-EH-reh* |
| bill | **banconota, biglietto di banca** *bahn-koh-nOH-tah bee-ly-AYt-toh dee bAHn-kah* |
| borrow (to) | **prendere a prestito** *prAYn-deh-reh ah prEHs-tee-toh* |

| | |
|---|---|
| cashier | **cassiere** *kahs-see-AY-reh* |
| capital | **capitale** *kah-pee-tAH-leh* |
| cashier's office | **cassa** *kAHs-sah* |
| checkbook | **libretto d'assegni** *lee-brAYt-toh dahs-sEH-ny-ee* |

| | |
|---|---|
| endorse (to) | **firmare** *feer-mAH-reh* |
| income | **reddito, entrata** *rEHd-dee-toh ehn-trAH-tah* |
| interest rate | **tasso d'interesse** *tAHs-soh deen-teh-rEHs-seh* |
| investment | **investimento** *een-vehs-tee-mEHn-toh* |
| lend (to) | **prestare** *preh-stAH-reh* |
| loss | **perdita** *pEHr-dee-tah* |
| make change (to) | **cambiare la moneta (i soldi)** *kahm-bee-AH-reh lah moh-nAY-tah (ee sOHl-dee)* |
| open an account (to) | **aprire un conto in banca** *ah-prEE-reh oon kOHn-toh een bAHn-kah* |
| premium | **l'interesse** *leen-teh-rEHs-seh* |
| safe | **cassaforte** *kahs-sah-fOHr-teh* |
| signature | **firma** *fEEr-mah* |
| window | **sportello** *spohr-tEHl-loh* |

# AT THE HOTEL

If you are unfamiliar with the city to which you are going, you'll probably find it best to make a hotel reservation in advance from home. All major credit cards are honored in Italy. You'll also find that some terminals have reservation desks, at which you may be able to reserve a room. Lastly, if you are unable to locate a hotel once you arrive, go to the tourist information office; someone there will be able to speak English and will help you in locating a suitable hotel. The following is a listing of the major types of hotels you will encounter. By law, the official price of the room must be posted in the room (usually found on the inside of a closet door). The final bill, however, will also include the value-added tax (IVA).

To make a call to Italy from the United States or Canada you start by dialing 011 (from the UK you dial 00). Then you add 39 (for Italy), add 06 (for Rome), followed by the local number. The phone numbers that follow are local numbers, to be dialed if you are *already* in Rome.

## ITALIAN HOTEL ASSOCIATIONS

Federalaberghi, Via Toscana 1, 00187 Roma
Phone: 4203610
Fax: 4203690
E-mail: *info@federalalberghi.it*

Asshotel – Associazione Italiana Imprenditori d'Albergo
Via Nazionale 60, 00184 Roma, Italy
Phone: 47251
Fax: 4746556
E-mail: *asshotel@confesercenti.it*

Federturismo (Federazione Nazionale Industria dei Viaggi e del Turismo)
Via Pasteur 10, 00144 Roma, Italy
Phone: 5911758
Fax: 5910390
E-mail: *federturismo@dada.it*

## YOUTH HOSTELS

AIG, Associazione Italiana Alberghi per la Gioventù (Italian Youth Hostels Association)
Via Cavour 44, 00184 Roma, Italy
Phone: 4871152
Fax: 4880492
*http://en.expopage.net/portal/stand.do?eboothid=17059*

CTS, Centro Turistico Studentesco (Tourist Student Center)
Via Andrea Vesalio 6, 00161 Roma, Italy
Phone: 441111
Fax: 44111400
E-mail: *ctsinfo@cts.it*

For budget travelers, try:
*www.budgethotels.com*
*www.hostels.com*
*www.hostelworld.com*
*www.cheaprooms.com*

CTG, Centro Turistico Giovanile (Youth Tourist Center)
Via della Pigna 13/a, 00186 Roma, Italy
Phone: 6795077
Fax: 6795078
E-mail: *ctg@ctg.it*

## TYPES OF LODGING

**albergo or hotel** Hotels are classified in six categories: 5-Star Deluxe, 5-Star, 4-Star, 3-Star, 2-Star, and 1-Star. The extent of the services and luxuriousness of the furnishings will vary with the class.

**motel** Situated near the autostrada, these are mostly new and getting better all the time.

**locanda** These are lovely, small country inns.

**pensione** Usually pretty casual, most of the time these are small residences similar to boardinghouses, in which you are customarily offered meals as well. **Pensione completa** refers to 3 meals a day, **mezza pensione** to 2 meals. Pensiones are also classed and vary in quality, but almost always are a good value. The term *pensione*, which describes a small hotel, is fading from everyday use in Italy. *Pensione* is now referred to as a 1-Star, 2-Star, or 3-Star hotel.

**albergo diurno** These are daytime hotels; that is, they are open during the day to travelers seeking showers, bathrooms, and other facilities. They do not offer beds, and they usually close at night.

## ALTERNATIVE ACCOMMODATIONS

If you are interested in experiences outside the range of standard hotels, you may wish to consider more or less expensive alternatives. You may check these suggested Internet sites and select the option that best fits your budget. Indicate whether you would like to be reached by e-mail or phone.

*http://www.italialodging.com/*
*http://www.vrbo.com/*

**affittacamere**

Neat and clean rental rooms close to most places. These are great deals for holiday rentals, from a room with a cot to a magnificent private studio. Located in most areas throughout the country, many offer in-house breakfast or, at worst, they are close to a local pizzeria, trattoria, or restaurant. Check *www.hostelbookers.com/hostels/italy/florence/33113/* or *www.tripadvisor.com/Hotel_Review-g187821-d668905-Reviews-*

**agriturismo**

Close to 19,000 farmers have converted their farms into inns. They offer major comfort services, from a simple bed and breakfast to full board. Dancing and live entertainment in some areas. Many include services for the disabled, swimming pools, restaurant facilities, oil and wine tasting, organic products, sport activities, and a pet-friendly atmosphere. Located in hospitable places in the countryside for lovers of nature and history. You may expect delicious food and wine with a family touch. Check *www.agriturismo.it/en/* or *www.agriturismo.com/englisch.htm*

**appartamenti/ condo**

These are comfortable rooms ranging from simple to luxurious. Located in all regions, rural and urban. Always close to a "tavola calda," trattoria, or local restaurant. Check *www.summerinitaly.com/* or *www.authentic-italy.co.uk/*

**cabine, cassette bungalow**

Cabins, cottages, and bungalows offered in clean, private, bucolic bungalow settings and equipped with air-conditioners, kitchenettes, showers, and wireless Internet access. You will find these in places outside the traditional tourist routes, such as hillsides, valleys, and sea shores, usually conveniently located near points of interest. You may cook your own food or eat at local eateries. Check *www.rvlinks.com/RV_Parks_Campgrounds-Italy-html* or *www.info.com/Bungalowsitaly*

**camping**

There are over 1,700 official camping sites in operation. You may get free location maps from the Federazione Italiana del Campeggio e del Caravanning, Federcampeggio at *www.worldtourismdirectory.com/adresse-19102-infos.htm* or check *www.reidsitalyy.com/planning/lodging/camping.html* or *www.camping.it/english/cartina.aspx*

**hotel a 4 zampe**

These are hotels that accept animals. After the successful opening of **spiagge per cani** (beaches for dogs), many hotels are accepting pets in their rooms, upon request, and some go as far as offering menus a la carte for dogs. Check *http://blog.hrs.it/leggi/europa/hotel-per-cani-italia/* or *www.booking.com/Italy/Emilia-Romagna/MisanoAdriatico*

**hotel per bambini e famiglia**

Such a hotel offers the best for families with children. The **Italy Family Hotel** logo is at the hotel entrance. Commodities include changing tables, baby baths, baby bottle warmers, cradles and cots with railings. There are dining rooms and restaurant facilities, medical and pediatric assistance, and baby-sitting services upon request. Inquire about customized family services. Located in all regions, they usually offer flexible meal times and have children's menus prepared by a chef according to parental guidelines. Obtain information from Italy Family Hotels, Via Macanno, 38 Q – 47900 Rimini (RN), Italy (*info@italyfamilyhotels.it*) or *http://www.italyfamilyhotels.it/en/baby-servizi/servizi-bambini.html*

**letto e colazione** These universally known bed and breakfast hostels provide a family atmosphere and offer local traditional dishes, wine and oil, and family breakfasts. Located everywhere, from the countryside to small villages and cities. Check *www.italialodging.com/*

**monasteri** Monasteries possess a serene atmosphere and unique beauty, and these are family-friendly, clean, and safe. Respect for monks, quiet, punctuality for meals, and curfew adherence are a must. Rooms come with narrow beds. Located in ideal city and regional surroundings, they guarantee peaceful environments as well as fresh and organic food. Check *www.go-to-italy.com* or *www.monasterystays.com/*

**rifugi** Mountain rentals of rooms with fabulous views and cozy blankets. You will find them in coastal areas, breathtaking mountainsides, and other enchanting landscapes. All meals include local and traditional dishes. Check *www.reidsitaly.com/planning/lodging/mountain_huts.html* or *www.cai.it/*

**ville**

If you can afford them, villas are the wonders of any Italian stay, providing a delightful mix of culture, folklore, art, and nature. You get an entire house with total privacy. Villas are located in every region of Italy, built in the most beautiful places of lively cities, beautiful countrysides, rolling hills, islands, lakes, and beaches. Meals represent genuine local cuisine and home cooking at its best. Check *www.villeinitalia.com* or *www.italianview.com/*

## GETTING TO YOUR HOTEL

I'd like to go to the _____ Hotel.

**Vorrei andare all'Hotel (all'Albergo) _____.** *vohr-rEH-ee ahn-dAH-reh ahl-loh-tEHl (ahl-lahl-bEHr-goh)*

Is it near (far)?

**È vicino (lontano)?** *EH vee-chEE-noh (lohn-tAH-noh)*

Where can I get a taxi?

**Dove posso prendere un taxi?** *dOH-veh pOHs-soh prAYn-deh-reh oon tahs-sEE*

What buses go into town?

**Quali autobus vanno in città?** *koo-AH-lee AH-oo-toh-boos vAHn-noh een cheet-tAH*

Where is the bus stop?

**Dov'è la fermata dell'autobus?** *doh-vEH lah fehr-mAH-tah dayl-lAH-oo-toh-boos*

How much is the fare?

**Quant'è la corsa? (il biglietto?)** *koo-ahn-tEH lah kOHr-sah (eel bee-ly-ee-AYt-toh)*

Can I rent a car? **Posso noleggiare una macchina?** *POHs-soh noh-lay-jee-AH-reh OO-nah mAH-key-nah?*

## CHECKING IN

Most first-class or deluxe hotels will have personnel who speak English. If you are checking into a smaller hotel, you might find these phrases useful in getting what you want. A room for two persons with a double bed is called **una camera matrimoniale** (*oo-nah kAH-meh-rah mah-tree-moh-nee-AH-leh*) and a room with twin beds is **una camera con due letti** (*oo-nah kAH-meh-rah kohn dOO-eh lEHt-tee*).

I'd like a single (double) room for tonight. **Vorrei una camera singola (doppia) per stanotte.** *vohr-rEH-ee OO-nah kAH-meh-rah sEEn-goh-lah (dOHp-pee-ah) pehr stah-nOHt-teh*

How much is the room _____? **Quant'è la camera _____?** *koo-ahn-tEH lah kAH-meh-rah*

- with a balcony **con terrazzino** *kohn tehr-rah-tsEE-noh*
- facing the sea **che dia sul mare** *kay dEE-ah sool mAH-reh*
- facing (away from) the street **che (non) dia sulla strada** *kay (nohn) dEE-ah sOOl-lah strAH-dah*
- facing the courtyard **che dia sul cortile** *kay dEE-ah sOOl kohr-tEE-leh*

Does it have _____? **Ha _____?** *ah*

- air-conditioning **l'aria condizionata** *lAH-ree-ah kohn-dee-tsee-oh-nAH-tah*
- hot water **l'acqua calda** *lAH-koo-ah kAHl-dah*
- television **la televisione** *lah teh-leh-vee-see-OH-neh*

| | |
|---|---|
| Can I get video games? | **Si possono avere videogiochi?**<br>*see pOHs-soh-noh ah-vAY-reh vee-deh-oh-jee-OH-key* |
| Can I rent movies? | **È possibile affittare dei film?**<br>*EH pohs-sEE-bee-leh ahf-feet-tAH-reh dAY-ee fEElm* |
| Do you receive satellite programs? | **Ricevete i programmi via satellite?**<br>*ree-chay-vAY-teh ee proh-grAHm-mee VEE-ah sah-tehl-lee-teh* |
| Do you have cable TV? | **Avete i programmi cable (via cavo)?**<br>*ah-vAY-teh ee proh-grAHm-mee kAH-bleh (vEE-ah kAH-voh)* |
| Do you get CNN? | **Ricevete le trasmissioni CNN?**<br>*ree-chay-vAY-teh leh trahs-mees-see-OH-nee CNN* |
| Are there any programs in English? | **Ci sono programmi in inglese?**<br>*chee sOH-noh proh-grAHm-mee een een-glAY-seh* |

Are there programs that should be blocked from children?

**Ci sono programmi che dovrebbero essere bloccati ai bambini?** *chee sOH-noh proh-grAHm-mee kay doh-vrAYb-beh-roh EHs-seh-reh bloh-kAH-tee ah-ee bahm-bEE-nee*

At what time are the adult programs?

**A che ora ci sono i programmi/spettacoli pornografici?** *ah kay OH-rah chee sOH-noh ee proh-grAHm-mee/speht-tAH-koh-lee pohr-noh-grAH-fee-chee*

On what channels?

**Su quali canali?** *soo koo-AH-lee kah-nAH-lee*

On which channels do you have ____?

**Su quale canale _____?** *Soo koo-AH-leh kah-nAH-leh*

- sports — **c'è lo sport** *chEH loh spOHrt*
- cartoons — **ci sono i cartoni animati** *chee sOH-noh ee kahr-tOH-nee ah-nee-mAH-tee*
- movies — **ci sono i film** *chee sOH-noh ee fEElm*
- soap operas — **c'è soap opera** *chEH sOHp OH-peh-rah*
- the news — **c'è il telegiornale** *chEH eel teh-leh-jee-ohr-nAH-leh*
- the weather — **c'è il meteo/"Che tempo fa"** *chEH eel mEH-teh-oh/"kay tEHm-poh fAH"*

Is voice mail available in the hotel room?

**È possibile ricevere voice mail in camera?** *eh pohs-sEE-bee-leh ree-chAY-veh-reh voice mail een kAH-meh-rah*

Do you have automatic checkout?

**Si può pagare il conto automaticamente e andarsene?** *see poo-OH pah-gAH-reh eel kOHn-toh ah-oo-toh-mah-tee-kah-mEHn-teh ay ahn-dAHr-seh-neh*

| | |
|---|---|
| I (don't) have a reservation. | **(Non) ho prenotazione.** *(nohn) oh preh-noh-tah-tsee-OH-neh* |
| Could you call another hotel to see if they have something? | **Potrebbe telefonare a un altro hotel per vedere se hanno qualcosa?** *poh-trAYb-beh teh-leh-foh-nAH-reh ah oon AHl-troh oh-tEHl pehr vay-dAY-reh say AHn-noh koo-ahl-kOH-sah* |
| May I see the room? | **Potrei vedere la camera?** *poh-trEH-ee veh-dAY-reh lah kAH-meh-rah* |
| I (don't) like it. | **(Non) mi piace.** *(nohn) mee pee-AH-cheh* |
| Do you have something _____? | **Ha qualche cosa _____?** *ah koo-AHl-keh kOH-sah* |
| ■ better | **di meglio** *dee mEH-ly-ee-oh* |
| ■ larger | **più grande** *pee-OO grAHn-deh* |
| ■ smaller | **più piccolo** *pee-OO pEEk-koh-loh* |
| ■ cheaper | **meno costoso** *mAY-noh koh-stOH-soh* |
| ■ quieter | **più quieto (tranquillo)** *pee-OO quee-EH-toh (trahn-hoo-EEl-loh)* |
| What floor is it on? | **A che piano è?** *ah kay pee-AH-noh EH* |
| Is there an elevator (lift)? | **C'è l'ascensore?** *chEH lah-shehn-sOH-reh* |
| How much is the room _____? | **Quanto si paga per una camera _____?** *koo-AHn-toh see pAH-gah pehr OO-nah kAH-meh-rah* |

| | |
|---|---|
| ■ with the American plan (three meals a day) | **con pensione completa** *kohn pehn-see-OH-neh kohm-plEH-tah* |
| ■ with breakfast | **con colazione** *kohn koh-lah-tsee-OH-neh* |
| ■ with no meals | **senza i pasti** *sEHn-tsah ee pAH-stee* |
| Is everything included? | **È tutto compreso?** *EH tOOt-toh kohm-prAY-soh* |
| The room is very nice. I'll take it. | **La camera è molto bella. La prendo.** *lah kAH-meh-rah EH mOHl-toh bEHl-lah lah prAYn-doh* |
| We'll be staying _____. | **Resteremo _____.** *rehs-teh-rAY-moh* |
| ■ one night | **una notte** *OO-nah nOHt-teh* |
| ■ a few nights | **alcune notti** *ahl-kOO-neh nOHt-tee* |
| ■ one week | **una settimana** *OO-nah seht-tee-mAH-nah* |
| How much do you charge for children? | **Quanto fanno pagare per i bambini?** *koo-AHn-toh fAHn-noh pah-gAH-reh pehr ee bahm-bEE-nee* |
| Could you put another bed in the room? | **Si potrebbe avere un altro letto nella camera?** *see poh-trAYb-beh ah-vAY-reh oon AHl-troh lEHt-toh nAYl-lah kAH-meh-rah* |
| Is there a charge? How much? | **C'è da pagare? Quanto?** *chEH dah pah-gAH-reh koo-AHn-toh* |

## TRAVELERS WITH SPECIAL NEEDS

There are strict regulations for travelers regarding special needs in Italy for access to restrooms, ticket counters at airports, hotels, rail stations, and most restaurants. Nonetheless, always call ahead to check for accessibility to places of worship, monuments, gardens, and public offices.

| | |
|---|---|
| Do you have facilities for the disabled? | **Ci sono servizi per disabili?** *chee sOH-noh sayr-vEE-tzee pehr dee-sAH-bee-lee* |
| Is there a special rate for the handicapped? | **Ci sono tariffe speciali per disabili?** *chee sOH-noh tah-rEEf-feh speh-chee-AH-lee pehr dee-sAH-bee-lee* |
| Can you provide _____? | **È possibile avere _____?** *EH pohs-sEE-bee-leh ah-vAY-reh* |
| ■ a wheelchair | **una sedia a rotelle** *OO-nah seh-dee-ah ah roh-tEHl-leh* |
| ■ an assistant | **un assistente** *OOn ahs-see-stEHn-teh* |
| Is there room in the elevator for a wheelchair? | **C'è posto in ascensore per una sedia a rotelle?** *chEH pOHs-toh een ah-shayn-sOH-reh pehr OO-nah seh-dee-ah roh-tEHl-leh* |
| Do you allow seeing-eye dogs? | **È permesso avere un cane da guida?** *EH pehr-mAYs-soh ah-VAY-reh oon KAH-neh dah goo-EE-dah* |
| I have asthma (heart problems). | **Ho l'asma (problemi cardiaci).** *oh lAHs-mah (proh-blEH-mee kahr-dEE-ah-chee)* |
| I'm diabetic. | **Sono diabetico.** *sOH-noh dee-ah-bEH-tee-koh* |

| | |
|---|---|
| I'm allergic to _____. | **Sono allergico _____.** *sOH-noh ahl-lEHr-jee-koh* |
| ■ dairy products | **ai latticini** *AH-ee laht-tee-chEE-nee* |
| ■ meat | **alla carne** *AHl-lah kAHr-neh* |
| ■ mold | **alla muffa** *AHl-lah mOOf-fah* |
| ■ peanuts | **alle noccioline americane** *AHl-leh noh-chee-oh-lEE-neh ah-meh-ree-kAH-neh* |
| ■ shellfish | **ai crostacei** *AH-ee kroh-stAH-cheh-ee* |
| I wanted it without _____. | **Lo volevo senza _____.** *loh voh-lAY-voh sEHn-tsah* |
| ■ alcohol | **alcol** *AHl-cohl* |
| ■ caffeine | **caffeina** *kahf-feh-EE-nah* |
| ■ meat | **carne** *kAHr-neh* |
| ■ sugar | **zucchero** *tsOO-keh-roh* |
| I am a vegetarian. | **Sono vegetariano (a).** *sOH-noh veh-jeh-tah-ree-AH-noh (nah)* |
| Do you have food _____? | **C'è cibo _____?** *chEH chEE-boh* |
| ■ low in calories | **con poche calorie** *kohn pOH-keh kah-loh-rEE-eh* |
| ■ low in cholesterol | **con poco colesterolo** *kohn pOH-koh koh-leh-steh-rOH-loh* |
| ■ low in fat | **con poco grasso** *kohn pOH-koh grAHs-soh* |
| Do you have an artificial sweetener? | **C'è qualche dolcificante artificiale?** *chEH koo-AHl-keh dohl-chee-fee-kAHn-teh ahr-tee-fee-chee-AHl-eh* |

Are there any _____?
**Ci sono _____?** *chee sOH-noh*

- escalators — **scale mobili** *skAH-leh mOH-bee-lee*
- ramps — **rampe** *rAHm-peh*

Are there any _____ we can contact in case of emergency?
**Ci sono _____ che possiamo contattare in caso d'emergenza?** *chee sOH-noh _____ kay pohs-see-AH-moh kohn-taht-tAH-reh een kAH-soh deh-mehr-jEHn-tzah*

- agencies — **agenzie** *ah-jehn-tzEE-eh*
- drugstores — **farmacie** *fahr-mah-chEE-eh*
- emergency rooms — **sale di pronto soccorso** *sAH-leh dee prOHn-toh soh-k-kOHr-soh*

Is there a(n) _____ available?
**C'è _____ disponibile?** *chEH _____ dees-poh-nEE-bee-leh*

- ambulance — **un'ambulanza** *oon-ahm-boo-lAHn-tzah*
- car service — **un servizio noleggio** *oon sayr-vEE-tzee-oh noh-lAY-jee-oh*
- taxi — **un taxi** *oon tahs-sEE*

Is there a doctor in the hotel?
**C'è un dottore nell'hotel?** *chEH oon doht-tOH-reh nayl-loh-tEHl*

How can we contact a doctor in case of emergency?
**Come possiamo contattare un medico in caso d'emergenza?** *KOH-meh pohs-see-AH-moh kohn-taht-tAH-reh oon mEH-dee-koh een kAH-soh deh-mehr-jEHn-tzah*

Do you have a toilet equipped for the handicapped?
**C'è un bagno equipaggiato per le persone disabili?** *chEH oon bAH-ny-oh ay-koo-ee-pah-jee-AH-toh pehr leh pehr-sOH-neh dee-sAH-bee-lee*

| | |
|---|---|
| Is there a kneeling bus available? | **È disponibile un autobus che facilita la salita e la discesa per disabili?** *EH dees-poh-nEE-bee-leh oon ah-oo-toh-bOOs kay fah-chEE-lee-tah lah sah-lEE-tah ay lah dee-shAY-sah pehr dee-sAH-bee-lee* |

## ORDERING BREAKFAST

Larger hotels will offer breakfast. The Italian breakfast is a simple one—coffee and a sweet roll or brioche, sometimes **focaccia**, and jam or marmalade. At hotels that cater to American or British tourists, you will also be able to order an English breakfast (juice, eggs, bacon, and toast). Larger hotels will have a dining room where you can eat breakfast, but the usual procedure is to have breakfast sent up to your room.

| | |
|---|---|
| We'll have breakfast in the room. | **Faremo colazione in camera.** *fah-rAY-moh koh-lah-tsee-OH-neh een kAH-meh-rah* |
| Please send up ____. | **Per favore mandino ____.** *pehr fah-vOH-reh mAHn-dee-noh* |
| ■ one (two) coffee(s) | **un (due) caffè** *oon (dOO-eh) kahf-fEH* |
| ■ tea | **un tè** *oon tEH* |
| ■ hot chocolate | **una cioccolata calda** *OO-nah chee-oh-koh-lAH-tah kAHl-dah* |
| ■ a sweet roll (brioche) | **un berlingozzo (una brioche)** *oon behr-leen-gOH-tsoh (oon-ah brEE-osh)* |
| ■ fruit (juice) | **(un succo di) frutta** *(oon sOO-koh dee) frOOt-tah* |
| ■ a carafe of tap water | **una caraffa di acqua semplice** *OO-nah kah-rAHf-fah dee AH-koo-ah sAYm-plee-che* |

| | |
|---|---|
| We'd both like _____. | **Noi due desideriamo _____.** *nOH-ee dOO-eh deh-see-deh-ree-AH-moh* |
| ■ bacon and eggs | **uova al tegamino con pancetta** *oo-OH-vah ahl teh-gah-mEE-noh kohn pahn-chAYt-tah* |
| ■ scrambled (fried, boiled) eggs | **uova al tegamino strapazzate (fritte, alla coque)** *oo-OH-vah ahl teh-gah-mEE-noh strah-pah-tsAH-teh (frEEt-teh ahl-lah kOHk)* |
| ■ toast | **pan tostato** *pAHn toh-stAH-toh* |
| ■ jam | **marmellata** *mahr-mehl-lAH-tah* |

NOTE: See the food section (pages 127–163) for more phrases dealing with ordering meals.

## HOTEL SERVICES

| | |
|---|---|
| Where is _____? | **Dov'è _____?** *doh-vEH* |
| ■ the dining room | **la sala da pranzo** *lah sAH-lah dah prAHn-tsoh* |
| ■ the bathroom | **il bagno (la toilette)** *eel bAH-ny-oh (lah too-ah lEHt)* |
| ■ the elevator (lift) | **l'ascensore** *lah-shehn-sOH-reh* |
| ■ the phone | **il telefono** *eel teh-lEH-foh-noh* |
| What is my room number? | **Qual è il numero della mia camera?** *koo-ah-lEH eel nOO-meh-roh dAYl-lah mEE-ah kAH-meh-rah* |

| | |
|---|---|
| May I please have my key? | **Può darmi la chiave, per favore?** *poo-OH dAHr-mee lah key-AH-veh pehr fah-vOH-reh* |
| I've lost my key. | **Ho perduto la chiave.** *oh pehr-dOO-toh lah key-AH-veh* |

## GETTING WHAT YOU NEED

| | |
|---|---|
| I need _____. | **Ho bisogno di _____.** *oh bee-sOH-ny-oh dee* |
| ■ a bellhop | **un fattorino** *oon faht-toh-rEE-noh* |
| ■ a chambermaid | **una cameriera** *OO-nah kah-meh-ree-EH-rah* |
| Please send _____ to my room. | **Per piacere mi mandi _____ in camera.** *pehr pee-ah-chAY-reh mee mAHn-dee _____ een kAH-meh-rah* |
| ■ a towel | **un asciugamano** *oon ah-shoo-gah-mAH-noh* |
| ■ a bar of soap | **una saponetta** *OO-nah sah-poh-nAYt-tah* |
| ■ some hangers | **delle grucce (degli attaccapanni)** *dAYl-lay grOO-cheh (dAY-ly-ee aht-AHk-kah-pAHn-nee)* |
| ■ a pillow | **un cuscino** *oon koo-shEE-noh* |
| ■ a blanket | **una coperta** *OO-nah koh-pEHr-tah* |
| ■ some ice cubes | **dei cubetti di ghiaccio** *dAY-ee koo-bAYt-tee dee ghee-AH-chee-oh* |
| ■ a bottle of mineral water | **una bottiglia d'acqua minerale** *OO-nah boht-tEE-ly-ee-ah dAH-koo-ah mee-neh-rAH-leh* |
| ■ toilet paper | **della carta igienica** *dAYl-lah kAHr-tah ee-jee-EH-nee-kah* |

| | |
|---|---|
| ■ a reading lamp | **una lampada per la lettura** *OO-nah lAHm-pah-dah pehr lah leht-tOO-rah* |
| ■ an electric adapter* | **un trasformatore elettrico** *oon trahs-fohr-mah-tOH-reh ay-lEHt-tree-koh* |

*NOTE: If you bring electric appliances with you from the U.S. (electric shaver, for example), you may need to have an adapter so that the voltage corresponds with that in the hotel. Newer hotels have 110-volt systems and an adapter isn't necessary.

## AT THE DOOR

| | |
|---|---|
| Who is (was) it? | **Chi è (era)?** *key-EH (EH-rah)* |
| Just a minute. | **Un momento.** *oon moh-mEHn-toh* |
| Come in. | **Entri (venga).** *AYn-tree (vEHn-gah)* |
| Put it on the table. | **Lo metta sul tavolo.** *loh mAYt-tah sool tAH-voh-loh* |
| Please wake me tomorrow at _____. | **Per favore mi svegli domani alle _____.** *pehr fah-vOH-reh mee svAY-ly-ee doh-mAH-nee AHl-leh* |

## COMPLAINTS

| | |
|---|---|
| There is no _____. | **Manca _____.** *mAHn-kah* |
| ■ running water | **l'acqua corrente** *lAH-koo-ah kohr-rEHn-teh* |
| ■ hot water | **l'acqua calda** *lAH-koo-ah kAHl-dah* |
| ■ electricity | **la luce elettrica** *lah lOO-cheh eh-lEHt-tree-kah* |
| The _____ doesn't work. | **_____ non funziona.** *____ nohn foon-tsee-OH-nah* |
| ■ air-conditioning | **l'aria condizionata** *lAH-ree-ah kohn-dee-tsee-oh-nAH-tah* |

| | |
|---|---|
| ■ fan | **il ventilatore** *eel vehn-tee-lah-tOH-reh* |
| ■ faucet | **il rubinetto** *eel roo-bee-nAYt-toh* |
| ■ light | **la luce** *lah lOO-cheh* |
| ■ radio | **la radio** *lah rAH-dee-oh* |
| ■ electric socket | **la presa della corrente** *lah prAY-sa dehl-lah kohr-rEHn-teh* |
| ■ light switch | **l'interruttore** *leen-tehr-root-tOH-reh* |
| ■ television | **la televisione** *lah teh-leh-vee-see-OH-neh* |
| Can you fix it? | **Può farlo(la) riparare?** *poo-OH fAHr-loh(ah) ree-pah-rAH-reh* |
| The room is dirty. | **La camera è sporca.** *lah kAH-meh-rah EH spOHr-kah* |
| Can you clean it _____? | **Può farla pulire _____?** *poo-OH fAHr-lah poo-lEE-reh* |
| ■ now | **subito** *sOO-bee-toh* |
| ■ as soon as possible | **il più presto possibile** *eel pee-OO prEH-stoh pohs-sEE-bee-leh* |

## AT THE DESK

| | |
|---|---|
| Are there (any) _____ for me? | **Ci sono _____ per me?** *chee sOH-noh _____ payr mAY* |
| ■ letters | **(delle) lettere** *(dAYl-leh) lAYt-teh-reh* |
| ■ messages | **(dei) messaggi** *(dAY-ee) mehs-sAH-jee* |
| ■ packages | **(dei) pacchi** *(dAY-ee) pAH-key* |
| Did anyone call for me? | **Mi ha cercato qualcuno?** *mee-AII chehr-kAH-toh koo-ahl-kOO-noh* |

I'd like to leave this in your safe. **Vorrei lasciare questo nella sua cassaforte.** *vohr-rEH-ee lah-shee-AH-reh koo-AYs-toh nAYl-lah sOO-ah kahs-sah-fOHr-teh*

Will you make this call for me? **Può farmi questa telefonata?** *poo-OH fAHr-mee koo-AYs-tah teh-leh-foh-nAH-tah*

## CHECKING OUT

I'd like the bill, please. **Vorrei il conto per favore.** *vohr-rEH-ee eel kOHn-toh pehr fah-vOH-reh*

I'll be checking out today (tomorrow). **Pagherò e partirò oggi (domani).** *pah-gheh-rOH ay pahr-tee-rOH OH-jee (doh-mAH-nee)*

Please send someone up for our baggage. **Per favore mandi qualcuno a prendere le valigie.** *pehr fah-vOH-reh mAHn-dee koo-ahl-kOO-noh ah prAYn-deh-reh leh vah-lEE-jee-eh*

## TIPPING

Usually tipping depends on the level and quality of service received. More often than not, simply round up the bill by a few euros.

In many instances, a service charge is included in the price of the service rendered. The added-on service charge usually comes to about 15 to 20 percent, most times indicated on the bill. It is customary, however, to leave some small change in addition to the service included on the bill. This usually consists of 40 to 70 cents, or whatever small change you receive from paying the bill.

It is customary, particularly at the large, deluxe hotels, to leave a tip for the maid and to tip the bellhop, desk attendant, and doorman as well. If you take a tour, the guide will expect a tip, as will taxi drivers, theater ushers, and other service personnel. The following is a table of the most appropriate amounts. You are now required by law to obtain an official receipt when eating at restaurants.

Avoid getting a fine, even if paying cash: always remember to get receipts, invoices, or bills. You may be stopped by plainclothes and/or uniformed police officers who may request to see such documents. It is the law!

| SERVICE | TIP |
|---|---|
| Barber, hairdresser | 5 to 10% of the total bill |
| Bathroom attendant | 50 cents to 1 euro |
| Bellhop, porter | 1 euro per bag |
| Cafes and bars | (at a table) 15% if service charge is not included in bill<br>(standing at a counter or bar drinking expresso, cappuccino, etc.) 20 to 30 cents<br>(standing at a counter or bar having alcoholic beverages, cocktails, desserts, pastries, sandwiches, etc.) up to 2 euros |
| Chambermaid | 1 to 2 euros a day |
| Concierge | 10 to 20 euros |
| Doorman (for calling a cab) | 50 to 70 cents |
| Hotel porters | 1 to 5 euros |
| Service station attendant | 50 to 70 cents or more for extra service (cleaning windshield, giving directions) |
| Sightseeing guide and driver | 2 euros minimum per person (for half-day tours)<br>3 euros minimum per person (for full-day tours) |
| Taxi driver | round up the bill and leave change |
| Theater usher | 50 cents (more for opera seats) |
| Waiter | 12–15% included in bill + (optional)<br>5–10% of check for good service |
| Waiter (room service) | 50 cents |

# GETTING AROUND TOWN

In smaller towns, you can walk to most places you want to visit, catching the flavor and color of the area at the same time. In the larger cities, you might want to get around using public transportation—another wonderful way to sample a country's way of life. For information on train or plane travel, see pages 73–82.

| | |
|---|---|
| **AUTOBUS** | City buses running from 6 A.M. to midnight. In larger cities they provide the **servizio notturno** *(sayr-vEE-tzee-oh noht-tOOr-noh)*, night runs. |
| **TRAM** | Trolley cars |
| **FILOBUS** | Trackless trolley (streetcar) |
| **METROPOLITANA** | Subway (underground) |
| **AUTOCORRIERA** | Bus services |
| **AUTOPULLMAN** | Orange is the color for city buses. Blue is the common color for **autopullman** |
| **EUROWAYS** | |
| **EUROPABUS** | |
| **ALISCAFO** | Hydrofoil |
| **NAVE TRAGHETTO** | Ferryboat **Grandi Traghetti**, **Moby Lines**, **Navarma**, **Sardinia Ferries**, and **Tirrenia** are some of the ferries that link Italy with its beautiful islands |
| **VAPORETTO** | Water buses |
| **MOTOSCAFO** | Slim, small, and fast boat |
| **MOTONAVE** | Two-tier boat |
| **GONDOLA** | Typical Venetian luxury form of transportation |

## THE SUBWAY (UNDERGROUND)

Getting around Rome, Milan, Naples, Turin, and Catania is made easier because of their **metropolitana** or **metro**. You'll find maps posted in every station, as well as in every train. The stops are clearly marked, and you should have no problems reaching your destination. On the street, the station entrances have a large **M** posted.

In Rome the **metro** (politana) runs roughly every 8–10 minutes every day from 5:30 A.M. till 11:30 P.M. and on Saturdays from 5:30 A.M. until 12:30 A.M. The Roman metro has only two lines and they cross at the Termini Central Station:

- the red line A
- the blue line B

**Look out!** Tickets must be bought in advance before going through the turnstile from vending machines using exact-change only. They can be purchased at metro and major bus stops or from bars, newsstands, and tabacchi. Tickets must be put through a scanner in order to get into the boarding area. Currently, the tickets may be:

- **biglietto semplice**, a time-integrated ticket valid for 75 minutes on any means of transportation.
- **biglietto giornaliero**, a ticket valid for 24 hours.
- **biglietto per 3 giorni**, a 3-day tourist integrated ticket.
- **biglietto settimanale**, a ticket valid for 7 days.

For details, check *www.rome.info/metro/* or *www.rome.info/transportation/tickets/*

Other Italian cities with subway systems follow:

**Milan:** The Milan Metro serves Milan and other surrounding cities. Most of the transport services run from 6:00 A.M. to 24:00 midnight. The major lines continue until about 02:00 A.M. There are 3 lines and 94 stations. Check *http://www.sea-aeroportimilano.it/en/pdf/mmferr.pdf* or *http://subway.umka.org/map-milan.html*

**Naples:** Italy's third largest city, has an integrated tariff system that allows travel across all forms of public transportation within Naples and the region of Campania. Trains run approximately every 8–10 minutes, from 6:00 A.M. until 23:00 P.M. every day of the year. Tickets are valid for use on metro, all buses, funiculars, and local railways in Naples and adjacent municipalities. This universal system is known as *Uniconapoli*. In addition, there are four funicular cable railways that complement the network. You may check *http://www.unicocampania.it/ita/home.htm* or *http://www.italyguide.com/index2.php?m=menu&htm=metro_napoli*

**Turin:** The MetroTorino is the first driverless, automated metro train line, with a total of 15 stations. It is known as Linea 1. The system is built with links to the city's tramway network. A second metro line is under construction. Check *http://www.railway-technology.com/projects/torino-metro/* or *www.tripadvisor.com/Travel.../turin:Italy:Public.Transportation.ht...*

**Catania:** The metro runs every 15 to 30 minutes. The current subway, Ferrovia Circumetnea, consists of just one line serving six stations. Other extensions are under construction and they will serve the city center, the airport, and the northwestern part of the city. Tickets can be bought from the vending mathines, tabacchi, or newsstands. Timetable: 7:00 A.M. to 20:45 (8:45 P.M.) on weekdays, and no service on Sundays (except on special events).

| | |
|---|---|
| Is there a subway (underground) in this city? | **C'è una metropolitana in questa città?** *chEH OO-nah meh-troh-poh-lee-tAH-nah een koo-AYs-tah cheet-tAH* |
| Do you have a map showing the stops? | **Ha una cartina che indica le fermate della metropolitana?** *ah OO-nah kahr-tEE-nah kay EEn-dee-kah lay fayr-mAH-teh dAYl-lah meh-troh-poh-lee-tAH-nah* |

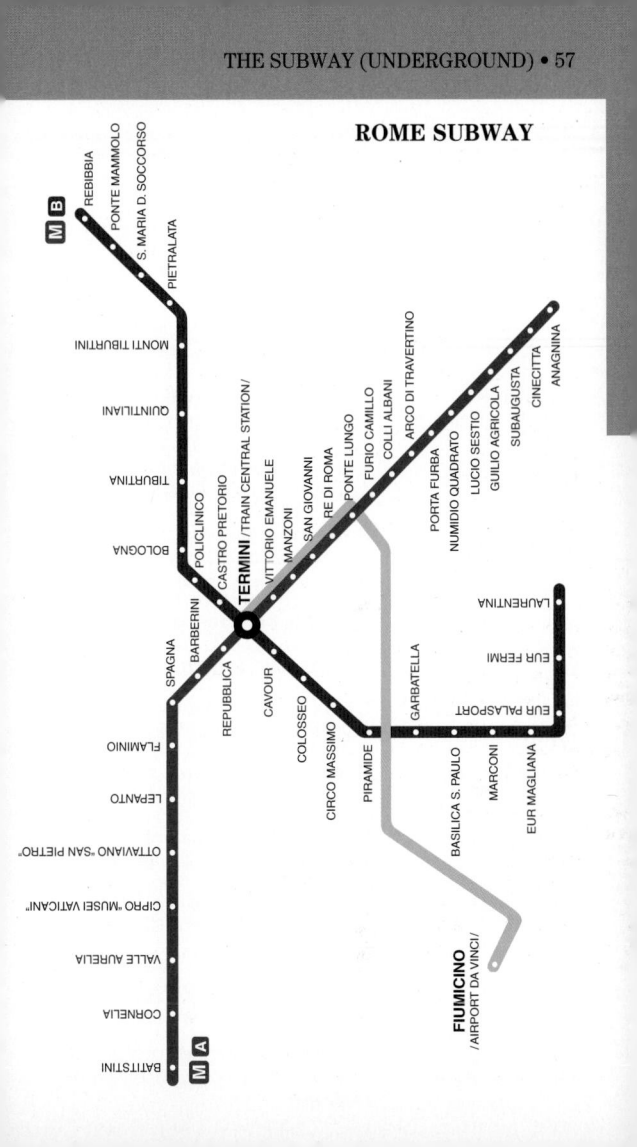
ROME SUBWAY
M A
BATTISTINI
CORNELIA
VALLE AURELIA
CIPRO "MUSEI VATICANI"
OTTAVIANO "SAN PIETRO"
LEPANTO
FLAMINIO
SPAGNA
BARBERINI
REPUBBLICA
BOLOGNA
TIBURTINA
QUINTILIANI
MONTI TIBURTINI
POLICLINICO
CASTRO PRETORIO
TERMINI /TRAIN CENTRAL STATION/
PIETRALATA
S. MARIA D. SOCCORSO
PONTE MAMMOLO
REBIBBIA
M B
CAVOUR
COLOSSEO
CIRCO MASSIMO
VITTORIO EMANUELE
MANZONI
SAN GIOVANNI
RE DI ROMA
PONTE LUNGO
PIRAMIDE
GARBATELLA
FURIO CAMILLO
COLLI ALBANI
ARCO DI TRAVERTINO
PORTA FURBA
NUMIDIO QUADRATO
LUCIO SESTIO
GUILIO AGRICOLA
SUBAUGUSTA
CINECITTA
ANAGNINA
EUR PALASPORT
EUR FERMI
LAURENTINA
BASILICA S. PAULO
MARCONI
EUR MAGLIANA
FIUMICINO
/AIRPORT DA VINCI/

Which line do I need to take for the Colosseum?

**Che linea si prende per il Colosseo?** *kay lEE-neh-ah see prAYn-deh pehr eel koh-lohs-sEE-oh*

Where is the closest subway (underground) station?

**Dov'è la stazione più vicina della metropolitana?** *doh-vEH lah stah-tsee-OH-neh pee-OO vee-chEE-nah dAYl-lah meh-troh-poh-lee-tAH-nah*

Where can I buy a ticket?

**Dove si fanno i biglietti?** *dOH-veh see fAHn-noh ee bee-lee-AY-tee*

I want a one way/round trip to ___.

**Voglio un biglietto di solo andata/di andata e ritorno per ____.** *VOH-ly-ee-oh oon bee-ly-ee-AYt-toh dee sOH-loh ahn-dAH-tah/dee ahn-dAH-tah ay ree-tOHr-noh pehr*

What time is the next train to ____ ?

**A che ora è il prossimo treno per ____?** *ah kay OH-rah EH eel prOHs-see-moh trEH-noh pehr*

Which platform for the train to ___?

**Da quale binario parte il treno per ___?** *dah koo-AH-leh bee-nAH-ree-oh pAHr-teh eel trEH-noh pehr*

Which is the train that goes to ___?

**Qual è il treno che va a ____?** *koo-ah-lEH eel trEH-noh kay vah ah*

Is this the train for ___?

**È questo il treno per ___?** *eh koo-AYs-toh eel trEH-noh pehr*

How many more stops?

**Quante fermate ancora?** *koo-AHn-teh fehr-mAH-teh ahn-kOH-rah*

What's the next station?

**Qual è la prossima stazione?** *koo-ah-lEH lah prOHs-see-mah stah-tsee-OH-neh*

The next stop is ____.

**La prossima stazione è ____.** *lah prOHs-see-mah stah-tsee-OH-neh EH*

The train is on time/delayed.

**Il treno è in orario/ritardo.** *eel trEH-no EH een oh-rAH-ree-oh/ree-tAHr-doh*

| | |
|---|---|
| Where should I get off? | **Dove dovrei scendere?** *dOH-vay doh-vrEH-ee shAYn-deh-reh* |
| Do I have to change trains? | **Devo cambiare treno?** *dAY-voh kahm-bee-AH-reh trEH-noh* |
| Can you tell me when we get there? | **Può farmi sapere quando siamo arrivati(e)?** *poo-OH fAHr-mee sah-pAY-reh koo-AHn-doh see-AH-moh ahr-ree-vAH-tee(eh)* |

## THE BUS (STREETCAR, TRAM)

Buses, trackless trolleys, and trams are the core of the Italian public transit network. Their routes crisscross the cities and extend into neighborhoods that tourists seldom visit. All stop at railroad stations that connect to trains, to airports, and cruise ports. Tickets must be bought at kiosks, cafes, newsstands, and tabacchi before boarding.

The buses that travel within the city limits are light grey or orange, with electronic destination signs in the front and the ATAC logo on the side. Regional and intercity buses are generally blue in color.

**Tickets:** In Rome, the **Metrobus** tickets are good for buses and trams. When stamped, a single ride ticket is valid for 75 minutes and travelers can transfer to other trams or buses using the same ticket on the trip. Once inside the car, validate the paper ticket by inserting it in the machine near the door. The radio frequency identification (RFID) tickets must be held against a round, yellow sensor, until the green light flashes.

| | |
|---|---|
| Where is the bus stop (bus terminal)? | **Dov'è la fermata dell'autobus (il capolinea)?** *doh-vEH lah fehr-mAH-tah dayl-lAH-oo-toh-boos (eel kah-poh-lEE-neh-ah)* |

| | |
|---|---|
| Which bus (trolley) do I take to get to _____? | **Quale autobus (tram) devo prendere per andare a _____?** *koo-AH-leh AH-oo-toh-boos (trAH-m) dAY-voh prAYn-deh-reh pehr ahn-dAH-reh ah* |
| In which direction do I have to go? | **In quale direzione devo andare?** *een koo-AH-leh dee-reh-tsee-OH-neh dAY-voh ahn-dAH-reh* |
| How often do the buses run? | **Ogni quanto tempo passano gli autobus?** *OH-ny-ee koo-AHn-toh tEHm-poh pAHs-sah-noh ly-ee AH-oo-toh-boos* |
| Do you go to _____? | **Va a _____?** *vAH ah* |
| I want to go to _____. | **Voglio andare a _____.** *vOH-ly-ee-oh ahn-dAH-reh ah* |
| Is it far from here? | **È lontano da qui?** *EH lohn-tAH-noh dah koo-EE* |
| How many stops are there? | **Quante fermate ci sono?** *koo-AHn-teh fehr-mAH-teh chee sOH-noh* |
| Do I have to change buses? | **Devo cambiare autobus?** *dAY-voh kahm-bee-AH-reh AH-oo-toh-boos* |

**Travel Tips** The Roma Pass Card for tourists. It's good for transportation and visits to museums.

In Milan, the *Radio Bus*, or "bus on request" service that picks up passengers and takes them within their areas of service without any waiting.

The *Tram Turistico Ciao Milano*, which for a reasonable fare lets you get acquainted with the city and to listen through a headset to comments in the language of your choice.

The *Eurotram*, the new modern Milan trams.

How much is the fare? **Quanto costa il biglietto?** *koo-AHn-toh kOH-stah eel bee-ly-ee-AYt-toh*

Where do I get off? **Dove devo scendere?** *dOH-vay dAY-voh shAYn-deh-reh*

Can you tell me where to get off? **Può dirmi dove devo scendere?** *poo-OH dEEr-mee dOH-veh dAY-voh shAYn-deh-reh*

## TAXIS

Taxis are an excellent means of transportation, from the airport to inner cities, hotels, historic sites, towns, villages, and even rural areas. Italian cab drivers make good "guides" especially when there is no language barrier. It is nice to greet them with a smile and a **Buon giorno!** *(boo-OHn jee-OHr-noh)*.

Make sure to use licensed taxis. They are white or yellow, carry a sign on the roof, have a meter, and an official number and sign on the driver's door that reads "Comune di Roma," or "Comune di Milano," etc. Also, make good use of taxi stands. Cabs are parked in designated areas or in the **piazza** *(pee-AH-tzah)*.

Is there a taxi stand near here? **C'è un posteggio dei taxi qui vicino?** *chEH oon poh-stAY-jee-oh dAY-ee tahs-sEE koo-EE vee-chEE-noh*

Please get me a taxi. **Per favore mi chiami un taxi.** *pehr fah-vOH-reh mee key-AH-mee oon tahs-sEE*

Taxi! Are you free? **Taxí! È libero?** *tahs-sEE EH lEE-beh-roh*

**Travel Tips** Ask how much it will cost to get to your destination. Get a quote and agree on the fare before getting into the cab!

Check if there will be an additional charge if you have more than one passenger riding with you.

When you call a cab, charges begin from the time the taxi is dispatched, not from the time of pick up.

Do not use unlicensed cars at terminal stations. They may not even have meters installed.

The taxi meter should show what the fare (**tariffa**—*tah-rEEf-fah)* is. If a cab has **Tariffa 1** and **Tariffa 2** it means that **Tariffa 1** is for immediate, short, nearby trips and **Tariffa 2** is for longer trips.

Make sure that the cab driver sets the meter for the correct **Tariffa!**

There will be a supplemental charge for each piece of luggage that the cab driver will handle.

There will be a surcharge for night service.

There is **no** smoking in any taxi in Italy!

| | |
|---|---|
| Take me (I want to go) _____. | **Mi porti (voglio andare) _____.** *mee pOHr-tee (vOH-ly-ee-oh ahn-dAH-reh)* |
| ■ to the airport | **all'aeroporto** *ahl-lah-eh-roh-pOHr-toh* |
| ■ to this address | **a questo indirizzo** *ah koo-AYs-toh een-dee-rEE-tsoh* |
| ■ to the station | **alla stazione** *AHl-lah stah-tsee-OH-neh* |
| ■ to _____ Street | **in via _____** *een vEE-ah* |
| Do you know where it is? | **Sa dove si trova?** *sah dOH-veh see trOH-vah* |
| How much is it to _____? | **Qual è la tariffa per _____?** *koo-ah-lEH lah tah-rEEf-fah pehr* |

Faster! I'm in a hurry.

**Più presto (veloce)! Ho fretta.** *pee-OO prEH-stoh (veh-lOH-cheh) oh frAYt-tah*

Please drive more slowly.

**Per cortesia guidi più piano.** *pehr kohr-tay-sEE-ah goo-EE-dee pee-OO pee-AH-noh*

Stop here at the corner.

**Si fermi qui all'angolo.** *see fAYr-mee koo-EE ahl-lAHn-goh-loh*

I think you are going the wrong way.

**Penso che lei stia andando nella direzione sbagliata.** *pEHn-soh kay lEH-ee stEE-ah ahn-dAHn-doh nAYl-lah dee-reh-tsee-OH-neh sbah-lyt-ee-AH-tah*

How much do I owe you?

**Quanto le devo?** *koo-AHn-toh leh dAY-voh*

This is for you.

**Questo è per lei.** *koo-AYs-toh EH pehr lEH-ee*

## SIGHTSEEING AND TOURS

In larger cities, you'll find facilities equipped for English-speaking tourists; in smaller towns, you may have to get along more on your own.

Where is the Tourist Information Office?

**Dov'è l'Ente Locale (Nazionale) per il Turismo?** *doh-vEH lEHn-teh loh-kAH-leh (nah-tsee-oh-nAH-leh) pehr eel too-rEEs-moh*

Where can I buy an English guidebook?

**Dove posso comprare una guida turistica in inglese?** *dOH-veh pOHs-soh kohm-prAH-reh OO-nah goo-EE-dah too-rEEs-tee-kah een een-glAY-seh*

I need an English-speaking guide.

**Ho bisogno di una guida che parli inglese.** *oh bee-sOH-ny-oh dee OO-nah goo-EE-dah kay pAHr-lee een-glAY-seh*

How much does he charge _____?

**Quanto si fa pagare _____?** *koo-AHn-toh see fah pah-gAH-reh*

- per hour — **all'ora** *ahl-lOH-rah*
- per day — **al giorno** *ahl jee-OHr-noh*

When does the tour begin?

**Quando inizia il tour (la gita)?** *koo-AHn-doh ee-nEE-tsee-ah eel tOOr (lah jEE-tah)*

How long is the tour?

**Quanto dura il tour (la gita)?** *koo-AHn-toh dOO-rah eel tOOr (lah jEE-tah)*

There are two (four, six) of us.

**Siamo in due (quattro, sei).** *see-AH-moh een-dOO-eh (koo-AHt-troh sEH-ee)*

Are there trips through the city?

**Si fanno (dei tour) delle gite turistiche della città?** *see fAHn-noh (dAY-ee tOOr) dAYl-leh jEE-teh too-rEE-stee-keh dAHl-lah cheet-tAH*

Where do they leave from?
**Da dove iniziano i tour (le gite)?** *dah dOH-veh ee-nEE-tsee-ah-noh ee tOOr (leh jEE-teh)*

We want to see ____.
**Vogliamo vedere ____.** *voh-ly-ee-AH-moh vay-dAY-reh*

- the botanical garden
  **il giardino botanico** *eel jee-ahr-dEE-noh boh-tAH-nee-koh*
- the business center
  **il centro commerciale** *eel chAYn-troh kohm-mehr-chee-AH-leh*
- the castle
  **il castello** *eel kahs-tEHl-loh*
- the cathedral
  **la cattedrale** *lah kaht-teh-drAH-leh*
- the church
  **la chiesa** *lah key-EH-sah*
- the concert hall
  **la sala dei concerti** *lah sAH-lah dAY-ee kohn-chEHr-tee*
- the downtown area
  **la zona del centro** *lah tsOH-nah dayl chAYn-troh*
- the fountains
  **le fontane** *leh fohn-tAH-neh*
- the library
  **la biblioteca** *lah bee-blee-oh-tEH-kah*
- the main park
  **il parco principale** *eel pAHr-koh preen-chee-pAH-leh*
- the main square
  **la piazza principale** *lah pee-AH-tsah preen-chee-pAH-leh*
- the market
  **il mercato** *eel mehr-kAH-toh*
- the mosque
  **la moschea** *lah moh-skEH-ah*
- the museum (of fine arts)
  **il museo (delle belle arti)** *eel moo-sEH-oh (dAYl-leh bEHl-leh AHr-tee)*
- a nightclub
  **un night club (locale notturno)** *oon nAH-eet klOOb (loh-kAH-leh noht-tOOr-noh)*
- the old part of town
  **la parte vecchia della città** *lah pAHr-teh vEHk-key-ah dAYl la cheet-tAH*
- the opera
  **il teatro dell'opera** *eel teh-AH-troh dayl-lOH-peh-rah*

- the palace — **il palazzo** *eel pah-lAH-tsoh*
- the stadium — **lo stadio** *loh stAH-dee-oh*
- the synagogue — **la sinagoga** *lah see-nah-gOH-gah*
- the university — **l'università** *loo-nee-vehr-see-tAH*
- the zoo — **il giardino zoologico (lo zoo)** *eel jee-ahr-dEE-no tsoh-oh-lOH-jee-koh (loh tsOH-oh)*

Is it open (closed)? — **È aperto (chiuso)?** *EH ah-pEHr-toh (key-OO-soh)*

At what time does it open (close)? — **A che ora aprono (chiudono)?** *ah kay OH-rah AH-proh-noh (key-OO-doh-noh)*

What's the admission price? — **Quant'è l'entrata?** *koo-ahn-tEH lehn-trAH-tah*

How much do children pay? — **Quanto pagano i bambini?** *koo-AHn-toh pAH-gah-noh ee bahm-bEE-nee*

Can they go in free? Until what age? — **Possono entrare gratis? Fino a quale età?** *pOHs-soh-noh ehn-trAH-reh grAH-tees fEE-noh ah koo-AH-leh eh-tAH*

Is it all right to take pictures? — **Si possono fare fotografie?** *see pOHs-soh-noh fAH-reh foh-toh-grah-fEE-eh*

How much extra does it cost to take pictures? — **Quanto costa in più per fare delle fotografie?** *koo-AHn-toh kOHs-tah een pee-OO pehr fAH-reh dAYl-leh foh-toh-grah-fEE-eh*

## A SIGHTSEEING ITINERARY

Italy has long attracted foreigners with its natural beauty and its visible reminders of a continuous history, a history that reaches back through the ages to the heights of Roman and Greek civilizations and beyond. Its rugged mountains, rolling plains, clear lakes, blue seas, flowery gardens, picturesque castles, imposing palaces and villas, great cathedrals and churches, busy city squares, narrow, winding streets, and ancient ruins and excavations—all these give pleasure to both the eye and the mind. Italy remains one of the world's richest treasuries of Western history, art, and civilization.

While retaining a strong sense of the past, present-day Italy is a thoroughly modern country, offering the tourist a vast and efficient network of superhighways and public transportation systems as well as the most advanced facilities for everyday comfort.

Even today, the visitor to Italy would need a lifetime to know the country, since there are thousands of places and things to see, each with its own flavor and history. The following is only a limited itinerary of principal points of interest to help the traveler become acquainted with this fascinating and seductive land.

### ROME

Rome is the heart of Italy. For unforgettable views of ancient Rome, its temples and monuments, see the Colosseum, the Roman Forum, the Capitol (**Campidoglio**), and the Pantheon, the most perfectly preserved ancient building. Visit St. Peter's, the Vatican Museums, and the Sistine Chapel. Descend the Spanish Steps to Via Condotti, Via del Babuino, Via Margutta (once an artists' quarter), and Piazza del Popolo. Smart boutiques, cafés, jewelry shops, and art galleries make this area very fashionable. Make a wish while tossing a coin in the famous Trevi Fountain. Piazza Navona, the old district of Trastevere, and the Sunday flea market at Porta Portese offer a glimpse of Roman daily life.

Near Rome, the gardens of Villa d'Este, with their water cascades and fountains, and the ruins of the Roman emperor Hadrian's Villa, both in Tivoli, are a must.

## FLORENCE

Florence is the seat of the Italian Renaissance. Visit the Cathedral of Santa Maria del Fiore and the Academia Museum to see Michelangelo's renowned *David.* Stroll through the Piazza della Signoria to the Uffizi, one of the world's most famous art museums. Cross the Ponte Vecchio, glancing in the gold- and silversmiths' shops lined up along the sides of the bridge, and from there walk to the Pitti Palace and through the Boboli Gardens. Ride to Piazzale Michelangelo for a bird's-eye view of the city with which such illustrious names as Dante, Michelangelo, Leonardo da Vinci, Giotto, Machiavelli, and Galileo are associated. Be sure to take a side trip to nearby Pisa to see the Leaning Tower and the Baptistry with its echo.

## MILAN

Italy's business and financial capital, Milan is also a historical city. Visit the Duomo, the dazzling Gothic cathedral with its hundred pinnacles; La Scala, the world-famous opera house; the Castello Sforzesco; and the Church of Santa Maria delle Grazie, to see Leonardo da Vinci's *Last Supper* in the refectory of the adjoining Dominican monastery. The shops in Via Montenapoleone are among the most elegant in Europe.

## MILAN TO VENICE

The route from Milan to Venice passes through the Po Valley, Italy's richest agricultural region. Stop off at Lake

Garda, which can probably be best viewed from the lovely little town of Sirmione near the southern end of the lake. On the way to Venice, stop in Verona to see "the house of Juliet," the Roman Arena (where operas are performed in the summer), and the well-preserved historical center of the city, especially Piazza dei Signori and Piazza delle Erbe (the old market square).

## VENICE

With its lagoons, canals, and palaces built on water, Venice inevitably enchants the visitor. Visit St. Mark's Square (Piazza San Marco) to see St. Mark's Church, its freestanding bell tower (Campanile), and the Palace of the Doges. Take a stroll through the narrow streets to the Rialto Bridge, which arches over the Grand Canal. A boat trip to the picturesque island towns of Murano and Burano, famous centers of glass and lace making, will prove fascinating.

## VENICE TO RAVENNA, SAN MARINO, AND ASSISI

Ravenna, on the coast south of Venice, is most famous for the magnificent mosaics in the Churches of San Vitale and Sant' Apollinare Nuovo and in the Mausoleum of Galla Placidia. A visit to the tomb of Dante, the father of Italian literature, will be interesting.

San Marino is an independent republic perched on a rocky pinnacle not far south of Ravenna. Tourists are attracted by its castles and picturesque old houses. This is an excellent place to buy stamps, coins, medieval armor, and gold jewelry.

The route from San Marino to Assisi passes through the Apennines, the rugged mountain chain that is called the backbone of Italy since it runs north-south down the Italian peninsula.

The town of Assisi is a very important pilgrimage center and tourist attraction. The old town is well preserved, with its medieval houses and narrow streets. Visit the magnificent Basilica of San Francesco, which contains celebrated frescoes by Giotto and Cimabue.

## ROME TO NAPLES

On the way to Naples, stop in Cassino to visit the Abbey of Montecassino, destroyed in World War II and rebuilt as a monument to faith, the arts, and culture.

Italy's third largest city, Naples is the gateway to the largely unspoiled beauty of southern Italy. Visit the Cathedral of San Gennaro (the city's patron saint), the steep, narrow-staired streets of the old quarter (Spaccanapoli), and the opera house of San Carlo. In the vicinity of Naples, discover the excavated Roman cities of Pompeii and Herculaneum in the shadow of Mt. Vesuvius. Take a ride on the breathtaking serpentine Amalfi Drive, or go out to the island of Capri.

## SICILY

From Naples there are direct airplane and boat connections to Palermo, Sicily. The island of Sicily is fascinating for its landscapes and the relics of its long, complex history. Visit the ancient Greek temples at Agrigento and Siracusa, reminders of the Greek foundations of Sicilian culture.

## SARDINIA

And on to Sardinia! You can get there from Genoa, Civitavecchia, Rome, Naples, Palermo, and Trapani. This picturesque island is ready to be discovered. Relax on the sand beaches of modern **Costa Smeralda**. Return to the Bronze and Iron Ages while standing and admiring the numerous and massive prehistoric towers called **nuraghi**.

Visit the pleasant metropolis of Cagliari and the partially submerged town of Nora. Listen to the sounds and voices of the inhabitants of Nuoro speaking a dialect very similar to Latin. And find the small treasures of old and modern times scattered throughout the island!

## RELIGIOUS SERVICES

In addition to viewing the churches and cathedrals throughout Italy, you may wish to attend services.

**Catholic Churches:** Torso and upper arms must be covered. Shorts and skirts must extend below the knee. Churches open early in the morning, close at 12 noon for about two hours, and then reopen till evening. More important cathedrals and basilicas are usually open all day.

**National Catholic Churches:**
**In Rome:**

- (American) The Church of Santa Susanna,
  Via XX (Venti) Settembre 15.
  Phone: 4201-4554

- (Canadian) Nostra Signora del Santísimo Sacramento e Santi Martiri Canadesi, Via G.B. de Rossi, 46.
  Phone: 44.23.79.84

**In Florence:**

- Santa Maria del Fiore, Piazza del Duomo.
  Phone 215380

- Church of Hospital St. John of God,
  Borgo Ognissanti 42.
  Phone/Fax: 218839

**Non-Catholic Churches**
**In Rome:**

- Anglican Church of All Saints
  Via del Babuino, 153
  Phone: 3600 1881

- Baptist Church
  Piazza San Lorenzo
  Lucina, 35
  Phone: 6876 652

- International Protestant
  Via Chiovenda, 57
  Phone: 745 400

- Methodist
  Via Firenze, 38
  Phone: 4743 695

**In Florence:**

- American Episcopal Church, St. James
  Via B. Rucellai, 9
  Phone: 294417

- Church of England
  Via Maggio, 16
  Phone: 294764

**In Milan:**

- Anglican Church of All Saints
  Via Solferino, 17
  Phone: 6552 258

- Christ Church
  Via del Bollo, 5
  Phone: 8056215

| Is there a _____ near here? | **C'è qui vicino una _____?** *chEH koo-EE vee-chEE-noh OO-nah* |
|---|---|
| ■ Catholic church | **chiesa cattolica** *key-EH-sah kaht-tOH-lee-kah* |
| ■ Protestant church | **chiesa protestante** *key-EH-sah proh-teh-stAHn-teh* |
| ■ synagogue | **sinagoga** *see-nah-gOH-gah* |
| ■ mosque | **moschea** *moh-skEH-ah* |

# PLANNING A TRIP

Check the Internet for direct international flights to major Italian cities or call a travel agent.

During your stay you may want to plan some excursions into the country or to other Italian cities. Visitors to Italy can move around the country by airplane, train, bus, boat, and car (see Driving a Car). For air travel within Italy, look for signs to the domestic terminal (sometimes separate from the international terminal).

## AIR SERVICE WITHIN ITALY

| | |
|---|---|
| **Aereo Trasporti Italiani, Aermediterranea, Air One, Air Dolomiti, Aligiulia, Alitalia, Alpi Eagles, Azurra Air, Federico II Airways, Meridiana, Pugliairbus, Transavia** | The national domestic airlines linking major cities |
| **Air Sicilia** | Flights to the island of Sicily |
| **Alisarda** | Flights to the island of Sardinia |

Look into . . .

- available connections to inner cities by train, bus, shuttle, or taxi.
- accessible services such as car rental, car hire, and minibus shuttle; hotel booking agencies; short- and long-term car parking (with reserved parking for disabled); exchange offices.
- charter flights.
- check-in time at Italian airports.
- Apex fares. Fares vary by season, airline, and holiday time.

When is there a flight to _____?

**Quando c'è un volo per _____?** *koo-AHn-doh chEH oon vOH-loh pehr*

I would like _____.

**Vorrei _____.** *vohr-rEH-ee*

- a round-trip (one-way) ticket _____.

**un biglietto di andata e ritorno (di andata)** *oon bee-ly-ee-AYt-toh dee ahn-dAH-tah ay ree-tOHr-noh (dee ahn-dAH-tah)*

- in tourist class

**in classe turistica** *een klAHs-seh too-rEE-stee-kah*

- in first class

**in prima classe** *een prEE-mah klAHs-seh*

Can I use this ticket for frequent flyer miles?

**Posso usare questo biglietto per il club "Mille miglia," frequent flyer miles?** *pOHs-soh oo-sAH-reh koo-AYs-toh bee-ly-AYt-toh pehr eel kloob mEEl-leh mEE-ly-ee-ah frequent flyer miles*

I would like a seat _____.

**Vorrei un posto _____.** *vohr-rEH-ee OOn pOH-stoh*

- next to the window

**accanto al finestrino** *ah-kAHn-toh ahl fee-neh-strEE-noh*

- on the aisle

**vicino al corridoio** *vee-chEE-noh ahl kohr-ree-dOH-ee-oh*

What is the fare?

**Qual è il prezzo del biglietto?** *koo-ah-lEH eel prEH-tsoh dAYl bee-ly-ee-EHt-toh*

Are meals served?

**Sono inclusi i pasti?** *sOH-noh een-klOO-see ee pAH-stee*

When does the plane leave (arrive)?

**A che ora parte (arriva) l'aereo?** *ah kay OH-rah pAHr-teh (ahr-ree-vAH) lah-EH-reh-oh*

When must I be at the airport?

**Quando dovrò trovarmi all'aeroporto?** *koo-AHn-doh doh-vrOH troh-vAHr-mee ahl-lah-eh-roh-pOHr-toh*

What is my flight number?

**Qual è il (mio) numero di volo?** *koo-AH-lEH eel (mEE-oh) nOO-meh-roh dee vOH-loh*

What gate do we leave from?

**Qual è la nostra porta d'uscita?** *koo-ah-lEH lah nOH-strah pOHr-tah doo-shEE-tah*

I want to confirm (cancel) my reservation for flight ____.

**Desidero confermare (cancellare) la mia prenotazione per il volo _____.** *day-sEE-deh-roh kohn-fayr-mAH-reh (kahn-chehl-lAH-reh) lah mEE-ah preh-noh-tah-tsee-OH-neh pehr eel vOH-loh*

I'd like to check my bags.

**Vorrei consegnare le valigie.** *vohr-rEH-ee kohn-say-ny-AH-reh leh vah-lEE-jee-eh*

I have only carry-on baggage.

**Ho soltanto bagagli a mano.** *oh sohl-tAHn-toh bah-gAH-ly-ee ah MAH-noh*

## TRAIN SERVICE

Call the **FS** (Italian Railway Network) at **1478-88088** for information on service, time schedules, and ticket prices all over Italy every day from 7:00 A.M. to 9:00 P.M. During the night, an automated answering machine will provide time schedule information only. You can contact the Internet site at *http://www.fs-on-line.com*

The Intercity-Eurostar trains and those trains displaying the seal for people in need of special assistance are equipped with special toilets and offer boarding and disembarking assistance.

The **Trenitalia** lines cover the entire country, whereas **Ferrovie Nord** runs in the northern regions. The Arrows (**Le Frecce**—*leh frAYc-ceh*) are high-speed trains with top service. They are elegant and have comfortable seats with plenty of leg room. The Red Arrow (**La Frecciarossa**—*lah frAYc-chee-ah rOHs-sah*) and the Silver Arrow (**La Frecciargento**—*lah frAYc-chee-ahr-gEHn-toh*) link Milan, Venice, Bologna, Rome, and Naples with access to the city centers and many towns and villages.

The following list describes the varieties of Italian trains.

| | | |
|---|---|---|
| **R** | **Rapido** | High-speed luxury train between major cities (supplementary fare required). |
| **E** | **Espresso** | Express train, for long routes within Italy. |
| **DD** | **Direttissimo** | Fast train, stopping only at main stations between large cities. |
| **R** | **Regionale** | Regional train (better known as **diretto**). |
| **I** | **Locale** | Local train, making all stops (also called **accelerato**). |
| **IR** | **Interregionale** | Train used between two or three regions. |
| **Il** | **Pendolino** | The "Leaning Train" is Italy's fastest train. |

| | | |
|---|---|---|
| **EC** | **Eurocity** | High-speed international luxury day trains. They stop in big cities only (Rome, Florence, Milan). Advance reservations are required. |
| **ES** | **Eurostar** | |
| **EN** | **Euronight** | International overnight trains with sleeping cars and berths (**cuccette**—*koo-chEHt-teh*). Booking in advance is advisable if you want to find a seat. |
| **EN** | **Espresso notte** | |
| **IC/IC plus** | **Intercity** | Domestic express trains within Italy. First-class cars are air-conditioned. |
| **ICN** | **Intercity notte** | Payment of a supplementary fare may be waived for holders of BTLC or Eurailpasses. Reservations are advisable. |
| **CIS** | **Cisalpino** | Train between Italy and Switzerland. It is as fast as **Eurostar** but as expensive as **Intercity**. |

Refunds for unused train tickets can be received within a year from the date of purchase. Unused tickets must be stamped "unused" by an official of the European Rail Roads. Administration fees and a 15% cancellation charge are added. Rates are subject to change without notice and refunds for tickets purchased in Europe cannot be obtained in the United States.

**Important symbols:**

| | |
|---|---|
| **R** | Reservation required. |
| **R** | Reservation optional (with charge if you want to reserve a seat). |
| **Ⓡ** | Reservation required (without charge) for passengers traveling in first class; reservation optional (with charge) for passengers traveling in second class. |
| **Handicap symbol** | Train with facilities for disabled. |

## DISCOUNTS

### Seniors

Currently, **Carta d'Argento/Silver Card** (free for passengers 75 and over) offers 10% off wagon lits and couchettes for travelers over 60, 15% off base fares for first or second class on all national trains, and 25% off all international connections.

**Green and Silver cards** can be purchased at station ticket desks or from authorized travel agencies. Cards are valid for one year.

### Youth

**Carta Verde/Green Card** offers a 10% discount for base fares on all national trains and 25% for first- or second-class tickets when traveling around Europe.

**Tessera Inter Rail/Inter Rail Card** is valid for up to eight days or one month in second class for travelers under 26, with a discount of up to 50%.

**Euro Domino Junior** is a junior fare on Italian trains (for second class only and for travelers up to 26 years old), with a 20% discount given at time of purchase.

### Travelers with special needs

**Carta Blu/Dark-Blu Card** is issued to those who present a valid medical certificate and is valid for five years. The price of the ticket includes an escort and a 20% discount.

### Group discounts

10% to 20% for groups of 10 to 42 passengers. Savings depend on the time of year and day of week of travel.

### Other discounts

- Italy rail passes with **Trenitalia** allow tourists to travel throughout Europe all year round.
- Italy's **Rail's Drive** includes four days of unlimited train travel in Italy and a two-day Hertz car rental with unlimited mileage plus choice of manual or automatic transmission.
- The **Carnet 10 viaggi** (10-trip voucher) saves 20% on the **Frecciarossa**, **Frecciargento**, and **ES** city trains.

- Discounts are available with cards such as the **Frecciarossa**, **Frecciargento**, **Cartafreccia Oro and Cartafreccia Platino**, and **Cartafreccia**.
- Telecom Italia and Trenitalia provide free Wi-Fi on board (**Wi-Fi Frecciarossa**). For help contact **Numero Verde Telecomitalia** at 800.287515.
- **Flexi Rail Card** at Trenitalia is valid for unlimited train travel within six months. Special saver prices for two or more traveling together.
- **Italian Pass Flexi Rail Card Saver** (aka Trenitalia Pass Saver)

Check *www.trenitalia.com/.../International* or *www.trenitalia.com/Home/Offer and deals/*

| | |
|---|---|
| Where is the train station? | **Dov'è la stazione ferroviaria?** *doh-vEH lah stah-tsee-OH-neh fehr-roh-vee-AH-ree-ah* |
| When does the train leave (arrive) for (from) _____? | **Quando parte (arriva) il treno per (da) _____?** *koo-AHn-doh pAHr-teh (ahr-rEE-vah) eel trEH-noh pehr (dah)* |
| Does this train stop at _____? | **Questo treno si ferma a _____?** *koo-AYs-toh trEH-noh see fAYr-mah ah* |

## BUYING A TICKET

Look into . . .

- the age range for a child to have a train ticket.
- sleeping accommodations for kids on overnight trains.
- the best train passes to buy for couples or groups, such as **Italy Group Discount**, the basic **Eurailpass**, **Britrail** tickets through the Chunnel, **Eurostar** rail passes.
- making reservation(s) on sleeper cars.
- **Eurostar** and **Trenitalia** trains. They give more flexibility, cover more trips, and save time at ticket offices. But make advanced reservations to avoid standing in a fully booked train.
- the different types of **Euro Rail** passes. They vary depending on the age of the traveler, the number of countries to be visited, and the total number of people on the trip.

Look out!

- Before using Italian train tickets, whether domestic or international, travelers must get them stamped at the machines on the platforms before getting on the trains.
- There is a penalty of up to 200 euros for riding with an unvalidated ticket.
- Before boarding your train, check
  - the track number (**binario**—*bee-nAH-ree-oh*).
  - if you have to use the underpass (**sottopassaggio**—*sOHt-toh pahs-sAh-jee-oh*) to get to the right track.

When making sleeper reservations, travelers

- must be very clear about the type(s) of accommodations(s) desired.
- have to request not to be placed in a cabin with a stranger of the opposite gender if so desired.

Passport and identification cards are mandatory and required when traveling on overnight trains and must be shown to the train conductor upon request.

Check *http://www.trenitalia.com/en* or *http://www.italiarail.com/trenitalia-network*

| | |
|---|---|
| I would like _____. | **Vorrei _____.** *vohr-rEH-ee* |
| ■ a first- (second-) class ticket for _____. | **un biglietto di prima (seconda) classe per _____.** *oon bee-ly-ee-AYt-toh dee prEE-mah (say-kOHn-dah) klAHs-seh pehr* |
| ■ a half-price ticket | **un biglietto a tariffa ridotta** *oon bee-ly-ee-AYt-toh ah tah-rEEf-fah ree-dOHt-tah* |
| ■ a one-way (round-trip) ticket | **un biglietto di andata (andata e ritorno)** *oon bee-ly-ee-AYt-toh dee ahn-dAH-tah (ahn-dAH-tah ay ree-tOHr-noh)* |
| ■ with supplement for the rapid train | **con supplemento rapido** *kohn soop-pleh-mEHn-toh rAH-pee-doh* |
| ■ with reserved seat | **con prenotazione** *kohn prey-noh-tAH-tzee-oh-neh* |

Are there discounts for _____?

- seniors
- youths
- groups
- travelers with special needs

**Ci sono sconti per _____?** *chee sOH-no skOHn-tee pehr*

**anziani** *ahn-tzee-AH-nee*

**giovani** *jee-OH-vah-nee*

**gruppi** *grOOp-pee*

**disabili** *dee-sAH-bee-lee*

Are there special passes?

- weekly
- monthly
- for groups
- for tourists

**Ci sono sconti speciali?** *chee sOH-noh skOHn-tee speh-chee-AH-lee*

**settimanali** *seht-tee-mah-nAH-lee*

**mensili** *mehn-sEE-lee*

**per gruppi** *pehr grOOp-pee*

**per turisti** *pehr too-rEEs-tee*

Is the train late?

**Il treno è in ritardo?** *eel trEH-noh EH een ree-tAHr-doh*

How long does it stop?

**Quanto tempo si ferma?** *koo-AHn-toh tEHm-poh see fAYr-mah*

## ON THE TRAIN

Is there time to get a bite?

**C'è tempo per comprare un boccone?** *chEH tEHm-poh pehr kohm-prAH-reh oon boh-kOH-neh*

Is there a dining car (a sleeping car)?

**C'è un vagone ristorante (un vagone letto)?** *chEH oon vah-gOH-neh ree-stoh-rAHn-teh (oon vah-gOH-neh lEHt-toh)*

Is this an express (local) train?

**È questo un treno rapido (locale)?** *EH koo-AYs-toh oon trEH-noh rAH-pee-doh (loh-kAH-leh)*

Do I have to change trains?

**Debbo cambiar treno?** *dAYb-boh kahm-bee-AHr trEH-noh*

| | |
|---|---|
| Is this seat taken? | **È occupato questo posto?** *EH oh-koo-pAH-toh koo-AYs-toh pOH-stoh* |
| Excuse me, but you are in my seat. | **Mi scusi ma lei ha occupato il mio posto.** *mee skOO-see mah lEH-ee ah oh-koo-pAH-toh eel mEE-oh pOHs-toh* |

## SHIPBOARD TRAVEL

If you want to visit some of the islands (Capri, Sicily, Sardinia), you will have to go by either ferry, hydrofoil (**aliscafo**—*ah-lee-skAH-phoh*), or ship. There are car ferries to Sicily and Sardinia. Genoa, Naples, and Palermo are the most common ports.

Some of the sea transport companies are Caremar, Corsica Ferris, European Sealines, Endeavor Lines, Grandi Navi Veloci, Medram, Minoan Lines, Moby Lines, Saremar, Siremar, Snav, Superfast ferries, SNCM, Tirrenia.

You can sail to or from Ancona, Bari, Brindisi, Capri, Corsica, Croatia, Ischia, Isola d'Elba, Greece, Morocco, Sardinia, Sicily, Spain, Tunis, Turkey.

| | |
|---|---|
| Where is the port (dock)? | **Dov'è il porto (molo)?** *doh-vEH eel pOHr-toh (mOH-loh)* |

## Travel Tips

- The Mediterranean is calmer and most favorable for sailing from April through November.
- You can take a ferry to Italy from Albania, Croatia, France, Greece, Montenegro, North Africa, and Spain.
- The Italian arrival ports are Ancona, Bari, Brindisi, Cagliari, Catania, Civitavecchia (for Rome), Livorno, Messina, Naples, Palermo, Trieste, Venice.
- There is a large number of cruise ships in the Mediterranean, including Cunard, Carnival, Costa Cruises, Emerald Princess, MSC Italian, Norwegian Cruise, and Silversea. Some can take you to Italy right from the United States!
- You may also charter a yacht when sailing to and around Italy with Charter World, Luxury Yacht Vacation, or Windward and Islands.

Check *www.traghettiweb.it/en/tw_index.php* or *www.traghettionline.com/* or *www.directferries.co.uk/italy.htm*

When does the next boat leave for ____?

**Quando parte il prossimo battello per _____?** *koo-AHn-doh pAHr-teh eel prOHs-see-moh baht-tEHl-loh pehr*

How long does the crossing take?

**Quanto dura la traversata?** *koo-AHn-toh dOO-rah lah trah-vehr-sAH-tah*

Do we stop at any other ports?

**Ci fermiamo in qualche altro porto?** *chee fayr-mee-AH-moh een koo-AHl-keh AHl-troh pOHr-toh*

How long will we remain in port?

**Quanto tempo resteremo in porto?** *koo-AHn-toh tEHm-poh reh-stay-rEII-moh een pOHr-toh*

When do we land?

**Quando sbarcheremo?** *koo-AHn-do sbahr-keh-rAY-moh*

| | |
|---|---|
| At what time do we have to go back on board? | **A che ora ritorniamo a bordo?** *ah kay OH-rah ree-tohr-nee-AH-moh ah bOHr-doh* |

## ITALY BY BUS

Tour operators, drivers, and tour escorts will entertain you and unravel in front of your eyes Italy's mythology, history, geography, arts, local events, fashion, cinema, and a world of culinary delicacies. Guided tours by motorcoaches leave from Bari, Bologna, Cagliari, Catania, Florence, Milan, Naples, Palermo, Pisa, Rome, Sorrento, and many other cities and towns.

You may choose among a variety of tours, such as guided tours, partially escorted tours, private tours, cross-regional tours, gastronomic and art tours, and cruise extension tours. Once you start doing the research, you will discover a world of possibilities for different budgets.

Look into . . .

- package tours.
- modern, air-conditioned and comfortable bus(es).
- security.
- hotel accommodations.
- reservations and entrance fees at palaces and museums.
- travel schedules.
- transfers to ferries and trains.
- organizing your own bus tour if you have at least eight people traveling with you.

Look out!

- Get up early! Don't miss the bus! Be on time and keep to the tour schedule.
- There may be a hidden extra cost for additional visits to places that are not included in the original itinerary. They may be optional!

Check *www.viator.com/rome-bus-tours* or *www.collettevacations.com* or *www.italytourbus.com/* or *www.coachtoursitaly.com/*

# DRIVING A CAR

To drive in Italy you will be best off with an International Driving Permit (equivalent to a regular driver's license), best obtained before you leave home. You will need the car's registration documents with the **bollo** *(bOHl-loh)*, the annual circulation charge, and a hazard triangle. Insurance is compulsory.

Motorways are indicated by the letter "A" followed by a number written in white on a green background. Tolls are paid in cash or with Viacard or Viacard Telepass cards (an electronic pass system that makes automatic payment possible without stopping at the toll booths).

The road signs with the symbol of a wrench have buttons for emergency calls in case of breakdowns and those with a red cross symbol are for first aid.

Buckling up is mandatory for the driver and all passengers. The use of portable telephones is prohibited if they need to be held by hand when driving.

Service areas along the motorways are always open and provide gasoline, restrooms, restaurants, shopping areas, bars, banks, and information offices. Gasoline is called **benzina** *(behn-tsEE-nah)*. Unleaded gas is **benzina senza piombo** *(behn-tsEE-nah sEHn-tsah pee-Ohm-boh)*, and diesel fuel is **gasolio** *(gah-sOH-lee-oh)*.

The Italian police (**Polizia Stradale**, **Carabinieri**, and **Vigili**) *(poh-lee-tsEE-ah strah-dAH-leh, kah-rah-bee-nee-EH-ree, vEE-jee-lee)* can stop at will any car on the road for spot checks and for traffic offenses. Tickets are paid on the spot. The traffic moves on the right, and passing is on the left. The speed limit—90–140 kilometers per hour or 56–87 miles per hour—depends upon engine capacity.

The roads in Italy are classified as **Autostrade** *(ah-oo-toh-strAH-deh)* with "pay tolls" (motorways or expressways); **S.S., Strade Statali** *(strAH-deh stah-tAH-lee)*, state roads; **S.P., Strade Provinciali** *(strAH-deh proh-veen-chee-AII-lee)*, provincial roads; **S.C., Strade Comunali** *(strAH-deh koh-moo-nAH-lee)*, village roads.

For road emergency, dial 116.

For police and ambulance, dial 113.

The Head Office of ACI, Automobile Club of Italy, is Via Marsala 8—00185 Roma
Phone: 06 49981

## TRAVELING BY CAR

Driving is freedom and vice versa. Enjoy driving in Italy! But look into . . .

- the driver's license needed to drive in Italy. You can secure the international driving permit from any AAA (Automobile Association of America).
- the insurance coverage. Does your insurance carrier cover you 100% when driving in Italy?
- renting or buying a GPS and/or GPS speed camera detectors.
- the cost of gasoline, which is pricey.
- the roadways (**autostrada**, **strada statale**, **strada provinciale**, and **strada comunale**).
- the road and street signals. Quite often, road signals are painted on the asphalt and pavement.
- the posted speed limit.
- car rental specials at major rent-a-car companies.
- deals on seasonal airfare, hotel accommodation services, sports and luxury rentals, and chauffer services offered with a rental.

Look out!

- The Italian Police use a round stop signal (**paletta**—*pah-lAYt-tah*), a disc with a handle, to pull drivers over.
- Pay the Fines! Use your credit cards when paying to keep a record. (Remember that minor traffic violations must be paid on the spot.)
- There are speed cameras. Some iPhone applications may warn you of their presence.
- Radar detectors are illegal. Users are fined when caught.
- Parking is confusing and limited. Everyone parks in any available parking spot regardless of the direction posted by the street signals. One- or two-way street signals are ignored by drivers. If a free spot is there people grab it!

- Pay attention to the signs that read **zona traffico limitato** (**ZTL**). Don't park there if your vehicle is not permitted.
- Italians tend to be aggressive drivers. They tailgate and flash their high beams to make drivers ahead of them switch lanes and move out of the way.
- The left lane is for passing and speeding only!

At the service station, ask the attendant to fill up, please (**Il pieno, per favore!**—*eel pee-EH-noh pEHr fah-vOH-reh*). Automatic pumps function in the evening and at night. They accept banknotes of 10, 20, and 50 euros. Check *www.italychronicles.com/speeding-fines-in-italy/*

## CAR RENTALS

Rentals can be arranged before departure for Italy through a travel agent or upon arrival in Italy at a rental office in the major airports or in or near the railroad station in a larger city or town. Some automobile rental companies are nationwide or worldwide organizations (like Avis and Hertz), enabling you to pick up and drop off a rented car at local offices throughout Italy.

To rent an automobile, you must be at least 21 years old and have an International Driving Permit, obtainable before departure or in Italy at the nearest office of the Automobile Club of Italy.

Look into . . .
- rental terms and conditions.
- convenient pickup and drop-off locations.
- car rentals at airports and other sites in Italy.
- special deals for big families.
- services and road side assistance offered.

Look out!
- Does your credit card give you 100% coverage in Italy?
- Do you need to buy supplemental insurance to be totally covered?

What happens if you
- get parking tickets, moving violation tickets or get involved in an accident?
- are under 25 years old?
- return the vehicle late?

Are there any hidden drop-off charges?

Check *www.autoeurope.com* or *www.autoeurope.com/go/car-ITALY.html*

| | |
|---|---|
| Where can I rent _____? | **Dove posso noleggiare _____?** *dOH-veh pOHs-soh noh-leh-jee-AH-reh* |
| ■ a car | **una macchina** *OO-nah mAHk-kee-nah* |
| ■ a motorcycle | **una motocicletta** *OO-nah moh-toh-chEE-klAYt-tah* |
| ■ a motor scooter | **una vespa (una lambretta)** *OO-nah vEH-spah (OO-nah lahm-brAYt-tah)* |
| ■ a moped | **un motorino** *oon moh-toh-rEE-noh* |
| ■ a bicycle | **una bicicletta** *OO-nah bee-chee-klAYt-tah* |
| I want (I'd like) _____. | **Voglio (Vorrei) _____.** *vOH-ly-ee-oh (vohr-rEH-ee)* |
| ■ a small car | **una macchina piccola** *OO-nah mAHk-kee-nah pEE-koh-lah* |

- a large car — **una macchina grande** *OO-nah mAHk-kee-nah grAHn-deh*
- a sports car — **una macchina sportiva** *OO-nah mAHk-kee-nah spohr-tEE-vah*

I prefer automatic transmission. — **Preferisco il cambio automatico.** *preh-feh-rEE-skoh eel kAHm-bee-oh ah-oo-toh-mAH-tee-koh*

How much does it cost _____? — **Quanto costa _____?** *koo-AHn-toh kOH-stah*

- per day — **al giorno** *ahl jee-OHr-noh*
- per week — **alla settimana** *AHl-lah seht-tee-mAH-nah*
- per kilometer — **per chilometro** *pehr key-lOH-meh-troh*
- for unlimited mileage — **a chilometraggio illimitato** *ah key-loh-meh-trAH-jee-oh eel-lee-mee-tAH-toh*

How much is the (complete) insurance? — **Quant'è l'assicurazione (completa)?** *koo-ahn-tEH lahs-see-koo-rah-tsee-OH-neh (kohm-plEH-tah)*

Is gas included? — **È inclusa la benzina?** *EH een-klOO-sah lah behn-tsEE-nah*

Here's my (international) driver's license. — **Ecco la mia patente (internazionale) di guida.** *EHk-koh lah mEE-ah pah-tEHn-teh (een-tehr-nah-tsEE-oh-nAH-leh) dee goo-EE-dah*

Do I have to leave a deposit? — **Devo lasciare un acconto (un deposito)?** *dAY-voh lah-shee-AH-reh oon ahk-kOHn-toh (oon day-pOH-see-toh)*

Is there a drop-off charge?

**C'è un supplemento per la consegna dell'auto?** *chEH oon soop-pleh-mEHn-toh pehr lah kohn-sEH-ny-ee-ah dayl-lAH-oo-toh*

I want to rent the car here and leave it in Turin.

**Desidero noleggiare l'auto qui e consegnarla a Torino.** *day-sEE-deh-roh noh-lay-jee-AH-reh lAH-oo-toh koo-EE ay kohn-say-ny-ee-AHr-lah ah toh-rEE-noh*

What kind of gasoline does it take?

**Che tipo di carburante usa?** *kay tEE-poh dee kahr-boo-rAHn-teh OO-sah*

## PARKING

Parallel parking is prohibited in the centers of many Italian cities and towns, especially where the street is so narrow that parked cars would obstruct traffic. Moreover, the historical center (**centro storico**) of a city or town may sometimes be entirely or partly closed to automobile traffic (as, for example, in Rome and Verona).

In larger cities and towns, automobiles should be left in an attended parking place (**posteggio**) or in a garage (**autorimessa**). When an automobile is left in an attended outdoor parking place—often a square (**piazza**) or widening of the street (**largo**)—the driver must pay the attendant (**posteggiatore**) on leaving the vehicle (sometimes also leaving the keys) and tip him on reclaiming it.

## ON THE ROAD

Excuse me. Can you tell me _____?

**Mi scusi. Può dirmi _____?** *mee skOO-see poo-OH dEEr-mee*

- which way is it to _____

**qual'è la via per _____** *koo-ah-lEH lah vEE-ah pehr*

- how I get to _____

**come potrei raggiungere _____** *kOH-meh poh-trEH-ee rah-jee-OOn-jeh-reh*

I think we're lost.

**Penso che ci siamo perduti(e).** *pEHn-soh kay chee see-AH-moh pehr-dOO-tee(eh)*

Is this the road (way) to _____?

**È questa la strada (via) per _____?** *EH koo-AYs-tah lah strAH-dah (vEE-ah) pehr*

Where does this road go?

**Dove porta questa strada?** *dOH-veh pOHr-tah koo-AYs-tah strAH-dah*

How far is it from here to the next town?

**Quanto dista da qui la prossima città?** *koo-AHn-toh dEE-stah dah koo-EE lah prOHs-see-mah cheet-tAH*

How far away is _____?

**Quanto dista _____?** *koo-AHn-toh dEE-stah*

| | |
|---|---|
| Do you have a road map? | **Ha una cartina stradale?** *AH OO-nah kahr-tEE-nah strah-dAH-leh* |
| Can you show it to me on the map? | **Può indicarmelo sulla cartina?** *poo-OH een-dee-kAHr-meh-loh sOOl-lah kahr-tEE-nah* |
| Is it a good road? | **È buona la strada?** *EH boo-OH-nah lah strAH-dah* |
| Is this the shortest way? | **È questa la via più corta?** *EH koo-AYs-tah lah vEE-ah pee-OO kOHr-tah* |
| Are there any detours? | **Ci sono deviazioni?** *chee sOH-noh day-vee-ah-tsee-OH-nee* |
| Do I go straight? | **Posso proseguire diritto?** *pOHs-soh proh-seh-goo-EE-reh dee-rEEt-toh* |
| Turn to the right (to the left). | **Giri a destra (a sinistra).** *jEE-ree ah dEH-strah (ah see-nEE-strah)* |

## AT THE SERVICE STATION

Gasoline is sold by the liter in Europe, and for the traveler accustomed to gallons, it may seem confusing, especially if you want to calculate your mileage per gallon (kilometer per liter). Here are some tips on making those conversions.

**LIQUID MEASURES (APPROXIMATE)**

| Liters | US Gallons | Imperial Gallons | Liters | US Gallons | Imperial Gallons |
|---|---|---|---|---|---|
| 10 | $2\frac{3}{4}$ | $2\frac{1}{4}$ | 50 | $13\frac{1}{4}$ | 11 |
| 20 | $5\frac{1}{4}$ | $4\frac{1}{2}$ | 60 | $15\frac{3}{4}$ | 13 |
| 30 | 8 | $6\frac{1}{2}$ | 70 | $19\frac{1}{8}$ | $15\frac{1}{2}$ |
| 40 | $10\frac{1}{2}$ | $8\frac{3}{4}$ | 80 | 21 | $17\frac{1}{2}$ |

| DISTANCE MEASURES (APPROXIMATE) | | | |
|---|---|---|---|
| Kilometers | Miles | Kilometers | Miles |
| 1 | 0.62 | 50 | 31 |
| 5 | 3 | 60 | $37\frac{1}{4}$ |
| 10 | $6\frac{1}{4}$ | 70 | $43\frac{1}{2}$ |
| 20 | $12\frac{1}{2}$ | 80 | $49\frac{1}{2}$ |
| 30 | $18\frac{1}{2}$ | 90 | $55\frac{3}{4}$ |
| 40 | $24\frac{3}{4}$ | 100 | 62 |

Where is there a gas (petrol) station?

**Dov'è una stazione di servizio?** *doh-vEH OO-nah stah-tsee-OH-neh dee sayr-vEE-tsee-oh*

Give me 15 (25) liters.

**Mi dia quindici (venticinque) litri.** *mee dEE-ah koo-EEn-dee-chee (vayn-tee-chEEn-koo-eh) lEE-tree*

Fill'er up with _____.

**Faccia il pieno di _____ .** *fAH-chee-ah eel pee-AY-noh dee*

- diesel — **diesel** *dEE-eh-sehl* or **gasolio** *gash-sOH-lee-oh*
- regular (standard) — **normale** *nohr-mAH-leh* or **benzina verde** *behn-tzEE-nah vEYr-deh*
- super (premium) — **super** *sOO-pehr*

Please check _____.

**Per favore mi controlli _____.** *pehr fah-vOH-reh mee kohn-trOHl-lee*

- the antifreeze — **l'acqua** *lAH-koo-ah*
- the battery — **la batteria** *lah baht-teh-rEE-ah*
- the oil — **l'olio** *lOH-lee-oh*
- the spark plugs — **le candele** *leh kahn-dAY-leh*
- the tires — **i pneumatici (le gomme)** *ee pneh-oo-mAH-tee-chee (leh gOHm-meh)*

Guarded railroad crossing

Yield

Stop

Right of way

Dangerous intersection ahead

Gasoline (petrol) ahead

Parking

No vehicles allowed

Dangerous curve

Pedestrian crossing

Oncoming traffic has right of way

No bicycles allowed

No parking allowed

No entry

No left turn

No U-turn

No passing

Border crossing

Traffic signal ahead

Speed limit

Traffic circle (roundabout) ahead

Minimum speed limit (kilometers)

All traffic turns left

End of no passing zone

One-way street

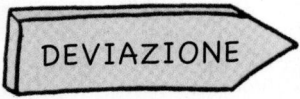


Detour

Danger ahead

Entrance to expressway

Expressway ends

| | |
|---|---|
| ■ the tire pressure | **la pressione delle gomme** *lah prehs-see-OH-neh dAYl-leh gOHm-meh* |
| Change the oil (please). | **Mi cambi l'olio (per favore).** *mee kAHm-bee lOH-lee-oh (pehr fah-vOH-reh)* |
| Charge the battery. | **Mi carichi la batteria.** *mee kAH-ree-key lah baht-teh-rEE-ah* |
| Change this tire. | **Mi cambi questa ruota.** *mee kAHm-bee koo-AYs-tah roo-OH-tah* |
| Wash the car. | **Mi faccia il lavaggio alla macchina.** *mee fAH-chee-ah eel lah-vAH-jee-oh AHl-lah mAHk-kee-nah* |
| Where are the restrooms? | **Dove sono i gabinetti?** *dOH-veh sOH-noh ee gah-bee-nAYt-tee* |

## ACCIDENTS AND REPAIRS

| | |
|---|---|
| My car has broken down. | **Mi si è guastata la macchina.** *mee see-EH goo-ah-stAH-tah lah mAHk-kee-nah* |
| It overheats. | **Si surriscalda.** *see soor-ree-skAHl-dah* |
| It doesn't start. | **Non si avvia.** *nohn see ahv-vEE-ah* |
| I have a flat tire. | **Ho una gomma bucata.** *oh OO-nah gOHm-mah boo-kAH-tah* |
| The radiator is leaking. | **Il radiatore perde acqua.** *eel rah-dee-ah-tOH-reh pEHr-deh AH-koo-ah* |

| TIRE PRESSURES | | | |
|---|---|---|---|
| LBS. PER SQ. IN. | KG. PER CM. | LBS. PER SQ. IN. | KG. PER CM. |
| 17 | 1.2 | 30 | 2.1 |
| 18 | 1.3 | 31 | 2.2 |
| 20 | 1.4 | 33 | 2.3 |
| 21 | 1.5 | 34 | 2.4 |
| 23 | 1.6 | 36 | 2.5 |
| 24 | 1.7 | 37 | 2.6 |
| 26 | 1.8 | 38 | 2.7 |
| 27 | 1.9 | 40 | 2.8 |
| 28 | 2.0 | | |

The battery is dead. **La batteria è scarica.** *lah baht-teh-rEE-ah EH skAH-ree-kah*

The keys are locked inside the car. **Le chiavi sono rimaste chiuse in macchina.** *leh key-AH-vee sOH-noh ree-mAH-steh key-OO-seh een mAHk-kee-nah*

Is there a garage near here? **C'è un'autorimessa qui vicino?** *chEH oon-ah-oo-toh-ree-mEHs-sah koo-EE vee-chEE-noh*

I need a mechanic (tow truck). **Ho bisogno di un meccanico (carroattrezzi).** *oh bee-sOH-ny-oh dee oon mehk-kAH-nee-koh (kAHr-roh-aht-trAY-tsee)*

Can you give me a push? **Può darmi una spinta?** *poo-OH dAHr-mee OO-nah spEEn-tah*

I don't have any tools. **Non ho gli attrezzi.** *nohn-OH ly-ee aht-trAY-tsee*

I need _____.
**Ho bisogno di _____.** *oh bee-sOH-ny-oh dee*

- a bulb
  **una lampadina** *OO-nah lahm-pah-dEE-nah*
- a filter
  **un filtro** *oon fEEl-troh*
- a fuse
  **un fusibile** *oon foo-sEE-bee-leh*

Can you fix the car?
**Può ripararmi la macchina?** *poo-OH ree-pah-rAHr-mee lah mAHk-kee-nah*

Can you repair it temporarily?
**Può farmi una riparazione provvisoria?** *poo-OH fAHr-mee OO-nah ree-pah-rah-tsee-OH-neh prohv-vee-sOH-ree-ah*

Do you have the part?
**Ha il pezzo di ricambio?** *ah eel pEH-tsoh dee ree-kAHm-bee-oh*

I think there's something wrong with _____.
**Penso che ci sia un guasto _____.** *pEHn-soh kay chee sEE-ah oon goo-AH-stoh*

- the adjustable driver's seat
  **al sedile di guida regolabile** *ahl say-dEE-leh dee goo-EE-dah reh-goh-lAH-bee-leh*
- the antilock brake system (ABS)
  **al l'antibloccaggio Abs** *ahl lahn-tee-blohk-kAH-jee-oh ah-bee-EHs-seh*
- the automatic transmission
  **al cambio automatico a controllo elettronico** *ahl kAHm-bee-oh ah-oo-toh-mAH-tee-koh ah kohn-trOHl-loh eh-leht-trOH-nee-koh*
- the climate control and dust/pollen filtration system
  **al climatizzatore con filtro antipolline e antipolvere** *ahl klee-mah-tee-tsAH-toh-reh kohn fEEl-troh ahn-tee-pOHl-lee-neh ay ahn-tee-pOHl-veh-ray*
- the compact disc changer
  **al lettore multiplo di compact disk** *ahl leht-tOH-reh mOOl-tee-ploh dee compact disc*

- the defogger/defroster — **al lo sbrinatore** *ahl loh sbree-nah-tOH-reh*
- the directional signal — **alla freccia** *AHl-lah frAY-chee-ah*
- the door handle — **alla maniglia della portiera** *AHl-lah mah-nEE-ly-ee-ah dAYl-la pohr-tee-EH-rah*
- the electrical system — **all'impianto elettrico** *ahl-leem-pee-AHn-toh eh-lEHt-tree-koh*
- the fan — **alla ventola** *AHl-lah vEHn-toh-lah*
- the fan belt — **alla cinghia del ventilatore** *AHl-lah chEEn-ghee-ah dayl vehn-tee-lah-tOH-reh*
- the fog lights — **al fendinebbia** *ahl fEHn-dee-nAYb-bee-ah*
- the fuel pump — **alla pompa della benzina** *AHl-lah pOHm-pah dAHl-lah behn-tsEE-nah*
- the gearshift — **al cambio** *ahl kAHm-bee-oh*
- the headlights — **agli abbaglianti** *AH-ly-ee ahb-bah-ly-ee-AHn-tee*

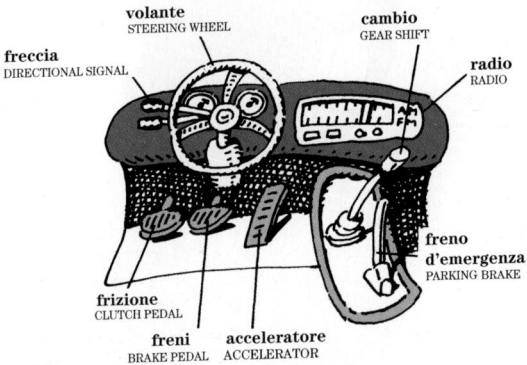

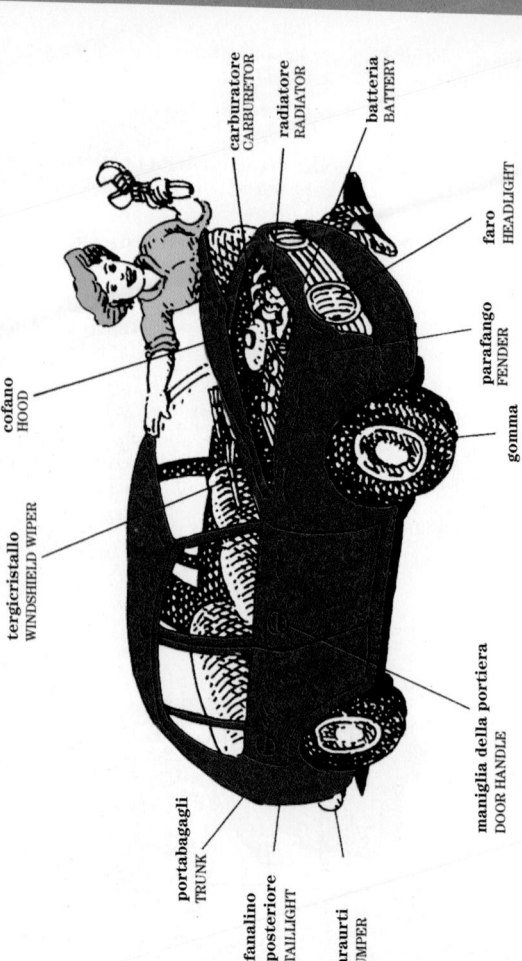
cofano
HOOD
tergicristallo
WINDSHIELD WIPER
portabagagli
TRUNK
fanalino posteriore
TAILLIGHT
paraurti
BUMPER
carburatore
CARBURETOR
radiatore
RADIATOR
batteria
BATTERY
faro
HEADLIGHT
parafango
FENDER
gomma
TIRE
maniglia della portiera
DOOR HANDLE

- the horn — **al clacson** *ahl klAH-ksohn*
- the ignition — **all'accensione** *ahl-lah-chehn-see-OH-neh*
- the lap-shoulder safety belts — **alle cinture di sicurezza a tre punti di ancoraggio** *AHl-leh cheen-tOO-reh dee see-koo-rEH-tzah ah tray pOOn-tee dee ahn-koh-rAH-jee-oh*
- the locking system with remote — **alla chiusura centralizzata con telecomando** *AHl-lah key-oo-sOO-rah chayn-trah-lee-tsAH-tah kohn tay-leh-koh-mAHn-doh*
- GPS — **al sistema di navigazione satellitare** *ahl see-stEH-mah dee nah-vee-gah-tsee-OH-neh sah-tehl-lee-tAH-reh*
- the power windows — **agli alzacristalli elettrici** *AH-ly-ee AHl-tsah-kree-stAHl-lee ay-lEHt-tree-chee*
- the radio — **alla radio** *AHl-lah rAH-dee-oh*
- the starter — **al motorino d'avviamento** *ahl moh-toh-rEE-noh dahv-vee-ah-mEHn-toh*
- the steering wheel — **al volante** *ahl voh-lAHn-teh*
- the steering wheel power adjustment — **al servosterzo elettrico** *ahl sehr-vo-stEHr-zoh eh-lEHt-tree-koh*
- the taillight — **al fanalino posteriore** *ahl fah-nah-lEE-noh poh-steh-ree-OH-reh*
- the theft protection system — **all'antifurto** *ahl-lahn-tee-fOOr-toh*
- the transmission — **alla trasmissione** *AHl-lah trah-smees-see-OH-neh*
- the water pump — **alla pompa dell'acqua** *AHl-lah pOHm-pah dayl-AH-koo-ah*

- the windshield (windscreen) wiper — **al tergicristallo** *ahl tehr-jee-kree-stAHl-loh*

Can you take a look at (check out) _____? — **Può dare un'occhiata (una controllata) _____?** *poo-OH dAH-reh oo-noh-key-AH-tah (OO-nah kohn-trohl-lAH-tah)*

- the brakes — **ai freni** *ah-ee frAY-nee*
- the bumper — **al paraurti** *ahl pah-rah-OOr-tee*
- the exhaust system — **al tubo di scappamento** *ahl tOO-boh dee skahp-pah-mEHn-toh*
- the gas tank — **al serbatoio (della benzina)** *ahl sehr-bah-tOH-ee-oh (dAYl-lah behn-tsEE-nah)*
- the hood — **al cofano** *ahl kOH-fah-noh*
- the trunk (boot) — **al portabagagli** *ahl pohr-tah-bah-gAH-ly-ee*

What's the matter? — **Che cosa c'è che non va?** *kay kOH-sah chEH kay nohn vAH*

Is it possible to (can you) fix it today? — **È possibile (può) aggiustarlo oggi?** *EH pohs-sEE-bee-leh (poo-OH) ah-jee-oo-stAHr-loh OH-jee*

How long will it take? — **Quanto tempo ci vorrà?** *koo-AHn-toh tEHm-poh chee vohr-rAH*

How much do I owe you? — **Quanto le devo?** *koo-AHn-toh leh dAY-voh*

# ENTERTAINMENTS AND DIVERSIONS

## MOVIES, THEATER, CONCERTS, OPERA, BALLET

Open-air festivals, ballets, and concerts echo the sound of music from majestic amphitheaters through old cities and squares where fountains and monuments are part of the enchanting stage called Italy. The Arena of Verona, the Baths of Caracalla in Rome, and the Theater of Taormina in Sicily enchant visitors. The summer **Festival dei Due Mondi** (in Umbria), the **Festival Roma Europa** in the Eternal City, and the **Festival della Canzone Napoletana** (Festival of Neapolitan Songs) in Naples are a few of the performances worth watching in the nightly view.

In Italy, foreign-language films shown in commercial theaters are dubbed rather than subtitled. Cinema houses are classified first run (**prima visione**), second run (**seconda visione**), and so on. All films are interrupted by an intermission (**intervallo**), during which refreshments are sold. No smoking is allowed by law. Not all cinemas are open at a given time in the summer, as each closes for a period (usually a month).

Most theater presentations are performed by repertory companies, some of which go on tour to smaller towns. Musical comedies are rare in Italy. In recent years, cabaret theater has become popular. Theaters are closed in the summer.

The opera season varies from place to place; however, most of the major opera houses offer out-of-season events (concerts, ballets).

Theater and opera tickets are easily purchased at the box office.

Ushers in cinemas, theaters, and opera houses expect to be tipped (see pages 52–53). You also must buy a program; you will not be given one.

Check *http://www.carnifest.com/carnivals/Romaeuropa-Festival.asp*

| | |
|---|---|
| Let's go to the _____. | **Andiamo al _____.** *ahn-dee-AH-moh ahl* |
| ■ movies (cinema) | **cinema** *chEE-neh-mah* |
| ■ theater | **teatro** *teh-AH-troh* |
| What are they showing today? | **Che spettacoli ci sono oggi?** *kay speht-tAH-koh-lee chee sOH-noh OH-jee* |
| Is it a _____? | **È _____?** *EH* |
| ■ mystery | **un giallo** *oon jee-AHl-loh* |
| ■ comedy | **una commedia** *OO-nah kohm-mEH-dee-ah* |
| ■ drama | **un dramma** *oon drAHm-mah* |
| ■ musical | **un'operetta** *oo-noh-peh-rAYt-tah* |
| ■ romance | **un romanzo** *oon roh-mAHn-tsoh* |
| ■ war film | **un film di guerra** *oon fEElm dee goo-EHr-ra* |
| ■ science fiction film | **un film di fantascienza** *oon fEElm dee fahn-tah-shee-EHn-tsah* |
| Is it in English? | **È parlato in inglese?** *EH pahr-lAH-toh een een-glAY-seh* |
| Has it been dubbed? | **È stato doppiato?** *EH stAH-toh dohp-pee-AH-toh* |
| Where is the box office? | **Dov'è il botteghino?** *doh-vEH eel boht-tay-ghEE-noh* |
| What time does the (first) show begin? | **A che ora comincia lo (il primo) spettacolo?** *ah kay OH-rah koh-mEEn-chee-ah loh (eel prEE-moh) speht-tAH-koh-loh* |

What time does the (last) show end?

**A che ora finisce lo (l'ultimo) spettacolo?** *ah kay OH-rah fee-nEE-sheh loh (lOOl-tee-moh) speht-tAH-koh-loh*

I want a seat near the middle (front, rear).

**Desidero un posto al centro (davanti, dietro).** *day-sEE-deh-roh oon pOHs-toh ahl chAYn-troh (dah-vAHn-tee dee-EH-troh)*

Can I check my coat?

**Posso consegnare (lasciare) il mio cappotto?** *pOHs-soh kohn-seh-ny-ee-AH-reh (lah-shee-AH-reh) eel mEE-oh kahp-pOHt-toh*

## BUYING A TICKET

I need _____ tickets for tonight (tomorrow night).

**Mi occorrono _____ biglietti per stasera (domani sera).** *mee oh-kOHr-roh-noh ____ bee-ly-ee-AYt-tee pehr stah-sAY-rah (doh-mAH-nee sAY-rah)*

- two orchestra seats — **due poltrone d'orchestra** *doo-eh pohl-trOH-neh dohr-kEHs-trah*
- two box seats — **due poltrone nei palchi** *doo-eh pohl-trOH-neh nAY-ee pAHl-kee*
- two mezzanine seats — **due poltrone** *doo-eh pohl-trOH-neh*
- two gallery seats — **due posti in galleria** *doo-eh pOHs-tee een gahl-leh-rEE-ah*

## MORE ABOUT MUSIC

How much are the front-row seats?

**Qual è il prezzo dei posti di prima fila?** *koo-ah-lEH eel prEH-tsoh dAY-ee pOH-stee dee prEE-mah fEE-lah*

What are the least expensive seats?

**Quali sono i posti meno costosi?** *koo-AH-lee sOH-noh ee pOH-stee mAY-noh koh-stOH-see*

Are there any seats for tonight's performance?

**Ci sono posti per lo spettacolo di stasera?** *chee sOH-noh pOH-stee pehr loh speht-tAH-koh-loh dee stah-sAY-rah*

We would like to attend _____.

**Vorremmo assistere ad _____.** *vohr-rEHm-moh ahs-sEE-steh-reh ahd*

- a ballet — **un balletto** *oon bahl-lAYt-toh*
- a concert — **un concerto** *oon kohn-chEHr-toh*

- an opera — **un'opera** *oo-nOH-peh-rah*

What are they playing (singing)?

**Che cosa recitano (cantano)?** *kay kOH-sah rEH-chee-tah-noh (kAHn-tah-noh)*

Who is the conductor?

**Chi è il direttore d'orchestra?** *key-EH eel dee-reht-tOH-reh dohr-kEH-strah*

I prefer _____.

**Preferisco _____.** *preh-feh-rEE-skoh*

- classical music — **la musica classica** *lah mOO-see-kah clAHs-see-kah*
- popular music — **la musica popolare** *lah mOO-see-kah poh-poh-lAH-reh*
- ballet — **il balletto** *eel bahl-lAYt-toh*

Should I get the tickets in advance?

**Debbo comprare i biglietti in anticipo?** *dAYb-boh kohm-prAH-reh ee bee-ly-ee-AYt-tee een ahn-tEE-chee-poh*

Do I have to dress formally?

**È prescritto l'abito da sera?** *EH preh-skrEEt-toh lAH-bee-toh dah sAY-rah*

May I buy a program?

**Posso comprare il programma di sala?** *pOHs-soh kohm-prAH-reh eel proh-grAHm-mah dee sAH-lah*

What opera (ballet) are they performing?

**Quale opera (balletto) danno?** *koo-AH-leh OH-peh-rah (bahl-lAYt-toh) dAHn-noh*

## NIGHTCLUBS, DANCING

Dance clubs, live concerts, discos, and live shows reflect the real multicultural aspects of contemporary Italy.

Look into . . .

- the dress code. Is it casual or are only certain types of clothing permitted?
- admission fees and payment options (some places are cash only).
- getting a free entrance card.
- the ambiance.

Look out!

- Is the place air-conditioned?
- Are you really paying a flat rate?
- The ticket may be used as a credit card, and at the end of the night you may be asked to pay for everything that is stamped on that ticket… drinks and anything else that is on it!
- Don't lose your ticket! There may be a fine of up to 50 euros.

Check *www.romeexplorer.com/club.html*

Let's go to a night-club.

**Andiamo al night club.** *ahn-dee-AH-moh ahl nAH-eet klOOb*

Is a reservation necessary?

**È necessaria la prenotazione?** *EH neh-chehs-sAH-ree-ah lah preh-noh-tah-tsee-OH-neh*

We haven't got a reservation.

**Non abbiamo la prenotazione.** *nohn ahb-bee-AH-moh lah preh-noh-tah-tsee-OH-neh*

Is there a good discotheque here?

**C'è una buona discoteca qui?** *chEH OO-nah boo-OH-nah dee-skoh-tEH-kah koo-EE*

Is there dancing at the hotel?

**Si balla in albergo (all'hotel)?** *see bAHl-lah een ahl-bEHr-goh (ahl-loh-tEHl)*

We'd like a table near the dance floor.

**Vorremmo un tavolo vicino alla pista (di ballo).** *vohr-rEHm-moh oon tAH-voh-loh vee-chEE-noh AHl-lah pEE-stah (dee bAHl-loh)*

Is there a minimum (cover charge)?

**C'è un prezzo minimo (per il tavolo)?** *chEH oon prEH-tsoh mEE-nee-moh (pehr eel tAH-voh-loh)*

Where is the checkroom?

**Dov'è il guardaroba?** *doh-vEH eel goo-ahr-dah-rOH-bah*

At what time does the floor show go on?

**A che ora comincia lo spettacolo (di varietà)?** *ah kay OH-rah koh-mEEn-chee-ah loh speht-tAH-koh-loh (dee vah-ree-eh-tAH)*

## SPORTS AND LEISURE ACTIVITIES

**Soccer** is the national sport. The national team, **gli Azzurri** *(ly-ee ah-tzOOr-ree)*, electrifies soccer fans worldwide. The games begin at the end of August and end in May. The soccer season culminates with the **Coppa Italia** *(kOHp-pah ee-tAH-lee-ah)*. The main stadiums are: Rome, **Stadio Olimpico**; Milan, **Stadio San Siro**; Turin, **Stadio delle Alpi**; Genoa, **Stadio Marassi**; Naples, **Stadio San Paolo**; and Bari, **Stadio Sant'Elia**.

**Bicycling** is also very popular. **Il Giro d'Italia** *(eel jEE-roh dee-tAH-lee-ah)* or Tour of Italy is a very prestigious cycling race that attracts competitors from all over the world.

**Skiing.** The Italian ski resorts are some of the best in Europe. Italy offers prime winter and summer skiing centers. Several, such as Cervinia, Cortina d'Ampezzo, Courmayer, and Sestriere are well known internationally. The Dolomites offer the best equipped ski resorts. Smaller ski centers are in the Apennines and in Sicily. For information on package ski holidays, contact the **Federazione Arrampicata Sportiva Italiana** *(feh-deh-rah-tzee-OH-neh ahr-rahm-pee-kAH-tah spohr-tEE-vah ee-tah-lee-AH-nah)*, the Italian Sport Climbing Federation.

Golf, fishing, flying and hang gliding, horseback riding, scuba diving and spear fishing, tennis, walking, water skiing and yachting, etc. are accessible throughout Italy. Swimming pools are very expensive in Italy but water parks provide pools, slides, games, and wave machines. You may want to contact the **Aeroclub d'Italia** *(ah-EH-roh-kloob dee-tAH-lee-ah)* for hang gliding and flying courses; the **Federazione Italiana di Canoa e Kayak** *(feh-deh-rah-tzee-OH-neh ee-tah-lee-AH-nah dee kah-nOH-ah ay kah-ee-AHk)* for canoeing and kayaking; the **Federazione Italiana di Vela** *(feh-deh-rah-tzee-OH-neh ee-tah-lee-AH-nah dee vAY-lah)* for sailing; the **Federazione Italiana di Sport Equestre** *(feh-deh-rah-tzee-OH-neh ee-tah-lee-AH-nah de spOHrt eh-koo-EHs-treh)* for riding lessons, trips, and outings; the **Federazione Italiana di Attività Subacque** *(feh-deh-rah-tzee-OH-neh ee-tah-lee-AH-nah dee aht-tee-vee-tAH soob-AHk-oo-eh)* for underwater diving courses; the **Club Alpino Italiano (CAI)** *(klEHb ahl-pEE-noh ee-tah-lee-AH-noh)* for trekking and climbing; the **Italian Birds Protection League** for nature walks and bird watching; and the **World Wide Fund for Nature (WWF)** for walking and trekking.

## SPECTATOR SPORTS

I'd like to watch a soccer game.

**Vorrei vedere una partita di calcio.** *vohr-rEH-ee veh-dAY-reh OO-nah pahr-tEE-tah dee kAHl-chee-oh*

Where's the stadium?

**Dov'è lo stadio?** *doh-vEH loh stAH-dee-oh*

At what time does the match begin?

**A che ora comincia la partita?** *ah kay OH-rah koh-mEEn-chee-ah lah pahr-tEE-tah*

What teams are playing?

**Quali squadre giocano?** *koo-AH-lee skoo-AH-dreh jee-OH-kah-noh*

What is the score?

**Qual è il punteggio?** *koo-ah-lEH eel poon-tAY-jee-oh*

Go!

**Forza!** *fOHr-tsah*

Is there a racetrack here?

**C'è un ippodromo qui?** *chEH oon eep-pOH-droh-moh koo-EE*

Is there a track and field stadium (sports arena) in this city?

**C'è uno stadio con piste e campo sportivo in questa città?** *chEH OO-noh stAH-dee-oh kohn pEEs-teh ay kAHm-poh spohr-tEE-voh een koo-AY-stah cheet-tAH*

What are the main events today (tomorrow)?

**Quali sono gli spettacoli principali di oggi (domani)?** *koo-AH-lee sOH-noh ly-ee speht-tAH-koh-lee preen-chee-pAH-lee dee OH-jee (doh-mAH-nee)*

| | |
|---|---|
| Do you think I can get a ticket? | **Pensa che è possibile avere un biglietto?** *pEHn-sah kay-EH pohs-sEE-bee-leh ah-vAY-reh oon bee-ly-ee-AYt-toh* |
| How much is a ticket? | **Quanto costa un biglietto?** *koo-AHn-toh kOHs-tah oon bee-ly-ee-AYt-toh* |

## SPORTS VOCABULARY

| | |
|---|---|
| I like to _____. | **Mi piace _____.** *mee pee-AH-cheh* |
| ■ do aerobics | **fare esercizi aerobici** *fAH-reh eh-sehr-chEE-tzee ah-eh-rOH-bee-chee* |
| ■ play basketball | **giocare a pallacanestro** *jee-oh-kAH-reh ah pAHl-lah-kah-nAY-stroh* |
| ■ go bicycling | **andare in bicicletta** *ahn-dAH-reh een bee-chee-klAYt-tah* |
| ■ go boating | **andare in barca** *ahn-dAH-reh een bAHr-kah* |
| ■ go canoeing | **andare in canoa** *ahn-dAH-reh een kah-nOH-ah* |
| ■ go diving | **fare immersioni** *fAH-reh eem-mehr-see-OH-nee* |
| ■ fish | **pescare** *pay-skAH-reh* |
| ■ play golf | **giocare a golf** *jee-oh-kAH-reh ah gOHlf* |
| ■ play hockey | **giocare ad hockey** *jee-oh-kAH-reh ahd OH-key* |
| ■ go horseback riding | **andare a cavallo** *ahn-dAH-reh ah kah-vAHl-loh* |
| ■ go hunting | **andare a caccia** *ahn-dAH-reh ah kAH-chee-ah* |
| ■ ice-skate | **pattinare su ghiaccio** *paht-tee-nAH-reh soo ghee-AH-chee-oh* |
| ■ go mountain climbing | **fare alpinismo** *fAH-reh ahl-pee-nEEs-moh* |

- roller-skate — **pattinare** *paht-tee-nAH-reh*
- go sailing — **andare in barca** *ahn-dAH-reh een bAHr-kah*
- scuba dive — **fare il nuoto subacqueo** *fAH-reh eel noo-OH-toh soob-AH-koo-eh-oh*
- ski — **sciare** *shee-AH-reh*
- surf — **surf** *sOOrf*
- swim — **nuotare** *noo-oh-tAH-reh*
- play tennis — **giocare a tennis** *jee-oh-kAH-reh ah tEHn-nees*
- play volleyball — **giocare a palla a volo** *jee-oh-kAH-reh ah pAHl-lah ah vOH-loh*

## PLAYING FIELDS

Shall we go to the _____. — **Andiamo _____?** *ahn-dee-AH-moh*

- beach — **alla spiaggia/al mare** *ahl-lah spee-AH-jee-ah/ahl mAH-reh*
- court — **in cortile** *een kohr-tEE-leh*
- tennis court — **sul campo da tennis** *sool kAHm-poh dah tEHn-nees*
- field — **al campo sportivo** *ahl kAHm-poh spohr-tEE-voh*
- golf course — **al campo di golf** *ahl kAHm-poh dee gOHlf*
- gymnasium — **in palestra** *een pah-lEH-strah*
- mountain — **in montagna** *een mohn-tAH-ny-ee-ah*
- ocean — **in oceano** *een oh-chEH-ah-noh*
- park — **al parco (ai giardini pubblici)** *ahl pAHr-koh (ah-ee jee-ahr-dEE-nee pOOb-blee-chee)*
- path — **sul sentiero (viottolo)** *sool sehn-tee-EH-roh (vee-OHt-toh-loh)*

- pool — **in piscina** *een pee-shEE-nah*
- rink — **in pista** *een pEE-stah*
- sea — **al mare** *ahl mAH-reh*
- stadium — **allo stadio** *AHl-loh stAH-dee-oh*
- track — **in pista** *een pEE-stah*

## SPORTS EQUIPMENT

I need _____. — **Ho bisogno di _____.** *oh bee-sOH-ny-oh dee*

- a ball — **una palla** *OO-nah pAHl-lah*
- a bat — **una mazza** *OO-nah mAHt-zah*
- a bicycle — **una bicicletta** *OO-nah bee-chee-clAYt-tah*
- a boat — **una barca** *OO-nah bAHr-kah*
- a canoe — **una canoa** *OO-nah kah-nOH-ah*
- a diving suit — **una tuta da sub** *OO-nah tOO-tah dah soob*
- a fishing rod — **una canna da pesca** *OO-nah kAHn-nah dah pAY-skah*
- golf clubs — **mazze da golf** *mAHt-zeh dah gOHlf*
- a hockey stick — **un bastone da hockey** *oon bah-stOH-neh dah OH-key*
- ice skates — **pattini per il ghiaccio** *pAHt-tee-nee pehr eel ghee-AH-chee-oh*
- jogging shoes — **scarpette da corsa (per jogging)** *skahr-pAYt-teh dah kOHr-sah (pehr jogging)*
- a jogging suit — **una tuta da ginnastica (da jogging)** *OO-nah tOO-tah dah jeen-nAH-stee-kah (dah jogging)*
- a puck — **un disco di gomma per hockey** *oon dEE-skoh dee gOHm-mah pehr OH-key*

- a racket — **una racchetta** *OO-nah rahk-kAYt-tah*
- rollerblades — **pattini-roller blades** *pAHt-tee-nee-rOHl-lehr blAY-deh*
- a sailboard — **una tavola a vela (un windsurf)** *OO-nah tAH-voh-lah ah vAY-lah (oon wEEn-soorf)*
- scuba gear — **un equipaggiamento per il nuoto subacqueo** *oon eh-koo-ee-pah-jee-ah-mEHn-toh pehr eel noo-OH-toh soob-AH-koo-eh-oh*
- a skateboard — **un monopattino** *oon moh-noh-pAHt-tee-noh*
- skis — **sci** *shee*
- a surfboard — **una tavola da surf** *OO-nah tAH-voh-lah dah sOOrf*
- a wet suit — **una muta da sub (per immersioni)** *OO-nah mOO-tah dah sOOb (pehr eem-mehr-see-OH-nee)*

## ACTIVE SPORTS

Do you play tennis? — **Gioca a tennis?** *jee-OH-kah ah tEHn-nees*

I (don't) play very well. — **(Non) gioco molto bene.** *(nohn) jee-OH-koh mOHl-toh bEH-neh*

Do you play singles (doubles)? — **Gioca il singolo (in doppio)?** *jee-OH-kah eel sEEn-goh-loh (een dOHp-pee-oh)*

Do you know where there is a court? — **Sa dove c'è un campo da tennis?** *sAH doh-veh-chEH oon kAHm-poh dah tEHn-nees*

Is it a private club? I'm not a member.

**È un club privato? Io non sono socio.** *EH oon clEHb pree-vAH-toh EE-oh nohn sOH-noh sOH-chee-oh*

How much do they charge per hour?

**Quanto si paga all'ora?** *koo-AHn-toh see pAH-gah ahl-lOH-rah*

Can I rent a racquet?

**Posso affittare una racchetta?** *pOHs-soh ahf-feet-tAH-reh OO-nah rahk-kAYt-tah*

You play very well.

**Lei gioca molto bene.** *lEH-ee jee-OH-kah mOHl-toh bEH-neh*

Let's play another set.

**Giochiamo un altro set.** *jee-oh-key-AH-moh oon AHl-troh seht*

Where is a safe place to run (to jog)?

**Dov'è un posto buono dove si può correre (fare del footing)?** *doh-vEH oon pOHs-toh boo-OH-noh dOH-veh see poo-OH kOHr-reh-reh (fAH-reh dayl fOO-teeng)*

Where is there a health club?

**Dove si può trovare un centro fitness?** *dOH-veh see poo-OH troh-vAH-reh oon chAYn-tro feet-nEHs*

Where can I play bocci?

**Dove posso giocare alle bocce?** *dOH-veh pOHs-soh jee-oh-kAH-reh AHl-leh bOH-cheh*

Where can I rent a _____?

**Dove posso noleggiare _____?** *dOH-veh pOHs-soh noh-lay-jee-AH-reh*

- bicycle

**una bicicletta** *OO-nah bee-chee-klAYt-tah*

- mountain bike

**un rampichíno (una mountain bike)** *oon rahm-pee-kEE-noh (OO-nah mAH-oon-tahn bAH-eek)*

- racing bike

**una bicicletta da corsa** *OO-nah bee-chee-klAYt-tah dah kOHr-sah*

| | |
|---|---|
| ■ touring bike | **una bicicletta da passeggio** *OO-nah bee-chee-klAYt-tah dah pahs-sAY-jee-oh* |
| Where can I rent _____? | **Dove posso affittare _____?** *dOH-veh pOHs-soh ahf-feet-tAH-reh* |
| ■ (inline) skates | **i roller blade** or **pattini a rotelle (in linea)** *ee rOHl-lehr blAY-deh* or *pAHt-tee-nee ah roh-tEHl-leh (een lEE-neh-ah)* |
| ■ skateboards | **monopattini** *moh-noh-pAHt-tee-nee* |

## AT THE BEACH/POOL

| | |
|---|---|
| Is there a beach nearby? | **C'è una spiaggia qui vicino?** *chEH OO-nah spee-AH-jee-ah koo-ee vee-chEE-noh* |
| Let's go to the beach (to the pool). | **Andiamo alla spiaggia (in piscina).** *ahn-dee-AH-moh AHl-lah spee-AH-jee-ah (een pee-shEE-nah)* |
| Which bus will take us to the beach? | **Quale autobus ci porterà alla spiaggia?** *koo-AH-leh AH-oo-toh-boos chee pohr-teh-rAH AHl-lah spee-AH-jee-ah* |
| Is there an indoor (outdoor) pool in the hotel? | **C'è una piscina coperta (scoperta) nell'hotel?** *chEH OO-nah pee-shEE-nah koh-pEHr-tah (skoh-pEHr-tah) nayl-loh-tEHl* |
| I (don't) know how to swim well. | **(Non) so nuotare bene.** *(nohn) soh noo-oh-tAH-reh bEH-neh* |
| Is it safe to swim here? | **Si può nuotare qui senza pericolo?** *see poo-OH noo-oh-tAH-reh koo-EE sEHn-tsah peh-rEE-koh-loh* |

Are there big waves? **Ci sono onde alte?** *chee sOH-noh OHn-deh AHl-teh*

Are there sharks? **Ci sono pescecani?** *chee sOH-noh pay-sheh-kAH-nee*

Is it dangerous for children? **È pericoloso per i bambini?** *EH peh-ree-koh-lOH-soh pehr ee bahm-bEE-nee*

Is there a lifeguard? **C'è un bagnino?** *chEH oon bah-ny-EE-noh*

Help! I'm drowning! **Aiuto! Affogo!** *ah-ee-OO-toh! Ahf-fOH-goh*

Where can I get _____? **Dove posso trovare _____?** *dOH-vey pOHs-soh troh-vAH-reh*

- an air mattress **un materassino pneumatico** *oon mah-teh-rahs-sEE-noh pneh-oo-mAH-tee-koh*
- a bathing suit **un costume da bagno** *oon koh-stOO-meh dah bAH-ny-oh*
- a beach chair **una sedia per la spiaggia** *OO-nah sEH-dee-ah pehr lah spee-AH-jee-ah*
- a beach towel **una tovaglia da spiaggia** *OO-nah toh-vAH-ly-ee-ah dah spee-AH-jee-ah*
- diving equipment **un equipaggiamento subacqueo** *oon ay-koo-ee-pah-jee-ah-mEHn-toh soob-AH-koo-eh-oh*
- sunglasses **degli occhiali da sole** *dAY-ly-ee oh-key-AH-lee dah sOH-leh*
- suntan lotion **una lozione per l'abbronzatura** *OO-nah loh-tsee-OH-neh pehr lahb-brohn-tsah-tOO-rah*

## ON THE SLOPES

Ski lovers can find the best Italian ski resorts in the Alps, Dolomites, and Apennines. The resorts are family-friendly and offer excellent accommodations and delicious food. In the north, they can have spectacular views of Mont Blanc and Mont Rosa. Enjoy the classic and charming slopes of the Apennines and ski down Mont Etna, the active volcano in Sicily. Hotels, ski chalets, and apartments are widely available.

Ski enthusiasts may arrange for the so-called Adventure Vacation Packages, under the supervision of experienced Alpine guides. Such packages can include climbing, bridging, canoeing, hiking, mountain biking, parasailing, rafting, and trekking.

While the northern part of Italy is better known for its skiing, it is also possible to ski in many other regions such as Abruzzo (Campo Imperatore), Tuscany (Abetone), and Mount Etna in Sicily.

Skiing in Italy is a relaxing, social, and friendly activity, involving a lot of eating, drinking, sunbathing, and chatting. The resorts' after-ski and nightlife are usually excellent and diverse.

### MINI SKI GLOSSARY

| | |
|---|---|
| chairlift | **seggiovia** *seh-jee-oh-vEE-ah* |
| cross-country skiing | **sci di fondo** *shee dee phOHn-doh* |
| first-aid service | **pronto soccorso** *prOHn-toh soh-kOHr-soh* |
| ski run map | **cartina delle piste** *kahr-tEE-nah dAYl-leh pEE-steh* |
| ski instructor | **maestro/istruttore di sci** *mah-AY-stroh/ee-stroot-tOH-reh dee shEE* |
| ski lift | **ski lift/sciovia** *ski lift/shee-oh-vEE-ah* |

| | |
|---|---|
| snowboard | **snowboard/tavola** *snowboard/tAH-voh-lah* |
| snowshoe | **ciaspola/racchetta da neve** *cee-AH-spoh-lah/rah-kEHt-tah dah nAY-veh* |

Look into …
- having a valid passport.
- ski vacation packages.
- travel insurance and travel insurance services.
- lodging/accommodations.
- getting Superski passes.
- entertainment/excursions.
- cooking classes.

Look out!
- Will prices change without notice even after booking?
- Does the trip price include departure taxes, fuel surcharges, and security fees?
- Are full-course dinners included?
- Are
  - airport ground transfers in Italy built-in?
  - daily transports to and from main lift stations free?
  - single supplements available?
  - discounts available for nonskiers?
  - there discounts for children under 12?

Check *goitaly.about.com/od/wintersportsinitaly/a/ski_italy.htm*

## POPULAR SKI AREAS

**Abruzzi**

The slopes of **Cinquemiglia** are located among the medieval hill towns of Castel del Sangro, Palena, Pescocostanza, Rivisondoli, and Roccaraso. The **Gran Sasso** area also has good skiing slopes, cross-country skiing, and many winter sports.
Check *www.lifeinabruzzo.com/skiing-in-abruzzo*

**Lazio**

**Monte Terminillo**, in the province of Rieti, is known as the Mountain of Rome. Its slopes provide fun for beginners and expert skiers with alpine skiing, cross-country, and snowboarding. It is part of the Apennine range in central Italy, 20 km from Rieti and 100 km from Rome. It can easily be reached by car and public transportation. Top-rated hotels and restaurants surround the area.
Google Search: Lazio Monte Terminillo

**Lombardy/ Valtellina**

This area has the ski resorts of **Aprica** and **Bormio**. Alta Valtellina is best known for the ski resorts of Livigno, Ponte di Legno, Santa Caterina Valfurva and Santa Caterina.
Check *www.j2ski.com › European Ski Resorts › Italian Ski Resorts-*

**Piedmont**

This northwestern region has 53 ski resorts and 1300 km of runs. **La Via Lattea** has 400 km of ski runs that include Cesena, Claviere, Sansicario, Sauze d'Oulx, and Sestriere. **Cervinia** has 30 ski lifts and a run over 20-km long. **Courmayeur,** in the Mont Blanc slopes, offers great skiing, good Italian restaurants, great shopping, and a lively nightlife.
Check *goitaly.about.com/od/ piemontepiedmont/a/ski_piemonte_2.htm*

**Sardinia**

Although the mountain of **Gennargentu** is located on a Mediterranean island, it has snow that falls every winter. The only ski resort is in Fonni, close to the peak of Bruncu Spina.
Check *travel.italyitalia.com/guides/ sardinia/skiing-sardinia-*

**Sicily**

During the winter, the slopes of the Mount Etna volcano are covered with deep snow. **Rifugio Sapienza** and **Liguaglossa** are the two ski areas to enjoy.
Check *www.gotaormina.com/en/sports/ skiing.html*

**Tuscany**

**Abetone,** in the Pistoia mountains of central Italy, is a very important ski resort. The slopes of **Val di Luce**, **Valle dello Scoltenna**, **Valle del Sestalone**, and **Valle di Lima** are interconnected. Fresh snow is provided by recently installed snow-making machines. The ski resorts of **Corlo ale Scale**, **Cimone**, and **Abetone** offer the Big Snow Pass that allows skiers to access the slopes of all three resorts.
Check *www.florencevillas.com/newsletter/nl_24.htm-*

**Trentino**

**Madonna di Campiglio** is a well-known ski resort area located in the Dolomites (the northeast corner of Italy), with slopes for all levels and good lodging choices.
Check *www.skiingitaly.net/ski_resort_info_madonna_di_campiglio.html-*

**Aosta**

**Cervinia** sits in the shadow of Monte Cervino (Matterhorn). This ski resort provides access to a variety of winter sports and the town has boutiques, discos, and nightclubs. Once there, take a hop to the **Gran Paradiso** national park.
Check *www.knowital.com › Italy*

**Veneto**

The Dolomites' resorts of Cortina d'Ampezzo, Val Gardena, and Val di Sole offer good restaurants, ice skating, and many indoor sports activities.
Check *www.dolomitemountains.com*

Which ski area do you recommend?

**Quali campi di sci consiglia?** *koo-AH-lee kAHm-pee dee shee kohn-sEE-ly-ee-ah*

I am a novice (intermediate, expert) skier.

**Sono uno sciatore (una sciatrice) (principiante, dilettante, esperto(a)).** *sOH-noh OO-noh shee-ah-tOH-reh (OO-nah shee-ah-trEE-ceh) (preen-chee-pee-AHn-teh dee-leht-tAHn-teh ehs-pEHr-toh(ah))*

| | |
|---|---|
| What kind of lifts are there? | **Come sono le sciovie?** *kOH-meh sOH-noh leh shee-oh-vEE-eh* |
| How much does the lift cost? | **Quant'è il biglietto per la sciovia?** *koo-ahn-tEH eel bee-ly-ee-AYt-toh pehr lah shee-oh-vEE-ah* |
| Do they give lessons? | **Danno lezioni?** *dAHn-noh leh-tsee-OH-nee* |
| Is there enough snow this time of the year? | **C'è abbastanza neve in questo periodo dell'anno?** *chEH ahb-bah-stAHn-tsah nAY-veh een koo-AYs-toh peh-rEE-oh-doh dayl-lAHn-noh* |
| Is there any cross-country skiing? | **C'è anche lo sci di fondo?** *chEH AHn-keh loh shee dee fOHn-doh* |
| How do I get there? | **Come ci si va?** *kOH-meh chee see vAH* |
| Can I rent _____ there? | **Posso affittare _____ sul posto?** *pOHs-soh ahf-feet-tAH-reh ____ sOOl pOH-stoh* |
| ■ equipment | **l'attrezzatura** *laht-treh-tsah-tOO-rah* |

- poles — **le racchette da sci** *leh rah-kAYt-teh dah shEE*
- skis — **gli sci** *ly-ee shEE*
- ski boots — **gli scarponi da sci** *ly-ee skahr-pOH-nee dah shEE*

## ON THE LINKS

Is there a golf course here? — **C'è un campo di golf (qui)?** *chEH oon kAHm-poh dee gOHlf (koo-EE)*

Can one rent clubs? — **Si possono affittare le mazze?** *see pOHs-soh-noh ahf-feet-tAH-reh leh mAH-tseh*

## CAMPING

Italy offers good and varied camping opportunities. Check *www.initaly.com/travel/info/camping.htm* or *www.canvasholidays.co.uk/destinations/italy-620-0.aspx*

Is there a camping area near here? — **C'è un campeggio qui vicino?** *chEH oon kahm-pAY-jee-oh koo-EE vee-chEE-noh*

Do we pick our own site? — **Possiamo scegliere il posto che ci piace?** *pohs-see-AH-moh shay-ly-ee-EH-reh eel pOHs-toh kay chee pee-AH-cheh*

We only have a tent. — **Noi abbiamo solo una tenta.** *nOH-ee ahb-bee-AH-moh sOH-loh OO-nah tEHn-tah*

Where is it on this map? — **Dov'è su questa cartina?** *doh-vEH soo koo-AY-stah kahr-tEE-nah*

| | |
|---|---|
| Can we park our trailer (caravan)? | **Possiamo posteggiare la nostra roulotte?** *pohs-see-AH-moh poh-steh-jee-AH-reh lah nOH-strah roo-lOH-te* |
| Can we camp for one night only? | **Possiamo accamparci per una notte solamente?** *pohs-see-AH-moh ahk-kahm-pAHr-chee pehr OO-nah nOHt-teh soh-lah-mEHn-teh* |
| Is (are) there ____? | **C'è (ci sono) _____?** *cheh (chee sOH-noh)* |
| ■ drinking water | **acqua potabile** *AH-koo-ah poh-tAH-bee-leh* |
| ■ showers | **docce** *dOH-cheh* |
| ■ grills | **caminetti** *kah-mee-nAYt-tee* |
| ■ picnic tables | **tavoli per il pic-nic** *tAH-voh-lee pehr eel peek-nEEk* |
| ■ electricity | **l'elettricità** *leh-leh-tree-chee-tAH* |
| ■ a grocery store | **un negozio di generi alimentari** *oon nay-gOH-tsee-oh dee jEH-neh-ree ah-lee-mehn-tAH-ree* |
| ■ a children's playground | **un posto dove far giocare i bambini** *oon pOH-stoh dOH-veh fahr jee-oh-kAH-reh ee bahm-bEE-nee* |
| ■ flush toilets | **gabinetti** *gah-bee-nAYt-tee* |
| How much do they charge per person (per car)? | **Quanto si paga a persona (per macchina)?** *koo-AHn-toh see pAH-gah ah pehr-sOH-nah (pehr mAHk-key-nah)* |
| We intend to stay _____ days (weeks). | **Pensiamo di stare _____ giorni (settimane).** *pehn-see-AH-moh dee stAH-reh _____ jee-OHr-nee (seht-tee-mAH-neh)* |

## IN THE COUNTRYSIDE

| | |
|---|---|
| Are there tours to the countryside? | **Si organizzano gite in campagna?** *see ohr-gah-nEE-tsah-noh jEE-teh een kahm-pAH-ny-ah* |
| What a beautiful landscape! | **Che bel panorama!** *kay bEHl pah-noh-rAH-mah* |
| Look at _____. | **Osserva (guarda) _____.** *ohs-sAYr-vah (goo-AHr-dah)* |
| ■ the barn | **la stalla** *lah stAHl-lah* |
| ■ the birds | **gli uccelli** *ly-ee oo-chEHl-lee* |
| ■ the bridge | **il ponte** *eel pOHn-teh* |
| ■ the castle | **il castello** *eel kah-stEHl-loh* |
| ■ the cottages | **i villini** *ee veel-lEE-nee* |
| ■ the farm | **la fattoria** *lah faht-toh-rEE-ah* |
| ■ the fields | **i campi** *ee kAHm-pee* |
| ■ the flowers | **i fiori** *ee fee-OH-ree* |
| ■ the forest | **il bosco** *eel bOH-skoh* |
| ■ the hill | **la collina** *lah kohl-lEE-nah* |
| ■ the lake | **il lago** *eel lAH-goh* |
| ■ the mountains | **le montagne** *leh mohn-tAH-ny-eh* |
| ■ the plants | **le piante** *leh pee-AHn-teh* |
| ■ the pond | **lo stagno** *loh stAH-ny-oh* |
| ■ the river | **il fiume** *eel fee-OO-meh* |
| ■ the sea | **il mare** *eel mAH-reh* |
| ■ the stream | **il ruscello** *eel roo-shEHl-loh* |
| ■ the trees | **gli alberi** *ly-ee AHl-beh-ree* |
| ■ the valley | **la valle** *lah vAHl-leh* |

- the village — **il paese (il villaggio)** *eel pah-AY-seh (eel veel-lAH-jee-oh)*
- the waterfall — **la cascata** *lah kah-skAH-tah*

**Travel Tips** Touring on a budget? Then it pays to do your homework. Look for hotels or bed-and-breakfast places that include a morning meal in the price of a room. Often the breakfast is hearty enough to allow a light lunch. Carry nutrition bars from home in your tote bag for snacking when only expensive airport or restaurant food is available. Use public transportation whenever possible. Rail and air passes are sold for Europe and other regions but often can only be purchased in the U.S. before departure. If you must rent a car and have booked one from home, double-check local prices. Sometimes better deals can be arranged on the spot. When you first arrive in a country, check with a visitors' bureau. Agents there will explain discount cards or money-saving packets offered by local governments or merchants. The discount plans often cover transportation, food, lodging, museums, concerts, and other entertainment.

# FOOD AND DRINK

How wonderful it is when a tourist can not only appreciate the sights and sounds of a country, but also enjoy its wonderful flavors. The food of Italy is world famous, and justifiably so. To savor the great range of culinary delights, you must first understand the differences among places that serve food and drink as well as the customs of the country. Always ask for **un posto dove si mangia bene**, a place where you can eat well.

| | |
|---|---|
| **Bar or Snack Bar** | Ice cream, coffee, pastries, and drinks are served. This is also a favorite place for a quick breakfast consisting of a hot, foamy **cappuccino** and a **mottino**, or a **maritozzo**, a **cornetto**, a **tramezzino**, or other pastry. |
| **Trattoria or Osteria** | Small, family-operated inn serving simple but delicious local dishes prepared while you wait. |
| **Tavola Calda** | Small, self-service cafeteria with simple, hot dishes that you choose from a hot table. In some places local specialties and dishes from other countries are prepared. |
| **Rosticceria** | Generally a take-out place for grilled meats. |
| **Pizzeria** | Small, family-operated pizza parlor. Local pizza specialties and other simple dishes are served. In some places they are called **pizzeria-rosticceria**, where you can sit and enjoy a nice meal. |
| **Paninotéca** | A sandwich bar, where a quick meal can be served. |
| **Autogrill** | A self-service cafeteria or snack area on the **autostrade** (motorway, turnpike) with bar, restaurant, tourist market, souvenirs, telephones, and bedrooms. |

**Ristorante** Elegant place classified by stars (some restaurants are rated according to their decor, others by the quality of their cuisine). *Often closed on Mondays.*

Most tourists will have their breakfast in the hotel, so much of the information that follows applies to lunch and dinner. Breakfast, **la prima colazione**, for an Italian consists of **caffelatte** (coffee with milk) and a **croissant**, **panini** (rolls) with butter (**burro**) and jam or marmalade (**marmellata**) or cheese (**formaggio**). If your hotel doesn't serve breakfast, or you prefer to go out, you'll find a suitable Italian breakfast at a caffé or bar.

## LUNCH—IL PRANZO

Lunch is served from about noon or 12:30 to 3 P.M. (Usually siesta time is after **il pranzo**.) A regular **pranzo** includes:

| | | |
|---|---|---|
| **antipasto** | *ahn-tee-pAH-stoh* | appetizer |
| **primo** | *prEE-moh* | pasta or soup **(minestra in brodo)** |
| **secondo** | *say-kOHn-doh* | a meat or fish dish with vegetable, wine, and water |
| **formaggi** | *fohr-mAH-jee* | cheese course |
| **dolci** | *dOHl-chee* | sweet dessert |
| **frutta** | *frOOT-ta* | fruit |
| **caffé** | *kahf-fEH* | coffee |

## DINNER—LA CENA

Dinner follows the same general arrangement as lunch. It is served from around 7 P.M. to 10 P.M. In Northern Italy, dinner is served earlier than in Southern Italy.

## THE MENU

Many restaurants offer a special plate of the day (**il piatto del giorno**) or have a tourist menu at a set price (**il menù turistico a prezzo fisso**). These are usually very good values. You should also watch for the specialty of the chef or of the restaurant (**la specialità del cuoco o del ristorante**). Often the local wine is included in the price of a meal **(vino incluso)**.

The bill may or may not include a service charge (**servizio**), which is usually 12 to 15 percent of the bill. Other items that may appear on the bill are the tip (**mancia**), bread and cover charge (**pane e coperto**), and a surcharge (**supplemento**). Even if the service and tip are included, you should leave some remaining change; it is a token of your appreciation for good service and excellent food.

## EATING OUT

| | |
|---|---|
| Do you know a good restaurant? | **Scusi, conosce un buon ristorante?** *skOO-see koh-nOH-sheh oon boo-OHn ree-stoh-rAHn-teh* |
| Is it very expensive (dressy)? | **È molto costoso (elegante)?** *eh mOHl-toh koh-stOH-soh (eh-leh-gAHn-teh)* |
| Do you know a restaurant that serves typical dishes? | **Conosce un ristorante tipico (del luogo)?** *koh-nOH-sheh oon res-toh-rAHn-teh tEE-pee-koh (dAYl loo-OH-goh)* |
| Waiter! | **Cameriere!** *kah-meh-ree-EH-reh* |
| A table for two, please. | **Un tavolo per due, per favore.** *oon tAH-voh-loh pehr dOO-eh pehr fah-vOH-reh* |
| ■ in the corner | **all'angolo** *ahl-lAHn-goh-loh* |
| ■ near the window | **vicino alla finestra** *vee-chee-noh AHl-lah fee-nEHs-trah* |
| ■ on the terrace | **sul terrazzo** *sOOl tehr-rAH-tsoh* |
| I'd like to make a reservation ____. | **Vorrei fare una prenotazione _____.** *vohr-rEH-ee fAH-reh oon-ah preh-noh-tah-tsee-OH-neh* |
| ■ for tonight | **per stasera** *pehr stah-sAY-rah* |
| ■ for tomorrow evening | **per domani sera** *pehr doh-mAH-nee sAY-rah* |
| ■ for two (four) persons | **per due (quattro) persone** *pehr dOO-eh (koo-AHt-troh) pehr-SOH-neh* |
| ■ at 8 P.M. | **per le venti** *pehr leh vAYn-tee* |
| ■ at 8:30 P.M. | **per le venti e trenta** *pehr leh vAYn-tee ay trEHn-tah* |

We'd like to have lunch (dinner) now.
**Vorremmo pranzare adesso.** *vohr-rAYm-moh prahn-tsAH-reh ah-dEHs-soh*

The menu, please.
**Il menù, per piacere.** *eel may-nOO pehr pee-ah-chAY-reh*

I'd like the set menu.
**Vorrei il menù turistico. (Il menù a prezzo fisso.)** *vohr-rEH-ee eel meh-nOO too-rEEs-tee-koh (eel meh-nOO ah prEH-tsoh fEEs-soh)*

What's today's special?
**Qual è il piatto del giorno?** *koo-ah-lEH eel pee-AHt-toh dayl jee-OHr-noh*

What do you recommend?
**Che cosa mi consiglia lei?** *kay kOH-sah mee kohn-sEE-ly-ee-ah lEH-ee*

What's the house specialty?
**Qual è la specialità della casa?** *koo-ah-lEH lah speh-chee-ah-lee-tAH dAYl-lah kAH-sah*

Do you serve children's portions?
**Si servono porzioni per bambini?** *see sEHr-voh-noh pohr-tsee-OH-nee pehr bahm-bEE-nee*

I'm (not) very hungry.
**(Non) ho molta fame.** *(nohn) oh mOHl-tah fAH-meh*

Are the portions small (large)?
**Le porzioni sono piccole (grandi)?** *leh pohr-tsee-OH-nee sOH-noh pEE-koh-leh (grAHn-dee)*

To begin with, please bring us _____.
**Per cominciare, ci porti _____.** *pehr koh-meen-chee-AH-reh chee pOHr-tee*

■ an aperitif
**un aperitivo** *oon ah-peh-ree-tEE-voh*

| | |
|---|---|
| ■ a cocktail | **un cocktail** *oon kOHk-tayl* |
| ■ some white (red) wine | **del vino bianco (rosso)** *dayl vEE-noh bee-AHn-koh (rOHs-soh)* |
| ■ some water | **dell'acqua** *dayl-LAH-koo-ah* |
| ■ a bottle of mineral water, carbonated (noncarbonated) | **una bottiglia d'acqua minerale gassata (naturale)** *OO-nah boht-tEE-ly-ee-ah dAH-koo-ah mee-neh-rAH-leh gahs-sAH-tah (nah-too-rAH-leh)* |
| ■ a beer | **una birra** *OO-nah bEEr-rah* |
| I'd like to order now. | **Vorrei ordinare adesso** *vohr-rEH-ee ohr-dee-nAH-reh ah-dEHs-soh* |
| I'd like _____. | **Vorrei _____.** *vohr-rEH-ee* |

(See the listings that follow for individual dishes, and also the regional specialties noted on pages 150–159.)

| | |
|---|---|
| Do you have a house wine? | **Hanno il vino della casa?** *AHn-noh eel VEE-noh dAYl-lah kAH-sah* |
| Is it dry (mellow, sweet)? | **È vino secco (amabile, dolce)?** *EH vEE-noh sAY-koh (ah-mAH-bee-leh dOHl-cheh)* |
| Please also bring us _____. | **Per piacere ci porti anche _____.** *pehr pee-ah-chAY-reh chee pOHr-tee AHn-keh* |
| ■ a roll | **un panino** *oon pah-nEE-noh* |
| ■ bread | **il pane** *eel pAH-neh* |
| ■ bread and butter | **pane e burro** *pAH-neh ay bOOr-roh* |
| Waiter, we need _____. | **Cameriere(a), abbiamo bisogno di _____.** *kah-meh-ree-EH-reh(ah) ahb-bee-AH-moh bee-sOH-ny-oh dee* |

| | |
|---|---|
| ■ a knife | **un coltello** *oon kohl-tEHl-loh* |
| ■ a fork | **una forchetta** *OO-nah fohr-kAYt-tah* |
| ■ a spoon | **un cucchiaio** *oon koo-key-AH-ee-oh* |
| ■ a teaspoon | **un cucchiaino** *oon koo-key-ah-EE-noh* |
| ■ a soup spoon | **un cucchiaio per la minestra (il brodo)** *oon koo-key-AH-ee-oh pehr lah mee-nEHs-trah (eel brOH-doh)* |
| ■ a glass | **un bicchiere** *oon bee-key-EH-reh* |
| ■ a cup | **una tazza** *OO-nah tAH-tsah* |
| ■ a saucer | **un piattino** *oon pee-aht-tEE-noh* |
| ■ a plate | **un piatto** *oon pee-AHt-toh* |
| ■ a napkin | **un tovagliolo** *oon toh-vah-ly-ee-OH-loh* |

## APPETIZERS (STARTERS)

**Antipasti** mostly consist of raw salads, cooked chilled vegetables dressed with a vinaigrette, and massive varieties of sausages and salamis. Some key terms are:

| | | |
|---|---|---|
| **acciughe** | *ah-chee-OH-gheh* | anchovies |
| **antipasto misto** | *ahn-tee-pAHs-toh mEEs-toh* | assorted appetizers |
| **carciofi** | *kahr-chee-OH-fee* | artichoke |
| **mortadella** | *mohr-tah-dEHl-lah* | cold sausage, similar to bologna |
| **prosciutto crudo** | *proh-shee-OOt-toh krOO-doh* | dry-cured spiced ham |
| **tartufi** | *tahr-tOO-fee* | truffles (white) |

## SOUPS

Soups can be either thick or thin, and thus are given different names. **Brodi** are generally broths, while **zuppe** are thick and hearty.

| | | |
|---|---|---|
| **brodo di manzo** | *brOH-doh dee mAHn-tsoh* | broth, generally meat-based |
| **brodo di pollo** | *brOH-doh dee pOHl-loh* | chicken broth |
| **brodo magro di vegetali** | *brOH-doh mAH-groh dee veh-jeh-tAH-lee* | vegetable broth |
| **crema di _____** | *krEH-mah dee* | creamed _____ soup |
| **buridda** | *boo-rEEd-dah* | fish stew |
| **cacciucco** | *kah-chee-OO-koh* | seafood chowder |
| **minestra in brodo** | *mee-nEHs-trah een brOH-doh* | pasta in broth |
| **minestrone** | *mee-nehs-trOH-neh* | thick vegetable soup |
| **zuppa di _____** | *tsOOp-pah dee* | thick soup |

## PASTA OR RICE COURSE

A pasta course normally precedes your entree, so it is usually a small serving offered in a special presentation. Since the varieties of pasta are almost endless, you'll find them offered on menus as **agnellotti**, **cappelletti**, **fettuccine**, **lasagne**, **tagliatelle**, **tortellini**, and many more. It will be sauced, perhaps with a cream and cheese mixture or with a tomato sauce. It may also be stuffed or baked, or served in a soup.

In parts of northern Italy, rice is often substituted for pasta. These dishes are generally less well known, but are no less tasty. Generally you'll find it on a menu as a plain rice dish (**riso**) or as a **risotto**, a creamy rice mixture often combined with cheese, fruit, vegetables, or meat.

A few other "pasta" dishes you will find on some menus are **polenta** *(poh-lEHn-tah)*—a cornmeal mush often sliced and served with sausages or chicken—and **gnocchi** *(ny-OH-key)*—dumplings made from potatoes and often mixed with spinach, cheese, or cornmeal. Egg dishes are also often offered for this course. A **frittata** *(free-tAH-tah)* is an omelet, often filled with vegetables.

## ENTREES (MEAT AND FISH DISHES)

The "main course" of an Italian meal is usually somewhat plain, either a sautéed or grilled meat or a baked fish or chicken. Along the coast and in Sicily and Sardinia, you'll find unusual and exciting varieties of seafood.

| | | |
|---|---|---|
| **acciughe** | *ah-chee-OO-gheh* | anchovies |
| **anguille** | *ahn-goo-EEl-leh* | eel |
| **aragosta** | *ah-rah-gOHs-tah* | lobster (spiny) |
| **aringa** | *ah-rEEn-gah* | herring |
| ■ **affumicata** | *ahf-foo-mee-kAH-tah* | smoked |
| **baccalà** | *bah-kah-lAH* | dried salt cod |
| **branzino (nasello)** | *brahn-tsEE-noh (nah-sEHl-loh)* | bass (hake) |
| **calamari (seppie)** | *kah-lah-mAH-ree (sAYp-pee-eh)* | squid |
| **cozze** | *kOH-tseh* | mussels |
| **gamberetti** | *gAHm-beh-rAY-tee* | prawns |

| | | |
|---|---|---|
| **granchi** | *grAHn-key* | crabs |
| **lumache** | *loo-mAH-keh* | snails |
| **merluzzo** | *mayr-lOOt-tsoh* | cod |
| **ostriche** | *OHs-tree-keh* | oysters |
| **polipo** | *pOH-lee-poh* | octopus |
| **salmone** | *sahl-mOH-neh* | salmon |
| **sardine** | *sahr-dEE-neh* | sardines |
| **scampi** | *skAHm-pee* | shrimps |
| **sogliola** | *sOH-ly-ee-oh-lah* | flounder (sole) |
| **trota** | *trOH-tah* | trout |
| **tonno** | *tOHn-noh* | tuna |
| **vongole** | *vOHn-goh-leh* | clams |
| **trance di pesce alla griglia** | *trAHn-cheh dee pAY-sheh AHl-lah grEE-ly-ee-ah* | grilled fish steaks |
| **fritto misto di pesce** | *frEEt-toh mEEs-toh dee pAY-sheh* | mixed fried fish |

Meat dishes are often sauced or served with some type of gravy. Here are some basic terms you'll encounter on Italian menus.

| | | |
|---|---|---|
| **agnello (abbacchio)** | *ah-ny-EHl-loh (ahb-bAH-key-oh)* | lamb |
| **capretto** | *kah-prAHy-toh* | goat |
| **maiale** | *mah-ee-AH-leh* | pork |
| **manzo** | *mAHn-tsoh* | beef |
| **montone** | *mohn-tOH-neh* | mutton |
| **vitello** | *vee-tEHl-loh* | veal |

And some common cuts of meat, plus other terms you'll find on a menu:

| | | |
|---|---|---|
| **affettati** | *ahf-fayt-tAH-tee* | cold cuts |
| **costate** | *kohs-tAH-teh* | chops |
| **animelle** | *ah-nee-mEHl-leh* | sweetbreads |
| **cervello** | *chehr-vEHl-loh* | brains |
| **fegato** | *fAY-gah-toh* | liver |
| **bistecca** | *bees-tAY-kah* | steak |
| **lingua** | *lEEn-goo-ah* | tongue |
| **pancetta** | *pahn-chAYt-tah* | bacon |
| **polpette** | *pohl-pAYt-teh* | meatballs |
| **prosciutto cotto** | *proh-shee-OOt-toh kOHt-toh* | ham (cooked) |
| **rognoni** | *roh-ny-OH-nee* | kidneys |

And some terms for fowl and game:

| | | |
|---|---|---|
| **anitra** | *AH-nee-trah* | duck |
| **beccaccia** | *bay-kAH-chee-ah* | woodcock |
| **cappone** | *kahp-pOH-neh* | capon |
| **carne di cervo** | *kAHr-neh dee chEHr-voh* | venison |
| **coniglio** | *koh-nEE-ly-ee-oh* | rabbit |
| **fagiano** | *fah-jee-AH-noh* | pheasant |
| **faraona** | *fah-rah-OH-nah* | guinea fowl |
| **lepre** | *lEH-preh* | hare |
| **oca** | *OH-kah* | goose |
| **pernice** | *pehr-nEE-cheh* | partridge |

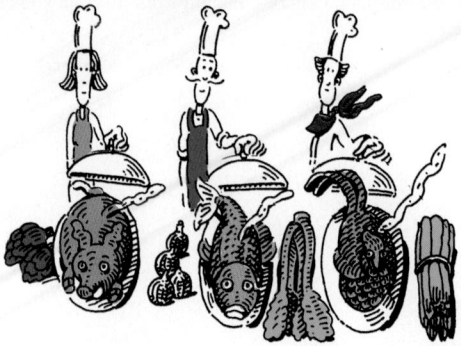

| | | |
|---|---|---|
| **piccioncino** | *pEE-chee-ohn-chEE-noh* | squab (pigeon) |
| **pollo** | *pOHl-loh* | chicken |
| **porcellino di latte** | *pohr-chehl-lEE-noh dee lAHz-teh* | suckling pig |
| **quaglia** | *koo-AH-ly-ee-ah* | quail |
| **tacchino** | *tah-kEY-noh* | turkey |

| I like it _____. | **Mi piace _____.** *mee pee-AH-cheh* |
|---|---|
| ■ baked | **al forno** *ahl fOHr-noh* |
| ■ boiled | **bollito** *bohl-lEE-toh* |
| ■ braised | **brasato al forno** *brah-sAH-toh ahl fOHr-noh* |
| ■ breaded | **impanato** *eem-pah-nAH-toh* |
| ■ broiled (grilled) | **alla griglia** *AHl-lah grEE-ly-ee-ah* |
| ■ browned | **rosolato** *roh-soh-lAH-toh* |
| ■ chopped | **tritato** *tree-tAH-toh* |

- fried — **fritto** *frEEt-toh*
- in its natural juices — **nei suoi succhi naturali** *nAY-ee soo-OH-ee sOO-key nah-too-rAH-lee*
- mashed — **passato (puré)** *pahs-sAH-toh (poo-rAY)*
- poached — **bollito** *bohl-lEE-toh*
- pureed — **passato (puré)** *pahs-sAH-toh (poo-rAY)*
- roasted — **arrosto** *ahr-rOHs-toh*
- with sauce — **in salsa** *een sAHl-sah*
- sautéed — **soffritto** *sohf-frEEt-toh*
- steamed — **al vapore** *ahl vah-pOH-reh*
- stewed — **stufato** *stoo-fAH-toh*
- wrapped in aluminum foil — **in cartoccio** *een kahr-tOH-chee-oh*

I prefer my eggs _____. — **Preferisco le uova ____.** *preh-feh-rEEs-koh leh oo-OH-vah*

- fried — **al tegame (fritte)** *ahl teh-gAH-meh (frEEt-teh)*
- hard-boiled — **sode** *sOH-deh*
- medium-boiled — **mollette** *mohl-lEH-teh*
- poached — **affogate (in camicia)** *ahf-foh-gAH-teh (een kah-mEE-chee-ah)*
- scrambled — **strapazzate** *strah-pah-tzAH-teh*
- soft-boiled — **alla coque (al guscio)** *AHl-lah kOHk (ahl gOO-shee-oh)*

I'd like an omelet. — **Vorrei una frittata.** *vohr-rEH-ee OO-nah freet-tAH-tah.*

I like the meat _____. — **La carne mi piace ____.** *lah kAHr-neh mee pee-AH-cheh*

- well done — **ben cotta** *bEHn kOHt-tah*
- medium — **cotta a puntino** *kOHt-tah ah poon-tEE-noh*

| | | |
|---|---|---|
| ■ rare | **al sangue** | *ahl sAHn-goo-eh* |
| ■ tender | **tenera** | *tEH-neh-rah* |

## VEGETABLES

Italians love vegetables, so you will find many types, prepared in a variety of ways.

| | | |
|---|---|---|
| **asparagi** | *ahs-pAH-rah-jee* | asparagus |
| **carciofi** | *kahr-chee-OH-fee* | artichoke |
| **carote** | *kah-rOH-teh* | carrots |
| **cavoli** | *kAH-voh-lee* | cabbage |
| **cavolfiori** | *kah-vohl-fee-OH-ree* | cauliflower |
| **ceci** | *chay-chee* | chickpeas |
| **cetriolo** | *cheh-tree-OO-loh* | cucumber |
| **fagioli** | *fah-jee-oh-lEE* | beans (dried) |
| **fagiolini** | *fah-jee-oh-lEE-nee* | green beans |
| **fave** | *fAH-veh* | broad beans |
| **finocchi** | *fee-nOH-key* | fennel |
| **funghi** | *fOOn-ghee* | mushrooms |
| **granturco** | *grahn-tOO-rkoh* | corn (maize) |
| **lattuga** | *laht-tOO-gah* | lettuce |
| **lenticchie** | *len-tEE-key-eh* | lentils |
| **melanzana** | *meh-lahn-tsAH-nah* | eggplant (aubergine) |
| **patate** | *pah-tAH-teh* | potatoes |
| ■ **patatine fritte** | *pah-tah-tEE-neh frEEt-teh* | French fries (chips) |

| | | |
|---|---|---|
| **peperoni** | *peh-peh-rOH-nee* | pepper |
| **piselli** | *pee-sEHl-lee* | peas |
| **pomodoro** | *poh-moh-dOH-roh* | tomato |
| **porcini** | *pohr-chEE-nee* | wild mushroom, similar to cèpes |
| **sedano** | *sAY-dah-noh* | celery |
| **spinaci** | *spee-nAH-chee* | spinach |
| **zucchini** | *tsoo-KEY-nee* | green squash (courgettes) |

## SEASONINGS

Although Italians season their food well, personal preferences sometimes intercede. Here's how to ask for what you want.

| | | |
|---|---|---|
| I'd like _____. | **Vorrei _____.** | *vohr-rEH-ee* |
| ■ butter | **burro** | *bOOr-roh* |
| ■ horseradish | **rafano** | *rAH-fah-noh* |
| ■ ketchup | **ketchup** | *keh-chOHp* |
| ■ margarine | **margarina** | *mahr-gah-rEE-nah* |
| ■ mayonnaise | **maionese** | *mah-ee-oh-nAY-seh* |
| ■ mustard | **senape** | *sEH-nah-peh* |
| ■ olive oil | **olio d'oliva** | *OH-lee-oh doh-lEE-vah* |
| ■ pepper (black) | **pepe (nero)** | *pAY-peh (nAY-roh)* |
| ■ pepper (red) | **pepe (rosso)** | *pAY-peh (rOHs-soh)* |

| | | |
|---|---|---|
| ■ salt | **sale** | *sAH-leh* |
| ■ sugar | **zucchero** | *tsOO-keh-roh* |
| ■ saccharin | **saccarina, dolcificante** | *sah-kah-rEE-nah dohl-chee-fee-kAHn-teh* |
| ■ vinegar | **aceto** | *ah-chAY-toh* |

## CHEESE

Every region has its own cheese or cheeses, which vary in shape, taste, and aging. As a dish, cheese is served at the beginning of a meal or before fruit and dessert. Wine is its best companion.

Many traditional dishes such as **la pastasciutta** *(lah pAH-stah-ah-shee-OOt-tah)*, **la trippa** *(lah trEEp-pah)*, **il minestrone** *(eel mee-nehs-trOH-neh)*, **i ravioli** *(ee rah-vee-OH-lee)*, **i risotti** *(ee ree-sOHt-tee)*, **i maccheroni** *(ee mahk-keh-rOH-nee)*, and some vegetable dishes owe their good taste and nutritional value to the grated cheese that is added when serving. The people from the Po River Valley region wouldn't even think about enjoying a dish of maccheroni, minestrone, ravioli, or risotto without adding grated cheese such as **grana** *(grAH-nah)*, **pecorino** *(peh-koh-rEE-noh)*, or sharp **provolone** *(proh-voh-lOH-neh)*.

The discovery of the use of fresh cheeses in recipes is partly attributed to Southern Italians. They love **mozzarella in carrozza** *(moh-tza-rEHl-lah een kah-rOH-tzah)*, **crostini di provatura** *(kroh-stEE-nee dee proh-vah-tOO-rah)*, **supplì "al telefono"** *(soop-lEE ahl teh-lEH-foh-noh)*, and **pizza**.

There are many, many varieties of Italian cheeses, and if you order a cheese course you will have the opportunity to try some that are never exported. Rather than give you the names of all the types, we offer a few useful words you can use in discussing your choices with the waiter.

| | | |
|---|---|---|
| Is the cheese _____? | **È il formaggio _____?** | *eh eel fohr-mAH-jee-oh* |
| ■ mild | **dolce** | *dOHl-cheh* |
| ■ sharp | **piccante** | *pee-kAHn-teh* |
| ■ hard | **duro** | *dOO-roh* |
| ■ soft | **molle** | *mOHl-leh* |

## FRUITS AND NUTS

Since the Italian meal is a filling one, often Italians will conclude their meal with a piece of fruit. Here are the names of some.

| | | |
|---|---|---|
| What kind of fruit do you have? | **Che frutta c'è?** | *kay frOOt-tah chEH* |
| **albicocca** | *ahl-bee-kOH-kah* | apricot |
| **ananasso** | *ah-nah-nAHs-soh* | pineapple |
| **anguria** | *ahn-gOO-ree-ah* | watermelon |
| **arancia** | *ah-rAHn-chee-ah* | orange |
| **castagne** | *kahs-tAH-ny-eh* | chestnuts |
| **cedro** | *chAY-droh* | lime |
| **ciliege** | *chee-lee-EH-jee-eh* | cherries |
| **datteri** | *dAHt-teh-ree* | dates |
| **fichi** | *fEE-key* | figs |
| **fragole** | *frAH-goh-leh* | strawberries |
| **lampone** | *lahm-pOH-neh* | raspberry |
| **limone** | *lee-mOH-neh* | lemon |
| **mandarini** | *mahn-dah-rEE-nee* | tangerines |
| **mandorle** | *mAHn-dohr-leh* | almonds |

| | | |
|---|---|---|
| **mela** | *mAY-lah* | apple |
| **melone** | *meh-lOH-neh* | melon |
| **more** | *mOH-reh* | mulberries |
| **noci** | *nOH-chee* | nuts |
| **nocciole** | *noh-chee-OH-leh* | hazelnuts (filberts) |
| **pera** | *pAY-rah* | pear |
| **pesca** | *pAYs-kah* | peach |
| **pompelmo** | *pohm-pEHl-moh* | grapefruit |
| **prugne** | *prOO-ny-eh* | plum |
| **uva** | *OO-vah* | grape |

## DESSERTS—SWEETS

Many restaurants do not serve elaborate desserts, since Italians don't generally eat pastries after a meal. We list below a few things you are likely to find on a menu. In particular, Italian ice cream is something not to be missed. Since it is not beaten with air, it is very rich and creamy.

| | | |
|---|---|---|
| **torta** | *tOHr-tah* | cake |
| **dolci** | *dOHl-chee* | sweets |
| **macedonia di frutta** | *mah-cheh-dOH-nee-ah dee frOOt-tah* | fresh fruit salad |
| **mousse al cioccolato** | *mOOs ahl chee-oh-koh-lAH-toh* | chocolate mousse |
| **crema inglese** | *krEH-mah een-glAY-seh* | custard |
| **crostata** | *kroh-stAH-tah* | pie |
| **budino** | *boo-dEE-noh* | pudding |

| | | |
|---|---|---|
| ■ **di pane** | *dee pAH-neh* | bread |
| ■ **di crema** | *dee krEH-mah* | cream |
| ■ **di riso** | *dee rEE-soh* | rice |
| **crema di caramello** | *crEH-mah dee kah-rah-mEHl-loh* | caramel custard |
| **gelato** | *jeh-lAH-toh* | ice cream |
| ■ **al cioccolato** | *ahl chee-oh-koh-lAH-toh* | chocolate |
| ■ **alla vaniglia** | *AHl-lah vah-nEE-ly-ee-ah* | vanilla |
| ■ **alla fragola** | *AHl-lah frAH-goh-lah* | strawberry |
| ■ **di caffè (con panna)** | *dee kahf-fEH (kOHn pAHn-nah)* | coffee (with whipped cream) |

## SPECIAL CIRCUMSTANCES

Many travelers have special dietary requirements, so here are a few phrases that might help you get what you need or avoid what does you wrong.

| | |
|---|---|
| I am on a diet. | **Sono a dieta.** *sOH-noh ah dee-EH-tah* |
| I'm a vegetarian. | **Sono vegetariano(a).** *SOH-noh veh-jeh-tah-ree-AH-noh(nah)* |
| I can't eat anything made with _____. | **Non posso mangiare niente con _____.** *nohn pOHs-soh mahn-jee-AH-reh nee-EHn-teh kohn* |
| I can't have any _____. | **Non posso avere ____.** *Nohn pOHs-soh ah-vAY-reh* |
| ■ alcohol | **sostanze alcoliche** *soh-stAHn-tzeh ahl-kOH-lee-keh* |
| ■ dairy products | **latticini** *laht-tee-chEE-nee* |
| ■ saturated fats | **grassi animali** *grAHs-see ah-nee-mAH-lee* |

| | |
|---|---|
| ■ seafood | **frutti di mare** *frOOt-tee dee mAH-reh* |
| I'm on a _____ diet. | **Faccio una dieta _____.** *fAH-chee-oh OO-nah dee-EH-tah* |
| ■ diabetic | **per diabetici** *pehr dee-ah-bEH-tee-chee* |
| ■ low-fat | **a basso contenuto di grassi** *ah bAHs-soh kohn-teh-nOO-toh dee grAHs-see* |
| ■ low-sodium | **a basso contenuto di sale** *ah bAHs-soh kohn-teh-nOO-toh dee sAH-leh* |
| ■ restricted | **stretta** *strAYt-tah* |
| ■ simple | **semplice** *sAYm-plee-cheh* |
| I'm looking for a dish _____. | **Cerco un piatto _____.** *chAYr-koh oon pee-AHt-toh* |
| ■ high in fiber | **ricco di fibra** *rEEk-koh dee fEE-brah* |
| ■ low in cholesterol | **a basso contenuto di colesterolo** *ah bAHs-soh kohn-teh-nOO-toh dee koh-leh-steh-rOH-loh* |
| ■ low in fat | **a basso contenuto di grassi** *ah bAHs-soh kohn-teh-nOO-toh dee grAHs-see* |
| ■ low in sodium | **a basso contenuto di sale** *ah bAHs-soh kohn-teh-nOO-toh dee sAH-leh* |
| ■ nondairy | **senza prodotti lattici** *sEHn-tsah proh-dOHt-tee lAHt-tee-chee* |
| ■ salt-free | **senza sale** *sEHn-tsah sAH-leh* |
| ■ sugar-free | **senza zucchero** *sEHn-tsah tsOO-keh-roh* |
| ■ without artificial coloring | **senza coloranti artificiali** *sEHn-tsah koh-loh-rAHn-tee ahr-tee-fee-chee-AHl-ee* |

| | |
|---|---|
| ■ without preservatives | **senza conservanti** *sEHn-tsah kohn-sayr-vAHn-tee* |
| I don't want anything fried (salted). | **Non posso mangiare cose fritte (salate).** *nohn pOHs-soh mahn-jee-AH-reh kOH-seh frEEt-teh (sah-lAH-teh)* |
| Is this very spicy? | **Questo è molto piccante?** *koo-AY-stoh eh mOHl-toh pee-kAHn-teh* |
| Do you have any dishes without meat? | **Hanno piatti (cibi) senza carne?** *AHn-noh pee-AHt-tee (chEE-bee) sEHn-tsah kAHr-neh* |

## CULINARY PROBLEMS

| | |
|---|---|
| It's _____. | **È _____.** *EH* |
| ■ bitter | **acre** *AH-kreh* |
| ■ burned | **bruciato(a)** *broo-chee-AH-toh(ah)* |
| ■ cold | **freddo(a)** *frAYd-doh(ah)* |
| ■ overcooked | **troppo cotto(a)** *trOHp-poh kOHt-toh(ah)* |
| ■ spoiled | **guasto(a)** *goo-AHs-toh(ah)* |
| ■ too rare | **non è cotto(a) abbastanza** *nohn eh kOHt-toh(ah) ahb-bah-stAHn-tzah* |
| ■ too salty | **troppo salato(a)** *trOHp-poh sah-lAH-toh(ah)* |
| ■ too spicy | **troppo piccante** *trOHp-poh pee-kAHn-teh* |
| ■ too sweet | **troppo dolce** *trOHp-poh dOHl-che* |
| ■ tough | **duro(a)** *dOO-roh(ah)* |
| It doesn't smell good. | **Non ha un odore gradevole.** *nohn ah oon oh-DOh-reh grah-dAY-voh-leh* |
| It smells bad. | **Ha un odore sgradevole.** *ah oon oh-DOh-reh sgrah-dEH-voh-leh* |

## BEVERAGES

See pages 161–163 for information on Italian wines. As for other beverages, we give you the following phrases to help you ask for exactly what you wish.

| | | |
|---|---|---|
| Waiter, please bring me _____. | **Cameriere(a), per piacere mi porti _____.** | *kah-meh-ree-EH-reh(ah) pehr pee-ah-chAY-reh mee pOHr-tee* |
| coffee (regular or American) | **caffè** | *kahf-fEH* |
| ■ with milk | **caffelatte** | *kahf-fEH-lAHt-teh* |
| ■ with sugar | **con zucchero** | *kohn tsOO-keh-roh* |
| ■ without sugar | **senza zucchero** | *sEHn-tsah tsOO-keh-roh* |
| ■ with saccharin | **con saccarina** | *kohn sah-kah-rEE-nah* |
| ■ with cream | **con panna** | *kohn pAHn-nah* |
| Italian coffee | **espresso** | *ehs-prEHs-soh* |
| ■ with anisette | **corretto all' anisetta** | *kohr-rEHt-toh ahl-lah-nee-sAYt-tah* |
| iced (coffee) | **freddo** | *frAYd-doh* |
| tea | **tè** | *tEH* |
| ■ with milk | **con latte** | *kohn lAHt-teh* |
| ■ with lemon | **con limone** | *kohn lee-mOH-neh* |
| ■ with sugar | **con zucchero** | *kohn tsOO-keh-roh* |
| ■ iced | **con ghiaccio** | *kohn ghee-AH-chee-oh* |

| | | |
|---|---|---|
| water | **acqua** | *AH-koo-ah* |
| ■ cold | **fredda** | *frAYd-dah* |
| ■ iced | **con ghiaccio** | *kohn ghee-AH-chee-oh* |
| ■ mineral | **minerale** | *mee-neh-rAH-leh* |
| ■ (carbonated) | **gassata** | *gahs-sAH-tah* |
| ■ (non-carbonated) | **naturale** | *nah-too-rAH-leh* |
| a glass of _____. | **un bicchiere di _____.** | *oon bee-key-EH-reh dee* |
| ■ milk (cold) | **latte (fresco)** | *lAHt-teh (frAY-skoh)* |
| ■ malted milk | **latte con malto** | *lAHt-teh kOHn mAHl-toh* |
| ■ milk shake | **frullato di latte** | *frool-lAH-toh dee lAHt-teh* |
| ■ orangeade | **aranciata** | *ah-rahn-chee-AH-tah* |
| ■ punch | **punch** | *pOHn-ch* |
| ■ soda | **bibita analcolica (soda)** | *bEE-bee-tah ah-nahl-kOH-lee-kah* |
| ■ (fruit) juice | **succo di (frutta)** | *sOO-koh dee (frOOt-tah)* |
| ■ lemonade | **limonata** | *lee-moh-nAH-tah* |

## SETTLING UP

The bill normally includes a surcharge for service. Tips are never included in the bill and customers leave from 10 to 15 percent of the bill in appreciation of courteous service, only 10 percent if the service wasn't that good.

| | | |
|---|---|---|
| The check, please. | **Il conto, per favore.** | *eel kOHn-toh pehr fah-vOH-reh* |

| | | |
|---|---|---|
| Separate checks. | **Conti separati.** | *kOHn-tee seh-pah-rAH-tee* |
| Is the service included? | **È incluso il servizio?** | *EH een-klOO-soh eel sehr-vEE-tsee-oh* |
| I haven't ordered this. | **Non ho ordinato questo.** | *nohn oh ohr-dee-nAH-toh koo-AY-stoh* |
| I don't think the bill is right. | **Non penso che il conto sia corretto.** | *nohn pEHn-soh kay eel kOHn-toh sEE-ah kor-rEHt-toh* |
| We're in a hurry. | **Abbiamo fretta.** | *ahb-bee-AH-moh frAYt-tah* |
| This is for you. | **Questo è per lei.** | *koo-AYs-toh EH pehr lEH-ee* |

## REGIONAL ITALIAN SPECIALTIES

We can give only a limited example of the extensive and varied cuisines of Italy. In whatever part of the country you are, ask for the local specialties and regional dishes.

There is no "Italian" cuisine; Italy is divided into regions, and each region has a cuisine based on its resources. Regions that border on the sea are often strong in seafood, while mountainous regions have wonderful meat dishes. Likewise, Italy can be divided somewhat gastronomically north and south, with favorites such as polenta and rice more to the north, while southern regions concentrate on pasta. Likewise, the lusher portions of Italy (mostly in the north) have a cuisine rich with meats and game, whereas the southern regions are poorer and consequently use more vegetables and fish in their dishes. The delicate pasta of the north is enriched with eggs, whereas in the south it is firmer and often factory-made.

There is another thing to note about Italian food, especially in contrast with French food. Italian food is basically from the home—that is, every good cook knows how to make a sauce at home, and the food you get in restaurants is founded on good home cooking. Just as every home has its favorite version of a sauce or soup, so Italian restaurants will differ greatly in their preparations of well-known Italian dishes, such as minestrone.

The following is a list of Italy's regions, along with some of the specialties you are likely to find there.

- VALLE D'AOSTA (Aosta) This northernmost area of Italy is actually French-speaking, but the food is quite coarse, with a lot of game, dark breads, and thick soups. Most famous is the **chamois**, a high mountain goat that is cooked in red wine and spiked with **grappa** (a dry, colorless brandy). **Motzetta** is the name for chamois when it is cured and sliced, served on bread. The sausages are also good here, mostly hard salami types. The **costoletta di vitello con fontina** is a veal chop stuffed with fontina cheese, coated with bread crumbs, and sautéed. Potatoes are usually served with these heavy game and meat dishes. The honey from this region is quite good, as is the butter.
- PIEMONTE (Torino) Turin is the center of this northern region of Italy. The area borders on Switzerland, so one of its famous dishes is **fonduta**, an Italian version of fondue, made with melted fontina cheese lightened with egg yolks and milk, and graced with slivers of white truffles. It is served like a soup, often poured over polenta. Also from this region is **bagna cauda**, a dipping sauce of oil and butter flavored with anchovies and sprinkled with white truffles. The mountain streams flow with trout, which these Italians prepare very simply—broiled or sautéed, sometimes with a touch of sage. **Riso alla piemontese** is stubby Italian rice with white truffles, topped with a meat sauce. For the pasta in this area, you'll most often be served **agnolotti**, small studded pillows. The **gnocchi** here are made with fontina cheese, and the polenta is often topped with melted fontina. For a sweet taste, the people in this region are fond of **gianduiotti**, chocolate drops from Turin.

- LOMBARDIA (Milano) This is a region very rich in good food. The inventiveness of Milanese cooks has made the cuisine famous throughout the world. It is also the region that produces the best-known cheeses, such as Bel Paese, Robiola, Gorgonzola (white), Mascarpone, and Stracchino. Some specialties you're likely to see on a menu are: **ossibuchi** (a veal shank braised in an herbed white wine and tomato sauce), **costoletta alla milanese** (a crisp-fried, breaded veal chop), **polenta** (a cornmeal mush, eaten as an accompaniment to stews and liver, or by itself with cheese or a sauce), **risotto** (a hearty rice dish in which rice is simmered in broth, often with butter, Parmesan cheese, and saffron), **riso con la luganega** (rice cooked with chopped Monza sausage and cheese), **busecca** (stewed tripe, served on French bread and covered with cheese), minestrone with rice, **lesso misto** (often called **bollito misto**, a boiled mixed meats dish in a rich broth), **stufato** (a tender and succulent beef stew), and **panettone** (a buttery yeast cake studded with raisins and candied fruits, usually enjoyed around Christmastime).

- TRENTINO ALTO ADIGE (Bolzano) This area of northern Italy borders on Austria and Switzerland, so don't be surprised to see sauerkraut (**crauti**) or Tirolean noodles. It is a German-speaking area, very mountainous with valleys where rye, corn, and wheat grow. They have what is called the Elephant Platter, an enormous quantity of food including at least 6 types of meats and 12 kinds of vegetables. There are also trout from the streams and much smoked pork. The **nockerln** are similar to gnocchi, offered as an accompaniment to meat dishes. There are also endless varieties of strudel, most of them involving fruits or cream wrapped in a paper-thin crust and sprinkled with chopped nuts.

- VENETO (Venezia, Padova, Verona) Early traders brought many unusual spices and seasonings to Venice, so the food from this area is very colorful. Saffron colors the polenta, while ginger and cloves accent the sweets. Seafood is prominent, with eels a favorite, either fried or marinated. Sardines, mullet, mussels, cuttlefish, and salted cod (**baccalà**) are the foundations for soups (**brodeto**). **Fegato alla veneziana** is a famous dish—thin slices of calf's liver lightly sautéed with onions and butter. Rice plays a prominent role, in **risi e bisi** (rice with peas), in **risotto nero** (rice with octopus), and in multiple other varieties. **Scampi** (shrimp) are served in a myriad of ways, sometimes fried, other times in a dish with rice, or in a soup. This is also an area for sweets, including **fritole di Venezia**, little fritters flavored with cinnamon, raisins, pignoli, and lemon peel. **Focaccia pasquale veneziana** is the traditional Easter cake in the shape of a dove, filled with eggs and sprinkled with kirsch and grappa.

- FRIULI-VENEZIA GIULIA (Trieste) This is not a rich area, so the food of the region reflects that, with an emphasis on poultry rather than meat, soups based on vegetables, and all of it served with a lot of bread. The prosciutto from San Daniele, however, is world famous. The **lujarnis** is their long and thin sausage, usually grilled. **Brovada** is a vegetable dish based on turnips. **Broeto** is a fish chowder, a variation of **brodetto**. In Trieste, the foods reflect some Austrian influences, with **liptauer** (a spreadable mixture of cheese and spices) made from gorgonzola and mascarpone instead. Trieste also has its own versions of calf's liver, flavored with cloves and lemon juice, and its own **risi e bisi**, more of a pea-and-rice puree served over pasta.

- LIGURIA (Genoa) This is a small region, dominated by the city of Genoa, but its foods are vast and varied. There is a lot of seafood, but not as much as you might expect from this seacoast region. From this area come some very famous Italian specialties, including **pesto**, that fragrant puree of basil leaves, olive oil, Parmesan cheese, and pignoli nuts. **Ravioli** is also from here, filled with minced meat and herbs. The minestrone is thick and creamy, varying as much among Ligurian cooks as it does throughout Italy. Also from this region are fish soups that are simply flavored with fennel and/or other herbs. The **focaccia** is a flatbread similar to a pizza without the topping. **Torta pasqualina** is their Easter cake made with many layers of puff pastry, filled with artichoke hearts, hard-cooked eggs, and cheese. For a sweet, **pandolce** is a yeast cake punctuated with grapes, raisins, and pignolis.
- EMILIA-ROMAGNA (Bologna, Ravenna) This region of northern Italy extends across the country following the ancient Emilian way. The fertile farmland produces a lot of wheat for pasta, but the sausages from this region are also famous, as is its prosciutto from Parma. **Zampone di Mantova** is a very large sausage of chopped seasoned meats and pork skin that is simmered, then sliced and served with lentils and onions. **Cotechina**, from Modena, is another sausage, simmered in wine and served with a thick sauce. From Bologna comes **mortadella**, a smooth, heavily spiced sausage that has traveled around the world as "bologna," and **tortellini**, circles of pasta that are stuffed with meat and cheese, then folded into rings and served with a sauce. **Tortellini mantovani** are bite-sized pastas stuffed with pureed pumpkin. When a pasta is served **alla bolognese**, expect a meat sauce thick with tomatoes.

  This region stretches to the Adriatic, and along the coast you'll find much seafood, particularly turbot (**rombo**), tuna (**tonno**), mackerel (**sgombero**), mullet (**barboni, triglie di scoglio**), angler fish (**rospo**), eel (**anguilla**), octopus (**seppia**), squid (**calamaro, totano**), spiny lobster (**agagosta**), crayfish (**gambero**), and scallops (**cappa santa**). For desserts, this area has to offer the **mandorlini**, an almond-flavored biscuit, and **crespelli**, strips of dough that are deep-fried, then dusted with sugar. But this is only a start of the wonderful foods of this region.

- TOSCANA (Firenze, Pisa) The food of Tuscany is hearty and simple. This is the region that produces the best olive oil in Italy, from Lucca. It is also where the finest beef in Italy is raised and so you will often see on a menu their Florentine steak, which is similar to a T-bone. It is served rare, unless you indicate otherwise. Chicken is served with a ginger sauce, **pollo alla diavola**; pork is slowly braised in broth and flavored with rosemary and garlic. **Stracotto alla fiorentina** is similar to pot roast, with carrots, celery, onions, and tomatoes. There aren't any exceptional fish dishes served here, although **baccalà** (salt cod) is popular, plumped in a tomato sauce. **Caciucco alla livornese** is a fish soup very similar to bouillabaisse that comes from Leghorn. In Pisa, you can eat **le cieche**, baby eels seared in hot oil. In contrast, **ribollita** is a dish of what is essentially leftovers, perked up with a helping of beans, which are a favorite ingredient in these parts. They can also be found in the minestrone, in their rice dishes, and served along with the steak. For dessert, these Italians like **castagnaccio**, a deep-fried chestnut cake.
- MARCHE (Ancona) This is actually several regions put together, so you won't find many unifying dishes; each area of the Marches has a proud cuisine of its own, mostly not known well outside of the area. Some of the famous foods from this region are the stuffed olives (**olive all'ascolana**) from Ascoli Piceno; the **brodetto** (fish chowder), which must always include the **scorfano** (hog fish); and the **porchetta** (roasted suckling pig). Also notable is **vincisgrassi**, a baked layered dish of lasagna, chicken livers, mushrooms, and onions, graced with a béchamel sauce.

- UMBRIA (Perugia) Saddled between the Marches and Lazio, Umbria has a cuisine that blends the heartiness of the mountains with the sophistication of the cities. The food is prepared fairly simply, but often includes some black truffles, which grow in this region. There are other wild mushrooms too, including the fleshy cèpes. Fennel flavors much of the cooking, including the **porchetta** (roast suckling pig). From here we also get **prosciutto di montagna**, a cured mountain ham, and some sheep's milk cheeses, **ravigiolo** and **caciotto**. From Norcia comes a liver sausage, **mazzafegati**. The sweets likely to be found here are **mostaccioli**, a spiced cake, and **pinoccata**, a chocolate-flavored cake made with pignolis.
- LAZIO (Roma) The food of this region centers on Rome, and in Rome you will find many specialties. One common one is **porchetta**, a spit-roasted suckling pig, and another is **abbacchio**, a baby lamb that is roasted with rosemary. **Saltimbocca** (slices of veal topped with prosciutto, then sautéed and sauced with Marsala) comes from Rome, although it appears on menus now in many parts of Italy. **Coda alla vaccinara** is oxtails in a tomato sauce, while **gnocchi alla romana** is that light dumpling, this time made without potatoes and instead with semolina and cheese. **Fettuccine all'Alfredo** is, of course, from Rome's infamous restaurant; this is tagliatelle noodles in a butter and cheese (Parmesan) sauce. Another popular pasta dish is **spaghetti alla carbonara**, in which spaghetti are tossed with bacon, garlic, oil, and Parmesan cheese. The Romans make a **stracciatelle**, which is a chicken or beef broth into which is beaten strands of egg—sort of an egg-drop soup. On menus you'll see some robust fish soups, plus a lot of other seafood: sardines stuffed with spinach, **baccalà** in a tomato sauce, grilled clams (**vongole**). **Stufatino** is a beef stew, **coppa** is head cheese, **trippa alla romana** is tripe that has been simmered with vegetables in a tomato sauce, along with parsley and mint. Vegetables are varied and plentiful, with several preparations for artichokes (including fried in oil until

they are black and opened out as a flower), eggplant, spinach, and peppers. For dessert, you'll probably be offered fruit or **budino di rocotta** (cheese pudding). At Christmastime, you'll see **pangiallo**, a fruit-studded cake, and at Easter, **quaresimali**, dry and crisp cookies. **Maritozzi** are soft breakfast buns with raisins.

- ABRUZZO (Pescara, l'Aquila) This is very rugged country, with a coastline that drops sharply to the Adriatic. Therefore, in the food you'll find an abundance of trout from mountain streams, and **scapece**, a pickled fish, flavored with saffron. **Polpi in purgatorio** is a highly spiced cuttlefish; **triglie ripiene** is red mullet, stuffed and baked. The area produces a **prosciutto aquilano** and also liver sausages (**fegati dolci, fegati pazzi**), one sweet and one hot. **Agnello con sottaceti** is a stewed lamb, done up with rosemary and pickled vegetables. This area is famous for its **panarda**, which is a celebratory meal of at least 30 courses.
- MOLISE (Campobasso) This food follows Abruzzo in style, with a few additional specialties such as **capretti al forno** (roasted kid) and **maccheroni alla chitarra**, a homemade macaroni that is cut into slices with guitar strings. The mozzarella here is made from water buffalo milk. **Picellati** are round, crisp biscuits.
- CAMPANIA (Napoli) Much of the Italian food that has traveled to other countries comes originally from Naples. This is the home of the **pizza**, and also of the **calzoni**, basically a pizza that has been wrapped up and sealed around the edges. **Mozzarella** cheese comes from here, historically made from water buffalo milk but now more commonly from cow's milk; and also **provolone**, both smoked and fresh. Most of the pasta dishes are based on macaroni, made in factories, and in countless widths and lengths. Other dishes are **mozzarella in carrozza**, a simple sandwich of mozzarella cheese between two pieces of bread that is dipped in beaten egg and fried until crisp. There is little meat but a lot of fish on the menus, including **fritto di pesce**, any kind of seafood that has been breaded and

*Travel Tips* Save receipts on foreign purchases for declaring at customs on reentry to the U.S. Some countries return a sales or value-added tax to foreign visitors. Take receipts to a special office at the store or to a tax rebate window at the airport of departure. Americans who buy costly objects abroad may be surprised to get a bill from their state tax collector. Most states with a sales tax levy a "use" tariff on all items bought outside the home state, including those purchased abroad. Most tax agencies in these states will send a form for declaring and paying the assessment.

## SELECTING ITALIAN WINES

With the exception of some outstanding restaurants where there is a waiter who really knows wines, the waiter is not an expert. He is likely to ask "red wine or white?" as soon as you sit down and before you have decided what to eat. The rule of "red with dark meats and white with chicken, fish, and egg dishes" applies, of course. Wine is the Italian national drink, and if you want the most economical wine, ask for the local open wine (not in bottles but served from large flasks or pitchers) or **vino della casa**. Vintages also are not very important in Italy. The weather is usually good and, except for some dramatic disaster at harvest time, one year is as good as the other. White wines, however, are best when two years old at most; one year is even better.

| TYPE OF WINE | SUGGESTED VARIETIES | REGION OF ORIGIN | MAJOR CITY |
|---|---|---|---|
| | White Wines | | |
| Dry light-bodied whites | **Est! Est! Est!** **Frascati** **Marino** | Lazio | Rome |
| | **Lugana** | Lombardy | Milan |
| | **Pinot Bianco** **Pinot Grigio** | Veneto and Friuli-Venezia Giulia | Venice Trieste |
| Dry medium-bodied whites | **Orvieto Secco** | Umbria | Perugia |
| | **Soave** | Veneto | Venezia |
| | **Tocai** | Friuli-Venezia Giulia | Trieste |
| | **Trebbiano di Romagna** | Emilia-Romagna | Bologna |
| | **Verdicchio** | Marche | Ancona |
| Mellow whites | **Orvieto Abboccato** | Umbria | Perugia |
| | **Prosecco** | Veneto | Venice |

| TYPE OF WINE | SUGGESTED VARIETIES | REGION OF ORIGIN | MAJOR CITY |
|---|---|---|---|
| | Red Wines | | |
| Semidry reds | **Lambrusco** | Emilia Romagna | Bologna |
| Dry light-bodied reds | **Bardolino** | Veneto | Lake Garda |
| | **Valpolicella** | Veneto | |
| Dry medium-bodied reds | **Castel del Monte Rosso** | Apulia | Bari |
| | **Cabernet** | Trentino Alto Adige | Bolzano |
| | **Chianti** | Tuscany | Florence |
| | **Dolcetto**<br>**Freisa**<br>**Grignolino**<br>**Nebbiolo** | Piedmont | Turin |
| | **Montepulciano d'Abruzzo** | Abruzzo and Molise | L'Aquila Campobasso |
| | **Merlot** | Friuli-Venezia Giulia | Udine |
| | **Sangiovese di Romagna** | Emilia-Romagna | Bologna |
| | **Sassella** | Lombardy | Milan |
| | **Torgiano Rosso** | Umbria | Perugia |

| TYPE OF WINE | SUGGESTED VARIETIES | REGION OF ORIGIN | MAJOR CITY |
|---|---|---|---|
| | Robust Reds | | |
| | **Barbaresco**<br>**Barbera d'Asti**<br>**Barolo**<br>**Carema**<br>**Gattinara**<br>**Ghemme** | Piedmont | Turin |
| | **Brunello di Montalcino**<br>**Chianti Riserva**<br>**Vino Nobile di Montepulciano** | Tuscany | Florence |
| | **Inferno** | Lombardy | Milan |
| | Rosé Wines | | |
| | **Castel del Monte** | Apulia | Bari |
| | **Chiaretto** | Lombardy | Milan |

# MEETING PEOPLE

Italians are hospitable. They are curious and friendly, even desirous of getting acquainted with travelers.

## SMALL TALK

| | |
|---|---|
| My name is _____. | **Il mio nome è _____.** *eel mEE-oh nOH-meh EH* |
| Do you live here? | **Lei abita qui?** *lEH-ee AH-bee-tah koo-EE* |
| Where are you from? | **Lei di dov'è?** *lEH-ee dee doh-vEH* |
| I am _____. | **Vengo _____.** *vEHn-goh* |
| ■ from the United States | **dagli Stati Uniti** *dAH-ly-ee stAH-tee oo-nEE-tee* |
| ■ from Canada | **dal Canadà** *dAHl kah-nah-dAH* |
| ■ from England | **dall'Inghilterra** *dahl-lEEn-gheel-tEHr-rah* |
| I like Italy (Rome) very much. | **L'Italia (Roma) mi piace moltissimo.** *lee-tAH-lee-ah (rOH-mah) mee pee-AH-cheh mohl-tEEs-see-moh* |
| I would like to go there. | **Mi piacerebbe andarci.** *mee pee-ah-cheh-rAYb-beh ahn-dAHr-chee* |
| How long will you be staying? | **Quanto tempo resterà qui?** *koo-AHn-toh tEHm-poh reh-steh-rAH koo-EE* |
| I'll stay for a few days (a week). | **Resterò alcuni giorni (una settimana).** *reh-steh-rOH ahl-kOO-nee jee-OHr-nee (OO-nah seht-tee-mAH-nah)* |

| | |
|---|---|
| What hotel are you staying at? | **In quale hotel (albergo) sta?** *een koo-AH-leh oh-tEHl (ahl-bEHr-goh) stAH* |
| I think it's _____. | **Penso che sia _____.** *pEHn-soh kay sEE-ah* |
| ■ beautiful | **bello** *bEHl-loh* |
| ■ interesting | **interessante** *een-teh-rehs-sAHn-teh* |
| ■ wonderful | **stupendo** *stoo-pEHn-doh* |
| May I introduce _____? | **Posso presentarle _____?** *pOHs-soh preh-sehn-tAHr-leh* |
| ■ my brother (sister) | **mio fratello (mia sorella)** *mEE-oh frah-tEHl-loh (mEE-ah soh-rEHl-lah)* |
| ■ my father (mother) | **mio padre (mia madre)** *mEE-oh pAH-dreh (mEE-ah mAH-dreh)* |
| ■ my friend | **il mio amico** *eel mEE-oh ah-mEE-koh* |
| ■ my husband (wife) | **mio marito (mia moglie)** *mEE-oh mah-rEE-toh (mEE-ah mOH-ly-ee-eh)* |
| ■ my sweetheart | **il mio ragazzo (la mia ragazza)** *eel mEE-oh rah-gAH-tsoh (lah mEE-ah rah-gAH-tsah)* |
| ■ my son (daughter) | **mio figlio (mia figlia)** *mEE-oh fEE-ly-ee-oh (mEE-ah fEE-ly-ee-ah)* |
| Glad to meet you. | **Piacere. Lieto(a) di conoscerla.** *pee-ah-chAY-reh lee-EH-toh(ah) dee koh-nOH-shehr-lah* |
| How do you do? | **Come sta?** *kOH-meh stah* |
| I am a(n) _____. | **Sono _____.** *sOH-noh* |
| ■ accountant | **ragioniere** *rah-jee-oh-nee-EH-reh* |
| ■ artist | **artista** *ahr-tEEs-tah* |

| | |
|---|---|
| businessperson | **persona d'affari** *pehr-sOH-nah dahf-fAH-ree* |
| construction worker | **operaio edile** *oh-peh-rAH-ee-oh eh-dEE-leh* |
| cook | **cuoco** *koo-OH-koh* |
| dentist | **dentista** *dehn-tEE-stah* |
| doctor | **dottore (dottoressa)** *doht-tOH-reh (doht-toh-rAYs-sah)* |
| firefighter | **vigile del fuoco** *vEE-jee-leh dayl foo-OH-koh* |
| hairdresser | **parrucchiere(a)** *pahr-roo-key-AY-reh(ah)* |
| lawyer | **avvocato (avvocatessa)** *ahv-voh-kAH-toh (ahv-voh-kah-tAYs-sah)* |
| manager | **dirigente (manager)** *dee-ree-jEHn-teh (manager)* |
| nurse | **infermiere(a)** *een-fehr-mee-EH-reh(ah)* |
| police officer | **poliziotto(a)** *poh-lee-tzee-OHt-toh(ah)* |

| | |
|---|---|
| salesperson | **commesso(a)** *kohm-mAYs-soh(ah)* |
| secretary | **segretario(a)** *seh-greh-tAH-ree-oh(ah)* |
| student | **studente (studentessa)** *stoo-dEHn-teh (stoo-dehn-tAYs-sah)* |
| teacher | **maestro(a)** *mah-AYs-troh(ah)* |
| waiter (waittress) | **cameriere(a)** *kah-meh-ree-EH-reh(ah)* |

| | |
|---|---|
| Would you like a picture (snapshot)? | **Vuole che le scatti una foto (un'instantanea)?** *voo-OH-leh kay leh skAHt-tee OO-nah fOH-toh (oon-een-stahn-tAH-neh-ah)* |
| Stand here (there). | **Si metta qui (lì).** *see mAYt-tah koo-EE (lEE)* |
| Don't move. | **Non si muova.** *nohn see moo-OH-vah* |
| Smile. That's it. | **Sorrida. Ecco fatto.** *sohr-rEE-dah EH-koh fAHt-toh* |
| Will you take a picture of me (us)? | **Può farmi (farci) una foto?** *poo-OH fAHr-mee (fAHr-chee) OO-nah fOH-toh* |

## DATING AND SOCIALIZING

| | |
|---|---|
| May I have this dance? | **Le piacerebbe ballare con me?** *leh pee-ah-cheh-rAYb-beh bahl-lAH-reh kohn mAY* |
| With pleasure. | **Con piacere.** *kohn pee-ah-chAY-reh* |
| Would you like a drink? | **Potrei offrirle da bere?** *poh-trEH-ee ohf-frEEr-leh dah bAY-reh* |
| May I call you? | **Posso telefonarle?** *pOHs-soh teh-leh-foh-nAHr-leh* |

| | |
|---|---|
| May I take you home? | **L'accompagno a casa?** *lahk-kohm-pAH-ny-oh ah kAH-sah* |
| Are you doing anything tomorrow? | **Che fa domani?** *kay fAH doh-mAH-nee* |
| Are you free this evening? | **È libero(a) stasera?** *EH lEE-beh-roh(ah) stah-sAY-rah* |
| Would you like to go to _____ together? | **Le piacerebbe andare insieme a _____?** *leh pee-ah-cheh-rEHb-beh ahn-dAH-reh een-see-EH-meh ah* |
| I'll wait for you in front of the hotel. | **L'aspetterò davanti all'hotel (all'albergo).** *lah-speht-teh-rOH dah-vAHn-tee ahl-loh-tEHl (ahl-lahl-bEHr-goh)* |
| I'll pick you up at your house (hotel). | **La verrò a prendere a casa sua (all'hotel).** *lah vehr-rOH ah prAYn-day-reh ah kAH-sah sOO-ah (ahl-loh-tEHl)* |
| What is your telephone number? | **Qual è il suo numero di telefono?** *koo-ahl-EH eel sOO-oh nOO-meh-roh dee teh-lEH-foh-noh* |
| Here's my telephone number (address). | **Ecco il mio numero di telefono (indirizzo).** *EHk-koh eel mEE-oh nOO-meh-roh dee teh-lEH-foh-noh (een-dee-rEE-tsoh)* |
| I'm single (married). | **Sono scapolo nubile (sposato[a]).** *sOH-noh scAH-poh-loh nOO-bih-leh (spoh-sAH-toh[ah])* |
| Is your husband (wife) here? | **Sta qui suo marito (la signora)?** *stAH koo-EE sOO-oh mah-rEE-toh (lah see-ny-OH-rah)* |
| I'm here with my family. | **Sono qui con la mia famiglia.** *sOH-noh koo-EE kohn lah mEE-ah fah-mEE-ly-ee-ah* |

| | |
|---|---|
| Do you have any children? | **Ha bambini?** *AH bahm-bEE-nee* |
| How many? | **Quanti?** *koo-AHn-tee* |
| How old are they? | **Quanti anni hanno?** *koo-AHn-tee AHn-nee AHn-noh* |

## SAYING GOOD-BYE

| | |
|---|---|
| Nice to have met you. | **È stato un piacere conoscerla.** *EH stAH-toh oon pee-ah-chAY-reh koh-nOH-shehr-lah* |
| The pleasure was mine. | **Il piacere è stato mio.** *eel pee-ah-chAY-reh EH stAH-toh mEE-oh* |
| Regards to _____. | **Saluti a _____.** *sah-lOO-tee ah* |
| Thanks for the evening. | **Grazie della serata.** *grAH-tsee-eh dAYl-lah say-rAH-tah* |
| I must go home now. | **Adesso devo andarmene a casa.** *ah-dEHs-soh dAY-voh ahn-dAHr-meh-neh ah kAH-sah* |
| You must come to visit us. | **Deve venire a farci visita.** *dAY-veh veh-nEE-reh ah fAHr-chee vEE-see-tah* |

# SHOPPING

Italian retail stores close for the mid-afternoon, usually between 1 and 4 P.M., but the closing hours vary slightly from place to place and according to the season.

Pharmacies (chemists) also observe the middle-of-the-day closing, but they are open on a rotation basis on holidays (see page 258), including Sundays, when the name and address of the nearest one open is posted on the front door of each pharmacy that is closed.

During the summer, especially from July 15 to September 1, most smaller stores close for vacation periods of their own choosing. For this reason, tourists will find that not all stores are open at a given time during the summer vacation period.

## TYPICAL ARTS AND CRAFTS

Italy offers a wide range of traditional arts and crafts. Each region, city, village, and town has its own variety of products. Bargaining for the item you wish is apt to be a new experience but the shopkeepers and merchants expect it. Here are some tips on what to look for in Italy's different regions.

- VALLE D'AOSTA (Aosta)—Laces, embossed copper wares, leather articles, and wood-carved jugs.
- PIEMONTE (Torino)—Wood-carved chamois and steenbok, woodworked boxes of Gran San Bernardo, and local pottery.
- LOMBARDIA (Milano)—Pottery of Laveno, printed silk of Como, rubber toys, shoes of Vigevano, laces of Cantù, accordions, and carpets. Best buys: silk dresses, latest fashions in the boutiques, leather goods.
- TRENTINO ALTO ADIGE (Bolzano, Trento)—Woodworks of Val Gardena, cuckoo clocks, knick-knacks made of onyx and horn, straw hats of Bessanone, bowls of Martello.
- VENETO (Venezia)—Glass and crystals of Murano, laces of Burano, wrought iron, mosaics, leather

articles, woodworks, kettles, and pipes. Best buys: glassware, antiques.

- FRIULI-VENEZIA GIULIA (Trieste)—Knives, mosaics, hempen clothes, linen, and wooden shoes.
- LIGURIA (Genova)—Embroidered silk shawls, laces of Santa Margherita, bottled miniature vessels, pottery of Albisona and Savona.
- EMILIA-ROMAGNA (Bologna, Ravenna)—Pottery of Faenza, wrought iron and woodwork of Grazzano Visconti, laces of Forlì, and copper engravings of Ravenna.
- TOSCANA (Firenze, Pisa)—Alabaster of Volterra, statuettes made with marble sawdust of Lucca, straw hats, prime light-grain florentine leather goods, pottery, and embroidery. Best buys: shoes, cameos, brushed gold (*satinato*), jewelry, silk.
- MARCHE (Ancona)—Accordions of Castelfidardo, Osimo, Numana, and Recanati; pottery of Urbino, Ascoli, and Pesaro; laces of Offida, in the province of Ascoli Piceno; and articles of straw.
- UMBRIA (Perugia)—Artistic pottery of Orvieto, Gubbio, Deruta, Perugia, Gualdo Tadino, and Città di Castello; textiles and laces of Assisi; inlaid furniture, wood carving, and wrought iron of Perugia, Gubbio, and Todi.
- LAZIO (Roma)—Copper wares of Fiuggi, carpets of Veroli, pottery of Civita Castellana, wrought iron of Ciociaria, and pillow laces. Best buys: luggage, leather goods, shoes, antiques, old books and prints.
- ABRUZZO (Pescara, L'Aquila)—Embossed copper wares, wrought iron, wood carving, carpets, textiles, laces, jeweler's wares, and artistic pottery.
- MOLISE (Campobasso)—Multicolored pottery, laces, dressed stones, wrought iron, watermarked papers, and jeweler's wares.
- CAMPANIA (Napoli)—Porcelain of Capodimonte, leather gloves of Naples, corals of Torre del Greco, pearls, textiles and silk, straw and wicker works, wrought iron and inlaid furniture. Best buys: coral

items, cameos. Note: Do not buy tortoiseshell; the U.S. forbids you to bring it in.

- PUGLIA (Bari)—Textiles (particularly woolens), tobacco pipes, embroidery, carpets, and tapestry.
- BASILICATA (Potenza)—Pottery of Potenza, woodworks, copper wares and wrought iron, embroidery, and handwoven textiles.
- CALABRIA (Reggio Calabria, Catanzaro)—Leather articles, laces, inlaid furniture, painted amphorae, and hand-woven textiles; string instruments of Bisignano and gold of Crotone.
- SICILIA (Palermo)—Sicilian handcarts, puppets of Palermo, corals, mandolins and guitars of Catania, marble sculptures, and articles of alabaster.
- SARDEGNA (Cagliari)—Carpets, textiles, blankets of lively colors, baskets made with reeds and rush, laces, earthenware, pottery, and wrought iron.

## FLEA MARKETS

In Italy, flea markets are a shopper's paradise. People can stroll, chat, browse around, and sniff out good deals. Vendors shout to promote the sale of their wares while tourists and bargain hunters look for the unusual. The objects on display may be centuries old!

Look into . . .
- the Italian law that forbids the purchase of illegal goods from unauthorized street vendors.

Look out!
- Learn the art of bargaining.
- Prices are not fixed.
- Walk away from persistent vendors.
- Be aware of wallet and bag snatchers!

Ask the hotel concierge about flea markets at every new town or city you visit, and you will not be disappointed: from centuries-old antiques that include jewelry, art, and exquisite linens to odd trinkets and amusing collectibles, Italian flea markets provide hours of entertainment and occasionally some real bargains.

## GOING SHOPPING

No matter what you are looking for, shopping in Italy is a fantastic and thrilling adventure! Italian products will fascinate you! The Made in Italy label brings immediately to mind the concepts of art and quality. Wander the streets in search of the unimaginable, from jewelry, leather goods, perfumes, designer shoes, gold, ceramics, laces, glasses, antiques, old and modern art works, cars, motorcycles, bicycles and food, wine and sweets, to famous Italian designers such as Armani, Bulgari, Cavalli, Dolce & Gabbana, Fendi, Ferragamo, Gucci, Krizia, Prada, Pucci, Valentino, Zegna, and many others.

On the other hand, watch out for imitation products of inferior quality that are flooding the market. Also, compare prices, for there may be a double standard: one for locals, another for the unsuspecting tourist!

Check *http://goitaly.about.com/od/shoppinginitaly/Shopping_in_Italy.htm* or *http://goitaly.about.com/od/florenceitaly/a/florence-shopping.htm*

| | |
|---|---|
| Where can I find _____? | **Dove posso trovare _____?** *dOH-veh pOHs-soh troh-vAH-reh* |
| ■ a bakery | **un fornaio** *oon fohr-nAH-ee-oh* |
| ■ a bookstore | **una libreria** *OO-nah lee-bray-rEE-ah* |
| ■ a butcher | **una macelleria** *OO-nah mah-chehl-leh-rEE-ah* |
| ■ a camera shop | **un negozio di fotocine** *oon neh-gOH-tsee-oh dee foh-toh-chEE-neh* |

- a candy store — **un sale e tabacchi** *oon sAH-leh ay tah-bAH-key*
- a clothing store — **un negozio di abbigliamento** *oon neh-gOH-tsee-oh dee ahb-bee-ly-ee-ah-mEHn-toh*
  - for children's clothes — **per bambini** *pehr bahm-bEE-nee*
  - men's store — **per uomini** *pehr oo-OH-mee-nee*
  - women's boutique — **per signore** *pehr see-ny-OH-reh*
- a delicatessen — **una salumeria** *OO-nah sah-loo-meh-rEE-ah*
- a department store — **i grandi magazzini** *ee grAHn-dee mah-gah-tsEE-nee*

- a pharmacy (chemist) — **una farmacia** *OO-nah fahr-mah-chEE-ah*
- a florist — **un fioraio** *oon fee-oh-rAH-ee-oh*
- a gift (souvenir) shop — **un negozio di regali (souvenir)** *oon neh-gOH-tsee-oh dee reh-gAH-lee (soo-vay-nEEr)*
- a grocery store — **un negozio di alimentari** *oon neh-gOH-tsee-oh dee ah-lee-mehn-tAH-ree*

| | |
|---|---|
| ■ a hardware store (ironmonger) | **un negozio di ferramenta** *oon neh-gOH-tsee-oh dee fehr-rah-mEHn-tah* |
| ■ a jewelry store | **una gioielleria** *OO-nah jee-oh-ee-ehl-leh-rEE-ah* |
| ■ a liquor store | **una enoteca** *OO-nah eh-noh-tEH-kah* |
| ■ a newsstand | **un'edicola (il giornalaio)** *oo-neh-dEE-koh-lah (eel jee-ohr-nah-lAH-ee-oh)* |
| ■ a supermarket | **un supermercato** *oon soo-pehr-mehr-kAH-toh* |
| ■ a tobacco shop | **una tabaccherìa** *OO-nah tah-bahk-keh-rEE-ah* |
| ■ a toy store | **un negozio di giocattoli** *oon neh-gOH-tsee-oh dee jee-oh-kAHt-toh-lee* |
| ■ a wine shop | **una mescita, una cantina, una enoteca** *OO-nah mAY-shee-tah OO-nah kahn-tEE-nah OO-nah eh-noh-tEH-kah* |
| Young man, can you wait on me? | **Giovanotto, può occuparsi di me?** *jee-oh-vah-nOHt-toh poo-OH ohk-koo-pAHr-see dee meh* |
| Miss, can you help me? | **Signorina, può aiutarmi?** *see-ny-oh-rEE-nah poo-OH ah-ee-oo-tAHr-mee* |
| Do you take credit cards? | **Accettano carte di credito?** *ah-chEHt-tah-noh kAHr-teh dee krEH-dee-toh* |
| Can I pay with a traveler's check? | **Posso pagare con un traveler's check?** *pOHs-soh pah-gAH-reh kohn oon trAH-veh-lehs chEH-keh* |

## BOOKS

| | |
|---|---|
| Is there a store that carries English-language books? | **C'è un negozio dove si vendono libri in lingua inglese?** *chEH oon neh-gOH-tsee-oh dOH-veh see vAYn-doh-noh lEE-bree een lEEn-goo-ah een-glAY-seh* |
| I'm looking for a copy of _____. | **M'interessa una copia di _____.** *meen-teh-rEHs-sah OO-nah kOH-pee-ah dee* |
| The author of the book is _____. | **L'autore del libro è _____.** *lah-oo-tOH-reh dayl lEE-broh EH* |
| I'm just looking. | **Sto solo guardando.** *stoh sOH-loh goo-ahr-dAHn-doh* |
| Do you have books (novels) in English? | **Ha libri (romanzi) in inglese?** *ah lEE-bree (roh-mAHn-tsee) een een-glAY-seh* |
| I want _____. | **Desidero _____.** *deh-sEE-deh-roh* |
| ■ a guide book | **una guida** *OO-nah goo-EE-dah* |
| ■ a map of this city | **una pianta di questa città** *OO-nah pee-AHn-tah dee koo-AYs-tah cheet-tAH* |
| ■ a pocket dictionary | **un dizionario tascabile** *oon dee-tsee-oh-nAH-ree-oh tah-skAH-bee-leh* |
| ■ an Italian-English dictionary | **un dizionario italiano-inglese** *oon dee-tsee-oh-nAH-ree-oh ee-tah-lee-AH-noh een-glAY-seh* |
| Where can I find _____? | **Dove posso trovare _____?** *dOH-veh pOHs-soh troh-vAH-reh* |
| ■ detective stories | **romanzi gialli** *roh-mAHn-tsee jee-AHl-lee* |
| ■ comics | **fumetti** *foo-mAYt-tee* |

| | |
|---|---|
| history books | **libri di storia** *lEE-bree dee stOH-ree-ah* |
| short stories | **una raccolta di novelle** *OO-nah rahk-kOHl-tah dee noh-vEHl-leh* |
| cookbooks | **libri di cucina** *lEE-bree dee koo-chEE-nah* |
| I'll take these books. | **Prendo questi libri.** *prAYn-doh koo-AYs-tee lEE-bree* |
| Will you wrap them, please? | **Me l'incarta, per favore?** *meh leen-kAHr-tah pehr fah-vOH-reh* |

## CLOTHING

Italians are into fashion, and they have an unspoken dress code that is based on good sense. Even common Italian people may like to wear jeans, shorts, miniskirts, and sneakers, but not for dinner.

Look out!

- Don't be sloppy. Look nice and dress age-appropriate.
- Always carry suitable clothing: skirts/pants and short/long sleeves.
- Cover shoulders and knees when visiting churches.
- Dress accordingly when going to upscale restaurants, theaters, political and social gatherings. Gentlemen should wear a jacket and tie.
- Men should wear long pants when eating at an elegant restaurant.
- Bring a hat and a small umbrella to protect yourself from the hot summer sun!

| | |
|---|---|
| Is this the _____ department? | **È questo il reparto (la sezione) di _____?** *EH koo-AYs-toh eel ray-pAHr-toh (lah say-tzee-OH-neh) dee* |

| | |
|---|---|
| Would you please show me _____? | **Per favore, può mostrarmi _____?** *pehr fah-vOH-reh poo-OH moh-strAHr-mee* |
| ■ a bathing suit | **un costume da bagno** *oon koh-stOO-meh dah bAH-ny-ee-oh* |
| ■ a man's (lady's) belt | **una cintura per uomo (per signora)** *OO-nah cheen-tOO-rah pehr oo-OH-moh (pehr see-ny-OH-rah)* |
| ■ a blouse | **una blusa (camicetta)** *OO-nah blOO-sah (kah-mee-chAYt-tah)* |
| ■ boots | **degli stivali** *dAY-ly-ee stee-vAH-lee* |
| ■ a bra | **un reggiseno** *oon reh-jee-sAY-noh* |
| ■ a dress | **una veste** *OO-nah vEH-steh* |
| ■ an evening gown | **un abito da sera** *oon AH-bee-toh dah sAY-rah* |
| ■ leather (suede) gloves | **dei guanti di pelle (scamosciata)** *dAY-ee goo-AHn-tee dee pEHl-leh (skah-moh-shee-AH-tah)* |
| ■ handkerchiefs | **dei fazzoletti** *dAY-ee fah-tsoh-lAYt-tee* |
| ■ a hat | **un cappello** *oon kahp-pEHl-loh* |
| ■ a jacket | **una giacca** *OO-nah jee-AHk-kah* |
| ■ jeans | **dei jeans** *dAY-ee jeans* |
| ■ a jogging suit | **un completo per jogging** *oon kohm-plEH-toh pehr jogging* |
| ■ an overcoat | **un soprabito** *oon soh-prAH-bee-toh* |
| ■ pajamas | **dei pigiama** *dAY-ee pee-jee-AH-mah* |
| ■ panties | **delle mutandine** *dAYl-leh moo-tahn-dEE-neh* |
| ■ pants | **dei pantaloni** *dAY-ee pahn-tah-lOH-nee* |
| ■ panty hose | **un collant** *oon koh-lAHn* |
| ■ a raincoat | **un impermeabile** *oon eem-pehr-meh-AH-bee-leh* |

- a robe (woman's) — **una vestaglia** *OO-nah veh-stAH-ly-ee-ah*
- a robe (man's) — **una veste da camera** *OO-nah vEH-steh dah kAH-meh-rah*
- sandals — **dei sandali** *dAY-ee sAHn-dah-lee*
- sneakers — **delle scarpette** *dAYl-leh skahr-pAYt-teh*
- a shirt — **una camicia** *OO-nah kah-mEE-chee-ah*
- (a pair of) shoes — **un paio di scarpe** *oon pAH-ee-oh dee skAHr-peh*
- shorts (briefs) — **dei pantaloncini (delle mutande)** *dAY-ee pahn-tah-lohn-chEE-nee (dAYl-leh moo-tAHn-deh)*
- a skirt — **una gonna** *OO-nah gOHn-nah*
- a slip — **una sottoveste** *OO-nah soht-toh-vEH-steh*
- slippers — **delle pantofole** *dAYl-leh pahn-tOH-foh-leh*
- socks — **dei calzini** *dAY-ee kahl-tsEE-nee*
- stockings — **delle calze** *dAYl-leh kAHl-tseh*
- a suit — **un vestito** *oon veh-stEE-toh*
- a sweater — **una maglia** *OO-nah mAH-ly-ah*
- a tee-shirt — **una maglietta** *OO-nah mah-ly-ee-AYt-tah*
- a tie — **una cravatta** *OO-nah krah-vAHt-tah*
- an undershirt — **una canottiera** *OO-nah kah-noht-tee-EH-rah*
- underwear — **della biancheria intima** *dAYl-lah bee-ahn-keh-rEE-ah EEn-tee-mah*
- a wallet — **un portafoglio** *oon pohr-tah-fOH-ly-ee-oh*

| | |
|---|---|
| Is there a special sale today? | **Oggi c'è una vendita d'occasione?** *OH-jee chEH OO-nah vAYn-dee-tah dohk-kah-see-OH-neh* |
| I'd like a shirt with short (long) sleeves. | **Vorrei una camicia con le maniche corte (lunghe).** *vohr-rEH-ee OO-nah kah-mEE-chee-ah kohn leh mAH-nee-keh kOHr-teh (lOOn-gheh)* |
| I need a bigger (smaller) size. | **Mi serve la taglia più grande (piccola).** *mee sEHr-veh lah tAH-ly-ah pee-OO grAHn-deh, pEEc-coh-lah* |
| Do you have this in another color? | **C'è in altri colori?** *chEH een AHl-tree koh-lOH-ree* |
| Can I pay by credit card? | **Posso pagare con la carta di credito?** *pOHs-soh pah-gAH-reh kohn lah kAHr-tah dee krEH-dee-toh* |
| I'd like a receipt, please. | **Mi dà lo scontrino, per favore?** *mee dAH loh skohn-trEE-noh pehr fah-vOH-reh* |
| Can I have a refund? | **Rimborsa(te) i soldi?** *ree-bOHr-sah (teh) ee sOHl-dee* |
| Do you have anything _____? | **Ha qualche cosa _____?** *AH koo-AHl-keh kOH-sah* |
| ■ else | **altro** *AHl-troh* |
| ■ larger | **più grande** *pee-OO grAHn-deh* |
| ■ less expensive | **meno costoso** *mAY-noh koh-stOH-soh* |
| ■ longer | **più lungo** *pee-OO lOOn-goh* |
| ■ of better quality | **di migliore qualità** *dee mee-ly-ee-OH-reh koo-ah-lee-tAH* |
| ■ shorter | **più corto** *pee-OO kOHr-toh* |
| ■ smaller | **più piccolo** *pee-OO pEE-koh-loh* |

| | |
|---|---|
| I don't like the color. | **Non mi piace il colore.** *nohn mee pee-AH-cheh eel koh-lOH-reh* |
| Do you have it in _____? | **Lo ha in _____?** *loh AH een* |
| ■ black | **nero** *nAY-roh* |
| ■ blue | **blu** *blOO* |
| ■ brown | **marrone** *mahr-rOH-neh* |
| ■ gray | **grigio** *grEE-jee-oh* |
| ■ green | **verde** *vAYr-deh* |
| ■ pink | **rosa** *rOH-sah* |
| ■ red | **rosso** *rOHs-soh* |
| ■ white | **bianco** *bee-AHn-koh* |
| ■ yellow | **giallo** *jee-AHl-loh* |

## SALE SIGNS

| | |
|---|---|
| SVENDITA | (sale) |
| SALDI DI FINE STAGIONE | (end-of-season sale) |
| LIQUIDAZIONE | (everything must go) |
| VENDITA TOTALE | |
| PREZZI FISSI | (fixed prices) |

| | |
|---|---|
| I want something in _____. | **Voglio qualche cosa _____.** *vOH-ly-ee-oh koo-AHl-keh kOH-sah* |
| ■ chiffon | **di chiffon** *dee sheef-fOHn* |
| ■ corduroy | **di velluto a coste** *dee vehl-lOO-toh ah kOH-steh* |
| ■ cotton | **di cotone** *dee koh-tOH-neh* |
| ■ denim | **di denim** *dee dEH-nim* |
| ■ felt | **di feltro** *dee fAYl-troh* |
| ■ flannel | **di flanella** *dee flah-nEHl-lah* |
| ■ gabardine | **di gabardine** *dee gah-bahr-dEE-neh* |
| ■ lace | **in pizzo** *een pEE-tsoh* |
| ■ leather | **in pelle** *een pEHl-leh* |
| ■ linen | **di lino** *dee lEE-noh* |
| ■ nylon | **di nylon** *dee nAH-ee-lohn* |
| ■ permanent press | **con piega permanente** *kohn pee-EH-gah pehr-mah-nEHn-teh* |
| ■ satin | **di raso** *dee rAH-soh* |
| ■ silk | **di seta** *dee sAY-tah* |

| | |
|---|---|
| ■ suede | **di renna** *dee rAYn-nah* |
| ■ polyester | **in poliestere** *een poh-lee-EH-steh-reh* |
| ■ terrycloth | **in tessuto spugnoso** *een tehs-sOO-toh spoo-ny-OH-soh* |
| ■ velvet | **di velluto** *dee vehl-lOO-toh* |
| ■ wool | **di lana** *dee lAH-nah* |
| ■ wash-and-wear | **che non si stira** *kay nohn see stEE-rah* |
| Show me something _____. | **Mi faccia vedere qualche cosa _____.** *mee fAH-chee-ah veh-dAY-reh koo-AHl-kay kOH-sah* |
| ■ in a solid color | **a tinta unita** *ah tEEn-tah oo-nEE-tah* |
| ■ with stripes | **a righe** *ah rEE-gheh* |
| ■ with polka dots | **a pallini** *ah pahl-lEE-nee* |
| ■ in plaid | **a quadri** *ah koo-AH-dree* |
| Could you take my measurements? | **Può prendermi le misure?** *poo-OH prEHn-dayr-mee leh mee-sOO-reh* |
| I take size (my size is) _____. | **La mia taglia è _____.** *lah mEE-ah tAH-ly-ee-ah EH* |
| ■ small | **piccola** *pEEk-koh-lah* |
| ■ medium | **media** *mEH-dee-ah* |
| ■ large | **grande** *grAHn-deh* |
| Can I try it on? | **Posso provarmelo(la)?** *pOHs-soh proh-vAHr-meh-loh(lah)* |
| Can you alter it? | **Può aggiustarmelo(la)?** *poo-OH ah-jee-oo-stAHr-meh-loh(lah)* |
| Can I return the article (if I change my mind)? | **(Se non mi va), posso portarlo indietro?** *(say nohn mee vAH) pOHs-soh pohr-tAHr-loh een-dee-EH-troh* |

| CLOTHING MEASUREMENTS | | | | | | | | |
|---|---|---|---|---|---|---|---|---|
| WOMEN | | | | | | | | |
| Shoes | | | | | | | | |
| American | 4 | 5 | 6 | 7 | 8 | 9 | | |
| British | 3 | 4 | 5 | 6 | 7 | 8 | | |
| Continental | 35 | 36 | 37 | 38 | 39 | 40 | | |
| Dresses, suits | | | | | | | | |
| American | 8 | 10 | 12 | 14 | 16 | 18 | | |
| British | 10 | 12 | 14 | 16 | 18 | 20 | | |
| Continental | 36 | 38 | 40 | 42 | 44 | 46 | | |
| Blouses, sweaters | | | | | | | | |
| American | 32 | 34 | 36 | 38 | 40 | 42 | | |
| British | 34 | 36 | 38 | 40 | 42 | 44 | | |
| Continental | 40 | 42 | 44 | 46 | 48 | 50 | | |
| MEN | | | | | | | | |
| Shoes | | | | | | | | |
| American | 7 | 8 | 9 | 10 | 11 | 12 | | |
| British | 6 | 7 | 8 | 9 | 10 | 11 | | |
| Continental | 39 | 41 | 43 | 44 | 45 | 46 | | |
| Suits, coats | | | | | | | | |
| American | 34 | 36 | 38 | 40 | 42 | 44 | 46 | 48 |
| British | 44 | 46 | 48 | 50 | 54 | 56 | 58 | 60 |
| Continental | 44 | 46 | 48 | 50 | 52 | 54 | 56 | 58 |
| Shirts | | | | | | | | |
| American | 14 | $14\frac{1}{2}$ | 15 | $15\frac{1}{2}$ | 16 | $16\frac{1}{2}$ | 17 | $17\frac{1}{2}$ |
| British | 14 | $14\frac{1}{2}$ | 15 | $15\frac{1}{2}$ | 16 | $16\frac{1}{2}$ | 17 | $17\frac{1}{2}$ |
| Continental | 36 | 37 | 38 | 39 | 40 | 41 | 42 | 43 |

| | |
|---|---|
| Do you have something handmade? | **Non c'è nulla che sia fatto a mano?** *nohn chEH nOOl-lah kay sEE-ah fAHt-toh ah mAH-noh* |
| The zipper doesn't work. | **La cerniera non funziona.** *lah chehr-nee-EH-rah nohn fOOn-tsee-OH-nah* |
| It doesn't fit me. | **Non mi sta bene.** *nohn mee stAH bEH-neh* |
| It fits very well. | **Mi sta molto bene.** *mee stAH mOHl-toh bEH-neh* |
| I'll take it. | **Lo(la) prendo.** *loh(lah) prAYn-doh* |
| Will you wrap it? | **Me lo(la) impacchetta?** *meh loh(lah) eem-pahk-kEHt-tah* |
| I'd like to see the pair of shoes (boots) in the window. | **Vorrei vedere il paio di scarpe (stivali) in vetrina.** *vohr-rEH-ee veh-dAY-reh eel pAH-ee-oh dee skAHr-peh (stee-vAH-lee) een vay-trEE-nah* |
| They're too narrow (wide). | **Sono troppo strette (larghe).** *sOH-noh trOHp-poh strAYt-teh (lAHr-gheh)* |
| They pinch me. | **Mi stanno strette.** *mee stAHn-noh strAYt-teh* |
| They fit me. | **Mi stanno bene.** *mee stAHn-noh bEH-neh* |
| I'll take them. | **Le compro.** *leh kOHm-proh* |
| I also need shoelaces. | **Ho bisogno anche dei lacci.** *oh bee-sOH-ny-oh AHn-keh dAY-ee lAH-chee* |
| That's all I want for now. | **Questo è tutto quello che voglio per ora.** *koo-AYs-toh EH tOOt-toh koo-AYl-loh kay vOH-ly-ee-oh pehr OH-rah* |

## ELECTRICAL APPLIANCES

Electric current in the U.S. is 110V AC, whereas in Italy it is 220V AC. Unless your electric shaver or alarm clock is able to handle both currents, you will need to purchase an adapter. When making a purchase, please be aware that some Italian products are engineered to work with either system whereas others will require an adapter.

| | |
|---|---|
| I what to buy _____. | **Vorrei comprare _____.** *vohr-rEH-ee kohm-prAH-reh* |
| ■ an adapter | **un trasformatore** *oon trahs-fohr-mah-tOH-reh* |
| ■ a battery | **una pila** *OO-nah pEE-lah* |
| ■ a curling iron | **una spazzola riscaldante elettrica per fare la messa in piega** *OO-nah spAH-tzoh-lah ree-skahl-dAHn-teh eh-lEHt-tree-kah pehr FAH-reh lah mAYs-sah een pee-EH-gah* |
| ■ an electric shaver | **un rasoio elettrico** *oon rah-sOH-ee-oh eh-lEHt-tree-koh* |
| ■ an electric water pick | **un idropulsore elettronico per la pulizia dei denti** *oon ee-droh-pool-sOH-reh eh-leht-trOH-nee-koh pehr lah poo-lee-tzEE-ah dAY-ee dEHn-tee* |
| ■ a hair dryer | **un asciugacapelli** *oon ah-shee-OO-gah-kah-pAYl-lee* |
| ■ a manicure set | **un completo per manicure** *oon kohm-plEH-toh pehr mah-nee-kOO-reh* |
| ■ a plug | **una spina (elettrica)** *OO-nah spEE-nah (eh-lEHt-tree-kah)* |
| ■ a transformer | **un trasformatore** *oon trahs-fohr-mah-tOH-reh* |

## FOODS AND HOUSEHOLD ITEMS

See also pages 127–159 and the dictionary (pages 284–334) for more food words. When you go to a food market or shop, bring your own bag along with you to tote home your groceries. A collapsible net bag is very useful.

| | |
|---|---|
| I'd like _____. | **Vorrei _____.** *vohr-rEH-ee* |
| Could you give me _____? | **Potrebbe darmi _____?** *poh-trAYb-beh dAHr-mee* |
| ■ a bar of soap | **una saponetta** *OO-nah sah-poh-nEHt-tah* |
| ■ a bottle of juice | **un succo di frutta** *oon sOO-koh dee frOOt-tah* |
| ■ a box of cereal | **una scatola di cereali** *OO-nah skAH-toh-lah dee cheh-reh-AH-lee* |
| ■ a can (tin) of tomato sauce | **una scatola di conserva di pomodoro** *OO-nah skAH-toh-lah dee kohn-sEHr-vah dee poh-moh-dOH-roh* |
| ■ a dozen eggs | **una dozzina d'uova** *OO-nah doh-tsEE-nah doo-OH-vah* |
| ■ a jar of coffee | **un vasetto di caffè** *oon vah-sAYt-toh dee kahf-fEH* |

| | |
|---|---|
| ■ a half-kilo of cherries (just over 1 pound) | **mezzo chilo di ciliege** *mEH-tsoh kEE-loh dee chee-lee-EH-jeh* |

## JEWELRY

| | |
|---|---|
| I'd like to see _____. | **Vorrei vedere _____.** *vohr-rEH-ee veh-dAY-reh* |
| ■ a bracelet | **un braccialetto** *oon brah-chee-ah-lAYt-toh* |
| ■ a brooch | **un fermaglio (una spilla)** *oon fehr-mAH-ly-ee-oh (OO-nah spEEl-lah)* |
| ■ a chain | **una catenina** *OO-nah kay-teh-nEE-nah* |
| ■ a charm | **un ciondolo** *oon chee-OHn-doh-loh* |
| ■ some earrings | **degli orecchini** *dAY-ly-ee oh-rehk-kEE-nee* |
| ■ a necklace | **un monile** *oon moh-nEE-leh* |
| ■ a pin | **una spilla** *OO-nah spEEl-lah* |
| ■ a ring | **un anello** *oon ah-nEHl-loh* |
| ■ a rosary | **una corona del rosario** *OO-nah koh-rOH-nah dayl roh-sAH-ree-oh* |
| ■ a (wrist) watch | **un orologio da polso** *oon oh-roh-lOH-jee-oh dah pOHl-soh* |
| Is this _____? | **Questo è ____?** *koo-AYs-toh EH* |
| ■ gold | **d'oro** *dOH-roh* |
| ■ platinum | **di platino** *dee plAH-tee-noh* |
| ■ silver | **d'argento** *dahr-jEHn-toh* |
| ■ stainless steel | **d'acciaio inossidabile** *dah-chee-AH-ee-oh ee-nohs-see-dAH-bee-leh* |
| Is it solid gold or gold plated? | **È oro massiccio oppure oro placcato?** *EH OH-roh mahs-sEE-chee-oh ohp-pOO-reh OH-roh plahk-kAH-toh* |

| | |
|---|---|
| How many carats is it? | **Di quanti carati è?** *dee koo-AHn-tee kah-rAH-tee EH* |
| What is that (precious) stone? | **Che pietra (preziosa) è?** *kay pee-EH-trah (preh-tsee-OH-sah) EH* |
| I want _____. | **Vorrei (voglio) _____.** *vohr-rEH-ee (vOH-ly-ee-oh)* |
| ■ an amethyst | **un'ametista** *oo-nah-meh-tEE-stah* |
| ■ an aquamarine | **un'acquamarina** *oo-nah-koo-ah-mah-rEE-nah* |
| ■ a coral | **un corallo** *oon koh-rAHl-loh* |
| ■ a diamond | **un diamante** *oon dee-ah-mAHn-teh* |
| ■ an emerald | **uno smeraldo** *OO-noh smeh-rAHl-doh* |
| ■ ivory | **una cosa d'avorio** *OO-nah kOH-sah dah-vOH-ree-oh* |
| ■ jade | **una giada** *OO-nah jee-AH-dah* |
| ■ onyx | **un'onice** *oon-OH-nee-cheh* |
| ■ pearls | **delle perle** *dAYl-leh pEHr-leh* |
| ■ a ruby | **un rubino** *oon roo-bEE-noh* |
| ■ a sapphire | **uno zaffiro** *OO-noh tsahf-fEE-roh* |
| ■ a topaz | **un topazio** *oon toh-pAH-tsee-oh* |
| ■ a turquoise | **un turchese** *oon toor-kAY-seh* |
| How much is it? | **Quanto costa?** *koo-AHn-toh kOH-stah* |
| I'll take it. | **Lo(a) prendo.** *loh(ah) prAYn-doh* |

## AUDIOVISUAL EQUIPMENT

Please see the note under Electrical Appliances on page 186. In addition, Europe uses broadcasting and recording systems that are often incompatible with those of the U.S. Unless expressly warranted, Italian TVs, DVD player/recorders, computers, and telephone answering systems will not operate properly in the U.S.

Is there an audio/video store in the neighborhood?

**C'è qui vicino un negozio di articoli audio/video?** *chEH koo-ee vee-chEE-noh oon neh-gOH-tsee-oh dee ahr-tEE-koh-lee AH-oo-dee-oh/VEE-deh-oh*

Where is the _____ section?

**Dov'è la sezione _____?** *doh-vEH lah seh-tsee-OH-neh*

- classical music — **di musica classica** *dee mOO-see-kah clAHs-see-kah*
- popular music — **di musica popolare** *dee mOO-see-kah poh-poh-lAH-reh*
- latest hits — **degli ultimi successi** *dAY-ly-ee OOl-tee-mee soo-chEHs-see*
- Italian music — **della musica italiana** *dAYl-lah mOO-see-kah ee-tah-lee-AH-nah*
- opera — **di musica d'opera** *dee mOO-see-kah dOH-peh-rah*

Do you have any songs of _____?

**Avete la canzone di _____?** *ah-vay-teh lah kahn-tzOH-neh dee*

I would like to buy _____.

**Vorrei comprare _____.** *vohr-rEH-ee kohm-prAH-reh*

- a portable CD player — **un lettore CD portatile** *oon leht-tOH-reh see-dEE pohr-tAH-tee-leh*
- a CD recorder — **un registratore CD** *oon reh-jee-strah-tOH-reh see-dEE*

| | |
|---|---|
| CDs | **dei CD** *dAY-ee see-dEE* |
| headphones | **una cuffia** *OO-nah kOOf-fee-ah* |
| recordable CDs | **dei compact disks vuoti (registrabili, vergini)** *dAY-ee compact disks voo-OH-tee (reh-jee-strAH-bee-lee vAYr-jee-nee)* |
| wireless headphones | **delle cuffie senza filo** *dAYl-leh kOOf-fee-eh sEHn-tsah fEE-loh* |
| I need _____. | **Ho bisogno di _____.** *oh bee-sOH-ny-oh dee* |
| a camcorder | **una videocamera** *OO-nah vEE-deh-oh-kAH-meh-rah* |
| digital videofilm | **un videofilm digitale** *oon vee-deh-oh-fEElm dee-jee-tAH-leh* |

| | |
|---|---|
| DVD movies | **dei film DVD** *dAY-ee fEElm dee-vee-dee* |
| a DVD player | **un registratore DVD** *oon reh-jee-strah-tOH-reh dee-vee-dee* |
| videofilm | **un film registrato su nastro video** *oon fEElm reh-jee-strAH-toh soo nAH-stroh vEE-deh-oh* |
| Do you have DVD movies with subtitles in English? | **Avete film con sottotitolo in inglese per DVD?** *ah-vAY-teh fEElm kohn soht-toh-tEE-toh-loh een een-glAY-seh pehr dee-vee-dee* |
| Will the warranty be honored in the U.S.? | **La garanzia sarà valida (accettata) negli Stati Uniti?** *lah gah-rahn-tsEE-ah sah-rAH vAH-lee-dah (ah-cheht-tAH-tah) nAYly-ee stAH-tee oo-nEE-tee* |

| | |
|---|---|
| Whom shall I contact if this malfunctions? | **Chi dovrò contattare se non funziona bene?** *key doh-vrOH kohn-taht-tAH-reh say nohn foon-tsee-OH-nah bEH-neh* |

## PHOTOGRAPHIC EQUIPMENT

For phrases dealing with camera repairs, see page 209.

| | |
|---|---|
| Where is there a camera shop? | **Dov'è un negozio di fotocine (macchine fotografiche)?** *doh-vEH oon neh-GOH-tsee-oh dee foh-toh-chEE-neh (mAHk-kee-neh foh-toh-grAH-fee-keh)* |
| I need _____. | **Ho bisogno di _____.** *oh bee-sOH-ny-oh dee* |
| ■ a camera bag | **una custodia della macchina fotografica** *OO-nah koo-stOH-dee-ah dAYl-lah mAH-key-nah foh-toh-grAH-fee-kah* |
| ■ camera batteries | **pile per la macchina fotografica** *pEE-leh pehr lah mAH-key-nah foh-toh-grAH-fee-kah* |
| ■ a disposable camera | **una macchina fotografica usa e getta** *OO-nah mAH-key-nah foh-toh-grAH-fee-kah OO-sah ay jEHt-tah* |
| ■ an expensive (inexpensive) camera | **una buona macchina fotografica (a buon mercato).** *OO-nah boo-OH-nah mAHk-kee-nah foh-toh-grAH-fee-kah (ah boo-OHn mayr-kAH-toh)* |
| ■ a flash | **un flash** *oon flash* |
| ■ a lens | **una lente** *OO-nah lEHn-teh* |
| ■ a memory card | **una memory card** *OO-nah memory card* |

| | |
|---|---|
| ■ a point-and-shoot camera | **una macchina fotografica "vai e clicca"** *OO-nah mAHk-kee-nah foh-toh-grAH-fee-kah vAH-ee ay klEEk-kah* |
| ■ an SLR camera | **una macchina fotografica SLR** *OO-nah mAHk-kee-nah foh-toh-grAH-fee-kah EHs-seh Ehl-leh Ehr-reh* |
| ■ a tripod | **un treppiede** *oon trehp-pee-EH-deh* |
| ■ a zoom lens | **un obiettivo con zoom** *oon oh-bee-ayt-tEE-voh kohn zoom* |
| I want one print of each. | **Voglio una copia per ogni fotografia.** *vOH-ly-ee-oh OO-nah kOH-pee-ah pehr OH-ny-ee foh-toh-grah-fEE-ah* |
| I want _____. | **Vorrei (voglio) _____.** *vohr-rEH-ee (vOH-ly-ee-oh)* |
| ■ an enlargement | **un ingrandimento** *oon een-grahn-dee-mEHn-toh* |
| with a glossy (matte) finish | **su carta lucida (opaca, matta)** *soo kAHr-tah lOO-chee-dah (oh-pAH-kah mAHt-tah)* |
| When can I pick up the pictures? | **Quando vengo a ritirarle?** *koo-AHn-doh vEHn-goh ah ree-tee-rAHr-leh* |

## NEWSPAPERS AND MAGAZINES

| | |
|---|---|
| Do you carry English newspapers (magazines)? | **Ha giornali (riviste) in inglese?** *a jee-ohr-nAH-lee (ree-vEE-steh) een een-glAY-seh* |
| I'd like to buy some (picture) postcards. | **Vorrei comprare delle cartoline (illustrate).** *vohr-rEH-ee kohm-prAH-reh dAYl-leh kahr-toh-lEE-neh (eel-loo-strAH-teh)* |

## SOUVENIRS, HANDICRAFTS

| | |
|---|---|
| I'd like _____. | **Vorrei _____.** *vohr-rEH-ee* |
| ■ a pretty gift | **un bel regalo** *oon bEHl reh-gAH-loh* |
| ■ a small gift | **un regalino** *oon reh-gah-lEE-noh* |
| ■ a souvenir | **un souvenir** *oon soo-veh-nEEr* |
| It's for _____. | **È per _____.** *EH pehr* |
| I don't want to spend more than 20 (30) dollars. | **Non voglio spendere più di venti (trenta) dollari.** *nohn vOH-ly-ee-oh spEHn-deh-reh pee-OO dee vAYn-tee (trEHn-tah) dOHl-lah-ree* |
| Could you suggest something? | **Potrebbe suggerirmi qualche cosa?** *poh-trAYb-beh soo-jeh-rEEr-mee koo-AHl-keh kOH-sah* |
| Would you show me your selection of _____? | **Che cosa potrebbe mostrarmi di _____?** *kay kOH-sah poh-trAYb-beh moh-strAHr-mee dee* |
| ■ blown glass | **vetro soffiato** *vAY-troh sohf-fee-AH-toh* |
| ■ carved objects | **legno intagliato** *lAY-ny-oh een-tah-ly-ee-AH-toh* |
| ■ crystal | **cristallo** *kree-stAHl-loh* |
| ■ earthenware (pottery) | **ceramiche** *cheh-rAH-mee-keh* |
| ■ fans | **ventagli** *vehn-tAH-ly-ee* |
| ■ jewelry | **oggetti preziosi** *oh-jEHt-tee preh-tsee-OH-see* |
| ■ lace | **pizzi** *pEE-tsee* |
| ■ leather goods | **articoli in pelle** *ahr-tEE-koh-lee een pEHl-leh* |
| ■ liqueurs | **liquori** *lee-koo-OH-ree* |

| | |
|---|---|
| local handicrafts | **prodotti dell'artigianato locale?** *proh-dOHt-tee dayl-lahr-tee-jee-ah-nAH-toh loh-kAH-leh* |
| musical instruments | **strumenti musicali** *stroo-mEHn-tee moo-see-kAH-lee* |
| perfumes | **profumi** *proh-fOO-mee* |
| (miniature) pictures | **quadretti (in miniatura)** *koo-ah-drAYt-tee (een mee-nee-ah-tOO-rah)* |
| posters | **affissi, manifesti, poster** *ahf-fEEs-see mah-nee-fEH-stee pOH-stehr* |
| religious articles | **articoli religiosi** *ahr-tEE-koh-lee reh-lee-jee-OH-see* |

## STATIONERY ITEMS

| | |
|---|---|
| I want to buy _____. | **Voglio comprare _____.** *vOH-ly-ee-oh kohm-prAH-reh* |
| a ballpoint pen | **una penna a sfera** *OO-nah pAYn-nah ah sfEH-rah* |
| a deck of cards | **un mazzo di carte** *oon mAH-tsoh dee kAHr-teh* |
| envelopes | **delle buste** *dAYl-leh bOO-steh* |
| an eraser | **una gomma per cancellare** *OO-nah gOHm-mah pehr kahn-chehl-lAH-reh* |
| glue | **della colla** *dAYl-lah kOHl-lah* |
| a notebook | **un taccuino** *oon tahk-koo-EE-noh* |
| pencils | **delle matite** *dAYl-leh mah-tEE-teh* |
| a pencil sharpener | **un temperamatite** *oon tehm-peh-rah-mah-tEE-teh* |
| a ruler | **una riga** *OO-nah rEE-gah* |

| | |
|---|---|
| ■ Scotch tape | **un nastro adesivo (uno scotch)** *oon nAH-stroh ah-deh-sEE-voh (OO-noh skO-ch)* |
| ■ some string | **del filo** *dayl fEE-loh* |
| ■ typing paper | **della carta per battere a macchina** *dAYl-lah kAHr-tah pehr bAHt-teh-reh ah mAH-kee-nah* |
| ■ wrapping paper | **della carta da imballaggio** *dAYl-lah kAHr-tah dah eem-bahl-lAH-jee-oh* |
| ■ writing paper | **della carta da scrivere** *dAYl-lah kAHr-tah dah scrEE-veh-reh* |

## TOBACCO

You go to a **Sali e Tabacchi** (*SAH-lee eh tah-bAH-kee*) to buy cigarettes as well as local bus and subway tickets, a phone card (**scheda telefonica**—*skEH-dah teh-leh-phOH-nee-kah*), postcards, and stamps (**francobolli**—*frahn-koh-bOHl-lee*).

You can buy a SIM card, candy, chewing gums, cigarettes, lighters, watches, and other related items.

| | |
|---|---|
| A pack (carton) of cigarettes, please. | **Un pacchetto (una stecca) di sigarette, per piacere.** *oon pah-kAYt-toh (OO-nah stAYk-kah) dee see-gah-rAYt-teh pehr pee-ah-chAY-reh* |
| ■ filtered | **con filtro** *kohn fEEl-troh* |
| ■ unfiltered | **senza filtro** *sEHn-tsah fEEl-troh* |
| ■ menthol | **alla menta** *ahl-lah mEHn-tah* |
| ■ king-size | **lunghe** *lOOn-gheh* |
| Are these cigarettes (very) strong (mild)? | **Sono (molto) forti (leggere) queste sigarette?** *sOH-noh (mOHl-toh) fOHr-tee (leh-jEH-reh) koo-AYs-teh see-gah-rAYt-teh* |

| | |
|---|---|
| Do you have American cigarettes? | **Ha sigarette americane?** *AH see-gah-rAYt-teh ah-meh-ree-kAH-neh* |
| What brand? | **Di che marca?** *dee kay mAHr-kah* |
| Please give me a pack of matches also. | **Mi dia anche una scatola di fiammiferi, per piacere.** *mee dEE-ah AHn-kay OO-nah skAH-toh-lah dee fee-ahm-mEE-fay-ree pehr pee-ah-chAY-reh* |

## TOILETRIES

In Italy, drugstores (chemists) carry mostly actual drugs and medicines. For toiletries and perfumes, you would go to a **profumeria**.

| Do you have _____? | **Ha _____?** *ah* |
|---|---|
| ■ bobby pins | **delle forcine** *dAYl-leh fohr-chEE-neh* |
| ■ a brush | **una spazzola** *OO-nah spAH-tsoh-lah* |
| ■ cleansing cream | **della crema detergente** *dAYl-lah crEH-mah day-tehr-jEHn-teh* |
| ■ a comb | **un pettine** *oon pEHt-tee-neh* |
| ■ a deodorant | **un deodorante** *oon deh-oh-doh-rAHn-teh* |
| ■ (disposable) diapers | **dei pannolini usa e getta** *dAY-ee pahn-noh-lEE-nee OO-sah ay jEHt-tah* |
| ■ emery boards | **delle limette per le unghie** *dAYl-leh lee-mEHt-teh pehr leh OOn-ghee-eh* |
| ■ eyeliner | **un eye liner** *oon eye liner* |
| ■ eye shadow | **l'ombretto** *lohm-brAYt-toh* |

- eyebrow pencil — **una matita per le sopracciglia** *OO-nah mah-tEE-tah pehr leh soh-prah-chEE-ly-ee-ah*
- hair spray — **della lacca per capelli** *dAYl-la lAHk-kah pehr kah-pAYl-lee*
- lipstick — **il lipstick (rossetto per le labbra)** *eel lipstick (rohs-sEHt-toh pehr leh lAHb-brah)*
- make-up — **il make-up (trucco)** *eel make up (trOOk-koh)*
- mascara — **del mascara** *dAYl mah-skAH-rah*
- a mirror — **uno specchio** *OO-noh spEHk-key-oh*
- mouthwash — **del disinfettante per la bocca** *dayl dee-seen-feht-tAHn-teh pehr lah bOHk-kah*
- nail clippers — **dei tagliaunghie** *dAY-ee tah-ly-ee-ah-OOn-ghee-eh*
- a nail file — **una limetta per le unghie** *OO-nah lee-mAYt-tah pehr leh OOn-ghee-eh*
- nail polish — **dello smalto per le unghie** *dAYl-loh smAHl-toh pehr leh OOn-ghee-eh*
- nail polish remover — **dell'acetone** *dayl-lah-cheh-tOH-neh*
- a razor — **un rasoio di sicurezza** *oon rah-sOH-ee-oh dee see-koo-rAY-tsah*
- razor blades — **delle lamette** *dAYl-leh lah-mAYt-teh*
- rouge — **il rossetto (belletto)** *eel rohs-sEHt-toh (behl-lEHt-toh)*
- sanitary napkins — **degli assorbenti (igienici)** *dAY-ly-ee ahs-sohr-bEHn-tee (ee-jee-EH-nee-chee)*
- (cuticle) scissors — **delle forbicine** *dAYl-leh fohr-bee-chEE-neh*

- shampoo — **dello shampoo** *dAYl-loh ShAHm-poh*
- shaving lotion — **un dopobarba** *oon doh-poh-bAHr-bah*
- soap — **del sapone** *dayl sah-pOH-neh*
- a sponge — **una spugna** *OO-nah spOO-ny-ah*
- tampons — **dei tamponi** *dAY-ee tahm-pOH-nee*
- tissues — **dei fazzolettini di carta** *dAY-ee fah-tsoh-leht-tEE-nee dee kAHr-tah*
- toilet paper — **della carta igienica** *dAYl-lah kAHr-tah ee-jee-EH-nee-kah*
- a toothbrush — **uno spazzolino per i denti** *OO-noh spah-tsoh-lEE-noh pehr ee dEHn-tee*
- toothpaste — **un dentifricio** *oon dEHn-tee-frEE-chee-oh*
- tweezers — **delle pinzette** *dAYl-leh peen-tsEHt-teh*

# PERSONAL CARE AND SERVICES

## AT THE BARBER

| | |
|---|---|
| Where is there a good barbershop? | **Dove potrei trovare (una buona barberia) un buon parrucchiere?** *dOH-veh poh-trEH-ee troh-vAH-reh (OO-nah boo-OH-nah bahr-beh-rEE-ah) oon boo-OHn pahr-rook-key-EH-reh* |
| Do I have to wait long? | **C'è da aspettare molto?** *chEH dah-speht-tAH-reh mOHl-toh* |
| Am I next? | **È arrivato il mio turno?** *EH ahr-ree-vAH-toh eel mEE-oh tOOr-noh* |
| I want a shave. | **Voglio farmi la barba.** *vOH-ly-ee-oh fAHr-mee lah bAHr-bah* |
| I want a haircut. | **Voglio un taglio di capelli.** *vOH-ly-ee-oh oon tAH-ly-ee-oh dee kah-pAYl-lee* |
| Short in back, long in front. | **Corti dietro, lunghi davanti.** *kOHr-tee dee-EH-troh lOOn-ghee dah-vAHn-tee* |
| Leave it long. | **Me li lasci lunghi.** *meh-lee lAH-shee lOOn-ghee* |
| I want it (very) short. | **Li voglio (molto) corti.** *lee vOH-ly-ee-oh (mOHl-toh) kOHr-tee* |

| | |
|---|---|
| You can cut a little _____. | **Me li può tagliare un po' _____.** *meh lee poo-OH tah-ly-ee-AH-reh oon pOH* |
| ■ in back | **di dietro** *dee dee-EH-troh* |
| ■ in front | **sul davanti** *sool dah-vAHn-tee* |
| ■ off the top | **sopra** *sOH-prah* |
| Cut a little bit more here. | **Tagli un po'di più qui (per favore).** *tAH-ly-ee oon pOH dee pee-OO koo-EE (pehr fah-vOH-reh)* |
| That's enough. | **Basta così.** *bAH-stah koh-sEE* |
| It's fine that way. | **Così è magnifico.** *Koh-sEE EH mah-ny-EE-fee-koh* |
| I (don't) want _____. | **(Non) voglio _____.** *(nohn) vOH-ly-oh* |
| ■ hair spray | **la lacca** *lah lAHk-kah* |
| ■ lotion | **la lozione** *lah loh-tzee-OH-neh* |
| ■ shampoo | **lo shampoo** *loh shAHm-poh* |
| Please trim _____. | **Può spuntarmi _____.** *poo-OH spoon-tAHr-mee* |
| ■ my beard | **il pizzo (la barba)** *eel pEE-tsoh (lah bAHr-bah)* |
| ■ my moustache | **i baffi** *ee bAHf-fee* |
| ■ my sideburns | **le basette** *leh bah-sAYt-teh* |
| How much do I owe you? | **Quanto le devo?** *koo-AHn-toh leh dAY-voh* |

## AT THE BEAUTY PARLOR

| | |
|---|---|
| Is there a beauty parlor (hairdresser) near the hotel? | **C'è una parrucchiera vicino all'albergo?** *chEH OO-nah pahr-rook-key-EH-rah vee-chEE-noh ahl-lahl-bEHr-goh* |
| I'd like an appointment for this afternoon (tomorrow). | **Vorrei un appuntamento per questo pomeriggio (per domani).** *vohr-rEH-ee oon ahp-poon-tah-mEHn-toh pehr koo-AYs-toh poh-meh-rEE-jee-oh (pehr doh-mAH-nee)* |
| Can you give me _____? | **Può farmi _____?** *poo-OH fAHr-mee* |
| ■ a cut and blow dry | **taglio e asciugatura spazzola e phon** *tAH-ly-oh ay ah-shee-oo-gah-tOO-rah spAH-tzoh-lah ay phOHn* |
| ■ a color rinse | **un cachet** *oon kah-shEH* |
| ■ a facial massage | **un massaggio facciale** *oon mahs-sAH-jee-oh fah-chee-AH-leh* |
| ■ a haircut | **un taglio di capelli** *oon tAH-ly-oh dee kah-pAYl-lee* |
| ■ a blunt haircut | **una spuntatina** *OO-nah spoon-tah-tEE-nah* |
| ■ a layered haircut | **un taglio scalato** *oon tAH-ly-oh skah-lAH-toh* |
| ■ a manicure | **la manicure** *lah mah-nee-kOO-reh* |
| ■ a pedicure | **il pedicure** *eel peh-dee-kOO-reh* |
| ■ a permanent | **una permanente** *OO-nah pehr-mah-nAYn-teh* |
| ■ a shampoo | **lo shampoo** *loh shAHm-poh* |
| ■ a shave | **una depilazione** *OO-nah deh-pee-lah-tzee-OH-neh* |

| | |
|---|---|
| ■ a tint | **una tintura** *OO-nah teen-tOO-rah* |
| ■ a touch-up | **una ritoccatina** *OO-nah ree-tohk-kah-tEE-nah* |
| ■ a trim | **una spuntatina** *OO-nah spoon-tah-tEE-nah* |
| ■ a wash and set | **shampoo e messa in piega** *shAHm-poh ay mAYs-sah een pee-AY-gah* |
| ■ a waxing | **una depilazione mediante ceretta** *OO-nah deh-pee-lah-tzee-OH-neh meh-dee-AHn-teh cheh-rAYt-tah* |
| Do you offer reflexology, aromatherapy treatments? | **Fate riflessologia, aromaterapia?** *phAH-teh ree-flehs-soh-loh-jEE-ah ah-rOH-mah-teh-rah-pEE-ah* |
| I'd like to see a color chart. | **Vorrei vedere il cartellino dei colori.** *vohr-rEH-ee veh-dAY-reh eel kahr-tehl-lEE-noh dAY-ee koh-lOH-ree* |
| I want _____. | **Voglio _____.** *vOH-ly-ee-oh* |
| ■ auburn | **un color rame** *oon koh-lOHr rAH-meh* |
| ■ (light) blond | **un biondo (chiaro)** *oon bee-OHn-doh (key-AH-roh)* |
| ■ brunette | **un bruno** *oon brOO-noh* |
| ■ a darker color | **un colore più scuro** *oon koh-lOH-reh pee-OO skOO-roh* |
| ■ a lighter color | **un colore più chiaro** *oon koh-lOH-reh pee-OO key-AH-roh* |
| ■ the same color | **lo stesso colore** *loh stAYs-soh koh-lOH-reh* |
| ■ highlights | **i colpi di sole** *ee kOHl-pee dee sOH-leh* |

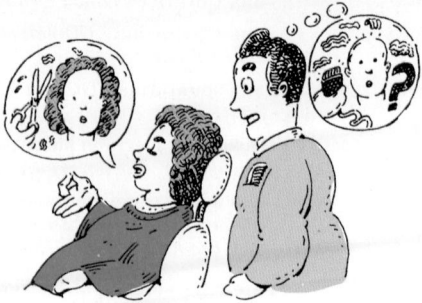

| | |
|---|---|
| Don't apply any hair spray. | **Non mi metta nessuna lacca.** *nohn mee mEHt-tah nays-sOO-nah lAHk-kah* |
| Not too much hair spray. | **Non troppa lacca.** *nohn trOHp-pah lAHk-kah* |
| I want my hair _____. | **Vorrei (voglio) i capelli _____.** *vohr-rEH-ee (vOH-ly-ee-oh) ee kah-pEHl-lee* |
| ■ with bangs | **con la frangia** *kohn lah frAHn-jee-ah* |
| ■ in a bun | **a nodo (a crocchia)** *ah nOH-doh (ah krOHk-key-ah)* |
| ■ in curls | **a boccoli** *ah bOHk-koh-lee* |
| ■ with waves | **ondulati** *ohn-doo-lAH-tee* |
| How much do I owe you? | **Quanto le devo?** *koo-AHn-toh leh dAY-voh* |

## LAUNDRY AND DRY CLEANING

Where is the nearest laundry (dry cleaner's)? **Dov'è la lavanderia (la tintoria) più vicina?** *doh-vEH lah lah-vahn-deh-rEE-ah (lah teen-toh-rEE-ah) pee-OO vee-chEE-nah*

I have a lot of (dirty) clothes to be _____. **Ho molta biancheria (sporca) da _____.** *oh mOHl-tah bee-ahn-keh-rEE-ah (spOHr-kah) dah*

- dry-cleaned — **lavare a secco** *lah-vAH-reh ah sAYk-koh*
- washed — **lavare** *lah-vAH-reh*
- mended — **rammendare** *rahm-mehn-dAH-reh*
- ironed — **stirare** *stee-rAH-reh*

Here's the list: **Ecco l'elenco:** *EHk-koh leh-lEHn-koh*

- 3 shirts (men's) — **tre camicie (da uomo)** *tray kah-mEE-chee-eh (dah oo-OH-moh)*
- 6 pairs of socks — **sei paia di calzini** *sAY-ee pAH-ee-ah dee kahl-tsEE-nee*
- 1 blouse (nylon) — **una blusa (di nylon)** *oo-nah blOO-sah (dee nAH-ee-lohn)*
- 4 shorts — **quattro mutande** *koo-AHt-tro moo-tAHn-deh*
- 2 pajamas — **due pigiama** *dOO-eh pee-jee-AH-mah*
- 2 suits — **due vestiti** *dOO-eh veh-stEE-tee*
- 3 ties — **tre cravatte** *tray krah-vAHt-teh*
- 2 dresses (cotton) — **due vesti (di cotone)** *dOO-eh vEH-stee (dee koh-tOH-neh)*

- 2 skirts — **due gonne** *dOO-eh gOHn-neh*
- 1 sweater (wool) — **una maglia (di lana)** *OO-nah mAH-ly-ah (dee lAH-nah)*

I need them (for) _____. — **Mi occorrono (per) _____.** *mee ohk-kOHr-roh-noh (pehr)*

- as soon as possible — **al più presto possibile** *ahl pee-OO prEH-stoh pohs-sEE-bee-leh*
- tonight — **stasera** *stah-sAY-rah*
- tomorrow — **domani** *doh-mAH-nee*
- next week — **la settimana prossima** *lah seht-tee-mAH-nah prOHs-see-mah*

When will you bring it (them) back? — **Quando lo (li) riporterà?** *koo-AHn-doh loh (lee) ree-pohr-teh-rAH*

There's a button missing. — **Manca un bottone.** *mAHn-kah oon boht-tOH-neh*

Can you sew it on? — **Può riattaccarlo?** *poo-OH ree-aht-tahk-kAHr-loh*

This isn't my laundry. — **Questa non è la mia biancheria.** *koo-AYs-tah nohn EH lah mEE-ah bee-ahn-keh-rEE-ah*

## SHOE REPAIRS

Can you fix these shoes (boots)? — **Può ripararmi queste scarpe (questi stivali)?** *poo-OH ree-pah-rAHr-mee koo-AYs-teh skAHr-peh (koo-AYs-tee stee-vAH-lee)*

Put on (half) soles and rubber heels. — **Ci metta le (mezze) suole e i tacchi di gomma.** *chee mEHt-tah leh (mEH-tseh) soo-OH-leh ay ee tAH-key dee gOHm-mah*

I'd like to have my shoes shined too.

**Vorrei anche che mi lucidasse le scarpe.** *vohr-rEH-ee AHn-keh kay mee loo-chee-dAHs-seh leh skAHr-peh*

When will they be ready?

**Quando saranno pronte?** *koo-AHn-doh sah-rAHn-noh prOHn-teh*

## CAMERA REPAIRS

Can you fix this camera (movie camera)?

**Può aggiustare questa macchina fotografica (questa cinepresa)?** *poo-OH ah-jee-oo-stAH-reh koo-AYs-tah mAH-kee-nah foh-toh-grAH-fee-kah (koo-AYs-tah chee-neh-prAY-sah)*

How much will the repair cost?

**Quanto mi costerà farla aggiustare?** *koo-AHn-toh mee koh-steh-rAH fAHr-lah ah-jee-oo-stAH-reh*

When can I come and get it?

**Quando posso venire a ritirarla?** *koo-AHn-doh pOHs-soh veh-nEE-reh ah ree-tee-rAHr-lah*

I need it as soon as possible.

**Ne ho bisogno al più presto possible.** *nay oh bee-sOH-ny-oh ahl pee-OO prEH-stoh pohs-sEE-bee-leh*

I think I need new batteries.

**Penso di aver bisogno delle pile nuove.** *pEHn-soh dee ah-vAYr bee-sOH-ny-oh dAYl-leh pEE-leh noo-OH-veh*

# MEDICAL CARE

Public and private organizations make up Italy's health care system. It is seen as one of the best in the world, with an excellent performance record.

For **Emergency Medical Service** (including ambulance and first aid), **dial 118.**

Look into . . .

- your own health insurance coverage before leaving for Italy.

Look out!

- If you are incapacitated, will your insurance cover the expenses to return home?
- Will your insurance pay up-front money for hospitalization in Italy?

Check *http://www.knowital.com/tourist/italy-health.html*

## THE PHARMACY (CHEMIST)

When you need immediate medical attention, go to the **Pronto Soccorso** *(prOHn-toh soh-kOHr-soh)*, the Emergency or First Aid Service. It is located at airports, hospitals, ports, and railway stations. Pharmacies carry various medical products and homeopathic supplies. The pharmacies may be open 24 hours in order to provide **servizio notturno** *(sehr-vEE-tsee-oh noht-tOOr-noh)* or night services. Their time schedules are displayed on the pharmacy door and their names and time schedules are listed in the local newspapers.

Usually, the opening hours are from 8:30 A.M. to 12:30 P.M. and 3:30 P.M. to 7:30 P.M. Pharmacies follow a system that guarantees an open pharmacy for medical emergencies in designated areas at night, Sundays, and holidays. Pharmacies display the sign of a red or green cross on a white background. In Italy, on an emergency basis, the pharmacists can give patients the medicine(s) they need if they remember their scientific or generic names. In some instances, the pharmacist can prescribe medications based on the description of specific symptoms.

Look into . . .

- dialing the toll-free number, **800-420-707** to inquire about an open pharmacy in the area.
- calling **118** for an ambulance. **It's a toll free** medical emergency telephone number.
- walking to a hospital's **Guardia Medica**, the **First Aid Service**.

Look out!

- Bring the original prescription written by your physician.
- Have a written description of your medical problem(s).
- Keep medications in their original flagons or containers.

Check *http://goitaly.about.com/od/planningandinformation/fr/pharmacies.htm*

| | |
|---|---|
| Where is the nearest (all-night) pharmacy (chemist)? | **Dov'è la farmacia (notturna) più vicina?** *doh-vEH lah fahr-mah-chEE-ah (noht-tOOr-nah) pee-OO vee-chEE-nah* |
| At what time does the pharmacy open (close)? | **A che ora apre (chiude) la farmacia?** *ah kay OH-rah AH-preh (key-OO-deh) lah fahr-mah-chEE-ah* |
| I need something for _____. | **Ho bisogno di qualche cosa per _____.** *oh bee-sOH-ny-oh dee koo-AHl-keh kOH-sah pehr* |
| ■ a cold | **il raffreddore** *eel rahf-frehd-dOH-reh* |
| ■ constipation | **la stitichezza** *lah stee-tee-kAY-tsah* |
| ■ a cough | **la tosse** *lah tOHs-seh* |
| ■ diarrhea | **la diarrea** *lah dee-ahr-rEH-ah* |
| ■ a fever | **la febbre** *lah fEHb-breh* |

| | |
|---|---|
| ■ hay fever | **una rinite da fieno** *OO-nah ree-nEE-teh dah fee-EH-noh* |
| ■ a headache | **il mal di testa** *eel mAHl dee tEHs-tah* |
| ■ insomnia | **l'insonnia** *leen-sOHn-nee-ah* |
| ■ motion sickness (seasickness) | **il mal d'auto (di mare)** *eel mAHl dAH-oo-toh (dee mAH-reh)* |
| ■ sunburn | **la scottatura solare** *lah skoht-tah-tOO-rah soh-lAH-reh* |
| ■ a toothache | **il mal di denti** *eel mAHl dee dEHn-tee* |
| ■ an upset stomach | **il mal di stomaco** *eel mAHl dee stOH-mah-koh* |
| I do not have a prescription. | **Non ho la ricetta medica.** *nohn OH lah ree-chEHt-tah mEH-dee-kah* |
| May I have it right away? | **Posso averla subito?** *pOHs-soh ah-vAYr-lah sOO-bee-toh* |
| It's an emergency. | **È un'emergenza.** *eh oo-neh-mehr-jEHn-tsah* |
| How long will it take? | **Quanto tempo ci vorrà?** *koo-AHn-toh tEHm-poh chee vohr-rAH* |
| When can I come for it? | **Quando potrò venire a prenderla?** *koo-AHn-doh poh-trOH veh-nEE-reh ah prAYn-dehr-lah* |
| I would like _____. | **Vorrei _____.** *vohr-rEH-ee* |
| ■ adhesive tape | **un nastro adesivo** *oon nAH-stroh ah-deh-sEE-voh* |
| ■ alcohol | **dell'alcol** *dayl-lAHl-kohl* |
| ■ an antacid | **un antiacido** *oon ahn-tee-AH-chee-doh* |
| ■ an antiseptic | **un antisettico** *oon ahn-tee-sEHt-tee-koh* |

- aspirins — **delle aspirine** *dAYl-leh ah-spee-rEE-neh*
- Band-Aids — **dei cerotti** *dAY-ee cheh-rOHt-tee*
- contraceptives — **dei contraccettivi** *dAY-ee kohn-trah-cheht-tEE-vee*
- corn plasters — **dei callifughi** *dAY-ee kahl-lEE-foo-ghee*
- cotton balls — **del cotone idrofilo** *dayl koh-tOH-neh ee-drOH-fee-loh*
- cough drops (syrup) — **delle pasticche (dello sciroppo) per la tosse** *dAYl-leh pahs-tEEk-keh (dAHl-loh shee-rOHp-poh) pehr lah tOHs-seh*
- eardrops — **delle gocce per gli orecchi** *dAYl-leh gOH-cheh pehr ly-ee oh-rAYk-key*
- eyedrops — **del collirio** *dayl kohl-lEE-ree-oh*
- iodine — **della tintura di iodio** *dAYl-lah teen-tOO-rah dee ee-OH-dee-oh*
- a (mild) laxative — **un lassativo (leggero)** *oon lahs-sah-tEE-voh (lay-jEH-roh)*
- milk of magnesia — **della magnesia** *dAYl-lah mah-ny-ee-EH-see-ah*
- prophylactics — **dei profilattici** *dAY-ee proh-fee-lAHt-tee-chee*
- sanitary napkins — **degli assorbenti (igienici)** *dAY-ly-ee ahs-sohr-bEHn-tee (ee-jee-EH-nee-chee)*
- suppositories — **delle supposte** *dAYl-leh soop-pOH-steh*
- talcum powder — **del borotalco** *dayl boh-roh-tAHl-koh*
- tampons — **dei tamponi** *dAY-ee tahm-pOH-nee*
- a thermometer — **un termometro** *oon tehr-mOH-meh-troh*
- vitamins — **delle vitamine** *dAYl-leh vee-tah-mEE-neh*

## WITH THE DOCTOR

Italy ranks number one in the world for the number of pro capita physicians. There is one for approximately every 160 people. **I medici italiani** (Italian doctors) are well trained and qualified professionals. The yellow pages list the family doctors under **Medici Generici** and the specialists under **Specialisti** with their area of expertise. More often than not, appointments are not needed to be seen by a doctor. Visits are based on a first come first served basis. It pays to arrive early! Doctors will write a **ricetta** (prescription) for needed drugs and medicines.

Look out!

- There may be an initial consultation fee for a first-time visit.
- An additional payment may be required for each follow-up visit.
- After treatment, patients are expected to pay in cash even though they have health insurance.
- Keep all medical receipts!

Check *www.justlanded.com/english/Italy/Italy-Guide/Health/Doctors*

| | |
|---|---|
| I don't feel well. | **Non mi sento bene.** *nohn mee sEHn-toh bEH-neh* |
| I feel sick. | **Mi sento male.** *mee sEHn-toh mAH-leh* |
| I need a doctor right away. | **Ho bisogno urgente del medico.** *oh bee-sOH-ny-oh oor-jEHn-teh dayl mEH-dee-koh* |
| Do you know a doctor who speaks English? | **Conosce un dottore che parli inglese?** *koh-nOH-sheh oon doht-tOH-reh kay pAHr-lee een-glAY-seh* |

Where is his office (surgery)? **Dov'è il suo ambulatorio?** *doh-vEH eel sOO-oh ahm-boo-lah-tOH-ree-oh*

Will the doctor come to the hotel? **Il dottore potrà venire all'hotel?** *eel doht-tOH-reh poh-trAH veh-NEE-reh ahl-loh-tEHl*

I feel dizzy. **Mi gira la testa (ho le vertigini).** *mee jEE-rah lah tEHs-tah (oh leh vehr-tEE-jee-nee)*

I feel weak. **Mi sento debole.** *mee sEHn-toh dAY-boh-leh*

I want to sit down for a while. **Vorrei sedermi un poco.** *vohr-rEH-ee seh-dAYr-mee oon pOH-koh*

My temperature is normal (37°C) (high). **La temperatura è normale (trenta sette gradi)(alta).** *lah tehm-peh-rah-tOO-rah EH nohr-mAH-leh (trEHn-tah sEHt-teh grAH-dee) (AHl-tah)*

I (think I) have _____. **(Credo che) ho _____.** *(kreh-doh kay) oh*

- an abscess **un ascesso** *oon ah-shEHs-soh*
- a fracture **una frattura** *OO-nah frat-tOO-rah*
- a bruise **una contusione** *OO-nah kohn-too-see-OH-neh*

| | |
|---|---|
| ■ a burn | **un'ustione** *oo-noo-stee-oH-neh* |
| ■ the chills | **i brividi** *ee brEE-vee-dee* |
| ■ a cold | **un raffreddore** *oon rahf-frehd-dOH-reh* |
| ■ constipation | **stitichezza** *stee-tee-kAY-tsah* |
| ■ a cut | **una ferita (un taglio)** *OO-nah feh-rEE-tah (oon tAH-ly-ee-oh)* |
| ■ diarrhea | **la diarrea** *lah dee-ahr-rEH-ah* |
| ■ a fever | **la febbre** *la fEHb-breh* |
| ■ a headache | **un mal di testa** *oon mAHl dee tEHs-tah* |
| ■ an infection | **un'infezione** *oo-neen-feh-tsee-OH-neh* |
| ■ a lump | **un gonfiore** *oon gohn-fee-OH-reh* |
| ■ rheumatism | **i reumatismi** *ee reh-oo-mah-tEE-smee* |
| ■ something in my eye | **qualche cosa nell'occhio** *koo-AHl-keh kOH-sah nayl-lOHk-key-oh* |
| ■ a sore throat | **un mal di gola** *oon mAHl dee gOH-lah* |
| ■ stomach cramps | **crampi allo stomaco** *krAHm-pee AHl-loh stOH-mah-koh* |
| ■ a stomachache | **un mal di stomaco** *oon mAHl dee stOH-mah-koh* |

## TELLING THE DOCTOR

| | |
|---|---|
| It hurts me here. | **Mi fa male qui.** *mee fah mAH-leh koo-EE* |
| My whole body hurts. | **Mi fa male dappertutto.** *Mee fah mAH-leh dahp-pehr-tOOt-toh* |
| I'm presently taking antibiotics. | **Sto prendendo degli antibiotici.** *stoh prayn-dEHn-doh dAY-ly-ee ahn-tee-bee-OH-tee-chee* |

I'm constipated. **Soffro di stitichezza.** *sOHf-froh dee stee-tee-kAY-tsah*

I need a laxative. **Ho bisogno di un lassativo.** *oh bee-sOH-ny-oh dee oon lahs-sah-tEE-voh*

I have (hay) fever. **Ho la febbre (da fieno).** *oh lah fEHb-breh (dah fee-EH-noh)*

My _____ hurts. **Mi fa male _____.** *mee fah mAH-leh*

- appendix **l'appendicite** *lahp-pehn-dee-chEE-teh*
- ankle **la caviglia** *lah kah-vEE-ly-ah*
- arm **il braccio** *eel brAH-chee-oh*
- back **la schiena** *lah skey-EH-nah*
- breast **il petto** *eel pEHt-toh*
- cheek **la guancia** *lah goo-AHn-chee-ah*
- ear **l'orecchio** *loh-rAY-key-oh*
- elbow **il gomito** *eel gOH-mee-toh*
- eye **l'occhio** *lOH-key-oh*
- face **la faccia** *lah fAH-chee-ah*
- finger **il dito** *eel dEE-doh*
- foot **il piede** *eel pee-EH-deh*
- hand **la mano** *lah mAH-noh*

| | |
|---|---|
| ■ head | **la testa** *lah tEHs-tah* |
| ■ heart | **il cuore** *eel koo-OH-reh* |
| ■ hip | **l'anca** *lAHn-kah* |
| ■ knee | **il ginocchio** *eel jee-nOH-key-oh* |
| ■ leg | **la gamba** *lah gAHm-bah* |
| ■ lip | **il labbro** *eel lAHb-broh* |
| ■ mouth | **la bocca** *lah bOH-kah* |
| ■ neck | **il collo** *eel kOHl-loh* |
| ■ nose | **il naso** *eel nAH-soh* |
| ■ shoulder | **la spalla** *lah spAHl-lah* |
| ■ throat | **la gola** *lah gOH-lah* |
| ■ thumb | **il pollice** *eel pOHl-lee-cheh* |
| ■ toe | **l'alluce** *lAHl-loo-cheh* |
| ■ tooth | **il dente** *eel dEHn-teh* |
| ■ wrist | **il polso** *eel pOHl-soh* |

| | |
|---|---|
| I've had this pain since yesterday. | **Ho questo dolore da ieri.** *oh koo-AYs-toh doh-lOH-reh dah ee-EH-ree* |
| There's a (no) history of asthma (diabetes, heart problems) in my family. | **(Non) c'è anamnesi di asma (diabete, problemi cardiaci) nella mia famiglia.** *(nohn) chEH ah-nahm-nEH-see dee AH-smah (dee-ah-bEH-teh proh-blEH-mee kahr-dEE-ah-chee) nAYl-lah mEE-ah fah-mEE-ly-ee-ah* |
| I'm (not) allergic to antibiotics (penicillin). | **(Non) sono allergico agli antibiotici (alla penicillina).** *(nohn) sOH-noh ahl-lEHr-jee-koh AH-ly-ee ahn-tee-bee-OH-tee-chee (AHl-lah peh-nee-cheel-lEE-nah)* |
| I have chest pains. | **Ho dolori al petto.** *oh doh-lOH-ree ahl pEHt-toh* |

| | |
|---|---|
| I had a heart attack _____. | **Ho avuto un attacco cardiaco _____.** *oh ah-vOO-toh oon aht-tAHk-koh kahr-dEE-ah-koh* |
| ■ last year | **l'anno scorso** *lAHn-noh skOHr-soh* |
| ■ (three) years ago | **(tre) anni fa** *trEH AHn-nee fah* |
| I'm taking this medicine (insulin). | **Sto prendendo questa medicina (insulina).** *stOH prehn-dEHn-doh koo-AYs-tah meh-dee-chEE-nah (een-soo-lEE-nah)* |
| I'm pregnant. | **Sono incinta.** *sOH-noh een-chEEn-tah* |
| I feel faint. | **Mi sento svenire.** *mee sEHn-toh sveh-nEE-reh* |
| I feel all right now. | **Mi sento bene adesso.** *mee sEHn-toh bEH-neh ah-dEHs-soh* |
| I feel better (worse). | **Mi sento meglio (peggio).** *mee sEHn-toh mEH-ly-ee-oh (pEH-jee-oh)* |
| Do I have _____? | **Ho _____?** *OH* |
| ■ appendicitis | **l'appendicite** *lahp-pehn-dee-chEE-teh* |
| ■ the flu | **l'influenza** *leen-floo-EHn-tzah* |
| ■ tonsilitis | **una tonsillite** *OO-nah tohn-seel-lEE-teh* |
| Is it serious (contagious)? | **È serio (contagioso)?** *EH sEH-ree-oh (kohn-tah-jee-OH-soh)* |
| Do I have to go to the hospital? | **Devo andare in ospedale?** *dAY-voh ahn-dAH-reh een oh-speh-dAH-leh* |
| When can I continue my trip? | **Quando potrò continuare la mia gita?** *koo-AHn-doh poh-trOH kohn-tee-noo-AH-reh lah mEE-ah jEE-tah* |

## QUESTIONS

Are you giving me a prescription?

**Mi darà una ricetta?** *mee dah-rAH OO-nah ree-chEHt-tah*

How often must I take this medicine (these pills)?

**Quante volte devo prendere questa medicina (queste pillole)?** *koo-AHn-teh vOHl-teh dAY-voh prAYn-deh-reh koo-AYs-tah meh-dee-chEE-nah (koo-AYs-teh pEEl-loh-leh)*

(How long) do I have to stay in bed?

**(Quanto) devo rimanere a letto?** *(koo-AHn-toh) dAY-voh ree-mah-nAY-reh ah lEHt-toh*

Thank you (for everything) doctor.

**Grazie (di tutto), dottore.** *grAH-tsee-eh (dee tOOt-toh) doht-tOH-reh*

How much do I owe you for your services?

**Quanto le devo per la visita?** *koo-AHn-toh leh dAY-voh pehr lah vEE-see-tah*

May I have a receipt?

**Può darmi la ricevuta?** *poo-OH dAHr-mee lah ree-chay-vOO-tah*

I have medical insurance.

**Ho l'assicurazione (l'assistenza) medica.** *oh lahs-see-koo-rah-tsee-OH-neh (lahs-sees-stEHn-tsah) mEH-dee-kah*

| | |
|---|---|
| Will you accept my medical insurance? | **Accetta la mia assicurazione (assistenza) medica?** *ah-chEHt-tah lah mEE-ah ahs-see-koo-rah-tsee-OH-neh (ahs-see-stEHn-tsah) mEH-dee-kah* |
| Is there a co-payment? | **C'è qualche pagamento a carica del paziente?** *chEH koo-AHl-kay pah-gah-mEHn-toh ah kaH-ree-kah dayl pah-tsee-EHn-teh* |

## IN THE HOSPITAL (ACCIDENTS)

In Italy, there is at least one **clinica** (clinic) or **ospedale** (hospital) in every city or large town. Public hospitals may refer patients to private clinics at no additional cost to the patient. Treatment is free in public hospitals. The cost in private clinics is quite expensive. Visiting hours are limited to two or three hours per day in public hospitals, but are waived at private clinics.

Look into . . .

- rooms with inside bathroom, shower, TV, telephone, and air-conditioning.
- visits by nurses.
- private hospitals run by the Roman Catholic Church. The atmosphere seems to be more pleasant!
- Hospitals designed for medical tourism.
- Hospitals with English-speaking doctors and staff. For example:

1. **Milan Clinic**, Via Cerva 25, Milan (Phone: 7601 6047)
2. **Rome American Hospital**, Via E. Longoni 69, Rome (Phone: 062 2551)
3. **Salvator Mundi International Hospital**, Viale Mura Gianicolensi 67, Rome (Phone: 588 961)

Look out!

- Patients need to bring dressing gowns, night dresses, pajamas, towels, and toiletries.
- In small towns, there may be six hospital beds in a room without private bathroom and shower.
- Single bedrooms with inside bathrooms may be available for a supplement.
- Food! Many patients receive food assistance from friends and relatives!

Check *www.italytravelescape.com/Health%20system.htm*

| | |
|---|---|
| Help! | **Aiuto!** *ah-ee-OO-toh* |
| Get a doctor, quick! | **Chiamate un medico, subito!** *key-ah-mAH-teh oon mEH-dee-koh sOO-bee-toh* |
| Call an ambulance! | **Chiamate un'ambulanza!** *key-ah-mAH-teh oo-nahm-boo-lAHn-tsah* |
| I've fallen. | **Sono caduto(a).** *sOH-noh kah-dOO-toh(ah)* |
| I think I've had a heart attack. | **Credo che ho avuto un collasso cardiaco.** *krEH-do kay oh ah-vOO-toh oon kohl-lAHs-soh kahr-dEE-ah-koh* |
| I burned myself. | **Mi sono ustionato(a).** *mee sOH-noh oo-stee-oh-nAH-toh(ah)* |
| I cut myself. | **Mi sono tagliato(a).** *mee sOH-noh tah-ly-ee-AH-toh(ah)* |
| I'm bleeding. | **Sto sanguinando.** *stOH sahn-goo-ee-nAHn-doh* |
| I think the bone is broken (dislocated). | **Penso che mi si sia fratturato (lussato) l'osso.** *pEHn-soh kay mee see sEE-ah fraht-too-rAH-toh (loos-sAH-toh) lOHs-soh* |
| The leg is swollen. | **La gamba è gonfia.** *lah gAHm-bah EH gOHn-fee-ah* |

The wrist is sprained (twisted).

**Mi si è slogato (storto) il polso.** *mee see-EH sloh-gAH-toh (stOHr-toh) eel pOHl-soh*

The ankle is sprained (twisted).

**Mi si è slogata (storta) la caviglia.** *mee see-EH sloh-gAH-tah (stOHr-tah) lah kah-vEE-ly-ee-ah*

I can't move my elbow (knee).

**Non posso muovere il gomito (il ginocchio).** *nohn pOHs-soh moo-OH-veh-reh eel gOH-mee-toh (eel jee-nOHk-key-oh)*

## AT THE DENTIST

I have to go to the dentist.

**Devo andare dal dentista.** *dAY-voh ahn-dAH-reh dAHl dehn-tEEs-tah*

Can you recommend a dentist?

**Può raccomandarmi un dentista?** *poo-OH rahk-koh-mahn-dAHr-mee oon dehn-tEEs-tah*

I would like an emergency appointment.

**Vorrei un appuntamento d'urgenza.** *vohr-rEH-ee oon ahp-poon-tah-mAYn-toh door-jEHn-tzah*

I have a toothache that's driving me crazy.

**Ho un mal di denti che mi fa impazzire.** *oh oon mAHl dee dEHn-tee kay mee fah eem-pah-tsEE-reh*

I have a cavity that's giving me a lot of pain.

**Ho una carie che mi fa molto male.** *oh OO-nah kAH-ree-eh kay mee fah mOHl-toh mAH-leh*

I've lost a filling.

**Ho perduto l'otturazione.** *oh payr-dOO-toh loht-too-rah-tsee-OH-neh*

I've a broken tooth.

**Mi son rotto un dente.** *mee sOHn rOHt-toh oon dEHn-teh*

My gums hurt me.

**Mi fanno male le gengive.** *mee fAHn-noh mAH-leh leh jehn-jEE-veh*

Is there an infection?

**C'è un'infezione?** *chEH oo-neen-feh-tsee-OH-neh*

Will you have to extract the tooth?

**Deve estrarre il dente?** *dAY-veh ehs-trAHr-reh eel dEHn-teh*

I'd prefer you filled it _____.

**Preferisco farlo otturare _____.** *preh-feh-rIH-skoh fAHr-loh oht-too-rAH-reh*

- with amalgam — **con l'algama** *kohn lAHl-gah-mah*
- with gold — **con oro** *kohn OH-roh*
- for now (temporarily) — **provvisoriamente** *prohv-vee-soh-ree-ah-mEHn-teh*

Can you fix _____? **Può riparare _____?** *poo-OH ree-pah-rAH-reh*

- this bridge **questo ponte** *koo-AYs-toh pOHn-teh*
- this crown **questa corona** *koo-AYs-tah koh-rOH-nah*
- these dentures **questi denti finti** *koo-AYs-tee dEHn-tee fEEn-tee*

When should I come back? **Quando dovrei ritornare?** *koo-AHn-doh doh-vrEH-ee ree-tohr-nAH-reh*

How much do I owe you for your services? **Quanto le devo per la visita?** *koo-AHn-toh leh dAY-voh pehr lah vEE-see-tah*

## WITH THE OPTICIAN

Can you repair these glasses (for me)? **Può aggiustar(mi) questi occhiali?** *poo-OH ah-jee-oo-stAHr (mee) koo-AYs-tee oh-key-AH-lee*

I've broken a lens (the frame). **Mi si è rotta una lente (la montatura).** *mee see-EH rOHt-tah OO-nah lEHn-teh (lah mohn-tah-tOO-rah)*

Can you put in a new lens? **Può metterci una lente nuova?** *poo-OH mAYt-tehr-chee OO-nah lEHn-teh noo-OH-vah*

| | |
|---|---|
| I do not have a prescription. | **Non ho la ricetta medica.** *nohn oh lah ree-chEHt-tah mEH-dee-kah* |
| Can you tighten the screw? | **Può stringere la vite?** *poo-OH strEEn-jeh-rEH lah vEE-teh* |
| I need the glasses as soon as possible. | **Ho bisogno degli occhiali al più presto possibile.** *oh bee-sOH-ny-oh dAY-ly-ee oh-key-AH-lee ahl pee-OO prEH-stoh pohs-sEE-bee-leh* |
| I don't have any others. | **Non ne ho altri.** *nohn nay-OH AHl-tree* |
| Do you sell _____? | **Vende _____?** *vAYn-deh* |
| ■ contact lenses | **lenti a contatto** *lEHn-tee ah kohn-tAHt-toh* |
| ■ sunglasses | **occhiali da sole** *oh-key-AH-lee dah sOH-leh* |
| ■ transition lenses | **lenti fotocromatiche** *lEHn-tee fOH-toh-kroh-mAH-tee-keh* |
| ■ progressive lenses | **lenti progressive** *lEHn-tee proh-grehs-sEE-veh* |
| ■ bifocal lenses | **lenti bifocali** *lEHn-tee bee-foh-kAH-lee* |
| ■ (disposable) contact lenses | **lenti a contatto (usa e getta)** *lEHn-tee ah kohn-tAHt-toh (OO-sah ay jEHt-tah)* |

| | |
|---|---|
| ■ color contact lenses | **lenti a contatto cromate** *lEHn-tee ah kohn-tAHt-toh kroh-mAH-teh* |
| ■ hearing aids | **apparecchi acustici per l'udito** *ah-pah-rAY-key ah-kOO-stee-chee pehr loo-dEE-toh* |
| I'm _____. | **Sono _____.** *SOH-noh* |
| ■ astigmatic | **astigmatico** *ah-steeg-mAH-tee-koh* |
| ■ farsighted | **presbiope** *prEH-sbee-oh-peh* |
| ■ nearsighted | **miope** *mEE-oh-peh* |
| I have lost a contact lens. | **Ho perduto una lente a contatto.** *oh pehr-dOO-toh oo-nah lEHn-teh ah kohn-tAHt-toh* |
| Can you replace it quickly? | **Può darmene un'altra subito?** *poo-OH dAHr-meh-neh oo-nAHl-trah sOO-bee-toh* |

## PHARMACEUTICALS—MINIDICTIONARY

| | |
|---|---|
| amphetamine | **l'anfetamina** *lahn-feh-tah-mEE-nah* |
| anaesthetic | **l'anestetico** *lah-neh-stEH-tee-koh* |
| analgesic | **l'analgesico** *lah-nahl-jEH-see-koh* |
| antacid | **l'antiacido** *lahn-tee-AH-chee-doh* |
| anti-inflammatory | **l'antiflogistico** *lahn-tee-floh-jEE-stee-koh* |
| antibiotic | **l'antibiotico** *lahn-tee-bee-OH-tee-koh* |
| antidepressant | **l'antidepressivo** *lahn-tee-deh-prehs-sEE-voh* |
| antiseptic | **l'antisettico** *lahn-tee-sEHt-tee-koh* |

| | |
|---|---|
| aspirin | **l'aspirina** *lah-spee-rEE-nah* |
| blood pressure monitoring kit | **un monitore per la pressione** *oon moh-nee-tOH-reh pehr lah prehs-see-OH-neh* |
| cough drop | **la pastiglia per la tosse** *lah pah-stEE-ly-ah pehr lah tOHs-seh* |
| cough syrup | **lo sciroppo per la tosse** *loh shee-rOHp-poh pehr lah tOHs-seh* |
| diuretic | **il diuretico** *eel dee-oo-rEH-tee-koh* |
| dose | **la dose** *lah dOH-seh* |
| drop | **la goccia** *lah gOH-chee-ah* |
| drug | **il fàrmaco** *eel fAHr-mah-koh* |
| eyedrop | **il collirio** *eel kohl-lEE-ree-oh* |
| injection | **l'iniezione (la puntura)** *lee-nee-eh-tzee-OH-neh (lah poon-tOO-rah)* |
| laxative | **il lassativo (il purgante)** *eel lahs-sah-tEE-voh (eel poor-gAHn-teh)* |
| ointment | **l'unguento (la pomata)** *loon-goo-EHn-toh (lah poh-mAH-tah)* |
| pill | **la pillola** *lah pEEl-loh-lah* |
| saccharin | **la saccarina** *lah sahk-kah-rEE-nah* |
| sedative | **il calmante** *eel kahl-mAHn-teh* |
| sleeping pill | **il sonnifero** *eel sohn-nEE-feh-roh* |
| stimulant | **lo stimolante** *loh stee-moh-lAHn-teh* |
| syringe | **la siringa** *lah see-rEEn-gah* |
| tablet | **la pastiglia (la compressa)** *lah pahs-tEE-ly-ah (lah kohm-prEHs-sah)* |

| | |
|---|---|
| thermometer | **il termometro** *eel tehr-mOH-meh-troh* |
| tranquilizer | **il tranquillante** *eel trahn-koo-eel-lAHn-teh* |
| vaccine | **il vaccino** *eel vah-chEE-noh* |
| vitamin | **la vitamina** *lah vee-tah-mEE-ah* |

**Travel Tips** Every traveler needs to carry a few small items for emergencies. Skip Swiss army knives or any objects that could be considered a weapon by airport security guards. All containers must be travel-size, i.e., very small.

# COMMUNICATIONS

## POST OFFICE

Post offices in Italy can be identified by a sign, **Poste e Telecomunicazioni**, or the initials **PT**. All post offices are generally open on weekdays from 8:00 A.M. to 1:30 or 2:00 P.M., and Saturdays from 8:00 A.M. to 11:45 A.M. In the largest cities (Rome, Milan, Turin, Naples, etc.) the central post office (**posta centrale**) is open until 9 P.M. Some counters (registered mail, telegrams, etc.) may have different hours and in the main cities they may also be open in the afternoon.

Stamps are sold at windows usually marked **Raccomandate/ Francobolli** (Registered Letters/Stamps). Always have the clerk weigh airmail letters since overweight letters will be sent surface mail rather than returned to the sender. Urgent letters may be sent **espresso** (special delivery) with additional postage.

Italian post offices are often very crowded because **conti correnti** (current bills for taxes, electricity and gas, and telephone) are paid at the post office.

Stamps for letters of normal weight and postcards can be purchased more conveniently at a tobacco shop (**tabaccheria**). The tobacconist has a schedule of postal rates. There are no stamp-dispensing machines in Italy.

Letter boxes, which are red and attached to the wall rather than freestanding, are found in front of post offices and in the vicinity of tobacco shops. If there are two letter boxes side by side, be sure *not* to put letters and postcards for other destinations, including overseas, in the box marked **Città** (City).

The post office also handles national and international money orders and currency exchange services.

| | |
|---|---|
| I want to mail a letter. | **Voglio spedire una lettera.** *vOH-ly-ee-oh speh-dEE-reh OO-nah lAYt-teh-rah* |
| Where's the post office? | **Dov'è l'ufficio postale?** *doh-vEH loof-fEE-chee-oh poh-stAH-leh* |
| Where's a letter box? | **Dov'è una cassetta postale?** *doh-vEH OO-nah kas-sAYt-tah poh-stAH-leh* |
| What is the postage on _____ to the United States (Canada, England, Australia)? | **Qual è l'affrancatura per _____ per gli Stati Uniti (Canadà, Inghilterra, Australia)?** *koo-ah-lEH lahf-frahn-kah-tOO-rah pehr ____ pehr ly-ee stAH-tee oo-nEE-tee (kah-nah-dAH een-gheel-tEHr-rah ahoo-strAH-lee-ah)* |
| ■ a letter | **una lettera** *OO-nah lAYt-teh-rah* |
| ■ an airmail letter | **una lettera via aerea** *OO-nah lAYt-teh-rah vEE-ah ah-EH-reh-ah* |
| ■ an insured letter | **una lettera assicurata** *OO-nah lAYt-teh-rah ahs-see-koo-rAH-tah* |
| ■ a registered letter | **una lettera raccomandata** *OO-nah lAYt-teh-rah rahk-koh-mahn-dAH-tah* |
| ■ a special delivery letter | **una lettera espresso** *OO-nah lAYt-teh-rah ehs-prEHs-soh* |
| ■ a package | **un pacco** *oon pAHk-koh* |
| ■ a postcard | **una cartolina postale** *OO-nah kahr-toh-lEE-nah poh-stAH-leh* |
| When will it arrive? | **Quando arriverà?** *koo-AHn-doh ahr-ree-veh-rAH* |

| | |
|---|---|
| Which is the _____ window? | **Qual è lo sportello per _____?** *koo-ah-lEH loh spohr-tEHl-loh pehr* |
| ■ general delivery | **il fermo posta** *eel fAYr-moh pOH-stah* |
| ■ money order | **i vaglia postali** *ee vAH-ly-ee-ah poh-stAH-lee* |
| ■ stamp | **i francobolli** *ee frahn-koh-bOHl-lee* |
| I'd like _____. | **Vorrei _____.** *vohr-rEH-ee* |
| ■ 10 postcards | **dieci cartoline postali** *dee-EH-chee kahr-toh-lEE-neh poh-stAH-lee* |
| ■ 5 (airmail) stamps | **cinque francobolli (via aerea)** *chEEn-koo-eh frahn-koh-bOHl-lee (vEE-ah ah-EH-reh-ah)* |
| Do I fill out a customs receipt? | **Devo compilare una ricevuta?** *dAY-voh kohm-pee-lAH-reh OO-nah ree-cheh-vOO-tah* |

## TELEPHONES

You'll find public telephones in cafés, bars, and station terminals. Obtain a prepaid phone card at a minimum charge of 3 euros. It can be bought almost everywhere (automatic distributors, Telecom shops, public phone locations, bars, newspaper stands, post offices, and tobacco shops). You may want to use a **tèlemat** (a public telephone that operates with coins and magnetic cards). As soon as you pick up the receiver, the directions for proper use will appear on the screen. You'll be able to select among four languages: Italian, English, French, and German. Remember to dial the area code for local calls, long-distance domestic, international, and intercontinental calls. To obtain information on rates, area codes, and phone numbers for foreign subscribers, dial **176**. (This service is on-line 24 hours a day.) You can access **Countrydirect** by dialing **172** + country code.

(The identity codes for various countries are listed in the official phone directories.) With this service, you can call abroad from Italy with assistance in your own language. Dial **800-020020** (Monday to Friday from 8:30 A.M. to 4:30 P.M.) to reach the International Contact Point Service for information in Italian or English on networks, telecommunication services, and relative charges. At several telephone centers there are "clicking" timers. You will pay after having completed the phone call and will be charged by the number of **scatti** *(skAHt-tee)* or "clicks" marked by the timer.

While the telephone is ringing, you'll be able to hear two different signals. The long *too, too* sounds signify that the line is free and the bell is ringing; the short and repeated *too, too, too* sounds signify that the line is busy.

If you have difficulty operating the telephone or feel you will not be able to understand the person who answers the call, ask the clerk at your hotel to make the call for you.

## MOBILE PHONES

Roaming can be expensive when using your own cell phone, and calls from a hotel may also be prohibitive. In addition, magnetic cards for local pay phones may not be easily available and overseas communications may be interrupted!

Unlocked cell phones let you use any SIM card. This tiny chip slides into a phone, is compatible with almost any cell phone, and contains as many minutes as you may want to buy. It is prudent to buy a prepaid card in Italy. You may get even better rates from dealers in the U.S. who sell and rent cell phones for use in most European countries. Purchasing an Italian SIM card along with a phone from Cellular Store Abroad may include a local phone number for calls to be made while staying in Italy. Other bonuses may be "free incoming calls" and an adapter for the charger. The telephone number is embedded in the SIM card.

## AREA CODES

Here are the dialing/area codes, **prefissi telefonici** *(preh-fEEs-see teh leh-phOH-nee-chee)*, for some of the principal cities in Italy. When you make a call from New York to Naples, you should dial as follows: 011 + 39 + 081 + phone number. When you call New York (Manhattan) from Italy, you dial 001 + 212 + phone number.

| | | | |
|---|---|---|---|
| Ancona | 071 | Lipari Islands | 090 |
| Alessandria | 0321 | Livorno (Leghorn) | 0586 |
| Aosta | 0165 | Messina | 090 |
| Assisi | 075 | Mantua | 0376 |
| Bari | 080 | Milan | 02 |
| Benevento | 0824 | Modena | 059 |
| Bergamo | 0461 | Monza | 039 |
| Biella | 035 | Naples | 081 |
| Bologna | 051 | Novara | 0321 |
| Bolzano | 0471 | Padua | 049 |
| Brescia | 0425 | Palermo | 091 |
| Brindisi | 0831 | Perugia | 075 |
| Cagliari | 070 | Pisa | 050 |
| Campobasso | 0874 | Potenza | 0971 |
| Capri | 081 | Reggio Calabria | 0965 |
| Caserta | 0823 | Rimini | 0541 |
| Catania | 095 | Rome | 06 |
| Catanzaro | 0961 | San Marino | 0549 |
| Como | 0432 | Sassari | 079 |
| Cortina d'Ampezzo | 0436 | Siena | 0577 |
| Ferrara | 0532 | Trento | 0461 |
| Florence | 055 | Trieste | 040 |
| Genoa | 010 | Turin | 011 |
| Ischia | 081 | Venice | 041 |
| La Spezia | 0187 | Verona | 045 |
| L'Aquila | 0862 | Viareggio | 0584 |

Where is _____? **Dov'è _____?** *doh-vEH*

■ a public telephone **un telefono pubblico** *oon teh-lEH-foh-noh pOOb-blee-koh*

| | |
|---|---|
| ■ a telephone booth | **una cabina telefonica** *OO-nah kah-bEE-nah teh-leh-fOH-nee-kah* |
| ■ a telephone directory | **un elenco telefonico** *oon eh-lEHn-koh teh-leh-fOH-nee-koh* |
| May I use your phone? | **Posso usare il suo telefono?** *pOHs-soh oo-sAH-reh eel sOO-oh teh-lEH-foh-noh* |
| Can I call direct? | **Posso telefonare direttamente?** *pOHs-soh teh-leh-foh-nAH-reh dee-reht-tah-mEHn-teh* |
| I want to reverse the charges. | **Desidero fare una riversibile.** *deh-sEE-deh-roh fAH-reh OO-nah ree-vehr-sEE-bee-leh* |
| I'd like a three-way call. | **Vorrei un collegamento in simultanea a tre.** *vohr-rEH-ee oon kohl-lay-gah-mEHn-toh een see-mool-tAH-neh-ah ah trAY* |
| Can you give me a phone card, please? | **Può darmi una scheda telefonica?** *poo-OH dAHr-mee OO-nah skEH-dah teh-leh-fOH-nee-kah* |
| I want to make a ____ to ____. | **Vorrei fare una _____ a _____.** *vohr-rEH-ee fAH-reh OO-nah____ ah ____* |
| ■ local call | **telefonata urbana** *teh-leh-foh-nAH-tah oor-bAH-nah* |
| ■ long-distance call | **una telefonata in teleselezione (interurbana, internazionale)** *OO-nah teh-leh-foh-nAH-tah een teh-leh-seh-leh-tsee-OH-neh (een-tehr-oor-bAH-nah een-tehr-nah-tsee-oh-nAH-leh)* |
| ■ person-to-person call | **una telefonata diretta con preavviso** *OO-nah teh-leh-foh-nAH-tah dee-rEHt-tah kohn preh-ahv-vEE-soh* |

| | |
|---|---|
| How do I get the operator? | **Come si ottiene il centralino?** *kOH-meh see oht-tee-EH-neh eel chehn-trah-lEE-noh* |
| Operator, can you give me _____? | **Signorina (signore, centralino), può darmi _____?** *see-ny-oh-rEE-nah (see-ny-OH-reh chehn-trah-lEE-noh) poo-OH dAHr-mee* |
| ■ number 23 345 | **il ventitrè trecentoquarantacinque** *eel vayn-tee-trEH treh-chEHn-toh-koo-ah-rahn-tah-chEEn-koo-eh* |
| ■ extension 19 | **interno diciannove** *een-tEHr-noh dee-chee-ahn-nOH-veh* |
| ■ area code ____ | **prefisso numero ____** *preh-fEEs-soh nOO-meh-roh* |
| ■ country code ____ | **prefisso internazionale ____** *preh-fEEs-soh een-tehr-nah-tzee-oh-nAH-leh* |
| ■ city code ____ | **prefisso interurbano ____** *preh-fEEs-soh een-tehr-oor-bAH-noh* |
| My number is _____. | **Il mio numero è _____.** *eel mEE-oh nOO-meh-roh EH* |
| May I speak to _____? | **Potrei parlare con _____?** *poh-trEH-ee pahr-lAH-reh kohn* |
| Is _____ in? | **C'è _____?** *chEH* |
| ■ Mr. ____ | **il signor ____** *EEl sy-nee-Ohr* |
| ■ Mrs. ____ | **la signora ____** *lah sy-nee-OH-rah* |
| ■ Miss ____ | **la signorina ____** *lah sy-nee-oh-rEE-nah* |
| Speaking. | **Sono io.** *sOH-noh EE-oh* |
| Hello. | **Pronto.** *prOHn-toh* |
| Who is it? | **Chi è?** *key EH* |

## PROBLEMS ON THE LINE

I can't hear. **Non si sente bene.** *nohn see sEHn-teh bEH-neh*

Speak louder (please). **Parli più forte (per favore).** *pAHr-lee pee-OO fOHr-teh (pehr fah-vOH-reh)*

Don't hang up. **Non appenda il ricevitore.** *nohn ahp-pEHn-dah eel ree-cheh-vee-tOH-reh*

This is _____. **Parla _____.** *pAHr-lah*

Do you have an answering machine? **Ha una segreteria telefonica?** *ah OO-nah seh-greh-teh-rEE-ah teh-leh-fOH-nee-kah*

The line is busy. **La linea è occupata.** *lah lEE-neh-ah EH ohk-koo-pAH-tah*

You gave me (that was) a wrong number. **Mi ha dato (era) un numero sbagliato.** *mee ah dAH-toh (EH-rah) oon nOO-meh-roh sbah-ly-ee-AH-toh*

| | |
|---|---|
| I was cut off. | **È caduta la linea.** *EH kah-dOO-tah lah lEE-neh-ah* |
| Please dial it again. | **Per favore, rifaccia il numero.** *pehr fah-vOH-reh ree-fAH-chee-ah eel nOO-meh-roh* |
| I want to leave a message. | **Voglio lasciare un (messaggio) appunto.** *vOH-ly-ee-oh lah-shee-AH-reh oon (mehs-sAH-jee-oh) ahp-pOOn-toh* |

## FAXES

| | |
|---|---|
| Do you have a fax machine? | **Ha un fax?** *ah oon fahcs* |
| What is your fax number? | **Qual è il numero del fax?** *koo-ahl-EH eel nOO-meh-roh dayl fahcs* |
| I'd like to fax _____. | **Vorrei faxare _____.** *vohr-rEH-ee fahc-sAH-reh* |
| ■ a document | **un documento** *oon doh-koo-mEHn-toh* |
| ■ an invoice | **una fattura** *OO-nah faht-tOO-rah* |
| ■ a letter | **una lettera** *OO-nah lAYt-teh-rah* |
| ■ a receipt | **una ricetta** *OO-nah ree-chEHt-tah* |
| May I fax it to you? | **Glielo posso faxare?** *ly-ay-loh pOHs-soh fahc-sAH-reh* |
| Fax it to me. | **Me lo faxi.** *may-loh fAHc-see* |
| I didn't get your fax. | **Non ho ricevuto il suo fax.** *nohn oh ree-cheh-vOO-toh eel sOO-oh fahcs* |

Did you receive my fax?

**Ha ricevuto il mio fax?** *ah ree-cheh-vOO-toh eel mEE-oh fahcs*

Your fax is illegible.

**Il suo fax è illegibile.** *eel sOO-oh fahcs EH eel-leh-jEE-bee-leh*

Please, send it again.

**Per favore, me lo(la) faxi di nuovo.** *pAYr fah-vOH-reh may-loh(lah) fahc-see dee noo-OH-voh*

## PHOTOCOPIES

Do you have a photocopier?

**C'è una fotocopiatrice?** *chEH OO-nah foh-toh-koh-pee-ah-trEE-ceh*

I would like to make a photocopy of this _____.

**Vorrei fare una fotocopia di _____.** *vohr-rEH-ee fAH-reh OO-nah foh-toh-kOH-pee-ah dee*

- page

**questa pagina** *koo-AYs-tah pAH-jee-nah*

- document

**questo documento** *koo-AYs-toh doh-koo-mEH-ntoh*

What is the cost per page?

**Quanto costa per pagina?** *koo-AHn-toh kOH-stah pehr pAH-jee-nah*

Can you enlarge it (by 25%)?

**Può ingrandirlo (del 25%)?** *poo-OH een-grahn-dEEr-loh (dayl vayn-tee-chEEn-koo-eh pehr chEHn-toh)*

Can you reduce it (by 50%)?

**Può ridurlo (del 50%)?** *poo-OH ree-dOOr-loh (dayl cheen-koo-AHn-tah pehr chEHn-toh)*

Can you make a color copy?

**Può fare una copia a colori?** *poo-OH fAH-reh OO-nah kOH-pee-ah ah koh-lOH-ree*

## COMPUTERS

We travel carrying laptops, cell phones, cameras, and a wide array of computerized gadgets that provide access to worldwide information. Travelers need to bear in mind that computer systems, electric voltages, computer accessories, and servers differ from country to country. Therefore, it is wise to know how to use the computer equipment in the countries that are going to be visited.

Look out!

- Italian wall sockets have a different shape. It's advisable to buy an adaptor that mates the Italian socket.
- In Italy, the electric supply is 220–230 volts, whereas in the United States and Canada it is 110–120 volts. Most computers automatically adapt to different currents, but make sure that your model does.
- Your modem is listening for an American or Canadian dial tone. Don't forget that you are plugged-in in Italy and the dial tone is different.
- Remember that an adaptor changes the plug shape while a transformer/converter changes the voltage.

Check *www.romebuddy.com/givesadvice/computers.html*

| | |
|---|---|
| What kind of computer do you have? | **Che sistema (tipo di computer) ha?** *kay see-stEH-mah (tEE-poh dee computer) ah* |
| What operating system are you using? | **Che sistema operativo usa?** *kay see-stEH-mah oh-peh-rah-tEE-voh OO-sah* |
| What word processing program are you using? | **Quale software applicativo usa?** *koo-AH-leh software ahp-plee-kah-tEE-voh OO-sah* |

| | |
|---|---|
| Are our systems compatible? | **Sono compatibili i nostri sistemi?** *sOH-noh kohm-pah-tEE-bee-lee ee nOHs-tree see-stEH-mee* |
| Do you have (use) an e-mail address? | **Ha (usa) un indirizzo di posta elettronica?** *ah (OO-sah) oon een-dee-rEE-tzoh dee pOH-stah eh-leht-trOH-nee-kah* |
| What is your e-mail address? | **Qual è il suo indirizzo e-mail?** *koo-ah-lEH eel sOO-oh een-dee-rEE-tzoh E-mail* |
| My e-mail address is _____. | **Il mio indirizzo e-mail è _____.** *eel mEE-oh een-dee-rEE-tzoh e-mail eh* |
| I'll e-mail it to you on Thursday. | **Glielo mando per e-mail giovedí.** *ly-EH-loh mAHn-doh pehr e-mail jee-oh-veh-dEE* |
| I'll send you the file as an attachment. | **Le mando il file in allegato.** *lay mAHn-doh eel file een ahl-lay-gAH-toh* |
| Download the file. | **Scarichi il file.** *skah-rEE-key eel file* |
| The information is on the website. | **Le informazioni si trovano sul sito web.** *leh een-fohr-mah-tzee-OH-nee see troh-vAH-noh sool sEE-toh web* |
| I have the broadband, dial-up. | **Ho la linea veloce, la connessione dial-up.** *oh lah lEE-nay-ah vay-lOH-cheh, lah kohn-nehs-see-OH-neh dial-up* |
| Do you have wireless Internet access? | **Avete (ha) accesso internet wireless?** *ah-vAY-teh (ah) ah-chEHs-soh internet wireless* |
| Can I check my e-mail here? | **Posso controllare l'e-mail qui?** *pOHs-soh kohn-troh-lAH-reh lee mail koo-EE* |

## COMPUTER TERMS—MINIDICTIONARY

| | |
|---|---|
| access | **accèsso (connessione)** *ah-chEH-soh (kohn-nehs-see-OH-neh)* |
| accessories | **accessori** *ah-chehs-sOH-ree* |
| boot, to | **accendere** *ah-chEHn-deh-reh* |
| brand name | **la marca (il nome di marca)** *lah mAHr-kah (eel nOH-meh dee mAHr-kah)* |
| cable | **cavo** *kAH-voh* |
| CDR | **CD registrabile** *see-dee ray-jee-strAH-bee-leh* |
| CD-ROM disk | **same as English** |
| CD-Writer | **masterizzatore** *mah-steh-ree-tzah-tOH-reh* |
| chip | **(micro) chip** *(mEE-kroh) cheep* |
| click, to | **cliccare** *kleek-kAH-reh* |
| computerize, to | **computerizzare** *kohm-poo-teh-ree-tzAH-reh* |
| cursor | **il cursore** *eel koor-sOH-reh* |
| database | **same as English** |
| disk drive | **same as English** |
| DOS | **same as English** |
| download, to | **scaricare** *skah-ree-kAH-reh* |
| e-mail | **la posta elettronica** *lah pOH-stah eh-leht-trOH-nee-kah* |
| file | **i file** *ee fAH-eel* |
| graphics | **la grafica** *lah grAH-fee-kah* |
| handhelds | **palmari** *pahl-mAH-ree* |

| | |
|---|---|
| hard drive | **disco rigido/fisso** *dEEs-koh rEE-jee-doh/fEEs-soh* |
| home page | **l'home page** *lOH-m page* |
| ink cartridge | **cartuccia** *kahr-tOO-chee-ah* |
| iPad | **(un) iPad** *(oon) iPad* |
| iPhone | **(un) iPhone** *(oon) iPhone* |
| key | **tasto** *tAHs-toh* |
| internet | **same as English** |
| joystick | **same as English** |
| keyboard | **tastiera** *tah-stee-EH-rah* |
| laptop computer | **pc portatile** *pee-see pohr-tAH-tee-lee* |
| link | **same as English** |
| memory | **la memoria** *lah meh-mOH-ree-ah* |
| memory disk | **same as English** |
| modem | **il modem** *eel mOH-dehm* |
| monitor | **same as English** |
| mouse | **same as English** |
| navigate, to | **navigare** *nah-vee-gAH-reh* |
| network | **same as English** |
| online service | **servizio in rete** *sayr-vEE-tsee-oh een rAY-teh* |
| paper | **carta** *kAHr-tah* |
| peripherals | **periferiche** *peh-ree-fEE-ree-keh* |
| power supply | **alimentatore** *ah-lee-mehn-tah-tOH-reh* |
| printer | **la stampante** *lah stahm-pAHn-teh* |
| ■ laser | **(il) laser** *eel laser* |
| ■ ink jet | **l'ink jet** *leenk jeht* |

| | |
|---|---|
| scanner | **lo scanner** *loh skAHn-neehr* |
| search engine | **sistema di ricerca** *see-stEH-mah dee ree-chAYr-kah* |
| site | **il sito** *eel sEE-toh* |
| software | **il software** *eel software* |
| speed | **la velocità** *lah veh-loh-chee-tAH* |
| spell checker | **il controllo ortografico** *eel cohn-trOHl-loh ohrtoh-grAH-fee-koh* |
| transformer/ converter | **trasformatore** *trahs-fohr-mah-tOH-reh* |
| video card | **scheda video** *skEH-dah vEE-deh-oh* |
| voltage | **voltaggio** *vohl-tAH-jee-oh* |
| web page | **pagina web** *pAH-jee-nah web* |

## BUSINESS SERVICES

| | |
|---|---|
| I need to send a fax. | **Devo mandare un fax.** *dAY-voh mahn-dAH-reh oon fahcs* |
| Are there telephone lines for computers in the rooms? | **Ci sono linee telefoniche per computers in camera?** *chee sOH-noh lEE-neh-eh teh-leh-fOH-nee-keh pehr computers een kAH-meh-rah* |
| Is there a (laptop) computer available? | **C'è un computer (pc portatile) disponibile?** *chee oon computer (pee-see pohr-tAH-tee-leh) dees-poh-nEE-bee-leh* |
| Does it have a ____? | **Ha _____?** *ah* |
| ■ CD-ROM/DVD drive | **un porto di CD-ROM e di DVD?** *oon pOHr-toh dee cd-rom ay dee dee-vee-dee* |

| | |
|---|---|
| modem | **un modem** *oon modem* |
| printer (in color)? | **una stampante (a colore)?** *OO-nah stahm-pAHn-teh (ah koh-lOH-reh)* |
| scanner | **uno scanner** *OO-noh scanner* |
| an anti-virus program | **un programma antivirus?** *oon proh-grAHm-mah antivirus* |
| Is it possible to get on the Internet? | **È possibile collegarsi ad internet?** *EH pohs-sEE-bee-leh kohl-lay-gAHr-see ahd internet* |
| Is the phone call charged as a local call? | **Si può usufruire della tariffa telefonica urbana?** *see poo-OH oo-soo-froo-EE-reh dAYl-lah tah-rEEf-fah teh-leh-fOH-nee-kah oor-bAH-nah* |
| Is there an e-mail address? | **C'è un indirizzo di posta elettronica?** *chEH oon een-dee-rEE-tzoh dee pOHs-tah eh-leht-trOH-nee-kah* |
| How can I send (receive) an e-mail? | **Come posso spedire (ricevere) una e-mail?** *kOH-meh pOHs-soh speh-dEE-reh (ree-chAY-vay-reh) OO-nah e-mail* |
| Is the telephone wireless? | **È un telefono senza fili?** *EH oon teh-lEH-foh-noh sEHn-tsah fEE-lee* |
| Does the telephone come with an answering machine? | **Il telefono ha anche la segreteria telefonica?** *eel teh-lEH-foh-noh ah AHn-keh lah seh-greh-teh-rEE-ah teh-leh-fOH-nee-kah* |
| Does the answering machine cost extra? | **C'è un costo extra (un supplemento) per la segreteria telefonica?** *chEH oon kOHs-toh EH-kstrah (oon soop-pleh-mAYn-toh) pehr lah seh-greh-teh-rEE-ah teh-leh-fOH-nee-kah* |
| Where can I rent (buy) _____? | **Dove posso noleggiare (comprare) _____?** *doH-veh pOHs-soh noh-lay-jee-AH-reh (kohm-prAH-reh)* |

# GENERAL INFORMATION

## TELLING TIME

What time is it? **Che ora è?** *kay OH-rah EH*

When telling time in Italian, *it is* is expressed by **è** for 1:00, noon, and midnight; **sono** is used for all other numbers.

Here's how to express afternoon and evening hours:

12:00 = noon = **Sono le dodici.** *sOH-noh leh dOH-dee-chee*

13:00 = 1:00 P.M. = **Sono le tredici.** *sOH-noh leh tray-dee-chee*

14:00 = 2:00 P.M. = **Sono le quattordici.** *sOH-noh leh koo-aht-tOHr-dee-chee*

15:00 = 3:00 P.M. = **Sono le quindici.** *sOH-noh leh koo-EEn-dee-chee*

16:00 = 4:00 P.M. = **Sono le sedici.** *sOH-noh leh sAY-dee-chee*

17:00 = 5:00 P.M. = **Sono le diciassette.** *sOH-noh leh dee-chee-ahs-sEHt-teh*

18:00 = 6:00 P.M. = **Sono le diciotto.** *sOH-noh leh dee-chee-OHt-toh*

Etc.

**La cena è alle 19 (diciannove)** (*lah chAY-nah EH AHl-leh dee-chee-ahn-nOH-veh*) means "Dinner is at 7:00 P.M."

Office hours, train schedules, movie timetables, entertainment, radio, and television programs follow the official Italian time.

It's 1:00. **È l'una.** *EH lOO-nah*

It's 12 o'clock (noon). **È mezzogiorno.** *EH meh-tsoh-jee-OHr-noh*

It's midnight. **È mezzanotte.** *EH meh-tsah-nOHt-teh*

It's early (late). **È presto (tardi).** *EH prEH-stoh (tAHr-dee)*

It's 2:00. **Sono le due.** *sOH-noh leh dOO-eh*

It's 3:00, etc. **Sono le tre.** *sOH-noh leh trAY*

The number of minutes after the hour is expressed by adding **e** ("and"), followed by the number of minutes.

It's 4:10. **Sono le quattro e dieci.** *sOH-noh leh koo-AHt-roh ay dee-EH-chee*

It's about 4:00. **Sono circa le quattro.** *sOH-noh chEEr-kah leh koo-AHt-troh*

It's exactly 4:00. **Sono le quattro in punto.** *sOH-noh leh koo-AHt-troh een pOOn-toh*

It's 5:20. **Sono le cinque e venti.** *sOH-noh leh chEEn-koo-eh ay vAYn-tee*

Fifteen minutes after the hour and half past the hour are expressed by placing **e un quarto** and **e mezzo** after the hour.

It's 6:15. **Sono le sei e un quarto.** *sOH-noh leh sEH-ee ay oon koo-AHr-toh*

It's 7:30. **Sono le sette e mezzo.** *sOH-noh leh sEHt-teh ay mEH-tsoh*

After passing the half-hour point on the clock, time is expressed in Italian by *subtracting* the number of minutes to the *next* hour.

It's 7:40. **Sono le otto meno venti.** *sOH-noh leh OHt-toh mEH-noh vAYn-tee*

It's 8:50. **Sono le nove meno dieci.** *sOH-noh leh nOH-veh mAY-noh dee-EH-chee*

At what time? **A che ora?** *ah kay OH-rah*

At 1:00. **All'una.** *ahl-lOO-nah*

## MONTHS OF THE YEAR

The months of the year are *not* capitalized in Italian.

| | | |
|---|---|---|
| January | **gennaio** | *jehn-nAH-ee-oh* |
| February | **febbraio** | *fehb-brAH-ee-oh* |
| March | **marzo** | *mAHr-tsoh* |
| April | **aprile** | *ah-prEE-leh* |
| May | **maggio** | *mAH-jee-oh* |
| June | **giugno** | *jee-OO-ny-ee-oh* |
| July | **luglio** | *lOO-ly-ee-oh* |
| August | **agosto** | *ah-gOH-stoh* |
| September | **settembre** | *seht-tEHm-breh* |
| October | **ottobre** | *oht-tOH-breh* |
| November | **novembre** | *noh-vEHm-breh* |
| December | **dicembre** | *dee-chEHm-breh* |
| What's today's date? | **Che data è oggi?** | *kay dAH-ta EH OH-jee* |

The first of the month is *il primo* (an ordinal number). All other dates are expressed with *cardinal* numbers.

| | | |
|---|---|---|
| Today is August *first.* | **Oggi è *il primo* di agosto.** | *OH-jee EH eel prEE-moh dee ah-gOH-stoh* |
| ■ second | **il due** | *eel dOO-eh* |
| ■ fourth | **il quattro** | *eel koo-AHt-troh* |
| ■ 25th | **il venticinque** | *eel vayn-tee-chEEn-koo-eh* |

| | | |
|---|---|---|
| This month | **Questo mese** | *koo-AYs-toh mAY-seh* |
| Last month | **Il mese scorso** | *eel mAY-seh skOHr-soh* |
| Next month | **Il mese prossimo** | *eel mAY-seh prOHs-see-moh* |
| Last year | **L'anno scorso** | *lAHn-noh skOHr-soh* |
| Next year | **L'anno prossimo** | *lAHn-noh prOHs-see-moh* |
| May 1, 1876 | **Il primo maggio, mille ottocento settanta sei** | *eel prEE-moh mAH-jee-oh mEEl-leh oht-toh-chEHn-toh seht-tAHn-tah sEH-ee* |
| July 4, 1984 | **Il quattro luglio, mille novecento ottanta quattro** | *eel koo-AHt-troh lOO-ly-ee-oh mEEl-leh noh-veh-chEHn-toh oht-tAHn-tah koo-AHt-troh* |

## THE FOUR SEASONS

| | | |
|---|---|---|
| Spring | **la primavera** | *lah pree-mah-vEH-rah* |
| Summer | **l'estate** | *leh-stAH-teh* |
| Fall | **l'autunno** | *lah-oo-tOOn-noh* |
| Winter | **l'inverno** | *leen-vEHr-noh* |

## THE WEATHER

| | |
|---|---|
| How is the weather today? | **Che tempo fa oggi?** *kay tEHm-poh fAH OH-jee* |
| It's good (bad) weather. | **Fa bel (cattivo) tempo.** *fah behl (kaht-tEE-voh) tEHm-poh* |
| It's hot. | **Fa caldo.** *fah kAHl-doh* |
| ■ cold | **freddo** *frAYd-doh* |
| ■ cool | **fresco** *frAY-skoh* |
| It's windy. | **Tira vento.** *tEE-rah vEHn-toh* |
| It's sunny. | **C'è il sole.** *chEH eel sOH-leh* |
| It's raining. | **Piove.** *pee-OH-veh* |
| It's snowing. | **Nevica.** *nAY-vee-kah* |
| It's drizzling. | **Pioviggina.** *pee-oh-vEE-jee-nah* |

## TEMPERATURE CONVERSIONS

To change Fahrenheit to Centigrade, subtract 32 and multiply by $\frac{5}{9}$.

To change Centigrade to Fahrenheit, multiply by $\frac{9}{5}$ and add 32.

## CLIMATE

| CITIES FROM N TO S IN ORDER OF LATITUDE | COLD MONTHS (JAN.–FEB.) | | HOT MONTHS (JULY–AUG.) | | AVERAGE ANNUAL TEMPERATURE | |
|---|---|---|---|---|---|---|
| | °C | °F | °C | °F | °C | °F |
| Bolzano | –1 | 30 | 23 | 72 | 12 | 54 |
| Trento | –3 | 23.5 | 23 | 72 | 11.5 | 53 |
| Trieste | 4 | 39 | 23.5 | 74 | 13.5 | 57 |
| Milan | –2 | 29 | 24 | 75 | 12.5 | 55 |
| Venice | 2.5 | 37 | 24.5 | 76 | 13.5 | 57 |
| Turin | –6 | 21 | 23 | 72 | 12 | 55 |
| Bologna | 1.5 | 35 | 24.5 | 76 | 13 | 56 |
| Genoa | 7.5 | 45 | 24 | 75 | 15.5 | 60 |
| Florence | 5 | 41 | 24.5 | 76 | 14.5 | 58 |
| Pisa | 6 | 43 | 23.5 | 74 | 14.5 | 58 |
| Ancona | 5.5 | 52 | 25.5 | 78 | 15.5 | 60 |
| Iesi | 6 | 43 | 26 | 79 | 16 | 61 |
| Siena | 4.5 | 40 | 23.5 | 74 | 13.6 | 57 |
| Perugia | 4 | 39 | 23 | 72 | 13 | 56 |
| L'Aquila | 1 | 34 | 21.5 | 71 | 11 | 52 |
| Rome | 6.5 | 43 | 25 | 77 | 15.5 | 60 |
| Sassari | 8.5 | 47 | 24 | 75 | 15 | 59 |
| Naples | 8 | 46 | 25 | 77 | 16 | 61 |
| Foggia | 6.5 | 43 | 26 | 79 | 16 | 61 |
| Bari | 8 | 46 | 24 | 75 | 16 | 61 |
| Potenza | 3 | 38 | 20.5 | 69 | 11 | 52 |
| Lecce | 9 | 48 | 25 | 77 | 16.5 | 62 |
| Cagliari | 9.5 | 49 | 25 | 77 | 16.5 | 62 |
| Reggio C. | 11.5 | 53 | 25 | 77 | 18 | 65 |
| Palermo | 10.5 | 51 | 25 | 77 | 17.5 | 64 |
| Catania | 11 | 52 | 26.5 | 80 | 18.5 | 66 |

## NATIONAL HOLIDAYS

Banks, post offices, retail stores, and public offices are closed on national holidays.

| | | |
|---|---|---|
| January 1 | New Year's Day | **Capodanno** |
| January 6 | Epiphany | **Epifania** |
| Varies | Easter Monday | **Lunedí dopo Pasqua** |
| April 25 | Liberation Day (1945) | **Festa della Resistenza** |
| May 1 | Labor Day | **Festa del Lavoro** |
| August 15 | Assumption Day (known as Ferragosto) | **Assunzione** |
| November 1 | All Saints Day | **Ognissanti** |
| December 8 | Immaculate Conception | **Immacolata Concezione** |
| December 25 | Christmas | **Natale** |
| December 26 | Saint Stephen | **Santo Stefano** |

## LOCAL HOLIDAYS

Stores and offices in some cities are closed on feast days honoring their patron saints.

| | | |
|---|---|---|
| Bari | December 6 | San Nicola |
| Bologna | October 4 | San Petronio |
| Cagliari | October 30 | San Saturnino |
| Florence and Genoa | June 24 | San Giovanni Battista (John the Baptist) |
| Milan | December 7 | Sant'Ambrogio |
| Naples | September 19 | San Gennaro |
| Palermo | July 15 | Santa Rosalia |
| Rome | June 29 | Santi Pietro e Paolo |
| Trieste | November 3 | San Giusto |
| Turin | June 24 | San Giovanni Battista |
| Venice | April 25 | San Marco |

## IMPORTANT SIGNS

| | |
|---|---|
| **Acqua (non) potabile** | (Not) drinking water |
| **Alt** | Stop |
| **Aperto** | Open |
| **Ascensore** | Elevator (Lift) |
| **Attenzione** | Caution, watch out |
| **Avanti** | Enter (come in, go, walk [at the lights]) |
| **Caldo** or **"C"** | Hot |
| **Cassa** | Cashier |
| **Chiuso** | Closed |
| **Divieto di sosta** | No parking |
| **Divieto di transito** | No entrance, keep out |
| **Freddo** or **"F"** | Cold |
| **Gabinetti (WC)** | Toilets |
| **Ingresso** | Entrance |
| **Libero** | Vacant |
| **Non calpestare le aiuole** | Keep off the grass |
| **Non ostruire l'ingresso** | Don't block entrance |
| **Non toccare** | Hands off, don't touch |
| **Occupato** | Occupied |
| **Pericolo** | Danger |
| **Riservato** | Reserved |
| **Si affitta (si loca)** | For rent |
| **Si vende** | For sale |
| **Donne** | Women's room |

| | |
|---|---|
| **Uomini** | Men's room |
| **Spingere** | Push |
| **Strada privata** | Private road |
| **Tirare** | Pull |
| **Uscita** | Exit |
| **Vietato fumare** | No smoking |
| **Vietato nuotare** | No bathing |
| **Vietato sputare** | No spitting |

## COMMON ABBREVIATIONS

| | | |
|---|---|---|
| **AA** | **Azienda Autonoma di Soggiorno e Turismo** | Local Tourist Information Center |
| **ACI** | **Automobile Club d'Italia** | Automobile Club of Italy |
| **Cap.** | **Capoluogo** | Province |
| **C.P.** | **Casella Postale** | Post Office Box |
| **CAP** | **Codice Postale** | Zip Code |
| **ENIT** | **Ente Nazionale per il Turismo** | Italian State Tourist Office |
| **EPT** | **Ente Provinciale per il Turismo** | Provincial Tourist Information Center |
| **F.lli** | **Brothers** | Inc. |
| **FS** | **Ferrovie dello Stato** | Italian State Railways |
| **IVA** | **Imposte sul Valore Aggiunto** | Italian State Tax |
| **N., n°** | **Numero** | Number |
| **Pro Loco** | **Ente Locale per il Turismo** | Local Tourist Information Office |
| **Prov.** | **Provincia** | Province |

| | | |
|---|---|---|
| **P.za** | **Piazza** | (City) Square |
| **S.** | **San, Santo(a)** | Saint |
| **S.A.** | **Società Anonima** | Inc. |
| **Sig.** | **Signor** | Mr. |
| **Sig.na** | **Signorina** | Miss |
| **Sig.ra** | **Signora** | Mrs. |
| **TCI** | **Touring Club Italiano** | Italian Touring Club |
| **v.** | **Via** | Street |
| **v.le** | **Viale** | Boulevard |

## CENTIMETERS/INCHES

It is usually unnecessary to make exact conversions from your customary inches to the metric system used in Italy, but to give you an approximate idea of how they compare, we have supplied the following guide.

To convert **centimetri** into inches, multiply by .39.

To convert inches into **centimetri**, multiply by 2.54.

**Centimetri**

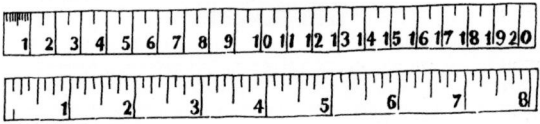


**Pollici**

## METERS/FEET

1 meter (metro) = 39.37 inches
= 3.28 feet
= 1.09 yards

1 foot = 0.3 meters
1 yard = 0.9 meters

How tall are you in meters? See for yourself.

| FEET-IN. | METERS-CM. | FEET-IN. | METERS-CM. |
|---|---|---|---|
| 5-0 | 1.52 | 5-7 | 1.70 |
| 5-1 | 1.54 | 5-8 | 1.73 |
| 5-2 | 1.57 | 5-9 | 1.75 |
| 5-3 | 1.59 | 5-10 | 1.78 |
| 5-4 | 1.62 | 5-11 | 1.80 |
| 5-5 | 1.64 | 6-0 | 1.83 |
| 5-6 | 1.68 | 6-1 | 1.85 |

## WHEN YOU WEIGH YOURSELF

| KILOS | POUNDS | KILOS | POUNDS |
|---|---|---|---|
| 40 | 88 | 75 | 165 |
| 45 | 99 | 80 | 176 |
| 50 | 110 | 85 | 187 |
| 55 | 121 | 90 | 198 |
| 60 | 132 | 95 | 209 |
| 65 | 143 | 100 | 220 |
| 70 | 154 | 105 | 231 |

## LIQUID MEASUREMENTS

1 liter = 1.06 quarts
4 liters = 1.06 gallons

For quick approximate conversion, multiply the number of gallons by 4 to get liters (**litri**). Divide the number of liters by 4 to get gallons.

NOTE: You will find other conversion charts on pages 92–93, 97, 184, 189, 256–257, and 261.

## MINIDICTIONARY FOR BUSINESS TRAVELERS

For other commercial terms, see Banking and Money Matters, pages 26–31 and Common Abbreviations, pages 260–261.

| | |
|---|---|
| amount | **ammontare, somma, totale** *ahm-mohn-tAH-reh sOHm-mah toh-tAH-leh* |
| appraise (to) | **stimare, valutare** *stee-mAH-reh vah-loo-tAH-reh* |
| authorize (to) | **autorizzare** *ah-oo-toh-ree-tsAH-reh* |
| ■ authorized edition | **edizione autorizzata** *ay-dee-tsee-OH-neh ah-oo-toh-ree-tsAH-tah* |
| bill | **fattura** *faht-tOO-rah* |
| ■ bill of exchange | **cambiale** *kahm-bee-AH-leh* |
| ■ bill of lading | **polizza di carico** *poh-lEE-tsah dee kAH-ree-koh* |
| ■ bill of sale | **atto di vendita** *AHt-toh dee vAYn-dee-tah* |

| | |
|---|---|
| business operations | **attività commerciali** *aht-tee-vee-tAH kohm-mehr-chee-AH-lee* |
| cash | **denaro, contanti** *deh-nAH-roh kohn-tAHn-tee* |
| ■ to buy, sell, for cash | **comprare, vendere in contanti** *kohm-prAH-reh vAYn-deh-reh een kohn-tAHn-tee* |
| cash a check (to) | **riscuotere un assegno** *ree-skoo-OH-teh-reh oon ahs-sAY-ny-oh* |
| certified check | **assegno vistato, autenticato** *ahs-sAY-ny-oh vees-tAH-toh ah-oo-tehn-tee-kAH-toh* |
| Chamber of Commerce | **Camera di Commercio** *kAH-meh-rah dee kohm-mEHr-chee-oh* |
| compensation for damage | **compenso (risarcimento) dei danni** *kohm-pEHn-soh (ree-sahr-chee-mEHn-toh) dAY-ee dAHn-nee* |
| competition | **concorrenza** *kohn-kohr-rEHn-tsah* |
| competitive price | **prezzo di concorrenza** *prEH-tsoh dee kohn-kohr-rEHn-tsah* |
| contract | **contratto** *kohn-trAHt-toh* |
| contractual obligation | **obbligazione (obbligo) contrattuale** *ohb-blee-gah-tsee-OH-neh (OHb-blee-goh) kohn-traht-too-AH-leh* |
| controlling interest | **controllo delle azioni** *kohn-trOHl-loh dAYl-leh ah-tsee-OH-nee* |
| co-owner | **comproprietario(a)** *kohm-proh-pree-eh-tAH-ree-oh(ah)* |
| co-partner | **consocio(a)** *kohn-sOH-chee-oh(ah)* |
| down payment | **acconto, anticipo, caparra** *ahk-kOHn-toh ahn-tEE-chee-poh kah-pAHr-rah* |

| | |
|---|---|
| due | **dovuto** *doh-vOO-toh* |
| enterprise | **impresa, iniziativa** *eem-prAY-sah ee-nee-tsee-ah-tEE-vah* |
| expedite delivery (to) | **sollecitare la consegna** *sohl-lay-chee-tAH-reh lah kohn-sAY-ny-ah* |
| expenses | **spese, indennità** *spAY-seh een-dehn-nee-tAH* |
| goods | **merci** *mEHr-chee* |
| infringement of patent | **contraffazione di brevetto** *kohn-trahf-fah-tsee-OH-neh dee breh-vAYt-toh* |
| ■ rights | **usurpazione di diritti** *oo-soor-pah-tsee-OH-neh dee dee-rEEt-tee* |
| insurance against all risks | **assicurazione comprendente tutti i rischi** *ahs-see-koo-rah-tsee-OH-neh kohm-prehn-dEHn-teh tOOt-tee ee rEEs-key* |
| international law | **legge internazionale** *lAY-jeh een-tehr-nah-tsee-oh-nAH-leh* |
| lawful possessor | **legittimo proprietario** *leh-jEEt-tee-moh proh-pree-eh-tAH-ree-oh* |
| lawsuit | **causa, processo** *kAHw-sah proh-chEHs-soh* |
| lawyer | **avvocato (avvocatessa)** *ahv-voh-kAH-toh (ahv-voh-kah-tAYs-sah)* |
| mail-order business | **ordinazione (di merci) per corrispondenza** *ohr-dee-nah-tsee-OH-neh (dee mEHr-chee) pehr kohr-rees-pohn-dEHn-tsah* |
| market value | **valore di mercato** *vah-lOH-reh dee mehr-kAH-toh* |

| | |
|---|---|
| manager | **direttore (direttrice)** *dee-reht-tOH-reh (dee-reht-trEE-cheh)* |
| payment | **pagamento** *pah-gah-mEHn-toh* |
| ■ part payment | **pagamento parziale** *pah-gah-mEHn-toh pahr-tsee-AH-leh* |
| past due | **arretrato** *ahr-reh-trAH-toh* |
| post office box | **casella postale** *kah-sEHl-lah pohs-tAH-leh* |
| property | **proprietà** *proh-pree-eh-tAH* |
| purchasing agent | **agente compratore** *ah-jEHn-teh kohm-prah-tOH-reh* |
| put (to) on the American market | **mettere in vendita sul mercato americano** *mAYt-teh-reh een vAYn-dee-tah sool mehr-kAH-toh ah-meh-ree-kAH-noh* |
| sale | **vendita, liquidazione, saldi** *vAYn-dee-tah lee-koo-ee-dah-tsee-OH-neh sAHl-dee* |
| sell (to) | **vendere** *vAYn-deh-reh* |
| send (to) | **mandare, inviare, spedire** *mahn-dAH-reh een-vee-AH-reh speh-dEE-reh* |
| ■ send back | **rinviare, mandare indietro** *reen-vee-AH-reh mahn-dAH-reh een-dee-AY-troh* |
| ■ send C.O.D. | **spedire contro assegno** *speh-dEE-reh kOHn-troh ahs-sEH-ny-oh* |
| shipment | **spedizione (di merci), carico** *speh-dee-tsee-OH-neh (dee mEHr-chee) kAH-ree-koh* |
| tax | **tassa, imposta** *tAHs-sah eem-pOHs-tah* |
| ■ tax-exempt | **esente da tasse** *ay-sEHn-teh dah tAHs-seh* |

| | |
|---|---|
| ■ sales tax | **imposta sulle vendite** *eem-pOHs-tah sOOl-leh vAYn-dee-teh* |
| ■ value-added tax | **imposta sui valori aggiunti** *eem-pOHs-tah sOO-ee vah-lOH-ree ah-jee-OOn-tee* |
| trade (n.) | **commercio** *kohm-mEHr-chee-oh* |
| ■ trade (to) | **commerciare** *kohm-mehr-chee-AH-reh* |
| transact business (to) | **trasferire** *trahs-feh-rEE-reh* |
| transportation charges | **spese di trasporto** *spAY-seh dee trahs-pOHr-toh* |
| via | **per, via** *pehr vEE-ah* |
| yield a profit (to) | **rendere interesse, fruttare un guadagno** *rEHn-deh-reh een-teh-rEHs-seh froot-tAH-reh oon goo-ah-dAH-ny-oh* |

# QUICK GRAMMAR GUIDE

Your facility with Italian will be greatly enhanced if you know a little of its grammar. Here are a few simple rules governing the use of the various parts of speech.

## NOUNS

In contrast with English, in which inanimate objects are considered neuter, Italian nouns are designated either masculine or feminine. In the singular, you'll find that feminine nouns often end in *a* while masculine nouns often end in *o*. Other nouns, which can be either masculine or feminine, often end in *e*. There are still others, however, that you simply have to learn as either masculine or feminine because their endings give you no clue as to their gender. With this in mind, you can follow these simple rules to make a singular noun plural.

**1.** When a feminine noun ends in *a*, make it plural by changing the *a* to *e*.
**2.** When a masculine noun ends in *o*, make it plural by changing the *o* to *i*.
**3.** For masculine or feminine nouns ending in *e*, make them plural by changing the *e* to *i*.
**4.** For masculine or feminine nouns with endings different from those above, keep the same ending for both singular and plural forms.

| GENDER | SINGULAR | PLURAL |
|---|---|---|
| feminine | cas*a* (house) | cas*e* (houses) |
| masculine | libr*o* (book) | libr*i* (books) |
| masculine or feminine | pied*e* (foot)<br>vest*e* (dress) | pied*i* (feet)<br>vest*i* (dresses) |
| masculine or feminine | bar (bar)<br>metropoli (city) | bar (bars)<br>metropoli (cities) |

Some nouns end in *co* or *go*; these change to *chi* and *ghi* in the plural. Other nouns ending in *ca* or *ga* change to *che* and *ghe* in the plural.

| | |
|---|---|
| **banco** (desk) | **banchi** (desks) |
| **fungo** (mushroom) | **funghi** (mushrooms) |
| **barca** (boat) | **barche** (boats) |
| **alga** (alga) | **alghe** (algae) |

## ARTICLES

Articles (*the*, *a*, *an*) agree in gender (masculine or feminine) and number (singular or plural) with the nouns they modify. Separate rules apply to the definite and indefinite articles.

The **definite article** (*the*) is different in both the singular and plural forms, depending on the noun it is being paired with. Select the proper word for *the*, depending on the sounds that are part of the noun.

| | |
|---|---|
| **il** (plural, **i**) | Use before consonants (except *s* followed by another consonant, *a*, *gn*, *ps*, and *x*): **il libro** (the book), **i libri** (the books); **il soldato** (the soldier), **i soldati** (the soldiers). |
| **lo (gli)** | Use before *z*, *gn*, *ps*, *x*, and *s* followed by another consonant: **lo zio** (the uncle), **gli zii** (the uncles); **lo stadio** (the stadium), **gli stadi** (the stadiums). |
| **lo (gli)** | Drops the *o* and becomes *l'* before vowels in the singular: **l'amico** (the friend), **gli amici** (the friends); **l'elefante** (the elephant), **gli elefanti** (the elephants). |
| **la (le)** | Use before consonants: **la casa** (the house), **le case** (the houses); **la ragazza** (the girl), **le ragazze** (the girls). |
| **la (le)** | Drops the *a* and becomes *l'* before vowels in the singular: **l'ora** (the hour), **le ore** (the hours); **l'edizione** (the edition), **le edizioni** (the editions). |

The **indefinite articles** (*a*, *an*) also follow certain rules. Use *un* or *uno* for masculine forms and *una* and *un'* for feminine ones. Use *qualche* to indicate the plural forms (*some*, *any*).

| | |
|---|---|
| **un** | Use before vowels and consonants (except *s* followed by another consonant, *z*, *gn*, *ps*, and *x*): **un amico** (a friend), **qualche amico** (some friends); **un dollaro** (a dollar), **qualche dollaro** (some dollars). |
| **uno** | Use before *s* followed by another consonant, *z*, *gn*, *ps*, and *x*: **uno specchio** (a mirror), **qualche specchio** (some mirrors); **uno zaino** (a knapsack), **qualche zaino** (some knapsacks). |
| **una** | Use before consonants: **una casa** (a house), **qualche casa** (some houses); **una chiesa** (a church), **qualche chiesa** (some churches). |
| **un'** | Use before vowel(s): **un'idea** (an idea), **qualche idea** (some ideas); **un'amica** (a girlfriend), **qualche amica** (some girlfriends). |

*Some* and *any* are often also expressed by *alcuni(e)* + the plural of the noun.

| | |
|---|---|
| **un piatto** (a dish) | **alcuni piatti** (some dishes) |
| **una ragazza** (a girl) | **alcune ragazze** (some girls) |

*Some* and *any* can also be indicated by using *di* + the definite article in a contracted form.

**una macchina** (a car) **delle macchine** (some cars)

To determine which contracted form is appropriate, use the following guide:

| | MASCULINE | | | FEMININE | |
|---|---|---|---|---|---|
| singular | di+il<br>del | di+lo<br>dello | di+l'<br>dell' | di+la<br>della | di+l'<br>dell' |
| plural | di+i<br>dei | di+gli<br>degli | | di+le<br>delle | |

**del (dei)** Use before consonants (except *x* followed by another consonant, *z*, *gn*, *ps*, and *x*): **del vino** (some wine), **dei vini** (some wines).

**dello (degli)** Use before *s* followed by another consonant, *z*, *gn*, *ps*, and *x*: **dello zucchero** (some sugar), **degli zuccheri** (some sugars).

**dello (degli)** Drops the *o* and becomes *dell'* before vowels in the singular: **dell'olio** (some oil), **degli olii** (some oils).

**della (delle)** Use before consonants: **della birra** (some beer), **delle birre** (some beers).

**della (delle)** Use before vowels: **dell'aranciata** (some orangeade), **delle aranciate** (some orangeades).

## ADJECTIVES

Adjectives agree in gender and in number with the nouns they modify. Descriptive adjectives are generally placed after the noun.

**la casa bianca (the white house)**

**il ragazzo alto (the tall boy)**

**le signore belle (the pretty women)**

**i libri costosi (the expensive books)**

The plurals of adjectives are formed following the same rules as for nouns.

**1.** For adjectives ending in *a*, change *a* to *e*.

2. For adjectives ending in *o*, change *o* to *i*.
3. For adjectives ending in *e*, change *e* to *i*.

The following shows the adjectives in their singular and plural forms.

**la carta azzurra** (the blue paper)

**le carte azzurre** (the blue papers)

**il vestito rosso** (the red dress)

**i vestiti rossi** (the red dresses)

**l'abito verde** (the green suit)

**gli abiti verdi** (the green suits)

Articles, possessives, and limiting adjectives agree in number and gender with the nouns they modify. Usually they are placed before the noun.

**molte cose** (many things)

**pochi americani** (few Americans)

In English, the possessive adjective agrees with the person who possesses the object, but in Italian, the possessive adjective agrees in gender and number with the object possessed. The possessive adjective is usually placed alongside the article.

**il mio libro** (my book)

**i miei libri** (my books)

**la mia amica** (my girlfriend)

**le mie amiche** (my girlfriends)

Use the following table to determine the correct form of the possessive, both for masculine and feminine forms and also for singular and plural forms.

| POSSESSIVE | MASCULINE | FEMININE |
|---|---|---|
| my | il mio (i miei) | la mia (le mie) |
| your | il tuo (i tuoi) | la tua (le tue) |
| his/her/your (formal) | il suo (i suoi) | la sua (le sue) |
| our | il nostro (i nostri) | la nostra (le nostre) |
| your | il vostro (i vostri) | la vostra (le vostre) |
| their/your (formal) | il loro (i loro) | la loro (le loro) |

There are a few exceptions to the above rules.

**mio padre** (my father) **mio zio** (my uncle)

**mia madre** (my mother) **mia zia** (my aunt)

**mio fratello** (my brother) **mio nonno** (my grandfather)

**mia sorella** (my sister) **mia nonna** (my grandmother)

Demonstrative adjectives (*this, these*) are placed in front of the nouns they modify. They agree in number and gender with the nouns that they modify. The adjective *this* has the following forms: **questo** (masculine singular), **questa** (feminine singular), **questi** (masculine plural), **queste** (feminine plural).

**questo libro** (this book) **questi libri** (these books)

**questa casa** (this house) **queste case** (these houses)

The demonstrative adjectives *that* and *those* are handled differently. **Quello** (that) has the following forms, depending on the article of the nouns being modified.

| | MASCULINE | | | FEMININE | |
|---|---|---|---|---|---|
| singular | que+il<br>quel | que+lo<br>quello | que+l'<br>quell' | que+la<br>quella | que+l'<br>quell' |
| plural | que+i<br>quei | que+gli<br>quegli | | que+le<br>quelle | |

For example, the singular forms.

**il ragazzo** (the boy) **quel ragazzo** (that boy)

**lo zio** (the uncle) **quello zio** (that uncle)

**l'albero** (the tree) **quell'albero** (that tree)

**l'oca** (the goose) **quell'oca** (that goose)

**la casa** (the house) **quella casa** (that house)

Now the plural forms.

| | |
|---|---|
| **i ragazzi** (the boys) | **quei ragazzi** (those boys) |
| **gli zii** (the uncles) | **quegli zii** (those uncles) |
| **gli alberi** (the trees) | **quegli alberi** (those trees) |
| **le oche** (the geese) | **quelle oche** (those geese) |
| **le case** (the houses) | **quelle case** (those houses) |

## PRONOUNS

Subject pronouns (*I, you, he, she,* etc.) have both singular and plural forms.

| | |
|---|---|
| **io** (I) | **noi** (we) |
| **tu** (you, familiar) | **voi** (you, familiar) |
| **Lei** (you, polite) | **Loro** (you, polite) |
| **egli, lui** (he) | **loro, essi** (they, masculine) |
| **ella, lei** (she) | **loro, esse** (they, feminine) |

Direct object pronouns (*me, you, him, it, us, them*) are used as direct objects of verbs. They have both singular and plural forms, and their placement before or after the verb varies. Italians usually place the direct object pronouns before the verb except for emphasis.

| SINGULAR | | PLURAL | |
|---|---|---|---|
| (me) | (You love me) | (us) | (You love us) |
| after verb | Tu ami *me* | after verb | Tu ami *noi* |
| before verb | Tu *mi* ami | before verb | Tu *ci* ami |
| (you) | (I love you) | (you) | (I love you) |
| after verb | Io amo *te* | after verb | Io amo *voi* |
| before verb | Io *ti* amo | before verb | Io *vi* amo |

| SINGULAR | | PLURAL | |
|---|---|---|---|
| (him/it) | (I love him) | (them, masc./ you, polite) | (I love them) |
| after verb | Io amo *lui* | after verb | Io amo *loro* |
| before verb | Io *lo* amo | before verb | Io *li* amo |
| (her/it/you, polite) | (I love her/ it/you) | (them, fem./ you, polite) | (I love them) |
| after verb | Io amo *lei/essa* | after verb | Io amo *loro* |
| before verb | Io *la* amo | before verb | Io *le* amo |

Indirect object pronouns are pronouns replacing nouns as indirect objects. They take the following forms, depending upon whether they are placed before or after the verb.

| SINGULAR | | PLURAL | |
|---|---|---|---|
| (to me) | (You give me a kiss) | (to us) | (You give us a kiss) |
| after verb | Tu dai un bacio *a me* | after verb | Tu dai un bacio *a noi* |
| before verb | Tu *mi* dai un bacio | before verb | Tu *ci* dai un bacio |
| (to you) | (I give you a kiss) | (to you) | (I give you a kiss) |
| after verb | Io do un bacio *a te* | after verb | Io do un bacio *a voi* |
| before verb | Io *ti* do un bacio | before verb | Io *vi* do un bacio |
| (to him) | (I give him a kiss) | (to them/you, polite) | (I give them/ you a kiss) |
| after verb | Io do un bacio *a lui* | after verb | Io do un bacio *a loro* |
| before verb | Io *gli* do un bacio | after verb | Io do *loro* un bacio |

| SINGULAR | | PLURAL | |
|---|---|---|---|
| (to her/you, polite) | (I give her/it a kiss) | (to them/you, polite) | (I give them/you a kiss) |
| after verb | Io do un bacio *a lei* | after verb | Io do un bacio *a loro* |
| before verb | Io *le* do un bacio | after verb | Io do *loro* un bacio |

## VERBS

In this phrase book, we limit the use of verbs to the present tense, since this is the most likely one for you to use as a tourist. Most Italian verbs in the infinitive end in either *are*, *ere*, or *ire*.

**parlare** (to speak)

**vedere** (to see)

**partire** (to leave)

In order to conjugate a verb, this infinitive ending must be removed and replaced by the appropriate ending found in the following table.

| PARLARE (TO SPEAK) | |
|---|---|
| io parlo (I speak) | noi parliamo (we speak) |
| tu parli (you speak, familiar) | voi parlate (you speak, familiar) |
| Lei parla (you speak, polite) | Loro parlano (you speak, polite) |
| egli parla (he speaks) lui | loro parlano (they speak, essi masculine) |
| ella parla (she speaks) lei | loro parlano (they speak, esse masculine) |

Two other examples of verbs with regular conjugations are:

| VEDERE (TO SEE) | |
|---|---|
| vedo (I see)<br>vedi (you see)<br>vede (he, she, you see(s)) | vediamo (we see)<br>vedete (you see)<br>vedono (they, you see) |
| PARTIRE (TO LEAVE) | |
| parto (I leave)<br>parti (you leave)<br>parte (he, she, you leave(s)) | partiamo (we leave)<br>partite (you leave)<br>partono (they, you leave) |

Some *ire* verbs add *sc* to the stem before the endings in the *io*, *tu*, *egli*, *essi* forms. For example, with the verb **finire** (to finish):

**io finisco** **egli finisce**

**tu finisci** **essi finiscono**

Not all verbs are regular. Here are some of the common irregular ones, with their conjugations.

| ANDARE (TO GO) | |
|---|---|
| vado (I go)<br>vai (you go)<br>va (he, she, you go) | andiamo (we go)<br>andate (you go)<br>vanno (they, you go) |
| DARE (TO GIVE) | |
| do (I give)<br>dai (you give)<br>da (he, she, you give) | diamo (we give)<br>date (you give)<br>danno (they, you give) |
| FARE (TO DO/TO MAKE) | |
| faccio (I do/make)<br>fai (you do/make)<br>fa (he, she, you do/make) | facciamo (we do/make)<br>fate (you do/make)<br>fanno (they, you do/make) |
| BERE (TO DRINK) | |
| bevo (I drink)<br>bevi (you drink)<br>beve (he, she, you drink(s)) | beviamo (we drink)<br>bevete (you drink)<br>bevono (they, you drink) |

| DOVERE (TO HAVE TO) | |
|---|---|
| devo (I have to) | dobbiamo (we have to) |
| devi (you have to) | dovete (you have to) |
| deve (he, she, you has (have) to) | devono (they, you have to) |
| POTERE (TO BE ABLE TO/CAN) | |
| posso (I am able to) | possiamo (we are able to) |
| puoi (you are able to) | potete (you are able to) |
| può (he, she, you is (are) able to) | possono (they, you are able to) |
| RIMANERE (TO STAY) | |
| rimango (I stay) | rimaniamo (we stay) |
| rimani (you stay) | rimanete (you stay) |
| rimane (he, she, you stay(s)) | rimangano (they, you stay) |
| SAPERE (TO KNOW) | |
| so (I know) | sappiamo (we know) |
| sai (you know) | sapete (you know) |
| sa (he, she, you know(s)) | sanno (they, you know) |
| VOLERE (TO WANT) | |
| voglio (I want) | vogliamo (we want) |
| vuoi (you want) | volete (you want) |
| vuole (he, she, you want(s)) | vogliono (they, you want) |
| USCIRE (TO GO OUT) | |
| esco (I go out) | usciamo (we go out) |
| esci (you go out) | uscite (you go out) |
| esce (he, she, you go(es) out) | escono (they, you go out) |
| VENIRE (TO COME) | |
| vengo (I come) | veniamo (we come) |
| vieni (you come) | venite (you come) |
| viene (he, she, you come(s)) | vengono (they, you come) |
| CONOSCERE (TO KNOW A PERSON) | |
| conosco (I know) | conosciamo (we know) |
| conosci (you know) | conoscete (you know) |
| conosce (he, she, you know(s)) | conoscono (they, you know) |

The verb **piacere** means to like something, but how it is conjugated depends on whether you like one thing or several. This is best shown as follows.

**mi piace** (I like—one thing)

**mi piacciono** (I like—several things)

Thus, the forms of **piacere** are as follows:

| | ONE THING | SEVERAL THINGS |
|---|---|---|
| I | mi piace | mi piacciono |
| you (familiar) | ti piace | ti piacciono |
| he<br>she | gli | gli |
| you (formal) | le piace | le piacciono |
| we | ci piace | ci piacciono |
| you (familiar) | vi piace | vi piace |
| they<br>you (formal) | piace a loro | piacciono a loro |

Used in sentences, they would be as follows:

**Le piace Venezia?** (Do you like Venice?)

**Le piace ballare?** (Do you like dancing?)

**Le piace Roma?** (Do you like Rome?)

**Le piacciono i monumenti?** (Do you like the monuments?)

Note the following constructions, which vary depending on the meaning intended.

**Ti piaccio?** (Am I pleasing to you?—familiar form of singular *you*)

**Le piaccio?** (Am I pleasing to you?—polite form of singular *you*)

**Vi piaccio?** (Am I pleasing to you?—familiar form of plural *you*)

**Piaccio a loro?** (Am I pleasing to them?—plural form of third person, polite form of plural *you*)

Or, in the form of a statement.

**Mi piaci.** (You are pleasing to me, I like you.—familiar form of singular *you*)

**Mi piace.** (You are pleasing to me. I like her/him.—singular form of third person, polite form of singular *you*)

**Mi piacete.** (You are pleasing to me, I like you.—familiar form of plural *you*)

**Mi piacciono.** (They are pleasing to me. I like them.—plural form of third person, polite form of plural *you*)

As in English, many verbs are used in conjunction with auxiliary verbs. Three of the most common are given below, with their conjugations.

| AVERE (TO HAVE) | |
|---|---|
| ho (I have)<br>hai (you have)<br>ha (he, she, you has(have)) | abbiamo (we have)<br>avete (you have)<br>hanno (they, you have) |
| ESSERE (TO BE) | |
| sono (I am)<br>sei (you are)<br>è (he, she, you is (are)) | siamo (we are)<br>siete (you are)<br>sono (they, you are) |
| STARE (TO BE) | |
| sto (I am)<br>stai (you are)<br>sta (he, she, you is (are)) | stiamo (we are)<br>state (you are)<br>stanno (they, you are) |

**Stare** is used when expressing an action in progress.

**Che cosa sta facendo?** (What are you doing?)

**Io sto camminando.** (I am walking.)

**Essere** is used mostly with intransitive verbs denoting motion such as *to go*. (The past participle with which it is linked agrees with its subject in gender and number.)

**Sono andato a fare la spesa.** (I have gone shopping.)

**Maria è appena arrivata.** (Mary has just arrived.)

**Avere** is used with verbs that may take an object, such as *to buy*.

**Che cosa ha comprato?** (What have you bought?)

**Ho comprato un regalo.** (I have bought a gift.)

To form the past participle of a verb, use the following patterns for all regular verbs.

| | |
|---|---|
| **parlare: parl + ato** (spoken) | **ho parlato** (I have spoken) |
| **vedere: ved + uto** (seen) | **ha veduto** (he, she, you has (have) seen) |
| **partire: part + ito** (left) | **sono partiti** (they, you have left) |

There are several idiomatic uses of the verb avere (*to have*), in which the verb is being used to express the English *to be*:

**aver freddo** (to be cold)

**aver sete** (to be thirsty)

**aver fame** (to be hungry)

**aver sonno** (to be sleepy)

**aver caldo** (to be hot)

**aver fretta** (to be in a hurry)

**aver paura** (to be afraid)

**aver ragione** (to be right)

**aver torto** (to be wrong)

Used in context, we have some examples of **avere**.

**Non ho caldo, ho freddo.** (I'm not hot, I'm cold.)

**Ha fame?** (Are you hungry?)

**No, ho sete.** (No, I am thirsty.)

**Abbiamo fretta.** (We're in a hurry.)

**Egli ha venti anni.** (He's 20 years old.)*

**Ho ragione.** (I'm right.)

*NOTE: In Italian, to express your age, you use the verb **avere**: to have _____ years.

## PREPOSITIONS

The following most common Italian prepositions are listed in the alphabetical order of their English equivalents.

| | |
|---|---|
| after | **dopo** *(dOH-poh)* |
| before (in time) | **prima** *(prEE-mah)* |
| before, in front of | **davanti** *(dah-vAHn-tee)* |
| behind, in back of | **dietro** *(dee-AY-troh)* |
| down | **giù** *(jee-oo)* |
| during | **durante** *(doo-rAHn-tay)* |
| for, through | **per** *(pehr)* |
| from | **da** *(dah)* |
| in | **in** *(een)* |
| in, into | **a** *(ah)* |
| inside | **dentro** *(dEHn-troh)* |
| outside | **fuori** *(foo-OH-ree)* |
| through, across | **attraverso** *(aht-trah-vEHr-soh)* |
| toward | **verso** *(vEHr-soh)* |
| until | **fino a** *(fEE-noh ah)* |
| up | **su** *(soo)* |
| without | **senza** *(sEHn-tsah)* |

## TO FORM NEGATIVE EXPRESSIONS

The most common negative word in Italian is *non*. It always precedes the verb.

**Io non ho soldi.** (I have no money; I don't have any money.)

Other negative words are:

**nessuno** (no one) — **Nessuno viene.** (No one is coming.)

**niente** (nothing) — **Non vedo niente.** (I don't see anything; I see nothing.)

**mai** (never) — **Mai mangiamo in casa.** (We never eat at home.)

**neppure** (neither) — **Lei non ha soldi e neppure io.** (She has no money and neither do I.)

Any one of the negative words except *non* may be used either before or after the verb. If one is used after the verb, *non* is also used before the verb (forming double negative).

**Nessuno parla.**
**Non parla nessuno.** (Nobody is speaking.)

**Mai vado da solo(a).**
**Non vado mai da solo(a).** (I never go alone.)

## TO FORM QUESTIONS

Some common interrogative words in Italian are the following:

**Dove?** (Where?)

**Come?** (How?)

**Quale?** (Which?)

**Quanto?** (How much?)

**Quanti?** (How many?)

**Per che cosa?** (What for?)

**Perché?** (Why?)

**Che (cosa)?** (What?)

**Chi?** (Who?)

To form a question in Italian, place the subject **after** the verb or raise your intonation at the end of the sentence.

**Lei parla italiano.** (You speak Italian.)
**Parla lei italiano?** (Do you speak Italian?)

**Maria ha il biglietto.** (Mary has the ticket.)
**Ha Maria il biglietto?** (Does Mary have the ticket?)

**Voi andate al cinema.** (You are going to the movies.)
**Andate voi al cinema?** (Are you going to the movies?)

# ENGLISH-ITALIAN DICTIONARY

## A

**a, an** un, uno, una *oon, OO-noh, OO-nah*
**about** circa *chEEr-kah*
**above** sopra *sOH-prah*
**abscess** ascesso *ash-EHs-soh*
**to accept** accettare *ah-cheht-tAH-reh*
**accessories** accessori *ah-chehs-sOH-ree*
**accountant** ragioniere(a) *rah-jee-oh-nee-EH-reh (ah)*
**ace** asso *AHs-soh*
**across** attraverso *aht-trah-vEHr-soh*
**address** indirizzo *een-dee-rEE-tsoh*
**adhesive tape** nastro adesivo *nAHs-troh ah-day-sEE-voh*
**advance** anticipo *ahn-tEE-chee-poh*
**adventure** avventura *ahv-vehn-tOO-rah*
**to adore** adorare *ah-doh-rAH-reh*
**after** dietro *dee-AY-troh;* dopo *dOH-poh*
**afternoon** pomeriggio *poh-may-rEE-jee-oh*
**again** ancora *ahn-kOH-rah*
**agency** agenzia *ah-jehn-tsEE-ah*
**air** aria *AH-ree-ah;*
**air-conditioned** aria condizionata *AH-ree-ah kohn-dee-tsee-oh-nAH-tah;*
**airmail** posta aerea *pOHs-tah ah-EH-reh-ah*
**airplane** aereo *ah-EH-reh-oh*
**airport** aeroporto *ah-eh-roh-pOHr-toh*
**aisle** corridoio *kohr-ree dOH-ee-oh*
**album** album *AHl-boom*
**alcohol** alcol *AHl-kohl*
**all** tutto *tOOt-toh*
**allergic** allergico *ahl-lEHr-jee-koh*
**to allow** permettere *pehr-mAYt-teh-reh*
**almond** mandorla *mAHn-dohr-lah*
**almost** quasi *kwAH-zee*
**alone** solo *sOH-loh*
**also** anche *AHn-keh*
**always** sempre *sEHm-preh*
**amalgam** amalgama *ah-mAHl-gah-mah*
**ambulance** autoambulanza *ah-oo-toh-ahm-boo-lAHn-tsah*
**American** americano *ah-may-ree-kAH-noh*
**amethyst** ametista *ah-may-tEEs-tah*
**among** fra *frAH;* tra *trAH*
**amount** ammontare *ahm-mohn-tAH-reh;* somma *sOHm-mah*
**anchovy** acciuga *ah-chee-OO-gah*
**and** e *ay*
**ankle** caviglia *kah-vEE-ly-ee-ah*
**another** un altro *oon AHl-troh*
**to answer** rispondere *rees-pOHn-day-reh*
**answering machine** segreteria telefonica *seh-greh-teh-rEE-ah teh-leh-fOH-nee-kah*
**antacid** antiacido *ahn-tee-AH-chee-doh*
**antibiotic** antibiotico *ahn-tee-bee-OH-tee-koh*

**antiseptic** antisettico *ahn-tee-sEHt-tee-koh*
**apartment** appartamento *ahp-pahr-tah-mEHn-toh*
**apéritif** aperitivo *ah-peh-ree-tEE-voh*
**appendicitis** appendicite *ahp-payn-dee-chEE-teh*
**appetizer** antipasto *ahn-tee-pAHs-toh*
**apple** mela *mAY-lah*
**appointment** appuntamento *ahp-poon-tah-mEHn-toh*
**apricot** albicocca *ahl-bee-kOH-kah*
**April** aprile *ah-prEE-leh*
**aquamarine** acquamarina *ah-koo-ah-mah-rEE-nah*
**Arab** arabo *AH-rah-boh*
**area code** prefisso *pray-fEEs-soh*
**arm** braccio *brAH-chee-oh*
**around** attorno *aht-toHr-noh*
**to arrive** arrivare *ahr-ree-vAH-reh*
**arrival** arrivo *ahr-rEE-voh*
**article** articolo *ahr-tEE-koh-loh*
**artificial sweetener** dolcificante artificiale *dohl-chee-fee-kAHn-teh ahr-tee-fee-chee-AH-leh*
**ashtray** portacenere *pohr-tah-chAY-nay-reh*
**to ask** chiedere *kay-AY-day-reh*
**asparagus** asparagi *ahs-pAH-ra-jee*
**aspirin** aspirina *ahs-pee-rEE-nah*
**to assist** assistere *ahs-sEEs-teh-reh*
**assistant** assistente *ahs-see-stEHn-teh*
**asthma** asma *AHs-mah*
**at** a *ah;* **at least** almeno *ahl-mAY-noh;* **at once** subito *sOO-bee-toh*
**attention** attenzione *aht-tehn-tsee-OH-neh*
**attentive** attento *aht-tEHn-toh*
**attraction** attrazione *aht-trah-tsee-OH-neh*
**auburn** castano *kahs-tAH-noh*
**August** agosto *ah-gOHs-toh*
**aunt** zia *tsEE-ah*
**author** autore *ah-oo-tOH-reh*
**automatic** automatico *ah-oo-toh-mAH-tee-koh*
**autumn** autunno *ah-oo-tOOn-noh*
**available** disponibile *dees-poh-nEE-bee-leh*
**awful** terribile *tehr-rEE-bee-leh*
**away** via *vEE-ah*

# B

**baby** bambino *bahm-bEE-noh*
**bachelor** scapolo *skAH-poh-loh*
**back** schiena *skee-AY-nah*
**backwards** dietro *dee-AY-troh*
**bacon** pancetta *pahn-chAYt-tah*
**bad** cattivo *kaht-tEE-voh*
**bag (handbag)** borsa *bOHr-sah;* borsetta *bohr-sAYt-tah;* **(suitcase)** valigia *vah-lEE-jee-ah;* **bag snatching** scippo *shEEp-poh*
**baggage** bagaglio *bah-gAH-lyee-oh*
**baked** al forno *ahl-fOHr-noh*
**bakery** fornaio *fohr-nAH-ee-oh*
**balcony (house)** balcone *bahl-kOH-neh;* **(theater)** galleria *gahl-leh-rEE-ah*
**ball (play ball)** palla *pAHl-lah*
**banana** banana *bah-nAH-nah*
**bandage** fascia *fAH-shee-ah*
**Band-Aid** cerotto *chay-rOHt-toh*
**bang(s) (hair)** frangia *frAHn-jee-ah*
**bangle** bracciale *brah-chee-AH-leh*
**bank** banca *bAHn-kah*
**bank note** banconota *bahn-koh-nOH-tah*
**barber** barbiere *bahr-bee-AY-reh;* parrucchiere *pahr-roo-key-AY-reh*

**baritone** baritono *bah-rEE-toh-noh*
**barley** orzo *OHr-tsoh*
**barn** stalla *stAHl-lah*
**bass (singer)** basso *bAHs-soh;* **(fish)** branzino *brahn-tsEE-noh*
**bath** bagno *bAH-ny-oh*
**bathing suit** costume da bagno *kohs-tOO-may dah bAH-ny-oh*
**bathrobe** accappatoio *ah-kahp-pah-tOH-ee-oh*
**bathroom** bagno *bAH-ny-oh*
**bathtub** vasca *vAHs-kah*
**battery** batteria *baht-teh-rEE-ah;* pila *pEE-lah* (for radio, camera, etc.)
**to be** essere *EHs-seh-reh;* stare *stAH-reh*
**beach** spiaggia *spee-AH-jee-ah*
**bean (shell)** fagiolo *fah-jee-OH-loh*
**beard** barba *bAHr-bah*
**beautiful** bello *bEHl-loh*
**because** perché *pehr-kAY*
**bed** letto *lEHt-toh;* **bedroom** camera da letto *kAH-meh-rah dah lEHt-toh*
**beef** manzo *mAHn-tsoh;* **(beef) steak** bistecca *bees-tAY-kah;* **(grilled)** ai ferri *ah-ee fEHr-ree;* **(medium)** a puntino *ah poon-tEE-noh;* **(rare)** al sangue *ahl sAHn-goo-eh;* **(well-done)** ben cotta *behn kOHt-tah*
**beer** birra *bEEr-rah;* **beer on tap** birra alla spina *bEEr-rah ahl-lah spEE-nah*
**before** prima *prEE-mah*
**to begin** cominciare *koh-meen-chee-AH-reh*
**behind** dietro *dee-AY-troh*
**Belgian** belga *bEHl-gah*
**to believe** credere *krAY-deh-reh*
**below** sotto *sOHt-toh*
**belt** cintura *cheen-tOO-rah*
**berth** cuccetta *koo-chAYt-tah*
**beside** accanto *ahk-kAHn-toh*
**best** il migliore *eel-mee-ly-ee-OH-reh*
**better** meglio *mEh-ly-ee-oh;* migliore *mee-ly-ee-OH-reh*
**between** fra *frAH;* tra *trAH*
**bicycle** bicicletta *bee-chee-klAYt-tah*
**bifocal lenses** lenti bifocali *lEHn-tee bee-foh-kAH-lee*
**big** grande *grAHn-deh;* grosso *grOHs-soh*
**bill** conto *kOHn-toh*
**bird** uccello *oo-chEHl-loh*
**birth** nascita *nAH-shee-tah*
**bite** boccone *boh-kOH-neh;* **to have a bite** mangiare un boccone *mahn-jee-AH-reh oon boh-kOH-neh*
**bitter** amaro *ah-mAH-roh*
**black** nero *nAY-roh*
**blade** lama *lAH-mah;* **razor blades** lamette *lah-mAYt-teh*
**blank** modulo *mOH-doo-loh*
**blanket** coperta *koh-pEHr-tah*
**blender** frullatore *frool-lah-tOH-reh*
**blond** biondo *bee-OHn-doh*
**blood** sangue *sAHn-goo-eh;* **I'm bleeding** Sto sanguinando *stOH sahn-goo-ee-nAHn-doh*
**blood test** analisi del sangue *ah-nAH-lee-see dAYl sAHn-goo-eh*
**blood pressure** la pressione *lah prehs-see-OH-neh*
**blouse** blusa *blOO-sah;* camicetta *kah-mee-chAYt-tah*
**blue** blu *blOO;* azzurro *ah-tsOOr-roh*
**body** corpo *kOHr-poh*
**boiled** bollito *bohl-lEE-toh*
**bolt** bullone *bool-lOH-neh*
**book** libro *lEE-broh;* **bookstore** libreria *lee-breh-rEE-ah*

**boot** stivale *stee-vAH-leh*
**booth** cabina telefonica *kah-bEE-nah teh-leh-fOH-nee-kah*
**botanic** botanico *boh-tAH-nee-koh*
**both** tutti e due *toot-tee ay dOO-eh*
**to bother** seccare *say-kAH-reh;* dare fastidio *dAH-reh fas-tEE-dee-oh;* **Don't bother me!** Non darmi fastidio! *nohn dAHr-mee fahs-tEE-dee-oh*
**bottle** bottiglia *boht-tEE-ly-ee-ah*
**box** scatola *skAH-toh-lah*
**bowling** bowling
**boy** ragazzo *rah-gAH-tsoh*
**bra, brassiere** reggiseno *reh-jee-SAY-noh*
**bracelet** bracciale *brah-chee-AH-leh*
**brain** cervello *chehr-vEHl-loh*
**brakes** freni *frAY-nee*
**bread** pane *pAH-neh;* **soft part of bread** mollica *mohl-lEE-kah;* **toasted bread** pan tostato *pAHn tohs-tAH-toh*
**to break** rompere *rOHm-pay-reh*
**breakdown (car)** guasto *goo-AHs-toh*
**breakfast** colazione *koh-lah-tsee-OH-neh*
**to breathe** respirare *rays-pee-rAH-reh*
**bridge** ponte *pOHn-teh*
**to bring** portare *pohr-tAH-reh;* **bring me . . .** mi porti . . . *mee pOHr-tee*
**broken** rotto *rOHt-toh*
**brooch** fermaglio *fehr-mAH-ly-ee-oh;* spilla *spEEl-lah*
**brook** ruscello *roo-shEHl-loh*
**broth** brodo *brOH-doh*
**brother** fratello *frah-tEHl-loh*
**brown** marrone *mahr-rOH-neh*
**bruise** contusione *kohn-too-see-OH-neh*
**brunette** bruna *brOO-nah;* brunetta *broo-nAYt-tah*
**brush** spazzola *spAH-tsoh-lah*
**bulb (light)** lampadina *lahm-pah-dEE-nah*
**bumper** paraurti *pah-rah-OOr-tee*
**bun (bread)** rosetta *roh-sAYt-tah;* **(hair)** crocchia *krOH-key-ah*
**to burn** bruciare *broo-chee-AH-reh*
**burn** ustione *oos-tee-OH-neh*
**burnt** ustionato *oos-tee-oh-nAH-toh*
**bus** autobus *ah-oo-toh-bOOs*
**business** affare *ahf-fAH-reh*
**busy** occupato *oh-koo-pAH-toh*
**but** ma *mah;* però *peh-rOH*
**butcher shop** macelleria *mah-chehl-leh-rEE-ah*
**butter** burro *bOOr-roh*
**button** bottone *boht-tOH-neh*
**to buy** comprare *kohm-prAH-reh*

# C

**cabbage** cavolo *kAH-voh-loh*
**cabin** cabina *kah-bEE-nah*
**cake** torta *tOHr-tah*
**calf** vitello *vee-tEHl-loh*
**to call** chiamare *key-ah-mAH-reh;* telefonare *teh-leh-foh-nAH-reh*
**camera** macchina fotografica *mAH-kee-nah foh-toh-grAH-fee-kah;* **camera store** negozio fotocine *neh-gOH-tsee-oh fOH-toh-chEE-neh;* negozio di articoli fotografici *neh-gOH-tsee-oh dee ahr-tEE-koh-lee foh-toh-grAH-fee-chee*
**camping** campeggio *kahm-pAY-jee-oh*
**Canadian** canadese *kah-nah-dAY-seh*
**cancel** cancellare *kahn-chehl-lAH-reh*

**candle** candela *kahn-dAY-lah*
**candy** dolci *dOHl-chee;* caramelle *kah-rah-mEHl-leh*
**cane** bastone *bah-stOH-neh*
**capon** cappone *kahp-pOH-neh*
**car (auto)** auto *AH-oo-toh;* **(train)** carrozza *kahr-rOH-tsah;* vagone *vah-gOH-neh;* **dining car** vagone ristorante *vah-gOH-neh rees-toh-rAHn-teh*
**car service** servizio noleggio *sehr-vEE-tsee-oh noh-lAY-jee-oh*
**carburetor** carburatore *kahr-boo-rah-tOH-reh*
**card (identification card)** carta d'identità *kAHr-tah dee-dEHn-tee-tAH;* **(playing) cards** carte da gioco *kAHr-teh dah jee-OH-koh;* **(deck of) cards** mazzo di carte *mAH-tsoh dee kAHr-teh*
**careful** attento *aht-tEHn-toh;* **be careful!** stia attento! *stEE-ah aht-tEHn-toh*
**carrot** carota *kah-rOH-tah*
**to carry** portare *pohr-tAH-reh*
**carton of cigarettes** stecca di sigarette *stAY-kah dee see-gah-rAYt-teh*
**carved** intagliato *een-tah-ly-ee-AH-toh*
**cashier** cassa *kAHs-sah;* cassiere *kahs-see-AY-reh*
**to catch** prendere *prAYn-day-reh*
**cathedral** cattedrale *kaht-tay-drAH-leh*
**Catholic** cattolico *kaht-tOH-lee-koh*
**cavity** carie *kAH-ree-eh*
**CD player** lettore CD *leht-tOH-reh see-dEE*
**CDR** CD registrabile *see-dee ray-jee-strAH-bee-leh*
**CD-Writer** masterizzatore *mah-steh-ree-tzah-tOH-reh*
**centimeter** centimetro *chayn-tEE-meh-troh*
**center** centrale *chayn-trAH-leh*
**ceramics** ceramiche *chay-rAH-mee-keh*
**cereals** cereali *cheh-reh-AH-lee*
**chain (gold)** catenina *kah-tay-nEE-nah*
**chair** sedia *sEH-dee-ah;* **chaise longue** sedia a sdraio *sEH-dee-ah ah sdrAH-ee-oh*
**chairlift** seggiovia *she-jee-oh-vEE-ah*
**chambermaid** cameriera *kah-meh-ree-AY-rah*
**to change** cambiare *kahm-bee-AH-reh*
**change (money)** resto *rEHs-toh;* **small change** spiccioli *spEE-chee-oh-lee*
**character** personaggio *pehr-soh-nAH-jee-oh*
**charm** ciondolo *chee-OHn-doh-loh*
**chart** cartellino *kahr-tehl-lEE-noh*
**cheap** a buon mercato *ah boo-OHn mehr-kAH-toh;* **cheaper** più a buon mercato *pee-OO ah boo-OHn mehr-kAH-toh*
**check** assegno *ahs-sAY-ny-oh*
**checkers** dama *dAH-mah*
**checkroom** guardaroba *goo-AHr-dah-rOH-bah*
**cheek** guancia *goo-AHn-chee-ah*
**cheers!** salute! *sah-lOO-teh*
**cheese** formaggio *fohr-mAH-jee-oh*
**chess** scacchi *skAH-key*
**chest** petto *pEHt-toh;* **a chest cold** un colpo d'aria al petto *oon kOHl-poh dAH-ree-ah ahl pEHt-toh*
**chestnuts** castagne *kahs-tAH-ny-eh*
**to chew** masticare *mahs-tee-kAH-reh;* **chewing gum**

gomma masticante *gOHm-mah mahs-tee-kAHn-teh*

**chicken** pollo *pOHl-loh*

**chiffon** chiffon *sheef-fOHn*

**child** bambino *bahm-bEE-noh*

**chill** brivido *brEE-vee-doh*

**chin** mento *mEHn-toh*

**chocolate** cioccolato *chee-oh-kOH-lah-toh*

**chop (meat)** cotoletta *koh-toh-lAYt-tah*

**Christmas** Natale *nah-tAH-leh*

**church** chiesa *key-AY-sah*

**cider** sidro *sEE-droh*

**cigar** sigaro *sEE-gah-roh;* **cigar store** tabaccaio *tah-bah-kAH-ee-oh;* tabaccheria *tah-bah-kEH-ree-ah*

**cigarette** sigaretta *see-gah-rAYt-tah;* **cigarette lighter** accendino *ah-chayn-dEE-noh*

**cinema** cinema *chEE-neh-mah*

**city** città *cheet-tAH*

**class** classe *klAHs-seh*

**to clean** pulire *poo-lEE-reh*

**clear** chiaro *key-AH-roh*

**clerk** impiegato *eem-pee-ay-gAH-toh*

**to climb** salire *sah-lEE-reh*

**to close** chiudere *key-OO-deh-reh;* **May I close?** Posso chiudere? *pOHs-soh key-OO-deh-reh;* **closed** chiuso *key-OO-soh*

**cloth** panno *pAHn-noh*

**clothing** vestiti *vays-tEE-tee;* **evening clothes** abiti da sera *AH-bee-tee dah sAY-rah*

**club** club *klOOb*; **nightclub** night club *nAH-eet klOOb*; **golf clubs** mazze da golf *mAH-tseh dah gOHlf*

**clutch** frizione *free-tsee-OH-neh*

**coat** cappotto *kahp-pOHt-toh*

**cocktail** cocktail *kOHk-tayl*

**coconut** noce di cocco *nOH-cheh dee kOH-koh*

**codfish** merluzzo *mehr-lOO-tsoh*

**coffee** caffè *kahf-fEH*

**cold** freddo *frAYd-doh;* **I have a cold** Ho il raffreddore *OH eel rahf-frayd-dOH-reh*

**cold cuts** affettati *ahf-fayt-tAH-tee;* salumi *sah-lOO-mee*

**color** colore *koh-lOH-reh;* **light color** color chiaro *koh-lOHr key-AH-roh*

**comb** pettine *pEHt-tee-neh*

**to come in** venire *vay-nEE-reh;* **come in!** entri! *AYn-tree* avanti! *ah-vAHn-tee*

**comedy** commedia *kohm-mEH-dee-ah*

**commercial** commerciale *kohm-mehr-chee-AH-leh*

**compartment** compartimento *kohm-pahr-tee-mEHn-toh*

**concert** concerto *kohn-chEHr-toh;* **concert hall** sala da concerti *sAH-lah dah kohn-chEHr-tee*

**to confirm** confermare *kohn-fayr-mAH-reh*

**consommé** consommé *kohn-sohm-mAY*

**constipation** stitichezza *stee-tee-kAY-tsah*

**consulate** consolato *kohn-soh-lAH-toh*

**to contact** contattare *kohn-taht-tAH-reh*

**contact lenses** lenti a contatto *lEHn-tee ah kohn-tAHt-toh*

**contagious** contagioso *kohn-tah-jee-OH-soh*

**to continue** continuare *kohn-tee-noo-AH-reh*

**contraceptive** contraccettivo *kohn-trah-cheht-tEE-voh*

**cooked** cotto *kOHt-toh*

**cookies** dolci *dOHl-chee*

**cool** fresco *frAYs-koh*

**copy** copia *kOH-pee-ah*

**coral** corallo *koh-rAHl-loh*

**corn plaster** callifugo *kahl-lEE-foo-goh*

**drinkable** potabile *poh-tAH-bee-leh*
**to drive** guidare *goo-ee-dAH-reh;* **driver's license** patente di guida *pah-tEHn-teh dee goo-EE-dah*
**to drown** affogare *ahf-foh-gAHr-reh*
**drugstore** farmacia *fahr-mah-chEE-ah*
**dry** secco *sAY-koh*
**to dry-clean** lavare a secco *lah-vAH-reh ah sAY-koh;* **dry cleaner** tintoria *teen-toh-rEE-ah*
**duck (bird)** anatra *AH-nah-trah*
**during** durante *door-AHn-teh*
**dust** polvere *pOHl-vay-reh*
**duty (customs)** dogana *doh-gAH-nah*
**dye** tintura *teen-tOO-rah*
**dysentery** dissenteria *dEEs-sehn-teh-rEE-ah*

# E

**each** ogni *OH-ny-ee*
**ear** orecchio *oh-rAY-key-oh*
**early** presto *prEHs-toh*
**earrings** orecchini *oh-ray-kEY-nee*
**earth** terra *tEHr-rah*
**east** est *ehst*
**easy** facile *FAH-chee-leh*
**to eat** mangiare *mahn-jee-AH-reh*
**eel** anguilla *ahn-goo-EEl-lah*
**egg** uovo *oo-OH-voh;* **hard-cooked eggs** uova sode *oo-OH-vah sOH-deh;* **scrambled eggs** uova strapazzate *oo-OH-vah strah-pah-tsAH-teh;* **soft-boiled eggs** uova alla coque *oo-OH-vah AHl-lah kOHk*
**eggplant** melanzana *may-lahn-tsAH-nah*
**eight** otto *OHt-toh;* **eight hundred** ottocento *OHt-toh-chEHn-toh*
**eighteen** diciotto *dee-chee-OHt-toh*
**eighth** ottavo *oht-tAH-voh*
**eighty** ottanta *oht-tAHn-tah*
**elbow** gomito *gOH-mee-toh*
**electric** elettrico *ay-lEHt-tree-koh;* **electricity** elettricità *ay-leht-tree-chee-tAH*
**elevator** ascensore *ah-shayn-sOH-reh*
**eleven** undici *OOn-dee-chee*
**emerald** smeraldo *smeh-rAHl-doh*
**emergency** emergenza *eh-mehr-jEHn-tsah*
**emergency room** pronto soccorso *prOHn-toh sohk-kOHr-soh*
**enamel** smalto *smAHl-toh*
**to end** finire *fee-nEE-reh*
**to endorse** firmare *feer-mAH-reh*
**English** inglese *een-glAY-seh*
**enlargement** ingrandimento *een-grahn-dee-mEHn-toh*
**enough** abbastanza *ahb-bah-stAHn-tsah;* **That's enough!** Basta! *bAHs-tah*
**to enter** entrare *ayn-trAH-reh*
**entrance** ingresso *een-grEHs-soh*
**envelope** busta *bOOs-tah*
**epileptic** epilettico *eh-pee-lEHt-tee-koh*
**equipment** equipaggiamento *ay-koo-ee-pah-jee-ah-mEHn-toh*
**eraser** gomma *gOHm-mah*
**escalator** scala mobile *skAH-lah mOH-bee-leh*
**even** pari *pAH-reh*
**evening** sera *sAY-rah;* **evening gown** abito da sera *AH-bee-toh dah sAY-rah*

**every** ogni *OH-ny-ee;* **everyone** ognuno *oh-ny-oo-noh;* **everything** tutto *tOOt-toh*
**to examine** esaminare *ay-sah-mee-nAH-reh*
**except** eccetto *ay-chEH-toh*
**to exchange** cambiare *kahm-be-AH-reh;* **the exchange rate** il cambio *eel kAHm-bee-oh;* **exchange office** ufficio di cambio *off-fEE-chee-oh dee kAHm-bee-oh*
**excursion** escursione *ays-koor-see-OH-neh;* gita *jEE-tah*
**to excuse** scusare *skoo-sAH-reh;* **Excuse me!** Mi scusi! *mee skOO-see*
**exhaust pipe** tubo di scappamento *tOO-boh dee skahp-pah-mEHn-toh*
**exit** uscita *oo-shEE-tah*
**expensive** caro *kAH-roh;* costoso *kohs-tOH-soh*
**express** espresso *ays-prEHs-soh*
**to extract** estrarre *ays-trAHr-reh*
**eye** occhio *OH-key-oh;* **eye doctor** oculista *oh-koo-lEEs-tah;* **eyedrops** collirio *kohl-lEE-ree-oh*
**eye shadow** ombretto *ohm-brAYt-toh*
**eyebrows** sopracciglia *soh-prah-chEE-ly-ee-ah*
**eyeglasses** occhiali *oh-key-AH-lee;* **sunglasses** occhiali da sole *oh-key-AH-lee dah sOH-leh*
**eyelashes** ciglia *chEE-ly-ee-ah*
**eyeliner** eyeliner

# F

**to face** dare su *dAH-reh soo*
**face** faccia *fAH-chee-ah*
**facial** facciale *fah-chee-AH-leh*
**to faint** svenire *svay-nEE-reh*
**fall (autumn)** autunno *ah-oo-tOOn-noh*
**to fall** cadere *kah-dAY-reh*
**family** famiglia *fah-mEE-ly-ee-ah*
**fan** ventaglio *vehn-tAH-ly-ee-oh;* ventola *vEHn-toh-lah;* **fan belt** cinghia del ventilatore *chEEn-ghee-ah dayl vehn-tee-lah-tOH-reh*
**far** lontano *lohn-tAH-noh*
**fare** corsa *kOHr-sah;* biglietto *bee-ly-ee-AYt-toh*
**farm** fattoria *faht-toh-rEE-ah*
**fast** veloce *vay-lOH-cheh;* **faster** più veloce *pee-OO vay-lOH-cheh*
**fat** grasso *grAHs-soh*
**father** padre *pAH-dreh*
**faucet** rubinetto *roo-bee-nAYt-toh*
**favor** favore *fah-vOH-reh*
**February** febbraio *fayb-brAH-ee-oh*
**to feel** sentire *sayn-tEE-reh;* **I don't feel well** Non mi sento bene *nohn mee sEHn-toh bEH-neh*
**felt (cloth)** feltro *fAYl-troh*
**fender** parafango *pah-rah-fAHn-goh*
**fever** febbre *fEHb-breh*
**few** alcuni *ahl-kOO-nee;* **a few** qualche *koo-AHl-keh*
**field** campo *kAHm-poh*
**fifteen** quindici *koo-EEn-dee-chee*
**fifth** quinto *koo-EEn-toh*
**fifty** cinquanta *cheen-koo-AHn-tah*
**fig** fico *fEE-koh*
**file (nail)** limetta *lee-mAYt-tah*
**to fill, to fill out** riempire *ree-ehm-pEE-reh*
**filling (tooth)** otturazione *oht-too-rah-tsee-OH-neh*
**film** film; pellicola *pehl-lEE-koh-lah*

**filter** filtro *fEEl-troh*
**to find** trovare *troh-vAH-reh*
**finger** dito *dEE-toh;* **fingers** dita *dEE-tah*
**to finish** finire *fee-nEE-reh*
**fire** fuoco *foo-OH-koh;* **Fire!** Al fuoco! *ahl foo-OH-koh*
**first** primo *prEE-moh;* **first class** prima classe *prEE-mah clAHs-seh;* **first aid** pronto soccorso *prOHn-toh soh-kOHr-soh*
**fish** pesce *pAY-sheh*
**five** cinque *chEEn-koo-eh;* **five hundred** cinquecento *chEEn-koo-eh-chEHn-toh*
**to fix** aggiustare *ah-jee-oos-tAH-reh;* riparare *ree-pah-rAH-reh*
**flannel** flanella *flah-nEHl-lah*
**flashlight** lampadina tascabile *lahm-pah-dEE-nah tahs-kAH-bee-leh*
**flat tire** gomma bucata *gOHm-mah boo-kAH-tah*
**flight** volo *vOH-loh*
**flint** pietrina *pee-ay-trEE-nah*
**florist** fioraio *fee-oh-rAH-ee-oh*
**flour** semola *sAY-moh-lah;* farina *fah-rEE-nah*
**flu** influenza *een-floo-EHn-tsah*
**fluid (for cigarette lighters)** benzina *bayn-tsEE-nah*
**folklore** folklore *fohl-klOH-ray;* **folkloric** folkloristico *fohl-kloh-rEEs-tee-koh*
**to follow** seguire *say-goo-EE-reh*
**foot** piede *pee-EH-deh;* **to go on foot, walk** andare a piedi *ahn-dAH-reh ah pee-EH-dee*
**for** per *pehr*
**forbidden** vietato *vee-ay-tAH-toh*
**forehead** fronte *frOHn-teh*
**forest** bosco *bOHs-koh;* foresta *foh-rEHs-tah*
**to forget** dimenticare *dee-mehn-tee-kAH-reh*
**fork** forchetta *fohr-kAYt-tah*
**form** modulo *mOH-doo-loh*
**fortune** fortuna *fohr-tOO-nah*
**forty** quaranta *koo-ah-rAHn-tah*
**to forward** spedire *spay-dEE-reh;* **forward (direction)** avanti *ah-vAHn-tee*
**fountain** fontana *fohn-tAH-nah*
**four** quattro *koo-AHt-troh;* **four hundred** quattrocento *koo-AHt-troh-chEHn-toh*
**fourteen** quattordici *koo-aht-tOHr-dee-chee*
**fourth** quarto *koo-AHr-toh*
**fracture** frattura *fraht-tOO-rah*
**frame** montatura *mohn-tah-tOO-rah*
**free** libero *lEE-beh-roh*
**fresh** fresco *frAYs-koh*
**Friday** venerdì *veh-nehr-dEE*
**fried** fritto *frEEt-toh*
**friend** amico *ah-mEE-koh*
**from** da *dah*
**front** davanti *dah-vAHn-tee*
**fruit** frutta *frOOt-tah;* **fresh-fruit salad** macedonia *mah-chay-dOH-nee-ah*
**fuel pump** pompa della benzina *pOHm-pah dAYl-lah bayn-tsEE-nah*
**fuel tank** serbatoio *sehr-bah-tOH-ee-oh*
**full** pieno *pee-AY-noh*
**fullback (sport)** terzino *tehr-tsEE-noh*
**furnished** ammobiliato *ahm-moh-bee-lee-AH-toh*

# G

**game (sports)** partita *pahr-tEE-tah;* **(birds)** selvaggina *sayl-vah-jEE-nah*

**garage** autorimessa *AH-oo-toh-ree-mAYs-sah*
**garden** aiuola *ah-ee-oo-OH-lah;* giardino *jee-ahr-dEE-noh*
**garlic** aglio *AH-ly-ee-oh*
**garnish** contorno *kohn-tOHr-noh*
**gasoline** benzina *bayn-tsEE-nah*
**gate** porta *pOHr-tah;* cancello *kahn-chAYl-loh;* uscita *oo-shEE-tah*
**gears** ingranaggi *een-grah-nAH-jee*
**general delivery** fermo posta *fAYr-moh pOHs-tah*
**gentleman** signore *see-ny-OH-reh*
**to get** ottenere *oht-teh-nAY-reh;* **to get back (to return)** ritornare *ree-tohr-nAH-reh;* **to get dressed** vestirsi *vays-tEEr-see;* **to get off** scendere *shAYn-day-reh;* **to get on** montare *mohn-tAH-ray;* **to get up** alzarsi *ahl-tzAHr-tsee*
**gift** regalo *ray-gAH-loh*
**girl** ragazza *rah-gAH-tsah*
**to give** dare *dAH-reh;* **to give back** ridare *ree-dAH-reh*
**glands** ghiandole *ghee-AHn-doh-leh*
**glass** vetro *vAY-troh;* **blown glass** vetro soffiato *vAY-troh sohf-fEE-ah-toh*
**glue** colla *kOHl-lah*
**goat (kid)** capra *kAH-prah;* capretto *kah-prAYt-toh*
**to go** andare *ahn-dAH-reh;* **Let's go!** Andiamo! *ahn-dee-AH-moh;* **Go!** Forza! *fOHr-tsah;* **to go back** ritornare *ree-tohr-nAH-reh;* **to go down** scendere *shAYn-day-reh;* **to go home** andare a casa *ahn-dAH-reh ah kAH-sah;* **to go in** entrare *ayn-trAH-reh;* **to go out** uscire *oo-shEE-reh;* **to go shopping** andare a fare la spesa *ahn-dAH-reh ah fAH-reh lah spAY-sah;* **to go up** salire *sah-lEE-reh*
**gold** oro *OH-roh;* **solid gold** oro massiccio *OH-roh mahs-sEE-chee-oh;* **gold plated** oro placcato *OH-roh plah-kAH-toh*
**good** buono *boo-OH-noh*
**good-bye** arrivederci *ahr-rEE-veh-dAYr-chee;* **(friendly)** ciao *chee-AH-oh*
**goose** oca *OH-kah*
**gram** grammo *grAHm-moh*
**grapefruit** pompelmo *pohm-pAYl-moh*
**grass** erba *EHr-bah*
**gray** grigio *grEE-jee-oh*
**to grease** lubrificare *loo-bree-fee-kAH-reh*
**Great!** Magnifico! *mah-ny-EE-fee-koh*
**green** verde *vAYr-deh*
**greetings** saluti *sah-lOO-tee*
**guide, guidebook** guida *goo-EE-dah*
**gums (teeth)** gengive *jayn-jEE-veh*

# H

**hair** capelli *kah-pAYl-lee;* **hair bleach** tintura per capelli *teen-tOO-rah pehr kah-pAYl-lee;* **hair dryer** asciugacapelli *ah-shee-OO-gah-kah-pAYl-lee;* fono *fOH-noh;* **hair lotion** frizione *free-tsee-OH-neh;* brillantina *breel-lahn-tEE-nah;* **hair rinse** cachet *kah-shEH;* **hair spray** lacca *lAH-kah*
**haircut** taglio di capelli *tAH-ly-ee-oh dee kah-pAYl-lee*

**hairdresser** parrucchiere per signore *pahr-roo-key-EH-reh pehr see-ny-OH-reh*
**hairpin** forcina *fohr-chEE-nah*
**hake (fish)** nasello *nah-sehl-loh*
**half** mezzo *mEH-tsoh*
**ham (cured)** prosciutto *proh-shee-OOt-toh*
**hamburger** hamburger
**hammer** martello *mahr-tEHl-loh*
**hand** mano *mAH-noh;* **Give me a hand** Mi dia una mano *mee dEE-ah OO-nah mAH-noh*
**handbag** borsetta *bohr-sAYt-tah*
**handhelds** palmari *pahl-mAH-ree*
**handicapped** disabile *dee-sAH-bee-leh*
**handkerchief** fazzoletto *fah-tsoh-lAYt-toh*
**handmade** fatto a mano *fAHt-toh ah mAH-noh*
**hanger** grucce *grOO-cheh;* attaccapanni *aht-tAH-kah-pAHn-nee*
**to happen** succedere *soo-chEH-deh-reh;* **What's happening?** Ma che cosa succede? *mah kay kOH-sah soo-chEH-deh*
**happy** lieto *lee-AY-toh*
**harbor** porto *pOHr-toh*
**hard** duro *dOO-roh*
**hard drive** disco rigido *dEEs-koh rEE-jee-doh*
**hardware store** ferramenta *fehr-rah-mEHn-tah*
**hare** lepre *lEH-preh*
**hat** cappello *kahp-pEHl-loh*
**to have** avere *ah-vAY-reh;* **to have to** dovere *doh-vAY-reh*
**hay fever** febbre del fieno *fEHb-breh dayl fee-AY-noh*
**hazelnuts** noccioline *noh-chee-oh-lEE-neh*
**he** egli *AY-ly-ee;* lui *lOO-ee*
**head** capo *kAH-poh;* **headache** mal di testa *mAHl dee tEHs-tah*
**headlights** fari abbaglianti *fAH-ree ahb-bah-ly-ee-AHn-tee*
**health** salute *sah-lOO-teh*
**to hear** sentire *sayn-tEE-reh*
**hearing aid** apparecchio acustico per l'udito *ahp-pah-rAY-key-oh ah-kOO-stee-koh pehr loo-dEE-toh*
**heart** cuore *koo-OH-reh;* **heart attack** attacco cardiaco *aht-tAHk-koh kahr-dEE-ah-koh*
**heat** calore *kah-lOH-reh*
**heaven** cielo *chee-EH-loh*
**heavy** pesante *pay-sAHn-teh*
**hectogram** ettogrammo *eht-toh-grAHm-moh*
**heel (foot)** tallone *tahl-lOH-neh;* **(shoe)** tacco *tAH-koh*
**Hello! (telephone)** Pronto! *prOHn-toh*
**to help** aiutare *ah-ee-oo-tAH-reh;* assistere *ahs-sEEs-tay-reh;* **Help!** Aiuto! *Ah-ee-OO-toh*
**her** lei *lEH-ee;* la *lah;* le *lay*
**here** qui *koo-EE;* qua *koo-AH;* **here is** ecco *EHk-koh*
**herring** aringa *ah-rEEn-gah*
**high** alto *AHl-toh*
**highway** autostrada *ah-oo-toh-strAH-dah*
**hill** collina *kohl-lEE-nah*
**him** lui *lOO-ee;* lo *loh*
**hip** anca *AHn-kah*
**to hold** tenere *tay-nAY-reh*
**home** casa *kAH-sah*
**hood (car)** cofano *kOH-fah-noh*
**horn (car)** clacson *klAH-ksohn*
**hors d'oeuvre** antipasto *ahn-tee-pAHs-toh*
**horse** cavallo *kah-vAHl-loh*
**hostel (youth)** ostello della gioventù *ohs-tEHl-loh dAYl-lah jee-oh-vehn-tOO*

**hot** caldo *kAHl-doh*
**hotel** hotel; albergo *ahl-bEHr-goh*
**hour** ora *OH-rah;* **at what time?** a che ora? *ah kay OH-rah*
**house** casa *kAH-sah;* **(to make) house calls** visitare i pazienti in casa *vee-see-tAH-reh ee pah-tzee-EHn-tee een kAH-sah*
**how** come *kOH-meh;* **How are you?** Come sta? *kOH-meh stAH;* **How far is it?** Quanto dista? *koo-AHn-toh dEEs-tah;* **How long does it take to get there?** Quanto tempo ci vuole per andarci? *koo-AHn-toh tEHm-poh chee voo-OH-leh pehr ahn-dAHr-chee;* **How much is it?** Quanto costa? *koo-AHn-toh kOHs-tah*
**however** però *peh-rOH*
**hundred** cento *chEHn-toh*
**hunger** fame *fAH-meh;* **I'm hungry** ho fame *OH fAH-meh*
**to hurry** sbrigarsi *sbree-gAHr-see;* **Hurry up!** Si sbrighi! *see sbrEE-ghee*
**to hurt** dolere *doh-lAY-reh;* far male *fahr mAH-leh*
**husband** marito *mah-rEE-toh*
**hydrofoil** aliscafo *ah-lee-skAH-phoh*
**hygienic** igienico *ee-jee-AY-nee-koh*

# I

**I** io *EE-oh*
**ice** ghiaccio *ghee-AH-chee-oh;* **ice cream** gelato *jeh-lAH-toh;* **ice cubes** cubetti di ghiaccio *koo-bAYt-tee dee ghee-AH-chee-oh;* **ice water** acqua ghiacciata *AH-koo-ah ghee-ah-chee-AH-tah*
**identification card** carta d'identità *kAHr-tah dee-dehn-tee-tAH*
**if** se *seh*
**ignition** accensione *ah-chehn-see-OH-neh*
**illness** malattia *mah-laht-tEE-ah*
**imagination** fantasia *fahn-tah-sEE-ah*
**important** importante *eem-pohr-tAHn-teh*
**impossible** impossibile *eem-pohs-sEE-bee-leh*
**in** in *een*
**included** incluso *een-klOO-soh*
**infection** infezione *een-feh-tsee-OH-neh*
**ink cartridge** cartuccia *kahr-tOO-chee-ah*
**inn** trattoria *traht-toh-rEE-ah*
**innocent** innocente *een-noh-chehn-teh*
**inside** dentro *dAYn-troh*
**insomnia** insonnia *een-sOHn-nee-ah*
**instead** invece *een-vAY-cheh*
**insulin** insulina *een-soo-lEE-nah*
**insurance** assicurazione *ahs-see-koo-rah-tsee-OH-neh*
**international** internazionale *een-tehr-nAH-tsee-oh-nAH-leh*
**interesting** interessante *een-teh-rehs-sAHn-teh*
**interpreter** interprete *een-TEHR-preh-teh*
**intersection** incrocio *een-krOH-chee-oh*
**into** in *een*
**iodine** iodio *ee-OH-dee-oh*
**iron** ferro *fEHr-roh*
**it** esso *AYs-soh;* essa *AYs-sah;* lo *loh;* la *lah*
**Italian** italiano *ee-tah-lee-AH-noh*

# J

**jack (car)** cricco *krEE-koh;* **(cards)** cavallo *kah-vAHl-loh*
**jacket** giacca *jee-AH-kah*
**jade** giada *jee-AH-dah*
**jam** marmellata *mahr-mehl-lAH-tah*
**January** gennaio *jehn-nAH-ee-oh*
**jar** vasetto *vah-sAYt-toh*
**jewel** gioiello *jee-oh-ee-EHl-loh;* **jeweler** gioielliere *jee-oh-ee-EHl-lee-EH-reh;* **jewelry shop** gioielleria *jee-oh-ee-EHl-leh-rEE-ah*
**Jewish** ebreo *ay-brEH-oh;* israeliano *ees-rah-eh-lee-AH-noh*
**juice** succo *sOO-koh*
**July** luglio *lOO-ly-ee-oh*
**June** giugno *jee-OO-ny-oh*

# K

**to keep** tenere *tay-nAY-reh;* **Keep off the grass** Non calpestare le aiuole *nohn kahl-pays-tAH-reh leh ah-ee-oo-OH-leh*
**key** chiave *key-AH-veh*
**kick** calcio *kAHl-chee-oh;* **kickoff** calcio d'inizio *kAHl-chee-oh dee-nEE-tsee-oh*
**kidney** rognone *roh-ny-OH-neh*
**kilogram** chilo *kEE-loh;* chilogrammo *key-loh-grAHm-moh*
**kilometer** chilometro *key-lOH-meh-troh*
**king** re *ray*
**to kiss** baciare *bah-chee-AH-reh*
**kiss** bacio *bAH-chee-oh*
**kitchen** cucina *koo-chEE-nah*
**knee** ginocchio *jee-nOH-key-oh*
**knife** coltello *kohl-tEHl-loh*
**knight (chess)** alfiere *ahl-fee-EH-reh*
**to know (facts)** sapere *sah-pAY-reh;* **to know (people)** conoscere *koh-nOH-shay-reh*

# L

**lace** merletto *mehr-lEHt-toh;* pizzo *pEE-tsoh*
**laces (shoe)** lacci *lAH-chee*
**lady** signora *see-ny-OH-rah;* **ladies' room** bagno per signora *bAH-ny-oh pehr see-ny-OH-rah*
**lake** lago *lAH-goh*
**lamb** agnello *ah-ny-EHl-loh*
**lamp** lampada *lAHm-pah-dah*
**land** terra *tEHr-rah*
**landscape** panorama *pah-noh-rAH-mah*
**language** lingua *lEEn-goo-ah*
**large** grande *grAHn-deh;* **larger** più grande *pee-OO grAHn-deh*
**to last** durare *doo-rAH-reh*
**last** ultimo *OOl-tee-moh*
**late** tardi *tAHr-dee;* **The train is late** Il treno è in ritardo *eel trEH-noh EH een ree-tAHr-doh;* **later** più tardi *pee-OO tAHr-dee;* **at the latest** al più tardi *ahl pee-OO tAHr-dee*
**lateness** ritardo *ree-tAHr-doh*
**to laugh** ridere *rEE-deh-reh*
**laundry** biancheria *bee-AHn-keh-rEE-ah*
**lawyer** avvocato *ahv-voh-kAH-toh*
**laxative** lassativo *lahs-sah-tEE-voh*
**to leak** perdere acqua *pEHr-deh-reh AH-koo-ah*
**to learn** apprendere *ahp-prAYn-deh-reh*
**leather** pelle *pEHl-leh*

**to leave** lasciare *lah-shee-AH-reh;* partire *pahr-tEE-reh*
**left** sinistro *see-nEEs-troh;* **to the left** a sinistra *ah see-nEEs-trah*
**leg** gamba *gAHm-bah*
**lemon** limone *lee-mOH-neh*
**lemonade** limonata *lee-moh-nAH-tah*
**lens** lente *lEHn-teh;* **contact lenses** lenti a contatto *lEHn-tee ah kohn-tAHt-toh*
**lentils** lenticchie *lehn-tEE-key-eh*
**letter** lettera *lAYt-teh-rah;* **airmail** via aerea *vEE-ah ah-EH-reh-ah;* **insured** assicurata *ahs-see-koo-rAH-tah;* **registered** raccomandata *rAH-koh-mahn-dAH-tah;* **special delivery** espresso *ehs-prehs-soh;* **with return receipt** con ricevuta di ritorno *kohn ree-chay-vOO-tah dee ree-tOHr-noh*
**lettuce** lattuga *laht-tOO-gah*
**library** biblioteca *bee-blee-oh-tEH-kah*
**to lie down** sdraiarsi *sdrah-eeAHr-see;* **Lie down!** Si sdrai! *see sdrAH-ee*
**life** vita *vEE-tah*
**lifeguard** bagnino *bah-ny-EE-noh*
**to lift** alzare *ahl-tsAH-reh*
**light (color)** chiaro *key-AH-roh;* **(electric)** luce *lOO-cheh;* **(weight)** leggero *lay-jEH-roh*
**lighter (cigarette)** accendino *ah-chayn-dEE-noh*
**to like** piacere *pee-ah-chAY-reh;* **I like it** Mi piace *mee pee-AH-cheh*
**lime** cedro *chAY-droh*
**line** linea *lEE-neh-ah*
**linen** biancheria *bee-AHn-keh-rEE-ah;* lino *lEE-noh*
**lips** labbra *lAHb-brah*
**lipstick** lipstick; rossetto *rohs-sAYt-toh*
**liqueur** liquore *lee-koo-OH-reh*
**list** elenco *eh-lEHn-koh;* lista *lEEs-tah*
**to listen** ascoltare *ah-skohl-tAH-reh*
**liter** litro *lEE-troh*
**little** piccolo *pEE-koh-loh*
**to live** abitare *ah-bee-tAH-reh*
**liver** fegato *fAY-gah-toh*
**to load** caricare *kah-ree-kAH-reh*
**loaf (of bread)** filone di pane *fee-lOH-neh dee pAH-neh*
**loan** prestito *prEHs-tee-toh*
**lobster** aragosta *ah-rah-gOHs-tah*
**local (train)** locale *loh-kAH-leh*
**long** lungo *lOOn-goh*
**to look** guardare *goo-AHr-dAH-reh;* **to take a look** dare un'occhiata *dAH-reh oo-noh-key-AH-tah;* **to look for** cercare *chayr-kAH-reh*
**to lose** perdere *pEHr-deh-reh*
**lotion** lozione *loh-tsee-OH-neh;* **suntan lotion** lozione per l'abbronzatura solare *loh-tsee-OH-neh pehr lahb-brohn-tsah-tOO-rah soh-lAH-reh*
**lots of** molto *mOHl-toh*
**loud** forte *fOHr-teh*
**love** amore *ah-mOH-reh*
**low** basso *bAHs-soh*
**lubricate** lubrificare *loo-bree-fee-kAH-reh*
**luck** fortuna *fohr-tOO-nah;* **Good luck!** Buona fortuna! *boo-OH-nah fohr-tOO-nah*
**luggage** bagaglio *bah-gAH-ly-oh;* **luggage rack** portabagagli *pohr-tah-bah-gAH-ly-ee*
**lump (swelling)** gonfiore *gohn-fee-OH-reh*
**lunch** pranzo *prAHn-tsoh*
**lung** polmone *pohl-mOH-neh*

# M

**machine** macchina *mAH-key-nah*
**mad** pazzo *pAH-tsoh*
**maid** cameriera *kah-meh-ree-AY-rah*
**mail** posta *pOHs-tah;* **mailbox** cassetta postale *kas-sAYt-tah pohs-tAH-leh*
**main** principale *preen-chee-pAH-leh*
**magazine** rivista *ree-vEEs-tah*
**magnetic phone card** scheda magnetica *skEH-dah mah-nyEH-tee-kah*
**major** maggiore *mah-jee-OH-reh*
**to make** fare *fAH-reh*
**malt** malto *mAHl-toh*
**man** uomo *oo-OH-moh*
**manager** direttore *dee-reht-tOH-reh*
**mango** mango *mAHn-goh*
**manicure** manicure *mah-nee-kOO-reh*
**many** molti *mOHl-tee*
**map** cartina *kahr-tEE-nah*
**March** marzo *mAHr-tsoh*
**margarine** margarina *mahr-gah-rEE-nah*
**market** mercato *mehr-kAH-toh*
**married** sposato *spoh-sAH-toh*
**Mass** Messa *mAYs-sah*
**massage** massaggio *mahs-sAH-jee-oh;* (hair) frizione *free-tsee-OH-neh*
**match** fiammifero *fee-ahm-mEE-feh-roh*
**to matter** importare *eem-pohr-tAH-reh;* **What's the matter with you?** Ma che cos'ha? *mah kay koh-sAH*
**mattress** materasso *mah-teh-rAHs-soh*
**May** maggio *mAH-jee-oh*
**maybe** forse *fOHr-seh*
**me** me *may*
**meal** pasto *pAHs-toh*
**to mean** significare *see-ny-ee-fee-kAH-reh;* **What does this mean?** Che cosa significa questo? *kay kOH-sah see-ny-EE-fee-kah koo-AYs-toh*
**means** mezzo *mEH-tsoh*
**measurements** misura *mee-sOO-rah*
**meat** carne *kAHr-neh*
**meatball** polpetta *pohl-pAYt-tah*
**mechanic** meccanico *meh-kAH-nee-koh*
**medical** medico *mEH-dee-koh*
**medicine** medicina *meh-dee-chEE-nah*
**to meet** incontrare *een-kohn-trAH-reh*
**melon** melone *may-lOH-neh*
**men** uomini *oo-OH-mee-nee;* **men's room** bagno per uomini (signore) *bAH-ny-oh pehr oo-OH-mee-nee (see-ny-OH-reh);* gabinetto *gah-bee-nAYt-toh*
**to mend** rammendare *rahm-mehn-dAH-reh*
**menu** menu *meh-nOO*
**message** messaggio *mehs-sAH-jee-oh*
**meter (length)** metro *mEH-troh*
**middle** mezzo *mEH-tsoh*
**midnight** mezzanotte *mEH-tsah-nOHt-teh*
**mileage** chilometraggio *key-loh-meh-trAH-jee-oh;* **unlimited mileage** chilometraggio illimitato *key-loh-meh-trAH-jee-oh EEl-lee-mee-tAH-toh*
**mild** leggero *lay-jEH-roh*
**milk** latte *lAHt-teh*
**million** milione *mee-lee-OH-neh*
**mind** mente *mEHn-teh;* **Do you mind?** Le dispiace? *lay dees-pee-AH-cheh*

**mineral water** acqua minerale *AH-koo-ah mee-neh-rAH-leh*
**minister** ministro *mee-nEEs-troh*
**minute** minuto *mee-nOO-toh*
**mirror** specchio *spEH-key-oh*
**Miss** signorina *see-ny-oh-rEE-nah*
**to miss** mancare *mahn-kAH-reh;* **I miss you** Mi manchi *mee mAHn-key*
**mistake** sbaglio *sbAH-ly-ee-oh*
**moment** momento *moh-mEHn-toh*
**Monday** lunedì *loo-nay-dEE*
**money** denaro *day-nAH-roh;* soldi *sOHl-dee;* **money order** vaglia *vAH-ly-ee-ah*
**month** mese *mAY-seh*
**moped** motorino *moh-toh-rEE-noh*
**more** più *pee-OO*
**morning** mattino *maht-tEE-noh*
**mosque** moschea *mohs-kEH-ah*
**mother** madre *mAH-dreh*
**motor** motore *moh-tOH-reh;* **motor coach** autopullman *AHoo-toh-pOOl-mahn;* **motor scooter** lambretta *lahm-brAYt-tah;* vespa *vEHs-pah*
**motorcycle** moto *mOH-toh*
**mountain** montagna *mohn-tAH-ny-ah*
**moustache** baffi *bAHf-fee*
**mouth** bocca *bOH-kah;* **mouthwash** disinfettante per la bocca *dee-seen-feht-tAHn-teh pehr lah bOH-kah*
**to move** muovere *moo-OH-vay-reh*
**movie** cinema *chEE-neh-mah;* **movie camera** cinepresa *chee-neh-prAY-sah*
**Mr.** signore *see-ny-OH-reh*
**Mrs.** signora *see-ny-OH-rah*
**much** molto *mOHl-toh;* **How much is it?** Quanto costa? *koo-AHn-toh kOHs-tah*
**museum** museo *moo-sEH-oh*
**mussels** cozze *kOH-tseh*
**music** musica *mOO-see-kah*
**must** dovere *doh-vAY-reh;* **I must go** Debbo andarmene *dAYb-boh ahn-dAHr-meh-neh*
**mustard** senape *sEH-nah-peh;* mostarda *moh-stAHr-dah*
**mutton** montone *mohn-tOH-neh*
**my** mio *mEE-oh;* miei *mee-AY-ee;* mia *mEE-ah;* mie *mEE-eh*
**mystery** mistero *mees-tEH-roh;* **It's a mystery!** È un giallo! *EH oon jee-AHl-loh*

# N

**nail** unghia *OOn-ghee-ah;* **nail clippers** tagliaunghie *tAH-ly-ee-ah-OOn-ghee-eh;* **nail polish** smalto per le unghie *smAHl-toh pehr leh OOn-ghee-eh;* **nail polish remover** acetone *ah-chay-tOH-neh*
**name** nome *nOH-meh;* **last name** cognome *koh-ny-OH-meh;* **My name is . . .** Mi chiamo . . . *mee key-AH-moh*
**napkin** tovagliolo *toh-vah-ly-ee-OH-loh;* **sanitary napkins** assorbenti igienici *ahs-sohr-bEHn-tee ee-jee-EH-nee-chee*
**nationality** nazionalità *nah-tsee-oh-nah-lee-tAH*
**near** accanto *ah-kAHn-toh*
**necessary** necessario *neh-chehs-sAH-ree-oh*
**necklace** catenina *kah-tay-nEE-nah;* collana *kohl-lAH-nah;* monile *moh-nEE-leh*
**necktie** cravatta *krah-vAHt-tah*
**to need** avere bisogno di *ah-vAY-reh bee-sOH-ny-oh dee;* **I need help** Ho bisogno d'aiuto *oh bee-sOH-ny-oh dah-eeOO-toh*
**needle** ago *AH-goh*

**new** nuovo *noo-OH-voh*
**newspaper** giornale *jee-ohr-nAH-leh*
**newsstand** edicola *ay-dEE-koh-lah;* giornalaio *jee-ohr-nah-lAH-ee-oh*
**next** prossimo *PROh-see-moh*
**next to** accanto *ah-kAHn-toh*
**nightclub** night club *nAH-eet klOOb*
**nine** nove *nOH-veh*
**nineteen** diciannove *dee-chee-ahn-nOH-veh*
**ninety** novanta *noh-vAHn-tah*
**ninth** nono *nOH-noh*
**Nonsense!** Sciocchezze! *shee-oh-kAY-tseh;* ma che! *mah kAY*
**noon** mezzogiorno *mEH-tsoh-jee-OHr-noh*
**normal** normale *nohr-mAH-leh*
**north** nord *nord*
**nose** naso *nAH-soh*
**not** non *nohn*
**notebook** taccuino *tah-koo-EE-noh;* block-notes *blOHk-nOH-tays*
**nothing** niente *nee-EHn-tay*
**now** adesso *ah-dEHs-soh;* ora *OH-rah*
**nuisance** seccatura *say-kah-tOO-rah*
**number** numero *nOO-meh-roh;* **numbered** numerato *noo-meh-rAH-toh*
**nut (fruit)** noce *nOH-chay;* **(mechanical)** dado *dAH-doh*
**nylon** nylon *nAH-ee-lohn*

# O

**to observe** osservare *ohs-sehr-vAH-reh*
**to obstruct** ostruire *ohs-troo-EE-reh*
**to obtain** ottenere *oht-tay-nAY-reh*
**occupied** occupato *oh-koo-pAH-toh*
**ocean** oceano *oh-chEH-ah-noh*
**October** ottobre *oht-tOH-breh*
**octopus** polipo *pOH-lee-poh*
**oculist** oculista *oh-koo-lEEs-tah*
**of** di *dee*
**office** ufficio *oof-fEE-chee-oh*
**often** spesso *spAYs-soh*
**oil** olio *OH-lee-oh*
**omelet** frittata *freet-tAH-tah*
**on** sopra *sOH-prah;* su *soo*
**once** una volta *OO-nah vOHl-tah*
**one** un *oon;* uno *OO-noh;* una *OO-nah;* un' *oon;* **one way** senso unico *sEHn-soh OO-nee-koh*
**onion** cipolla *chee-pOHl-lah*
**only** solamente *soh-lah-mEHn-teh*
**onyx** onice *OH-nee-cheh*
**to open** aprire *ah-prEE-reh*
**open** aperto *ah-pEHr-toh*
**opera** opera *OH-peh-rah;* **operetta** operetta *oh-peh-rAYt-tah*
**opposite** contrario *kohn-trAH-ree-oh*
**optician** ottico *OHt-tee-koh*
**or** o *oh*
**orange (fruit)** arancia *ah-rAHn-chee-ah;* **(tree)** arancio *ah-rAHn-chee-oh*
**orangeade** aranciata *ah-rahn-chee-AH-tah*
**orchestra** orchestra *ohr-kEHs-trah;* **(group) section** platea *plah-tEH-ah*
**to order** ordinare *ohr-dee-nAH-reh*
**other** altro *AHl-troh*
**Ouch!** Ahi! *AHee*
**outcome** risultato *ree-sool-tAH-toh*

**outside** fuori *foo-OH-ree*
**oven** forno *fOHr-noh*
**overcoat** soprabito *soh-prAH-bee-toh*
**to overheat** surriscaldare *soor-rEEs-kahl-dAH-reh*
**own** proprio *prOH-pree-oh*
**oyster** ostrica *OHs-tree-kah*

# P

**package** pacchetto *pah-kAYt-toh*
**pair** paio *pAH-ee-oh*
**palace** palazzo *pah-lAH-tsoh*
**panorama** panorama *pah-noh-rAH-mah*
**panties** mutandine *moo-tahn-dEE-neh*
**pants** pantaloni *pahn-tah-lOII-nee*
**panty hose** collant *kOHl-lahnt*
**paper** carta *kAHr-tah*
**parcel** pacco *pAH-koh*
**to park** parcheggiare *pahr-kay-jee-AH-reh;* **no parking** divieto di sosta *dee-vee-AY-toh dee sOHs-tah*
**park (garden)** parco *pAHr-koh*
**partridge** pernice *payr-nEE-cheh*
**parts (car)** pezzi di ricambio *pEH-tsee dee ree-kAHm-bee-oh*
**to pass** passare *pahs-sAH-reh*
**passport** passaporto *pahs-sah-pOHr-toh*
**pastry** pasticceria *pahs-tee-cheh-rEE-ah*
**pathway** sentiero *sayn-tee-AY-roh*
**to pay** pagare *pah-gAH-reh*
**peas** piselli *pee-sEHl-lee*
**peach** pesca *pAYs-kah*
**pear** pera *pAY-rah*
**pedestrian** pedone *peh-dOH-neh*
**pen** penna *pAYn-nah;* **ballpoint pen** penna a sfera *pAYh-nah ah sfEH-rah*
**pencil** matita *mah-tEE-tah;* **pencil sharpener** temperamatite *tEHm-peh-rah-mah-tEE-teh*
**penicillin** penicillina *pay-nee-cheel-lEE-nah*
**perfume** profumo *proh-fOO-moh*
**perhaps** forse *fOHr-seh*
**peripherals** periferiche *peh-ree-fEE-ree-keh*
**period** periodo *payr-EEoh-doh*
**to permit** permettere *pehr-mEHt-teh-reh*
**permit (license)** patente *pah-tEHn-teh*
**pharmacy** farmacia *fahr-mah-chEE-ah*
**pheasant** fagiano *fah-jee-AH-noh*
**phone card** scheda telefonica *skEH-dah teh-leh-phOH-nee-kah*
**to photograph** fotografare *foh-toh-grah-fAH-reh*
**photograph (picture)** fotografia *foh-toh-grah-fEE-ah*
**piece** pezzo *pEH-tsoh*
**pig (pork)** maiale *mah-ee-AH-leh*
**pill** pillola *pEEl-loh-lah*
**pillow** cuscino *koo-shEE-noh*
**pin** spilla *spEEl-lah*
**pineapple** ananasso *ah-nah-nAHs-soh*
**place** posto *pOHs-toh;* località *loh-kah-lee-tAH*
**plate** piatto *pee-AHt-toh*
**plant** pianta *pee-AHn-tah*
**plastic** plastica *plAHs-tee-kah*
**platform** piattaforma *pee-AHt-tah-fOHr-mah*
**platinum** platino *plAH-tee-noh*

**to play** giocare *jee-OH-kAH-reh*
**playground** zona giochi *tsOH-nah jee-OH-key*
**please** per favore *pehr fah-vOH-reh;* per piacere *pehr pee-ah-chAY-reh*
**pliers** pinze *pEEn-tseh*
**plug (electric)** spina per la corrente *spEE-nah pehr lah kohr-rEHn-teh;* **spark plug** candela *kahn-dAY-lah*
**plum** susina *soo-sEE-nah;* prugna *prOO-ny-ah*
**poker** poker *pOH-kehr*
**police** polizia *poh-lee-tsEE-ah;* **police station** stazione di polizia *stah-tsee-OH-neh dee poh-lee-tsEE-ah;* Commissariato *kOHm-mees-sah-ree-AH-toh;* caserma dei carabinieri *kah-sEHr-mah dAY-ee kah-rah-bee-nee-AY-ree*
**pond** stagno *stAH-ny-oh*
**pork** maiale *mah-ee-AH-leh*
**portable** portatile *pohr-tAH-tee-leh*
**porter** portabagagli *pOHr-tah-bah-gAH-ly-ee*
**portion** porzione *pohr-tsee-OH-nay*
**possible** possibile *pohs-sEE-bee-leh*
**post office** ufficio postale *oof-fEE-chee-oh pohs-tAH-leh*
**postage** affrancatura *ahf-frahn-kah-tOO-rah*
**postcard** cartolina postale *kahr-toh-lEE-nah pohs-tAH-leh;* **picture postcard** cartolina illustrata *kahr-toh-lEE-nah EEl-loos-trAH-tah*
**poster** poster; manifesto *mah-nee-fEHs-toh*
**potable** potabile *poh-tAH-bee-leh*
**potato** patata *pah-tAH-tah*
**power supply** alimentatore *al-lee-mehn-tah-tOH-reh*
**prayer** preghiera *pray-ghee-EH-rah*
**to prefer** preferire *preh-fay-rEE-reh*
**pregnant** incinta *een-chEEn-tah*
**to prepare** preparare *preh-pah-rAH-reh*
**prescription** ricetta *ree-chEHt-tah*
**to present** presentare *preh-sayn-tAH-reh*
**present (gift)** regalo *ray-gAH-loh*
**price** prezzo *prEH-tsoh*
**priest** prete *prEH-teh*
**print (photo)** copia *kOH-pee-ah*
**private** privato *pree-vAH-toh*
**profession** professione *proh-fehs-see-OH-neh*
**prophylactics** profilattici *proh-fee-lAHt-tee-chee;* preservativi *preh-sehr-vah-tEE-vee*
**program** programma *proh-grAHm-mah*
**progressive lenses** lenti progressive *lEHn-tee proh-grehs-sEE-veh*
**Protestant** protestante *proh-teh-stAHn-teh*
**to prove** provare *pro-vAH-reh*
**pudding** budino *boo-dEE-noh*
**to pull** tirare *tee-rAH-reh*
**pump** pompa *pOHm-pah;* **fuel pump** pompa della benzina *pOHm-pah dAYl-lah behn-tsEE-nah*
**to purchase** comprare *kohm-prAH-reh*
**purse** borsetta *bohr-sAYt-tah*
**to push** spingere *spEEn-jay-reh*
**to put** mettere *mAYt-tay-reh*

# Q

**quarter** quarto *koo-AHr-toh*
**queen (cards)** donna *dOHn-nah*
**question** domanda *doh-mAHn-dah*
**quick** presto *prEHs-toh*

# R

**rabbi** rabbino *rahb-bEE-noh*
**rabbit** coniglio *koh-nEE-ly-ee-oh*
**racetrack** ippodromo *eep-pOH-droh-moh*
**racquet** racchetta *rah-kAYt-tah*
**radiator (car)** radiatore *rah-dee-ah-tOH-reh*
**radish** ravanello *rah-vah-nEHl-loh*
**railroad** ferrovia *fehr-roh-vEE-ah;* **railroad station** stazione ferroviaria *stah-tsee-OH-neh fEHr-ro-vee-AH-ree-ah*
**to rain** piovere *pee-OH-veh-reh*
**raincoat** impermeabile *eem-pehr-may-AH-bee-leh*
**ramp** rampa *rAHm-pah*
**raspberry** lampone *lahm-pOH-neh*
**rate** tariffa *tah-rEEf-fah*
**razor** rasoio *rah-sOH-ee-oh;* **razor blades** lamette *lah-mAYt-teh*
**to reach** raggiungere *rah-jee-OOn-jay-reh;* arrivare *ahr-ree-vAH-reh*
**to read** leggere *lEH-jeh-reh*
**ready** pronto *prOHn-toh*
**receipt** ricevuta *ree-chay-vOO-tah*
**to receive** ricevere *ree-chAY-vay-reh*
**receiver (telephone)** destinatario *days-tee-nah-tAH-ree-oh*
**to recommend** consigliare *kohn-see-ly-ee-AH-reh;* raccomandare *rAH-koh-mahn-dAH-reh*
**record (phonograph)** disco *dEEs-koh;* **record player** giradischi *jEE-rah-dEEs-kee*
**reduced** ridotto *ree-dOHt-toh*
**red** rosso *rOHs-soh*
**referee** arbitro *AHr-bee-troh*
**refund** rimborso *reem-bOHr-soh*
**religious** religioso *ray-lee-jee-OH-soh*
**to remain** restare *rays-tAH-reh*
**to rent (car)** noleggiare *noh-lay-jee-AH-reh;* **(house)** affittare *ahf-feet-tAH-reh*
**to repair** aggiustare *ah-jee-oos-tAH-reh;* riparare *ree-pah-rAH-reh*
**repair shop** officina meccanica *ohf-fee-chEE-nah may-kAH-nee-kah*
**to repeat** ripetere *ree-pEH-teh-reh*
**reservation** prenotazione *preh-noh-tah-tsee-OH-neh*
**reserved** riservato *ree-sehr-vAH-toh;* prenotato *preh-noh-tAH-toh*
**to reside** risiedere *ree-see-AY-deh-reh*
**to rest** riposare *ree-poh-sAH-reh*
**restroom** gabinetto *gah-bee-nAYt-toh;* bagno *bAH-ny-oh;* toilette *too-AH-lEHt*
**restaurant** ristorante *rEEs-toh-rAHn-teh*
**result** risultato *ree-sool-tAH-toh*
**to return** ritornare *ree-tohr-nAH-reh*
**rice** riso *rEE-soh*

**refund** rimborso *reem-bOHr-soh*
**right** destro *dEHs-troh;* **That's all right** Va bene *vah bEH-neh;* **Right away** Subito *sOO-bee-toh*
**ring** anello *ah-nEHl-loh*
**river** fiume *fee-OO-meh*
**road** via *vEE-ah;* strada *strAH-dah;* **road map** cartina stradale *kahr-tEE-nah strah-dAH-leh*
**roadway** autostrada *ow-toh-strAH-dah*
**roast** arrosto *ahr-rOHs-toh*
**robe** accappatoio *ah-kAHp-pah-tOH-ee-oh*
**roll (film)** rullino *rool-lEE-noh*
**room** camera *kAH-meh-rah;* **bedroom** camera da letto *kAH-meh-rah dah lEHt-toh*
**rose** rosa *rOH-sah*
**rouge** rossetto *rohs-sAYt-toh*
**row (theater)** fila *fEE-lah*
**ruler** riga *rEE-gah*
**to run** correre *kOHr-ray-reh;* **running water** acqua corrente *ah-koo-ah kohr-rEHn-tay*
**rye** segala *sAY-gah-lah*

# S

**saccharin** saccarina *sah-kah-rEE-nah;* dolcificante *dohl-chee-fee-kAHn-teh*
**salad** insalata *een-sah-lAH-tah*
**salami** salame *sah-lAH-meh*
**sale** svendita *svAYn-dee-tah*
**salmon** salmone *sahl-mOH-neh*
**salt** sale *sAH-leh;* **salty** salato *sah-lAH-toh*
**same** stesso *stAYs-soh*
**sand** sabbia *sAHb-bee-ah*
**sandwich** panino (imbottito) *pah-nEE-noh (eem-boht-tEE-toh)*
**sapphire** zaffiro *tsahf-fEE-roh*
**sardine** sardina *sahr-dEE-nah*
**Saturday** sabato *sAH-bah-toh*
**sauce** salsa *sAHl-sah*
**saucer** piattino *pee-aht-tEE-noh*
**to say** dire *dEE-reh*
**schedule** orario *oh-rAH-ree-oh;* **on schedule** in orario *een oh-rAH-ree-oh*
**science fiction** fantascienza *fAHn-tah-shee-EHn-tsah*
**scissors** forbici *fOHr-bee-chee*
**score** punteggio *poon-tAY-jee-oh*
**Scotch tape** nastro adesivo *nAHs-troh ah-day-sEE-voh*
**Scram!** Si tolga dai piedi! *see tOH-lgah dAHee pee-EH-dee*
**screw** vite *vEE-teh*
**sea** mare *mAH-reh*
**seafood** frutti di mare *frOOt-tee dee mAH-reh*
**seasickness** mal di mare *mAHl dee mAH-reh*
**second** secondo *say-kOHn-doh*
**sedative** sedativo *say-dah-tEE-voh*
**to see** vedere *vay-dAY-reh*
**seeing-eye dog** cane da guida *kAH-neh dah goo-EE-da*
**selection** selezione *say-leh-tsee-OH-neh*
**to sell** vendere *vAYn-day-reh*
**to send** mandare *mahn-dAH-reh;* spedire *spay-dEE-reh*
**September** settembre *seht-tEHm-breh*
**series** serie *sEH-ree-eh*
**to serve** servire *sayr-vEE-reh*
**service** servizio *sehr-vEE-tsee-oh*
**seven** sette *sEHt-teh;* **seven hundred** settecento *sEHt-teh-chEHn-toh*
**seventeen** diciassette *dEE-chee-ahs-sEHt-teh*
**seventh** settimo *sEHt-tee-moh*

**seventy** settanta *sEHt-tAHn-tah*
**to sew** cucire *koo-chEE-reh*
**shade** ombra *OHm-brah;* **(window)** tendina *tehn-dEE-nah*
**shampoo** shampoo *shAHm-poh*
**to shave oneself** farsi la barba *fAHr-see lah bAHr-bah;* **aftershave** dopobarba *dOH-poh-bAHr-bah*
**shaving cream** crema per la barba *krEH-mah pehr lah bAHr-bah*
**she** lei *lEH-ee;* ella *AYl-lah;* essa *AYs-sah*
**sherry** sherry
**to shine shoes** lucidare le scarpe *loo-chee-dAH-reh leh skAHr-peh*
**ship** nave *nAH-veh*
**shirt** camicia *kah-mEE-chee-ah;* **man's shirt** camicia da uomo *kah-mEE-chee-ah dah oo-OH-moh*
**shoe** scarpa *skAHr-pah;* **shoe store** calzaturificio *kahl-tsah-too-ree-fEE-chee-oh*
**shoelaces** lacci per le scarpe *lAH-chee pehr leh skAHr-peh*
**shoemaker** calzolaio *kahl-tsoh-lAH-ee-oh*
**shop** negozio *neh-gOH-tsee-oh;* **shop window** vetrina *vay-trEE-nah*
**short** corto *kOHr-toh;* **(person)** basso(a) *bAHs-soh(ah);* **short story** novella *noh-vEHl-lah*
**shorts** pantaloncini *pahn-tah-lohn-chEE-nee*
**shoulder** spalla *spAHl-lah*
**to show** indicare *een-dee-kAH-reh*
**shower** doccia *dOH-chee-ah*
**shrimps** gamberetti *gahm-bay-rAYt-tee*
**to shuffle** mischiare *mees-key-AH-reh*
**Shut up!** Zitto! *tsEEt-toh*
**sick** malato *mah-lAH-toh*
**side (body)** fianco *fee-AHn-koh*
**sidewalk** marciapiede *mAHr-chee-ah-pee-EH-deh*
**to sign** firmare *feer-mAH-reh*
**signature** firma *fEEr-mah*
**silence** silenzio *see-lEHn-tsee-oh*
**silk** seta *sAY-tah*
**silly** sciocco *shee-OH-koh;* **silliness** sciocchezza *shee-oh-kAH-tsah*
**silver** argento *ahr-jEHn-toh*
**sin** peccato *peh-kAH-toh*
**since** siccome *see-kOHm-eh*
**to sing** cantare *kahn-tAH-reh*
**single (room)** camera a un letto *kAH-may-rah ah oon lEHt-toh*
**sister** sorella *soh-rEHl-lah*
**to sit** sedersi *say-dAYr-see*
**site** località *loh-kah-lee-tAH*
**six** sei *sEH-ee;* **six hundred** seicento *sEH-ee-chEHn-toh*
**sixteen** sedici *sAY-dee-chee*
**sixth** sesto *sEHs-toh*
**sixty** sessanta *says-sAHn-tah*
**size** misura *mee-sOO-rah;* taglia *tAH-ly-ee-ah*
**to ski** sciare *shee-AH-reh*
**ski (boots)** scarponi da sci *skahr-pOH-nee dah shEE;* **(lifts)** sciovie *shee-oh-vEE-eh;* **(slopes)** piste (per sciare) *pEEs-teh (pehr shee-AH-reh)*
**skiing (water)** sci acquatico *shEE ah-koo-AH-tee-koh*
**skin** pelle *pEHl-leh*
**skirt** gonna *gOHn-nah*
**to sleep** dormire *dohr-mEE-reh*
**sleeping car (train)** vagone letto *vah-gOH-neh lEHt-toh*

**sleeve** manica *mAH-nee-kah*
**slice** fetta *fAYt-tah;* **sliced** affettato *ahf-fayt-tAH-toh*
**slip** sottoveste *soht-toh-vEHs-teh*
**slippers** pantofole *pahn-tOH-foh-leh;* ciabatte *chee-ah-bAHt-teh*
**slowly** lentamente *layn-tah-mEHn-teh;* piano *pee-AH-noh*
**small** piccolo *pEE-koh-loh;* **smaller** più piccolo *pee-OO pEE-koh-loh*
**to smile** sorridere *sohr-rEE-day-reh;* fare un sorriso *fAH-reh oon sohr-rEE-soh;* **Smile!** Sorrida! *sohr-rEE-dah*
**to smoke** fumare *foo-mAH-reh;* **no smoking** vietato fumare *vee-ay-tAH-toh foo-mAH-reh*
**smoker** fumatore *foo-mah-tOH-reh*
**to snatch** scippare *sheep-pAH-reh*
**to snow** nevicare *nay-vee-kAH-reh*
**snow** neve *nAY-veh*
**so** cosi *koh-sEE*
**soap** sapone *sah-pOH-neh;* saponetta *sah-poh-nAYt-tah*
**soccer** calcio *kAHl-chee-oh;* **soccer game** partita di calcio *pahr-tEE-tah dee kAHl-chee-oh*
**socks** calzini *kahl-tsEE-nee;* calzettini *kahl-tsayt-tEE-nee*
**soft drink** bibita analcolica *bEE-bee-tah ah-nahl-koh-lEE-kah*
**sole (fish)** sogliola *sOH-ly-ee-oh-lah*
**soles (shoes)** suole *soo-OH-leh;* **half-soles** mezze suole *mEH-tseh soo-OH-leh*
**solid color** tinta unita *tEEn-tah oo-nEE-tah*
**some** alcuni *ahl-kOO-nee;* qualche *koo-AHl-keh;* **someone** qualcuno *koo-ahl-kOO-noh;* **something** qualche cosa *koo-AHl-keh kOH-sah;* **sometimes** qualche volta *koo-AHl-keh vOHl-tah*
**son** figlio *fEE-ly-ee-oh*
**soon** presto *prEHs-toh;* **as soon as possible** appena possibile *ahp-pAY-nah pohs-sEE-bee-leh*
**soprano** soprano
**sorry (to be sorry)** dispiacere *dees-pee-ah-chAY-reh;* **I'm sorry** Mi dispiace *mee dees-pee-AH-cheh*
**soup** minestra *mee-nEHs-trah*
**south** sud *sood*
**spades (cards)** picche *pEE-keh*
**spare tire** la ruota di scorta *lah roo-OH-tah dee skOHr-tah*
**spark plug** candela *kahn-dAY-lah*
**sparkling wine** spumante *spoo-mAHn-teh*
**to speak** parlare *pahr-lAH-reh*
**special** speciale *spay-chee-AH-leh*
**specialty** specialità *spEH-chee-ah-lee-tAH*
**to spend (money)** spendere *spEHn-deh-reh;* **(time)** passare *pahs-sAH-reh*
**spicy** piccante *peek-kAHn-teh*
**spinach** spinaci *spee-nAH-chee*
**sponge** spugna *spOO-ny-ah*
**spoon** cucchiaio *koo-key-AH-ee-oh;* **teaspoon** cucchiaino *koo-key-ah-EE-noh*
**sports car** macchina sportiva *mAH-key-nah spohr-tEE-vah*
**spot** posto *pOHs-toh*
**to sprain** slogare *sloh-gAH-reh*
**sprain (injury)** slogatura *sloh-gah-tOO-rah*

**spring** molla *mOHl-lah;* **(season)** primavera *pree-mah-vEH-rah*
**squab (pigeon)** piccioncino *pEE-chee-ohn-chEE-noh*
**square** piazza *pee-AH-tsah*
**squid** calamari *kah-lah-mAH-ree*
**stadium** stadio *stAH-dee-oh*
**stairs** scale *skAH-leh*
**stamp** francobollo *frahn-koh-bOHl-loh*
**to stand** stare in piedi *stAH-reh een pee-EH-dee*
**to start** cominciare *koh-meen-chee-AH-reh;* **(car)** avviare *ahv-vee-AH-reh*
**station** stazione *stah-tsee-OHn-neh*
**to steal** rubare *roo-bAH-reh*
**steel** acciaio *ah-chee-AH-ee-oh;* **stainless steel** acciaio inossidabile *ah-chee-AH-ee-oh een-OHs-see-dAH-bee-lah*
**steering wheel** volante *voh-lAHn-teh*
**still** ancora *ahn-kOH-rah*
**stocking** calza *kAHl-tsah*
**stomach** stomaco *stOH-mah-coh*
**stone** pietra *pee-EH-trah;* **precious stone** pietra preziosa *pee-EH-trah pray-tsee-OH-sah*
**to stop** fermare *fayr-mAH-reh*
**stop** fermata *fayr-mAH-tah;* **bus stop** fermata dell'autobus *fayr-mAH-tah dayl-lAH-oo-toh-boos*
**store** negozio *neh-gOH-tsee-oh*
**stories** racconti *rah-kOHn-tee;* storie *stOH-ree-eh*
**straight** diritto *dee-rEEt-toh*
**stream** ruscello *roo-shEHl-loh*
**street** strada *strAH-dah;* via *vEE-ah*
**streetcar** tram *trAHm;* tranvai *trahn-vAH-ee*
**string beans** fagiolini *fah-jee-oh-lEE-nee*
**strong** forte *fOHr-teh;* **stronger** più forte *pee-OO fOHr-teh*
**stuck** bloccato *bloh-kAH-toh*
**stupid** stupido *stOO-pee-doh;* **Don't be stupid** Non fare lo stupido *nohn fAH-reh loh stOO-pee-doh*
**subtitle** sottotitolo *sOHt-toh-tEE-toh-loh*
**subway** metropolitana *mEH-troh-poh-lee-tAH-nah*
**suede (leather)** renna *rAYn-nah;* pelle scamosciata *pEHl-lay skah-moh-shee-AH-tah*
**sugar** zucchero *tsOO-keh-roh;* **sugar substitute** dolcificante *dohl-chee-fee-kAHn-teh*
**suit** abito *AH-bee-toh;* vestito *vays-tEE-toh*
**suitcase** valigia *vah-lEE-jee-ah*
**summer** estate *ehs-tAH-teh*
**sun** sole *sOH-leh*
**sunburn** scottatura solare *skoht-tah-tOO-rah soh-lAH-reh*
**Sunday** domenica *doh-mAY-nee-kah*
**sunglasses** occhiali da sole *oh-key-AH-lee dah sOH-leh*
**supermarket** supermercato *sOO-pehr-mehr-kAH-toh*
**supper** cena *chAY-nah;* **to have supper** cenare *chay-nAH-reh*
**sweater** maglia *mAH-ly-ah*
**sweet** dolce *dOHl-cheh*
**swelling** gonfiore *gohn-fee-OH-reh*
**to swim** nuotare *nOO-oh-tAH-reh*
**swimming pool** piscina *pee-shEE-nah;* **(indoor)** piscina coperta *pee-shEE-nah koh-pEHr-tah;* **(outdoor)**

piscina scoperta *pee-shEE-nah skoh-pEHr-tah*

**switch** interruttore *een-tehr-root-tOH-reh*

**swollen** gonfio *gOHn-fee-oh*

**synagogue** sinagoga *see-nah-gOH-gah*

**synthetic** poliestere *poh-lee-EHs-tay-reh;* sintetico *seen-tEH-tee-koh*

**syrup** sciroppo *shee-rOHp-poh*

**system** sistema *sees-tEH-mah*

# T

**table** tavola *tAH-voh-lah*

**tablecloth** tovaglia *toh-vAH-lyee-ah*

**tablet** pasticca *pahs-tEE-kah*

**tag** cartellino *kahr-tayl-lEE-noh*

**tailor** sarto *sAHr-toh*

**to take** prendere *prayn-dAY-reh;* **(to a place)** portare *pohr-tAH-reh;* **to take off (airplane)** decollare *day-kohl-lAH-reh*

**taken (occupied)** occupato *oh-koo-pAH-toh*

**talcum powder** talco *tAHl-koh*

**tall** alto *AHl-toh*

**to talk** parlare *pahr-lAH-reh*

**tampons** tamponi igienici *tahm-pOH-nee EE-jee-EH-nee-chee*

**tangerine** mandarino *mahn-dah-rEE-noh*

**tariff** tariffa *tah-rEEf-fah*

**tavern** trattoria *traht-toh-rEE-ah*

**tax** tassa *tAHs-sah;* imposta *eem-pOH-stah*

**taxi** tassì *tahs-sEE*

**tea** tè *tEH*

**team** squadra *skoo-AH-drah*

**to telephone** telefonare *teh-leh-foh-nAH-reh;* **I want to make a phone call** Voglio fare una telefonata *vOH-ly-ee-oh fAH-reh OO-nah teh-leh-foh-nAH-tah;* **local call** urbana *oor-bAH-nah;* **long-distance** in teleselezione, *een teh-leh-say-leh-tsee-OH-neh;* interurbana *een-tayr-oor-bAH-nah;* **person-to-person** con preavviso *kohn prEH-ahv-vEE-soh;* **reverse-charge** riversibile *ree-vehr-sEE-bee-leh*

**telephone** telefono *teh-lEH-foh-noh;* **public telephone** telefono pubblico *teh-lEH-foh-noh pOOb-blee-koh*

**television** televisione *teh-leh-vee-see-OH-neh*

**to tell** dire *dEE-reh;* **Tell me** Mi dica *mee dEE-kah*

**temperature** temperature *tehm-peh-rah-tOO-rah*

**temporarily** provvisoriamente *prohv-vee-sOH-ree-ah-mEHn-teh*

**ten** dieci *dee-EH-chee*

**tennis** tennis *tEHn-nees*

**tenor** tenore *teh-nOH-reh*

**tenth** decimo *dEH-chee-moh*

**terminal (bus, tram, auto)** capolinea *kah-poh-lEE-neh-ah*

**terrace** terrazza *tehr-rAH-tsah*

**terrible** terribile *tehr-rEE-bee-leh*

**thanks** grazie *grAH-tsee-eh;* **Thank you very much** Molte grazie *mOHl-teh grAH-tsee-eh*

**that** che *kay;* **that one** quello *koo-AYl-loh*

**the** il *eel;* lo *loh;* la *lah;* i *ee;* gli *ly-ee;* le *leh*

**theater** teatro *teh-AH-troh*

**their** loro *lOH-roh*

**them** li *lee;* le *lay;* loro *lOH-roh*

**there** lì *lEE;* là *lAH;* **there are** ci sono *chee sOH-noh;* **there is** c'è *chEH*

**thermometer** termometro *tehr-mOH-meh-troh*
**these** questi *koo-AYs-tee;* queste *koo-AYs-teh*
**they** essi *AYs-see;* esse *AYs-say;* loro *lOH-roh*
**thief** ladro *lAH-droh*
**thigh** coscia *kOH-shee-ah*
**thin** sottile *soht-tEE-leh*
**thing** cosa *kOH-sah*
**to think** pensare *pehn-sAH-reh*
**third** terzo *tEHr-tsoh*
**thirsty** assetato *ahs-say-tAH-toh*
**thirteen** tredici *trAY-dee-chee*
**thirty** trenta *trEHn-tah*
**this** questo *koo-AYs-toh;* questa *koo-AYs-tah*
**those** quelli *koo-AYl-lee;* quelle *koo-AYl-leh*
**thousand** mille *mEEl-leh*
**thread** filo *fEE-loh*
**three** tre *tray*
**throat** gola *gOH-lah*
**thumb** pollice *pOHl-lee-cheh*
**Thursday** giovedì *jee-oh-vay-dEE*
**ticket** biglietto *bee-ly-ee-AYt-toh;* **a one-way ticket** un biglietto di andata *oon bee-ly-ee-AYt-toh dee ahn-dAH-tah;* **a round-trip ticket** un biglietto di andata e ritorno *oon bee-ly-ee-AYt-toh dee ahn-dAH-tah ay ree-tOHr-noh;* **ticket office** biglietteria *bee-ly-ee-AYt-tay-rEE-ah*
**to tighten** stringere *strEEn-jay-reh*
**time** tempo *tEHm-poh;* **timetable** orario *oh-rAH-ree-oh*
**tip** mancia *mAHn-chee-ah*
**tire** pneumatico *pneh-oo-mAH-tee-koh;* **flat tire** gomma bucata *gOHm-mah boo-kAH-tah*
**tired** stanco *stAHn-koh*
**to** a *ah*
**to toast (drink)** brindare *breen-dAH-reh*
**tobacco** tabacco *tah-bAH-koh;* **tobacco shop** tabaccheria *tah-bAH-kay-rEE-ah;* **snuff tobacco** tabacco da fiuto *tah-bAH-koh dah fee-OO-toh*
**today** oggi *OH-jee*
**toe** alluce *AHl-loo-cheh*
**together** insieme *een-see-EH-meh*
**toilet** gabinetto *gah-bee-nAYt-toh;* toilette *too-ah-lEHt;* bagno *bAH-ny-oh;* **toilet paper** carta igienica *kAHr-tah ee-jee-EH-nee-kah*
**token** gettone *jayt-tOH-nay*
**tomato** pomodoro *poh-moh-dOH-roh*
**tomorrow** domani *doh-mAH-nee;* **the day after tomorrow** dopodomani *dOH-poh-doh-mAH-nee;* **See you tomorrow** A domani *ah doh-mAH-nee*
**tonic** tonico *tOH-nee-koh*
**tonight** stasera *stah-sAY-rah*
**tonsils** tonsille *tohn-sEEl-leh*
**too** anche *AHn-keh*
**tools** attrezzi *aht-trAY-tsee*
**tooth** dente *dEHn-tah;* **toothache** mal di denti *mAHl dee dEHn-tee;* **toothbrush** spazzolino per i denti *spah-tsoh-lEE-noh pehr ee dEHn-tee;* **toothpaste** dentifricio *dehn-tee-frEE-chee-oh*
**top** cima *chEE-mah*
**topaz** topazio *toh-pAH-tsee-oh*
**to touch** toccare *toh-kAH-reh*
**tourist (for tourists)** turistico *too-rEEs-tee-koh*
**tow truck** carroattrezzi *kAHr-roh-aht-trAY-tsee*
**towel** asciugamano *ah-shee-OO-gah-mAH-noh*

**toy store** negozio di giocattoli *neh-gOH-tsee-oh dee jee-oh-kAHt-toh-lee*
**track (train)** binario *bee-nAH-ree-oh*
**traffic light** semaforo *seh-mAH-foh-roh*
**train** treno *trEH-noh*
**training** allenamento *ahl-lay-nah-mEHn-toh*
**transformer** trasformatore *trahs-fohr-mah-tOH-reh*
**transit** transito *trAHn-see-toh*
**transition lenses** lenti fotocromatiche *lEHn-tee foh-toh-kroh-mAH-tee-keh*
**travel** viaggio *vee-AH-jee-oh;* **travel agency** agenzia di viaggi *ah-jehn-tsEE-ah dee vee-AH-jee*
**traveler's check** assegno di viaggiatore *ahs-sAY-ny-oh dee vee-ah-jee-ah-tOR-reh*
**tree** albero *AHl-beh-roh*
**to trim (hair)** spuntare *spoon-tAH-reh*
**trip** viaggio *vee-AH-jee-oh;* gita *jEE-tah*
**trouble** fastidio *fahs-tEE-dee-oh*
**trout** trota *trOH-tah*
**true** vero *vEH-roh*
**to try** provare *proh-vAH-reh*
**Tuesday** martedì *mahr-teh-dEE*
**tuna** tonno *tOHn-noh*
**turkey** tacchino *tah-kEE-noh*
**to turn** girare *jee-rAH-reh;* **it's your turn** tocca a lei *tOH-kah ah lEH-ee*
**turquoise** turchese *toor-kAY-seh*
**tweezers** pinzette *peen-tsAYt-teh*
**twelve** dodici *dOH-dee-chee*
**twenty** venti *vAYn-tee;* **twenty-one** ventuno *vayn-tOO-noh;* **twenty-two** ventidue *vAYn-tee-dOO-eh*
**two** due *doo-eh;* **two hundred** duecento *doo-eh-chEHn-toh*
**typing paper** carta per battere a macchina *kAHr-tah pehr bAHt-teh-reh ah mAH-kee-nah*

# U

**umbrella** ombrello *ohm-brEH-loh*
**uncle** zio *tsEE-oh*
**under** sotto *sOHt-toh*
**underpass** sottopassaggio *sOHt-toh-pahs-sAH-jee-oh*
**undershirt** canottiera *kah-noht-tee-EH-rah*
**to understand** capire *kah-pEE-reh*
**underwear** biancheria intima *bee-AHn-kay-rEE-ah EEn-tee-mah*
**university** università *oo-nee-vayr-see-tAH*
**unless** a meno che *ah mAY-noh keh*
**until** fino a *fEE-noh ah*
**us** ci *chee*
**to use** usare *oo-sAH-reh*
**usher (theater)** maschera *mAHs-keh-rah*

# V

**vegetarian** vegetariano *veh-jeh-tah-ree-AH-noh*
**very** molto *mOHl-toh*
**video card** scheda video *skEH-dah vEE-deh-oh*
**view** panorama *pah-noh-rAH-mah*
**village** villaggio *veel-lAH-jee-oh*
**vinegar** aceto *ah-chAY-toh*
**to visit** visitare *vee-see-tAH-reh*
**voltage** voltaggio *vohl-tAH-jee-oh*

# W

**to wait** aspettare *ahs-peht-tAH-reh*
**waiter** cameriere *kah-meh-ree-EH-reh*
**waitress** cameriera *kah-meh-ree-EH-rah*
**to wake up** svegliare *svay-ly-ee-AH-reh*
**to walk** camminare *kahm-mee-nAH-reh*
**walker** il girello *eel jee-rEHl-loh*
**to want** volere *voh-lAY-reh*
**warm** caldo *kAHl-doh*
**to wash** lavare *lah-vAH-reh*
**to watch** guardare *goo-ahr-dAH-reh*
**watch** orologio *oh-roh-lOH-jee-oh;* **wristwatch** orologio da polso *oh-roh-lOH-jee-oh dah pOHl-soh;* **watchmaker** orologiaio *oh-roh-loh-jee-AH-ee-oh*
**water** acqua *AH-koo-ah;* **drinkable water** acqua potabile *AH-koo-ah poh-tAH-bee-leh;* **running water** acqua corrente *AH-koo-ah kohr-rEHn-teh*
**waterfall** cascata *kahs-kAH-tah*
**watermelon** cocomero *koh-kOH-may-roh;* anguria *ahn-gOO-ree-ah*
**wave** onda *OHn-dah*
**wavy hair** capelli ondulati *kah-pAYl-lee ohn-doo-lAH-tee*
**waxing** depilazione mediante ceretta *deh-pee-lah-tzee-OH-neh meh-dee-AHn-teh cheh-rAYt-tah*
**we** noi *nOH-ee*
**weak** debole *dAY-boh-leh*
**to wear** portare *pohr-tAH-reh;* indossare *een-dohs-sAH-reh*
**weather** tempo *tehm-poh*
**Wednesday** mercoledì *mehr-koh-lay-dEE*
**week** settimana *seht-tee-mAH-nah*
**well** bene *bEH-neh*
**west** ovest *OH-vehst*
**what** che *kay;* che cosa *kay kOH-sah*
**wheel** ruota *roo-OH-tah*
**wheelchair** sedia a rotelle *sEH-dee-ah ah roh-tEHl-leh*
**when** quando *koo-AHn-doh*
**where** dove *dOH-veh;* **Where is it?** Dov'è? *doh-vEH*
**which** quale *koo-AH-leh*
**whiskers** baffi *bAHf-fee*
**while** mentre *mEHn-treh*
**white** bianco *bee-AHn-koh*
**who** chi *key;* che *kay*
**why** perché *payr-kAY*
**wide** largo *lAHr-goh*
**wife** moglie *mOH-ly-ee-eh*
**to win** vincere *vEEn-chay-reh*
**window** finestra *fee-nEHs-trah*
**wine** vino *vEE-noh;* **wine shop** enoteca *AY-noh-teh-kah;* rivendita di vini *ree-vAYn-dee-tah dee vEE-nee*
**wing** ala *AH-lah*
**winter** inverno *een-vEHr-noh*
**to wish** desiderare *day-see-deh-rAH-reh*
**with** con *kohn;* **within** dentro *dEHn-troh;* **without** senza *sEHn-tsah*
**woman** donna *dOHn-nah*
**wonderful** fantastico *fahn-tAH-stee-koh;* stupendo *stoo-pEHn-doh*
**wool** lana *lAH-nah*
**word** parola *pah-rOH-lah*
**to work** lavorare *lah-voh-rAH-reh;* **(machinery)** funzionare *foon-tsee-oh-nAH-reh*
**to worship** adorare *ah-doh-rAH-reh*
**wound** ferita *fay-rEE-tah*

**to wrap** incartare *een-kahr-tAH-reh*
**to write** scrivere *skrEE-veh-reh*
**writing pad** blocchetto di carta *bloh-kAYt-toh dee kAHr-tah*

# Y

**yard** iarda *ee-AHr-dah*
**year** anno *AHn-noh*
**yellow** giallo *jee-AHl-loh*
**yes** sì *sEE*
**yesterday** ieri *ee-AY-ree*
**you** tu *too;* lei *lEH-ee;* voi *vOH-ee;* te *tay;* loro *lOH-roh*
**young** giovane *jee-OH-vAH-neh;* **young lady** signorina *see-ny-oh-rEE-nah;* **young man** giovanotto *jee-oh-vah-nOHt-toh*
**your** suo *sOO-oh;* sua *sOO-ah;* vostro *vOH-stroh;* loro *lOH-roh;* tuo *tOO-oh;* tua *tOO-ah*
**youth** gioventù *jee-oh-vayn-tOO;* **youth hostel** ostello della gioventù *ohs-tEHl-loh dAYl-lah jee-oh-vehn-tOO*

# Z

**zero** zero *tsEH-roh*
**zipper** cerniera *chayr-nee-EH-rah*
**zoo** zoo *tsOH-oh*

# ITALIAN-ENGLISH DICTIONARY

The following Italian words are presented here with accent marks to aid pronunciation. As there are actually very few accents used in Italian, you will find most of these words without accents when used in context.

## A

**a** to, at, in
**abbàcchio** lamb, spring lamb
**abbagliànti** headlights
**abbastànza** enough
**abbronazatúra** suntan
**abitàre** to live
**àbito** dress, suit; _____ **da séra** evening gown
**accànto** next to, near
**accappatòio** robe for man
**accèndere** to light
**accendíno** cigarette lighter
**accensióne** ignition
**accessori** accessories
**accettàre** to accept
**acciàio** steel; _____ **inossidàbile** stainless steel
**acciúga** anchovy
**accónto** deposit, partial payment
**accorciatòia** shortcut
**acéto** vinegar
**acetóne** nail polish remover
**àcqua** water; _____ **corrènte** running water; _____ **potàbile** drinkable water
**acquamarína** aquamarine
**adèsso** now
**adoràre** to adore, to worship
**aèreo** airplane
**aeropòrto** airport
**affàre** business
**affettàto** sliced; **affettàti** cold cuts
**affittàre** to rent; **si affítta** for rent
**affrancatúra** postage
**agenzía** agency; _____ **d'informazioni** information office; _____ **di viaggi** travel agency
**aggiustàre** to fix, to repair
**àglio** garlic
**àgnèllo** lamb
**ago** needle
**agósto** August
**aiuòla** flower bed, garden, grass
**aiutàre** to help
**aiùto** help
**àla** wing
**albèrgo** hotel, inn
**àlbero** tree
**albicòcca** apricot
**àlbum** album
**àlcol** alcohol
**alcúni** a few, some
**alfière** knight
**alimentatore** power supply
**aliscafo** hydrofoil
**allenaménto** training, practice
**allèrgico** allergic
**àlluce** big toe
**àlto** high
**àltro** other; **un àltro** another
**alzàre** to lift, to raise; _____ **il màzzo** to cut cards

**amàlgama** amalgam
**ambulatòrio** first-aid station, doctor's office
**americàno(a)** American
**ametísta** amethyst
**amíco(a)** friend
**amóre** love; **per l'amòr del cièlo!** my goodness!
**analcòlico** nonalcoholic; **bíbita analcòlica** soft drink
**ananàsso** pineapple
**ancóra** still
**andàre** to go; **Andiàmo!** Let's go!
**andàta** one-way trip; **____ e ritórno** round trip
**anèllo** ring
**àngolo** corner; **all'àngolo** at the corner
**anguílla** eel
**angùria** watermelon
**ànitra** duck
**ànno** year
**antiàcido** antacid
**antibiòtico** antibiotic
**antícipo** advance
**antipàsto** appetizers, hors d'oeuvre
**antisèttico** antiseptic
**aperitívo** aperitif
**apèrto** open
**appartamènto** apartment
**appéna** as soon as
**appendicíte** appendicitis
**apprèndere** to learn, to come to know of
**appuntaménto** appointment
**aprile** April
**apríre** to open; **È apèrto?** Is it open?
**aragósta** lobster
**aràncio(a)** orange tree (fruit)
**aranciáta** orangeade
**àrbitro** referee
**argènto** silver
**ària** air; **_____ condizionàta** air-conditioning
**arínga** herring
**arrivàre** to reach, to get to a place
**arrivedérci** good-bye
**arròsto** roast
**artícolo** item, article
**ascensóre** elevator (lift)
**ascèsso** abscess
**asciugacapélli** hair dryer
**asciugamàno** towel
**ascoltàre** to listen
**àsma** asthma
**aspàragi** asparagus
**aspettàre** to wait; **aspètti!** wait!
**aspirína** aspirin
**àsso** ace
**asségno** check
**assicurazióne** insurance
**assístere** to assist, to help
**assorbènti igiènici** sanitary napkins
**attàcco cardíaco** heart attack
**attènto(a)** attentive, careful; **Attènto!** Watch out!
**attenzióne** attention; **Stía attènto(a)!** Be careful!
**atterràre** to land
**attórno** around, roundabout
**attravèrso** across, through
**attrazióne** attraction
**attrézzi** tools
**àuto** car; **màl d'àuto** car sickness
**autoambulànza** ambulance
**àutobus** bus
**automàtico** automatic
**autopúllman** motor coach
**autoriméssa** garage
**autóre** author
**autostràda** highway
**autúnno** fall
**avére** to have; **Ma che còsa ha?** What's the matter with you?
**avànti** forward; **Avànti!** Come in!

**avventúra** adventure; **avventúre poliziésche** detective stories
**avviàre** to start
**avvocàto** lawyer
**azzúrro** blue

# B

**baciàre** to kiss
**bacíno** pelvis; basin
**bàcio** kiss
**bàffi** moustache
**bagníno** lifeguard
**bàgno** bathroom
**balcóne** balcony
**ballàre** to dance
**ballétto** ballet
**bàllo** dance
**bambíno** child, kid, baby
**bàmbola** doll
**banàna** banana
**bànca** bank
**banconòta** banknote
**bàrba** beard, shave
**barbería** barbershop
**barítono** baritone
**bàsso** low, short, bass voice
**bàsta** enough; **Bàsta (cosí)!** That's enough!
**battería** battery
**bellézza** beauty; **salóne di _____** beauty parlor
**bèl, bèllo(a)** beautiful, handsome, nice
**bène** well; **va bène** that's all right
**benzína** gasoline (petrol)
**bére** to drink
**bianchería** linen, laundry; **_____ íntima** underwear
**biànco(a)** white
**bíbita** drink
**bibliotèca** library
**bicchière** drinking glass
**biciclétta** bicycle
**biglietteria** ticket office
**bigliétto** ticket, banknote; **un _____ da mílle euro** a 1000-euro bill; **un _____ di andàta e ritórno** a round-trip ticket
**bióndo (chiàro)** (light) blond
**bírra** beer
**biscòtto** cookie
**bisognàre** to be necessary, to have to
**bisógno** need
**bistécca** beefsteak
**bloccàto(a)** stuck
**blocchétto (di càrta)** writing pad
**blu** blue
**blúsa** blouse
**bócca** mouth; **In _____ al lùpo!** Good luck!
**boccóne** bite; **mangiàre un _____** to have a bite
**bollíto** boiled
**bórsa** handbag
**botànico** botanic
**botteghíno** (theater) box office
**bottíglia** bottle
**bottóne** button
**bowling** bowling
**bracciàle** armlet, bangle, bracelet
**bràccio** arm
**branzíno** bass (fish)
**brívido** shiver, chills
**bròdo** broth
**bruciàto** burnt
**brúna** dark-haired woman, brunette
**budíno** pudding
**bullóne** bolt
**bugía** lie; **È una _____!** It's a lie!
**buòno(a)** good
**búrro** butter
**bústa** envelope

# C

**cabína** cabin; _____ **telefònica** phone booth
**cachèt** color rinse
**cadére** to fall; **sono cadùto(a)** I have fallen
**caffè** coffee; _____ **corrètto** with liquor
**calamàri** squid
**càlcio** kick, soccer; **il _____ d'inìzio** the kickoff; **una partìta di _____** a soccer game
**càldo** warm, hot
**callìfugo** corn plaster
**calpestàre** to crush underfoot; **È vietàto _____ l'èrba** Keep off the grass
**càlza** stocking
**calzaturifìcio** shoe store
**calzíni** socks
**calzolàio** shoemaker
**cambiàre** to change, to exchange
**càmbio** change; **l'uffìcio di _____** (money) exchange office
**càmera** room; _____ **da lètto** bedroom
**camerièra** maid, waitress
**camerière** waiter
**camícia** shirt; _____ **da uòmo** man's shirt
**campàgna** countryside
**campéggio** camping
**càmpo** field; _____ **di golf** golf course
**cancellàre** to erase
**candéla** spark plug, candle
**canottièra** man's undershirt
**cantàre** to sing
**capélli** hair; **un tàglio di _____** a haircut
**capíre** to understand; **io capísco** I understand
**càpo** head
**capolínea** (bus) terminal
**cappèllo** hat
**Càpperi!** Man alive!
**cappóne** capon
**capréttо** baby goat
**caramèlla** candy
**carburatóre** carburetor
**cariàto** decayed; rotten
**caricàre** to load
**càrne** meat
**caròta** carrot
**carroattrézzi** tow truck
**carròzza** railroad car; **In _____!** All aboard!; _____ **ristoràntе** dining car
**càrta** paper, map; _____ **di crèdito** credit card; _____ **d'identità** identification card; _____ **stradàle** road map; _____ **da giuòco** playing card; _____ **igiènica** toilet paper; _____ **da imballàggio** wrapping paper; _____ **per bàttere a màcchina** typing paper
**cartellíno** chart, tag
**cartolína** card; _____ **illustràta** picture postcard; _____ **postàle** postcard
**cartúccia** cartridge
**càsa** house
**cascàta** waterfall
**CD registrabile** CDR
**che** who, that; _____ **còsa?** What?
**chi** who; _____ **è?** Who is it?
**chiamàre** to call; **Mi chiàmo _____** My name is _____
**chiàro** clear, light-colored
**chiàve** key
**chièsa** church
**chíffon** chiffon
**chílo** kilogram
**chilòmetro** kilometer; **a chilometràggio illimitàto** unlimited mileage
**chiúdere** to close; **Pòsso _____?** May I close?
**chiúso** closed

**céci** chickpeas
**cetriólo** cucumber
**ciabàtte** slippers
**ciào** hi, hello, bye
**cièlo** heaven, sky; **Per l'amór del _____!** My goodness!
**cíglia** eyelash
**ciliègia** cherry
**cínema** cinema, movie house
**cineprésa** movie camera
**cinquànta** fifty
**cínque** five
**cinquecènto** five hundred
**cintúra** belt
**cioccolàta** chocolate
**ciòndolo** charm
**cipólla** onion
**città** city
**clàcson** (car) horn
**clàsse** class
**cocktail** cocktail
**cocómero** watermelon
**còfano** hood
**cognóme** last name
**colazióne** breakfast
**cólla** glue
**còllant** panty hose
**collína** hill
**collírio** eyedrops
**cólpo d'aria (al pètto)** (chest) cold
**coltèllo** knife
**cóme** as, how; **_____ sta?** How are you?
**cominciàre** to begin
**commèdia** comedy
**commerciàle** commercial
**commissariàto** police station
**compartiménto** compartment
**compràre** to buy
**complèto** complete, full
**compréso** included
**con** with
**concèrto** concert; **sàla da concèrti** concert hall
**confermàre** to confirm
**coníglio** rabbit
**conòscere** to know
**consegnàre** to deliver
**consèrva (di pomodòro)** (tomato) sauce
**consigliàre** to recommend, to suggest
**consolàto** consulate
**consommè** consommé
**contagiòso** contagious
**continuàre** to continue, to keep (doing something)
**cònto** bill, check; **cònti separàti** separate checks
**contòrno** garnish; **càrne con contòrno** meat and vegetables
**contracettívo** contraceptive
**contusióne** bruise
**copèrta** blanket
**còpia** copy, print
**coràllo** coral
**coròna** crown
**còrpo** body
**corrènte** current, running
**corrètto** correct; **caffè _____** coffee with liquor
**corridòio** aisle
**còrsa** fare
**cortìle** courtyard
**còrto(a)** short
**còsa** thing; **Che _____?** What?
**così** so, this way; **Bàsta _____!** That's enough!
**cosmètico** cosmetic
**costàta** rib
**costàre** to cost; **Quànto còsta?** How much is it?
**costóso** expensive; **méno _____** cheaper
**costúme da bàgno** bathing suit
**cotolétta** cutlet
**cotóne** cotton
**còtto** cooked; **ben còtto** well-done
**còzze** mussels
**cràmpi** cramps
**cravàtta** necktie

**crèdito** credit; **càrta di _____** credit card
**crèma** cream
**críccо** jack (car)
**cristàllo** crystal
**cròcchia** bun
**croissànt** croissant
**cròsta** crust
**cuccétta** berth
**cucchiàio** spoon
**cucchiaíno** teaspoon
**cucína** kitchen, cooking
**cucíre** to sew
**cuòre** heart
**cúrva** curve
**cuscíno** pillow

# D

**da** from, by, to, at the house of, since
**dàdo** nut
**dàma** checkers
**dàre** to give; **Mi sta dàndo _____** He (she) is giving me _____; **dàre le càrte** to deal
**dàta** date; **Qual è la dàta di òggi?** What is today's date?
**dàtteri** dates (fruit)
**davànti** before, in front of
**débole** weak
**dècimo** tenth
**decollàre** to take off
**denàro** money
**dènte** tooth; **mal di dènti** toothache
**dentifrício** toothpaste
**dentísta** dentist
**deodoránte** deodorant
**depòsito** deposit
**desideràre** to desire
**dessert** dessert
**destinatàrio** receiver; **a càrico del destinatàrio** collect call
**deviazióne** detour
**diabète** diabetes
**dèstro** right; **a dèstra** to the right
**detergènte** detergent
**diamànte** diamond
**diapositíve** slides
**diarrèa** diarrhea
**diàvolo** devil; **Ma che diàvolo vuòle?** What the devil do you want?
**dicèmbre** December
**dichiaràre** to declare
**diciannòve** nineteen
**diciassètte** seventeen
**diciòtto** eighteen
**dièci** ten
**dietro** in back of, after
**díre** to say; **Mi díca** Tell me; **Ha détto** He (she) has said
**dirètto** direct, express train
**direttóre** conductor, director, manager
**direzióne** direction; **In che direzióne?** Which way?
**dirítto** straight; **avànti dirítto** straight ahead
**dísco** disk, record
**disco rigido** hard drive
**discotèca** discotheque
**disinfettànte (per la bócca)** mouthwash
**dispiacére** to dislike; **Mi dispiàce** I'm sorry; **Le dispiàce?** Do you mind?
**dissenterìa** dysentery
**disturbàre** to disturb
**dito** finger
**dóccia** shower; **fàre la dóccia** to take a shower
**documénto** document
**dódici** twelve
**dogàna** customs; **pagàr dogàna** to pay duty
**dólci** sweets
**dolcificànte** sugar substitute
**dolére** to hurt; **Mi duòle** It hurts
**dòllaro** dollar

**domàni** tomorrow; **a domàni** see you tomorrow
**doménica** Sunday
**dòmino** dominoes
**dònna** woman; queen (card games)
**dopobàrba** aftershave lotion
**dopodomàni** the day after tomorrow
**dormìre** to sleep
**dottóre** doctor
**dóve** where; **Dov'è?** Where is it?
**dovére** to have to, to owe; **Quànto le devo?** How much do I owe you?
**dràmma** drama
**drìtto** straight
**dùbbio** doubt; **sènza dúbbio** without fail
**dùe** two
**duecènto** two hundred
**duránte** during
**duràre** to last

# E

**e** and
**ècco** here is (are), there is (are)
**edìcola** newsstand
**Eh!** Wow!
**égli** he
**elènco** list
**elettricità** electricity
**elèttrico** electric
**élla** she
**emergènza** emergency
**entràre** to enter; **Èntri!** Come in!
**equipaggiaménto** equipment
**èrba** grass
**esprèsso** espresso (coffee), express train, special delivery
**èssere** to be
**estàte** summer
**estràrre** to extract, to pull out
**ètto, ettogràmmo** 100 grams, hectogram

# F

**fàccia** face
**facciàle** facial; **massàggio facciàle** facial massage
**fagiàno** pheasant
**fagiòlo** bean
**fagiolíno** green bean
**fàme** hunger; **Ho fàme** I'm hungry
**famìglia** family
**fanalíni** (tail)lights
**fantascièǹza** science fiction
**fantasìa** imagination
**fantàstico** imaginary, fantastic, wonderful
**fàre** to do, to make; **Mi fàccio il bàgno** I'm taking a bath; **Fa fréddo** It is cold; **Fa càldo** It is warm; **fàre la fila** to stand in line
**farmacìa** pharmacy, drugstore
**fàscia** bandage
**fastìdio** trouble, nuisance
**fattorìa** farm
**favóre** favor; **per favóre** please
**fazzolétto** handkerchief; **fazzolétto di carta** paper handkerchief, "tissue"
**febbràio** February
**febbre** fever, temperature; **la fébbre del fièno** hay fever
**fégato** liver
**féltro** felt
**ferìta** wound, cut
**fermàglio** brooch
**fermàre** to stop
**fermàta** stop (bus stop, etc.)
**férmo (pòsta)** general delivery
**ferraménta** hardware store
**ferrovìa** railroad
**fétta** slice
**fiammìfero** match

**fìco (fìchi)** fig(s)
**figlia** daughter
**figlio** son
**fila** line, row
**filo** thread, wire
**film** film
**filóne** long loaf
**filtro** filter
**finèstra** window
**finestrìno** (train) window
**fioràio** florist
**fióre** flower; **fiori** clubs (cards)
**firma** signature
**firmàre** to sign, to endorse
**fiùme** river
**flanèlla** flannel
**folclorìstico** folkloric
**fontàna** fountain
**fòrbici** scissors
**forchétta** fork
**forcìna** hairpin
**forèsta** forest
**formàggio** cheese
**fórno** oven; **al fórno** baked
**fórse** perhaps, maybe
**fòrte** strong; **Più fòrte!** Faster!
**fortúna** fortune; **Buòna fortúna!** Good luck!
**Fòrza!** Go!
**fotografía** photograph
**fòto-òttica** camera store
**fra** between, among
**fràgole** strawberries
**francobòllo** postage stamp
**fràngia** bang(s)
**fratèllo** brother
**frattúra** fracture
**fréccia** direction indicator
**fréddo** cold
**fréno** brake
**frésco** cool, fresh
**frétta** hurry; **Ho frétta** I'm in a hurry
**frittàta** omelet
**frítto** fried; **frítto místo** fish fry
**frizióne** tonic, massage, clutch
**frónte** front, forehead
**frullàto (di làtte)** (milk) shake
**frullatóre** blender
**frútto(a)** fruit
**fumàre** to smoke
**fumatóre** smoker
**fúngo** mushroom, fungus
**funzionàre** to work
**fuòco** fire; **Al fuoco!** Fire!
**fuòri** outside; **Fuòri!** Get out!

# G

**gabardíne** gabardine
**gabinétto** toilet, rest room
**gàmba** leg
**gàmberi** prawns, shrimp
**gas** gas
**gassàta** with gas; **àcqua gassàta** carbonated water
**gelateria** ice-cream store
**gelàto** ice cream
**gengíve** gums
**gennàio** January
**gettóne** token
**ghiacciàto** iced; **àcqua ghiacciàta** ice water
**ghiàccio** ice; **cubétti di ghiàccio** ice cubes
**ghiàndole** glands
**giàcca** jacket
**giàda** jade
**giàllo** yellow; **è un giàllo** it's a mystery
**giàra** jar
**ginòcchio** knee
**giocattolería** toy store
**gioiellería** jewelry store
**giornàle** newspaper
**giórno** day; **buòn giórno** good morning
**giovanòtto** young man
**giovedì** Thursday
**gioventù** youth
**giradíschi** record player

**giràre** to turn; **giràre un asségno** to endorse a check; **Mi gíra la tèsta** I'm dizzy
**gíta** trip, tour
**giúgno** June
**giocàre** to play (games)
**gli** the, to him
**góla** throat; **mal di góla** sore throat
**gómito** elbow
**gómma** eraser; **gómma bucáta** flat tire
**gónfio** swollen
**gonfiòre** swelling, lump
**gónna** skirt
**gràmmo** gram
**gránchio** crab
**grànde** large, big; **più grànde** larger
**gràzie** thanks; **Mólte gràzie** Thank you very much
**grígio** gray
**grúcce** dress hangers
**guància** cheek
**guànto** glove
**guardàre** to look at, to watch
**guardaròba** checkroom
**guàsto** breakdown, trouble
**guàva** guava
**guída** guide, guidebook
**guidàre** to drive

# H

**hambúrger** hamburger
**hotèl** hotel

# I

**identità** identity; **càrta d'identità** identification card
**iàrda** yard
**ièri** yesterday
**igiénico** hygienic; **un ròtolo di càrta igiènica** a roll of toilet paper
**impaccàre** to wrap up, to pack
**impermeàbile** raincoat
**impiegàto** clerk
**importàre** to matter; **Non impòrta** It doesn't matter
**importànte** important
**impossíbile** impossible
**impòsta** tax
**in** into, in
**incartàre** to wrap in paper
**incínta** pregnant
**inclúso(a)** included
**incominciàre** to start
**incontràre** to meet
**incrócio** crossing, crossroad
**indicàre** to show, to point out
**indiètro** back, backward(s)
**indirízzo** address
**indossàre** to wear
**infezióne** infection
**influènza** flu
**inglèse** English
**ingranàggio (del càmbio)** gearshift
**ingrèsso** entrance
**iniziàre** to start
**innamoràto(a)** lover, sweetheart (girlfriend)
**innocènte** innocent
**insalàta** salad
**insième** together
**insònnia** insomnia
**insulína** insulin
**intaglìato** carved
**interessànte** interesting
**internazionàle** international
**interpretàre** to interpret
**intèrprete** interpreter
**interròmpere** to cut off (telephone)
**interruttóre** (electric light) switch
**interurbàna** long-distance call
**intórno** around
**invéce** instead

**investito(a)** run over (by a car)
**inviàre** to send
**io** I; **io stésso** myself
**iòdio** iodine
**ippòdromo** racetrack

# L

**la** the, her, you
**là** there
**làbbra** lips
**làcca** hair spray
**làcci (da scàrpe)** shoelaces
**làdro** thief
**làgo** lake
**lamétta** blade
**lambrétta** motor scooter
**làmpada** lamp
**lampóne** raspberry
**làna** wool
**lancétta** hand (of a watch)
**lasciàre** to leave; **Mi làsci in pàce!** Don't bother me!
**lassatívo** laxative
**làto** side
**làtte** milk
**lattúga** lettuce
**lavàggio** wash; **lavàggio a sécco** dry cleaner
**lavàre** to wash; **lavàre a sécco** to dry-clean
**le** the, them, to her, to you
**leggèro** light, mild
**lèi** she, her, you
**lentaménte** slowly
**lènte** lens; **lènte a contàtto** contact lens
**lentícchie** lentils
**lèpre** hare
**lèttera** letter; **per vía aèra** airmail; **assicuràta** insured; **raccomandàta** registered; **esprèsso** special delivery; **con ricevùta di ritórno** with return receipt
**lètto** bed
**li** them
**lì** there
**líbero** free, not occupied; **il líbero** halfback (soccer player)
**librería** bookstore
**líbro** book
**lièto** happy
**limétta (per le únghie)** (nail) file
**limóne** lemon
**línea** line
**língua** tongue
**líno** linen
**liquóre** liqueur
**lísta** list
**lítro** liter
**locàle** place
**località** site, place
**lontàno** distant, far away
**lóro** their, theirs; **a lóro** to them
**lozióne** lotion; **lozióne per l'abbronzatùra** suntan lotion
**lubrificàre** to lubricate, to grease, to oil
**lúce** light
**lucidàre** to shine (shoes)
**lùglio** July
**lùi** he, him
**lunedì** Monday
**lúngo** long

# M

**ma** but, yet, however; **Ma che!** Nonsense!
**màcchina** machine, automobile
**macedònia** fresh-fruit salad
**macellería** butcher shop
**màdre** mother
**magazzíno** department store
**mággio** May
**màglia** sweater
**magnífico** great
**maiàle** pig

**màle** ill, sick; **màl d'àuto** car sickness; **màl di mare** seasickness
**maledizióne** malediction, curse; **Maledizióne!** Darn it!
**màlto** malt
**mancàre** to be lacking, to be missing; **Tu mi mànchi!** I miss you!
**mància** tip
**mandàre** to send
**mandaríno** tangerine
**màndorle** almonds
**mangiàre** to eat
**màngo** mango
**mànica** sleeve
**manicúra** manicure
**manifésto** poster
**maníglia** doorknob
**màno** hand; **Mi día una màno** Give me a hand
**mànzo** beef
**màrca** brand
**màrcia** gear (car)
**marciapiède** sidewalk
**màre** sea; **che dà sul màre** facing the sea
**margarína** margarine
**maríto** husband
**marróne** brown
**martedí** Tuesday
**martèllo** hammer
**màrzo** March
**màschera** usher (theater)
**masterizzatore** CD-Writer
**masticàre** to chew
**materàsso** mattress
**matíta** pencil
**màzze (da golf)** (golf) clubs
**màzzo (di càrte)** deck (of cards)
**me** me
**meccànico** mechanic
**medicína** medicine
**mèdico** doctor
**mèglio** better
**méla** apple
**melanzàna** eggplant (aubergine)
**melóne** melon
**menù** menu
**meravigliόso** wonderful
**mercàto** market; **a buòn mercàto** cheap
**mercoledì** Wednesday
**merlétto** lace
**merlúzzo** codfish
**mése** month
**Méssa** Mass
**messàggio** message
**metà** half
**mètro** meter
**metropolitàna** subway
**méttere** to put
**mezzanótte** midnight
**mèzzo** half, means
**mezzogiórno** midday, noon
**mía** my
**mi** me
**miéi** my
**miglióre** better; **il miglióre** the best
**milióne** million
**mílle** one thousand
**mineràle** mineral
**minéstra** soup
**mínimo** minimum
**minístro** minister
**minúto** minute
**mío** my
**mischiàre** to shuffle
**misúra** measurement, size
**mobiliàto** furnished
**mòdulo** blank, form
**mòglie** wife
**mòlla** spring
**mólto** much, a lot
**moménto** moment
**moníle** necklace
**montàgna** mountain
**montatúra** frame
**montóne** mutton
**moschèa** mosque
**mostràre** to show; **mi mòstri** show me

**motociclétta** motorcycle
**motoríno** moped; **motoríno d'avviamènto** starter
**muòvere** to move
**musèo** museum
**mùsica** music; _____ **clàssica** classical music; _____ **modèrna** modern music
**mutànde** shorts, underwear
**mutandíne** panties

# N

**nàscita** birth; **dàta di nàscita** birth date
**nasèllo** hake (fish)
**nàso** nose
**nàstro (adesívo)** Scotch tape
**Natàle** Christmas
**Naturalménte!** Of course!
**nàve** ship
**nazionalità** nationality
**ne** of (something)
**necessàrio** necessary
**negòzio** store; **negòzio d'abbigliamènto** clothing store
**néro** black
**néve** snow
**nevicàre** to snow
**niènte** nothing
**night club** nightclub
**no** no
**nocciolíne** hazelnuts
**nóce (di còcco)** (coco)nut
**nói** we, us
**noleggiàre** to rent
**nóme** name
**non** not
**nòno** ninth
**normàle** normal
**nòstro(a)** our, ours
**nòtte** night; **buòna nòtte** good night
**novànta** ninety
**nòve** nine
**novecènto** nine hundred
**novèlla** short story
**novèmbre** November
**núlla** nothing
**numeràto** numbered
**número** number
**nuotàre** to swim
**nuòvo** new
**nylon** nylon

# O

**o** or
**òca** goose
**occhiàli** eyeglasses; **occhiàli da sóle** sunglasses
**occhiàta** look; **dàre un'occhiàta** to take a look
**òcchio** eye
**occórrere** to be necessary; **Mi occórrono** I need (them)
**occupàto** taken, busy
**ocèano** ocean
**oculísta** oculist, eye doctor
**officína meccànica** repair shop
**oggètti preziósi** jewelry
**òggi** today
**òlio** oil
**òmbra** shade
**ombrétto** eye shadow
**ónda** wave
**ondulàto** wavy; **capélli onduláti** wavy hair
**ònice** onyx
**òpera** opera
**operétta** operetta
**óra** hour, now; **A che óra?** At what time?
**oràrio** timetable; **in oràrio** on schedule
**ordinàre** to order
**orecchíno** earring
**òro** gold; **d'òro massíccio** solid gold; **d'òro placcàto** gold plated
**orologiàio** watchmaker
**orològio** watch, clock; **orològio da pólso** wristwatch

**òrzo** barley
**osservàre** to observe, to watch
**ostèllo (délla gioventù)** (youth) hostel
**ostería** wine shop, tavern
**òstrica** oyster
**ostruíre** to obstruct, to block up
**ottànta** eighty
**ottenére** to obtain
**òttico** optician
**òtto** eight
**ottocènto** eight hundred
**ottòbre** October
**otturàre** to fill (a tooth)

# P

**pacchétto** packet, small parcel, small package
**pàcco** package, parcel
**pàdre** father
**paése** village, town
**pagàre** to pay
**pàio** pair
**palàzzo** palace
**pàlla** ball
**pallíni** dots
**palmari** handhelds
**pancétta** bacon
**pàne** bread; **pàne tostàto** toasted bread
**panettería** bakery
**paníno** roll
**pànna** cream
**pànno** cloth
**pannolíno** linen, cloth diaper, sanitary napkin; **pannolíni ùsa e gètta** disposable diapers
**panoràma** view, panorama, landscape
**pantalóni** (a pair of) trousers, slacks, pants
**pantòfola** slipper
**pantaloncíni** shorts
**paraúrti** bumper
**parcheggiàre** to park
**parchéggio** parking
**pàrco** park
**paréggio** draw, tie (sport)
**parlàre** to speak, to talk
**parrucchière** hairdresser
**pàrte** part, section, area
**partíre** to depart, to leave
**partíta** game
**passàggio** passage, crossing; **diviéto di passàggio** no crossing
**passapòrto** passport
**passàre** to pass, to go by
**pàsta** pasta, pastry
**pastícca (per la tósse)** (cough) drop
**pàsto** meal
**patènte di guída** driver's license
**pàzzo** mad, crazy; **mi sta facèndo uscíre pàzzo** it's driving me crazy
**peccàto** sin; **Che peccàto!** What a shame!
**pedóne** pedestrian; pawn (chess)
**pèlle** skin, leather
**penicillína** penicillin
**pénna** pen; _____ **a sfèra** ballpoint pen
**pensàre** to think
**pensióne** private residence, usually with meals; **pensióne complèta** room with 3 meals a day
**pépe** pepper
**péra** pear
**per** for, through, about
**perché** why, what, because
**pèrdere** to lose
**perícolo** danger; **pericolóso** dangerous
**periferiche** peripherals
**período** period
**pèrla** pearl

**permésso** permitted, permit; **Con permésso!** Excuse me!
**perméttere** to permit, to allow
**perníce** partridge
**personàggio** character
**personàle** personal
**pesànte** heavy
**pèsca** peach
**pietrína** flint
**pèttine** comb
**pèzzo** piece; _____ **di ricàmbio** spare part
**piacére** pleasure; **per piacére** please; **con piacére** with pleasure
**piacére** to please, to like, to be fond of; **mi piàce** I like him/her
**piànta** plant, tree, map
**piàtto** plate, dish
**piattíno** saucer
**piccióne (implùme)** squab (pigeon)
**píccolo** small; **più píccolo** smaller
**piède** foot; **andare a pièdi** to walk
**pièno** full
**piètra preziósa** (precious) stone
**píllola** pill
**pínze** pliers
**pinzétta** tweezers
**piòvere** to rain
**piscína** swimming pool
**pisèlli** peas
**písta** dance floor; **le píste per sciàre** ski slopes
**più** more
**pízzo** lace; pointed beard
**plàstica** plastic
**platèa** orchestra (theater)
**plàtino** platinum
**pneumàtico** tire; **un materassíno pneumàtico** an air mattress
**pòco** little
**polièstere** synthetic
**pólipo** octopus
**polizía** police; **stazióne di polizía** police station
**pòllice** thumb, inch
**póllo** chicken
**polmóne** lung
**polpétta** meatball
**pólso** wrist
**pólvere** dust, powder
**pomeríggio** afternoon
**pomodòro** tomato
**pómpa** pump; **pómpa della benzína** fuel pump
**pompèlmo** grapefruit
**pónte** bridge
**pòrta** door, gate
**portabagàgli** luggage rack, porter
**portafòglio** wallet
**portàre** to bring; **Mi pòrti** _____ Bring me _____; **Dove pòrta quésta stràda?** Where does this road lead to?
**portàta** course (meal)
**pòrto** port, harbor
**porzióne** portion
**possíbile** possible
**pòsta** mail
**postàle** postal; **vàglia postàle** money order; **pòste e telègrafi** postal and telegraph services
**posteggiàre** to park
**postéggio** parking
**pósto** place, spot, seat
**potàbile** potable, drinkable
**potére** to be able to, can
**pranzàre** to dine, to have dinner
**pránzo** dinner, lunch
**preferíre** to prefer
**prefísso** area code
**preghièra** prayer
**prègo** you're welcome
**prèndere** to take; **Lo (la) prèndo!** I'll take it!
**prenotazióne** reservation

**présa di corrènte** electric outlet
**presentàre** to present
**prèstito** loan
**prèsto** early
**prète** priest
**prèzzo** price; **a prèzzo fìsso** fixed price
**primavèra** spring
**prímo** first
**principàle** main, principal
**privàto** private
**professióne** profession
**profilàttici** prophylactics
**profúmo** perfume
**prónto** ready; **prónto soccórso** first aid; **Prónto!** Hello! (telephone)
**pròprio** own, private
**prosciútto** ham
**pròssimo** near, next
**pròtesi dentària** dental prosthesis
**protestànte** protestant
**provàre** to prove, to try; **Pòsso provàrmelo?** May I try it on?
**prúgna** plum
**pulíre** to clean
**púllman** motor coach
**punch** punch
**puntéggio** score
**puntíno** dot; **a puntíno** medium (of meat)

# Q

**qua** here
**quàdro** picture, painting
**quàlche** a few, some, any
**qualcúno** somebody, someone, anybody
**qualità** quality
**quàndo** when
**quànto** how much; **Quànto còsta?** How much is it?
**quaràntа** forty
**quàrto** fourth, quarter
**quattórdici** fourteen
**quàttro** four
**quattrocènto** four hundred
**quéllo** that, that one; **Che cos'è quéllo?** What's that?
**quésto** this
**qui** here
**quíndici** fifteen
**quínto** fifth

# R

**rabbíno** rabbi
**racchétta** racquet; **racchétte da scí** ski poles
**raccommandàta** registered letter
**raccónti** stories
**ràdio portàtile** portable radio
**raffreddóre** cold
**ragàzza** girl
**ragàzzo** boy
**raggiúngere** to reach, to get to, to arrive at
**rammendàre** to mend
**rasóio** razor
**rattoppàre** to patch up, to mend
**ravanèllo** radish
**re** king
**recapitàre** to deliver
**regàlo** gift
**regalíno** little present
**reggiséno** brassiere, bra
**regína** queen
**religióso** religious
**rènna** suede
**respiràre** to breathe
**restàre** to stay, to remain
**rèsto** change (from a paid bill)
**rètro** behind; **sul rètro** in the back
**rícciolo** curl
**ricètta** prescription
**ricévere** to receive
**ricevúta** receipt
**ricreazióne** recreation

**ridótto** reduced; **a taríffa ridótta** half-price ticket
**ríga** ruler; **con rígbe** with stripes
**rigonfiaménto** swelling
**rimanére** to remain, to stay
**rimorchiàre** to tow
**riparàre** to repair, to fix
**riservàto** reserved
**risièdere** to reside, to live
**ríso** rice
**ristoràntе** restaurant
**risultàto** score, result, outcome
**ritàrdo** delay, lateness
**ritornàre** to return, to go back
**ritórno** return; **andàta e ritórno** round trip
**rivísta** magazine, periodical
**rognóne** kidney
**romànzo** love story, novel
**ròsa** rose, pink
**rosétta** small round bread, bun
**rossétto** rouge; _____ **per le làbbra** lipstick
**rósso** red
**roulòtte** trailer
**rubàre** to steal
**rubinétto** faucet
**rubíno** ruby
**rullíno** roll of film
**ruòta** wheel
**ruscèllo** brook, small stream

# S

**sàbato** Saturday
**sàbbia** sand
**saccarína** saccharin
**sacchétto** bag
**sàla** large room; **la sàla da prànzo** dining room
**salàto** salted, salty
**salàme** salami
**sàle** salt
**salmóne** salmon
**salóne di bellezza** beauty parlor
**salòtto** living room
**salumería** delicatessen
**salúte** health; **Salúte!** Cheers!
**salúti** greetings
**sàngue** blood; **Sto sanguinàndo** I'm bleeding
**sapére** to know; **Lo so!** I know it!
**saponétta** small bar of soap
**sardína** sardine
**sàrto** tailor
**sbaglière** to make a mistake, to go wrong in (something); **número sbaglièto** wrong number
**sbrigàrsi** to hurry up; **Si sbrígbi!** Hurry up!
**scàcchi** chess
**scamosciàto** suede
**scàmpi** shrimp
**scàpolo** bachelor
**scàrpa** shoe
**scarpóni da sci** ski boots
**scàtola** box
**scattàre una fòto** to take a picture
**scéndere** to go down, to get off
**scheda telefonica** phone card
**scheda video** video card
**sciène** back
**scí** skiing; **scí acquàtico** waterskiing
**sciàre** to ski
**sciocchézza** silliness; **Sciocchèzze!** Nonsense!
**sciòcco** silly, foolish
**sciovíe** ski lifts
**scíppo** bag snatching
**sciròppo** syrup
**scottatúra solàre** sunburn
**scrívere** to write
**scúro** dark
**scusàre** to excuse; **Mi scúsi!** Excuse me!

**sdraiársi** to lie down, to stretch; **Si sdràì!** Lie down!
**seccatúra** nuisance; **Ma che seccatúra!** What a nuisance!
**sécco** dry
**secóndo** second
**sèdano** celery
**sedatívo** sedative
**sedére** to sit, to be sitting; **Vòglio sedérmi** I want to sit
**sèdia** chair; **sèdia a sdràio** chaise longue
**sédici** sixteen
**ségala** rye
**seggiovia** chairlift
**seguíre** to follow
**sèi** six
**seicènto** six hundred
**selezióne** selection; **telefonàta in teleselezióne** long-distance call
**selvaggína** game
**semàforo** traffic light
**sémola** bran; **pàne integràle** whole wheat (whole meal) bread
**sentièro** path, pathway
**sentíre** to feel, to hear; **Non mi sènto bène** I don't feel well
**sènape** mustard
**sènza** without
**séppia** squid
**séra** evening, night; **buòna séra** good evening
**serbatóio** fuel tank
**sèrie** series; **in série A** major league (sport)
**servíre** to serve
**servízio** service; **servízi di traspòrti púbblici** public transportation
**sessànta** sixty
**séte** thirst; **ho séte** I'm thirsty
**settànta** seventy
**sètte** seven; **sètte e mèzzo** blackjack (card game)
**settecènto** seven hundred
**settimàna** week
**sèttimo** seventh
**shampoo** shampoo; **shampoo e méssa in pièga** wash and set
**sherry** sherry
**si** one, they, people, oneself, himself, herself, themselves
**sí** yes
**sídro** cider
**sigarétta** cigarette
**sígaro** cigar
**significàre** to mean, to signify; **Che còsa significa quésto?** What does this mean?
**signóra** lady, wife, Mrs.
**signóre** gentleman, Mr. (use *signór* when addressing the person); **Signór Róssi, come stà?** Mr. Rossi, how are you?
**signorína** young lady, Miss
**silènzio** silence
**sinagòga** synagogue
**sinístro** left, left-hand; **a sinístra** to the left
**sistèma** system
**slip** man's briefs, shorts
**slogàre** to sprain
**smàlto** enamel; **smàlto per le únghie** nail polish
**smeràldo** emerald
**soccórso** help, aid; **prónto soccórso** first aid
**sògliola** sole (fish)
**sòldi** money
**sóle** sun
**sólo** alone
**sópra** on, upon, upstairs
**sopràbito** overcoat
**sopràno** soprano
**sorèlla** sister
**sorrídere** to smile
**sósta** stop; **divièto di sósta** no parking

**sottopassaggio** underpass
**sottotítolo** subtitle
**sottovèste** slip, undergarment
**souvenir** souvenir
**spàlla** shoulder
**spàzzola** brush
**spazzolíno per i dènti** toothbrush
**spècchio** mirror
**specialità** specialty
**spedíre** to send, to mail
**spésso** often
**spettàcolo** show
**spiàggia** beach
**spíccioli** small change
**spílla** brooch
**spína per la corrènte** electric plug
**spinàci** spinach
**spíngere** to push
**splèndido** wonderful
**spogliàre** to undress
**spòrco** dirty
**sportèllo** window (bank, post office, ticket office)
**sportívo** sporting; **una màcchina sportíva** a sports car
**sposàto(a)** married
**spúgna** sponge
**spumànte** sparkling wine
**spuntàre** to trim
**sputàre** to spit
**squàdra** team
**stàdio** stadium
**stagióne** season
**stàgno** pond
**stàlla** barn
**stànco(a)** tired; **Mi sènto stànco** I'm tired
**stàre** to be, to stay, to remain
**staséra** this evening
**stazióne** station
**stécca** carton
**sterlíne** pounds (British pound sterling)
**stésso** same
**stiràre** to iron; **che non si stíra** permanent press
**stitichézza** constipation
**stivàle** boot
**stòmaco** stomach
**stórto** twisted
**stràda** street, road
**strétto** tight, narrow
**stríngere** to tighten
**stupèndo(a)** wonderful
**stúpido(a)** stupid; **Non èssere stúpido!** Don't be stupid!
**stuzzicadènti** toothpicks
**su** on, upon, up, upstairs
**súbito** at once, right away
**succèdere** to happen; **Che còsa succède?** What's up?
**suòle** soles (shoes)
**supermercàto** supermarket
**surf (tàvola da surf)** surf
**surriscaldàre** to overheat
**susína** plum
**svéndita** sale
**sveglìare** to wake up
**sveníre** to faint
**sviluppàre** to develop

# T

**tabacchería** tobacco shop
**tabàcco** tobacco
**tacchíno** turkey
**tàcchi** heels (shoes)
**taccuíno** notebook
**tàglia** size
**taglìare** to cut; **un tàglio di capélli** a haircut
**tagliaúnghie** nail clippers
**tàlco** talcum powder
**tampóni igiènici** sanitary tampons
**tànto** a lot, much
**tàrdi** late; **a più tàrdi** see you later; **al più tàrdi** at the latest
**taríffa** tariff, rate, fare
**tàxi** taxi

**tàvola** table
**tàzza** cup
**tè** tea
**teàtro** theater
**telefonàre** to telephone
**telefonàta** phone call; **interurbàna** long-distance; **teleselezióne** long-distance; **urbàna** local; **con prevvíso** person-to-person; **riversíbile** reverse-charge
**telèfono** telephone; **cabína telefónica** telephone booth; **elènco telefónico** telephone directory
**televisióne** television
**temperamatíte** pencil sharpener
**temperatúra** temperature
**tèmpo** time, weather
**temporaneamènte** temporarily
**tènnis** tennis
**tenóre** tenor
**tergicristàllo** windshield wiper
**termòmetro** thermometer
**tèrra** earth, land
**terràzza** terrace
**terríbile** terrible
**terzíno** fullback (sport)
**tèrzo** third
**tèssera** card, ticket, pass, identification card
**tèsta** head
**ti** you, yourself
**tínta uníta** solid color
**tintoría** dry cleaner
**tintúra** dye; **tintúra di iódio** tincture of iodine
**títolo** title
**toccàre** to touch
**toilette** rest room
**tònico** tonic
**tonsílle** tonsils
**tónno** tuna
**topàzio** topaz
**tornàre** to return, to come back
**tórta** cake, pie
**tósse** cough
**tossíre** to cough
**tour** trip, excursion
**tovàglia** tablecloth
**tovagliòlo** napkin
**transformatore** transformer
**tránsito** transit; **divièto di tránsito** no entrance
**tranvài** streetcar
**trascórrere** to spend, to pass
**trasmissióne** transmission
**trattoría** inn, tavern
**traversàta** crossing
**tre** three
**trecènto** three hundred
**trédici** thirteen
**trèno** train
**trènta** thirty
**trentúno** thirty-one
**trentadúe** thirty-two
**tròta** trout
**trúcco** makeup
**tu** you
**turchése** turquoise
**túbo di scappamènto** exhaust pipe
**turístico** for tourists
**túttо(a)** all, everything; **túttа l'estàte** all summer

# U

**uccèllo** bird
**uffício** office; **uffício postàle** post office
**último(a)** last
**úndici** eleven
**università** university
**un, úno, úna, un'** an, a, one
**uòvo** egg; **uòva sode** hard-cooked eggs; _____ **strapazzàte** scrambled eggs; _____ **alla coque** soft-boiled eggs

**urbàno** urban
**uscíre** to go out; **Esca!** Get out!
**uscíta** exit, gate
**ustióne** burn

# V

**vacànza** vacation
**vàglia** money order
**vagóne** railroad car; **vagóne lètto** sleeping car
**valígia** suitcase
**vallàta** valley
**valúta** currency
**vaníglia** vanilla
**vedére** to see
**vellúto** velvet
**velóce** fast; **più velóce** faster
**véndere** to sell
**venerdì** Friday
**vénti** twenty
**ventidúe** twenty-two
**ventimíla** twenty thousand
**vènto** wind; **Tíra vènto** It's windy
**ventàglio** fan
**ventúno** twenty-one
**vérde** green
**vèro** true, real
**vèspa** motor scooter
**vestàglia** robe
**vèste** dress
**vestírsi** to get dressed; **Si vèsta!** Get dressed!
**vestíto** dress, suit
**vetrína** shop window
**vétro** glass; **vétro soffiàto** blown glass
**vía** street, way; **vía aèrea** airmail
**viàggio** trip
**vicíno** near, next to
**vietàto** forbidden; **vietàto sputàre** no spitting
**villàggio** village
**villíno** cottage
**víncere** to win
**víno** wine
**vísita** visit
**vitamína** vitamin
**víte** screw
**vitèllo** calf; **cotoléttе di vitèllo** veal cutlets
**volànte** steering wheel
**volére** to want, to wish; **Vorrèi** _____ I'd like _____
**vólo** flight
**vòlta** time; **úna vòlta** once
**voltaggio** voltage
**vóngole** clams

# Z

**zàffiro** sapphire
**zèro** zero
**zía** aunt
**zío** uncle
**Zítto!** Shut up!
**zóna** zone, area
**zòo** zoo; **giardíno zoològico** zoological garden
**zúcchero** sugar

# INDEX

abbreviations, 260–261
accidents, 96–102, 206–208
*affittacamere*, 35
*agroturismo*, 35
air travel:
  carriers, 73
  flights within country, 73–75
*albergo* or hotel, 34
*albergo diurno*, 34
annoyances, 13–15
*appartamenti*/condo, 35
appetizers, 133
appliances, 186
area codes, 236
art, 170–173
arts and crafts, 170–172
ATMs, 27
*autogrill*, 127
automobile. *See* car

baggage, 23–25
ballet, 103–105
banks and banking. *See also* money
  hours of operation, 26
  terms, 30–31
bar/snack bar, 127
barber, 202–203
beach, 116–117
beauty parlor, 204–206
beverages, 148–149
boat. *See* ship
books, 176–177
breakfast, 47–48
bus, 38, 47, 54, 84
business dictionary, 263–267
business services, 246–248

*cabine*, 35
calendar, 253–255
camera, 194–195, 209
camping, 36, 123–124
car:
  accidents, 96–102
  driving information, 5–6, 85–92
  gasoline, 4–5, 92–93
  parking, 90–91
  parts of, 98–102
  rentals, 87–90
  repairs, 96–102
  road signs, 94–95
  service station, 85, 92–93, 96
Catania, 56
cheeses, 142–143, 188
churches:
  religious services, 71–72
  sightseeing, 65
cigarettes, 198–199
climate. *See* weather
clothing, 177–185
colloquialisms, 11–12
commercial terms, 263–267
communications, 7–8
complaints, 50–52
computers, 242–246
concerts, 103–107
conversation, 164–169

countryside, 125–126
crafts, 170–172, 196–197
currency, 3, 26–30
customs, 4, 20–22

dancing, 107–108
dating, 167–169
days, 253
dentist, 223–225
desserts, 144–145
dinner, 129
disabilities, 44–47
doctor, 214–221
documentation, 4
dry cleaning, 207–208

electrical appliances, 4, 186
e-mail, 244, 247
emergencies, 12, 234
entrees, 135–140
exchanging money, 28–30
exclamations, 11–12
expressions, 6–7

faxes, 240–241, 246
film, 193
fish, 135–136
flea markets, 172–173
Florence, 68, 72
food:
  breakfast, 47–48
  dietary restrictions, 145–147
  dining out, 130–133
  dinner, 129
  general types of, 173–174
  lunch, 129
  preparation of, 138–140
  problems, 147
  regional specialties, 150–159
  service, 149–150
foreign embassies, 23
fractions, 19
fruits, 143–144

gasoline, 4–5, 92–93
glasses, 225–227
golf, 123
good-byes, 169
grammar, 268–283

holidays, 258
hospitals, 221–223
hostels, 33
hotels:
  associations, 32–33
  breakfast, 47–48
  checking in/out, 39–43, 52
  complaints, 50–51
  general information, 5
  room service, 50–51
  services offered, 48–49
  special needs for disabled, 44–47
  staff, 49–50
  toiletries, 49–50, 199–201
  transportation to, 38–39
*hotel a 4 zampe*, 36
*hotel per bambini e famiglia*, 36

identity card, 22
Internet, 243, 245–248
introductions, 7–8

jet lag, 2
jewelry, 190–191

laundry, 207–208
*letto e colazione*, 37
*locanda*, 34
locations, 8–10
lodging, 33–38. *See also* Hotels
luggage, 23–25
lunch, 129

magazines, 195
mail, 230–232
measurements:
  clothing, 184
  distance, 93
  liquid, 92, 189, 263
  metric, 261–262
  solid, 189
meat, 136–140
meals, different types of, 47–48, 127–129, 133–138, 150–159
medical care, 5, 210–221
menu, 129
Milan, 55, 68, 72
*monasteri*, 37
money. *See also* banks and banking
  ATMs, 27
  exchanging, 28–30
  national currency, 3, 26
  tipping, 52–53
months, 254–255
motel, 34
movies, 103–105, 192–194
music, 103–108

Naples, 56, 70
newspapers, 195
nightclubs, 107–108
numbers, 16–19
nuts, 143–144

opera, 103–107
optician, 225–227

*paninotéca*, 127
papal audience, 5
parking, 90–91
passport, 20–21
pasta, 134–135
*pensione*, 34
pharmacies, 210–213, 227–229
photocopies, 241, 248
pizzeria, 127
pool, 116–117
population, 3
porters, 23–25
post office, 230–232
pronunciation guide, 1–2

quantities, 19
questions, 11

religious services, 71–72
renting a car, 87–90
repairs:
  car, 96–102
  shoe, 208
  road signs, 85, 94–95
*rifugi*, 37
*ristorante*, 128
Rome, 57, 67–68, 70
*rosticceria*, 127

Sardinia, 70
seasonings, 141–142
seasons, 255
service station, 92–93, 96
ship, 82–84
shoe repair, 208
shopping, 10, 170–185
  sales tax, 160
Sicily, 70
sightseeing, 64–71
signs and symbols:
  driving, 94–95
  important types of, 259–260
  road, 85, 94–95
  shopping-related, 182
  trains, 76–77
skiing, 118–123
soccer, 109–110
socializing, 164–169
soups, 134
souvenirs, 196–197
sports, 109–123
stationery, 197–198
subway, 55–59
symbols. *See* signs and symbols

*tavola calda*, 127
taxi, 38, 61–63
telephones, 232–240, 246–248
temperature, 256
tennis, 114–115
theater, 103–105
tickets:
  plane, 25, 74, 249
  opera, theater, 105
  train, 75–81
time, 250–252
tipping, 52–53
tobacco, 198–199
toiletries, 49, 199–201
trains:
  general information, 75–80
  ticket purchase, 75, 77, 78–81
  types of, 75–77
transportation:
  bus, 38, 54, 59–61
  car. *See* car
  hotel, to, 38–39
  subway, 55–59
  taxi, 38, 61–63
  train, 75–82
  types of, 54
*trattorie*, 127
trouble, 14–15

vegetables, 140–141
Venice, 68–69
*ville*, 38
visa, 4

weather, 3, 256–257
wine, 160–163

youth hostels, 33

BOLOGNA
N
Viale P. Pietramellara
Via Amendola
Via C. Boldrini
Viale Angelo Masini
Via Stalingrado
Via Milazzo
Via Serra
La Piazzola
Via del Pallone
Via Capo di Lucca
Mura P. ta Galliera
Viale Carlo
Piazza dei Martiri
Via Galliera
Via del Mille
Parco della Montagnola
Via Marconi
Via del Porto
Via Mascarella
Via del Borgo S. Pietro
Piazza Otto Agosto
Via Imerio
Via Menotti
Via Riva di Reno
Via A. Righi
Via dell'Indipendenza
Centrorreccento
Pinacoteca Nazionale
Via Belle Arti
Via Zamboni
Via de Castagnoli
Via Nazario Sauro
Via S. Giorgio
Via Marsala
Via Goito
Chiesa Metropolitana di S. Pietro
Basilica di San Martino
Teatro Comunale
Piazza Verdi
Via Ugo Bassi
Altabella
Palazzo Comunale
Via Rizzoli
Piazza Porta
Via San Vitale
Due Torri
Piazza Maggiore
Chiesa di S. Salvatore
Basilica di San Petronio
Strada Maggiore
Via Broccaindosso
Chiesa di S.G. Battista Oratorio
Archiginnasio
Via Farini
Basilica di S. Stefano
Via Guerrazzi
Basilica di S. Maria dei Servi
Via Castiglione
Chiesa di San Procolo
Via Tagliapietre
Piazza San Domenico
Via Rialto
Via Santo Stefano
Via Tovaglie
Viale XII Giugno
Via de Coltelli
Via Fondazza
Via Arienti
Via Orfeo
Viale E. Panzacchi
Santuario della Mad. del Baraccano
Viale G. Gozzadini
0 2.5 km. 5 km.
0 1.5 mi. 3 mi.

VENICE
Rio San Martino
Samoughe
Campocroce
A4
E70
Boschetta
Condula
Scorzè
Zona Industriale Scorzè
Cappella
Peseggia
Gardigiano
Mogliano Veneto
Golf Ca' Della Nave
Olmara
Ghetto
SS13
Cornarotta
Sant'Elena
Martellago
Capitello
Robegano
Marocco
Salzano
Trivignano
Maerne
Lugatti
Ca' Trevisan
Zona Industriale Cayino
Terraglio
E55
Olmo
Zelarino
Luneo
Zigaraga
Rossignago
SS13
Orgnano
Fossa
Spinea
Gazzera
Mirano
Mestre
Graspo d'Uva
E70
Crea
Chirignago
A4
Fornase
Marghera
Gidoni
Trescievoli
SS309
Marano
Malpaga
Zona Artigianale Oriago Nord
A57
E55
Borbiago
Oriago
Zona Industriale Porto Marghera
Zona Industriale Miralanza
Mira
Malcontenta
Molin Rotto
Moranzani
Gambarare
Piazza Vecchia
Dogaletto
Idrovia
SS309
E55
Curano

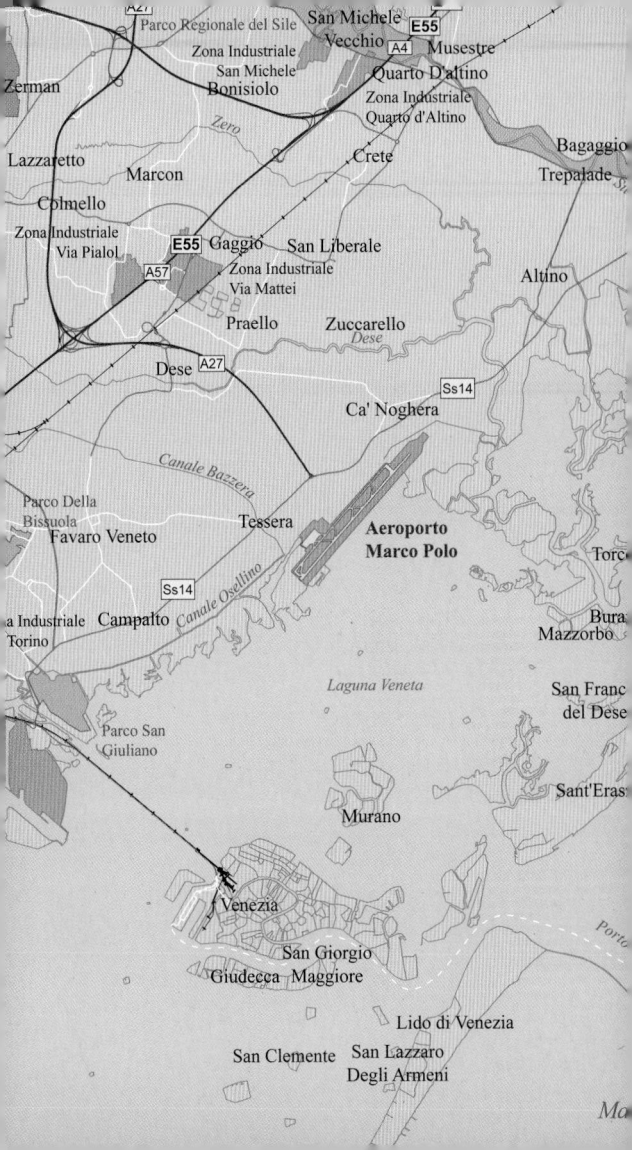
A27
Parco Regionale del Sile
San Michele
Vecchio
E55
A4
Musestre
Zona Industriale
San Michele
Bonisiolo
Quarto D'altino
Zerman
Zona Industriale
Quarto d'Altino
Zero
Bagaggio
Lazzaretto
Crete
Marcon
Trepalade
Colmello
Zona Industriale
Via Pialol
E55
Gaggio
San Liberale
A57
Zona Industriale
Via Mattei
Altino
Praello
Zuccarello
Dese
Dese
A27
Ss14
Ca' Noghera
Canale Bazzera
Parco Della
Bissuola
Tessera
Aeroporto
Marco Polo
Favaro Veneto
Torc
Ss14
Canale Osellino
a Industriale
Torino
Campalto
Bura
Mazzorbo
Laguna Veneta
San Franc
del Dese
Parco San
Giuliano
Sant'Eras
Murano
Venezia
Porto
San Giorgio
Giudecca
Maggiore
Lido di Venezia
San Clemente
San Lazzaro
Degli Armeni
Ma

MILAN
E35
E62
Innova Business Park
Grancia
Parco delle Groane
Castellazzo
Cassina Nuova
Cascina del Sole
Bollate
SP46
SS33
Cascina Papis
A8
SP233
Rho
Mazzo
Novate Milanese
Zona Industriale Alcide de Gasperi
Baranzate
Cerchiarello
Cerchiate
Lucernate
A4
E64
Pero
Cimitero Maggiore
Zona Industriale Via Carlo Pisacane
Cornaredo
Vighignolo
Figino
SS11
Bosco In Città
Parco di Trenno
Ippodromo di San Siro
Settimo Milanese
A50
Quinto Romano
Z. I. Via E. Fermi
Seguro
Villaggio Cavour
SP162
Parco Agricolo
Monzoro
Z.I. di Villaggio Cavour
Cusago
Cascina
Zona Industriale Cusago
Cesano Boscone
Via Lorenteggio
SS494
Robarello
Corsico
Quartiere Tessera
Buccinasco
Zona Industriale Tangenziale Ovest
San Vito
Bazzana Superiore
Zona Industriale Assago
Bonirola
Gaggiano
Assago
A7
SP38
SP139
SP184
Vallean
San Novo
Cascina Bazzanella
Cassino Scanasio
Barate
Vigano
SP203
San Pietro Cusico
Rozza

Cinisello Balsamo
A52
A4
E64
Brugherio
Cusano
Milanino
San Maurizio
Al Lambro
Aeroporto
di Bresso
Bresso
A52
Sesto San Giovanni
SP113
Cologno
Monzese
Parco
Nord
Milano
Molinetto C.C.
SS11
Vimodrone
Villaggio
Ambrosiano
A51
Milano Due
Rovagnasco
Viale Marche
Parco
Lambro
Milano Oltre
Lavanderie
Segrate
Rugaces
Redecesio
Corso
Venezia
Acquario
Tregarezzo
San Felice
Teatro Alla Scala
Parco
Forlanini
Novegro
La Scala
Piazza Duomo
Milano
Idroscalo
Aeroporto
di Linate
Porta
Romana
Viale Umbria
Linate
Mezzate
Ponte Lambro
Canzo
Zeloforomagno
SS9
Zona Industria
di Foramagno
San Donato
Milanese
Bellaria
Robbia
SS412
Chiaravalle
Milanese
A1
Lambro
Sorigherio
Poasco
Zona Industriale
di Civesio
Carpianello
Parco Agricolo
Sud Milano
Noverasco
Sesto Ulteriano
Civesio
San Giuliano
Milanese
A50
E35
Zivido
Zona Industriale
Sesto Ulteriano
Viboldone
Ponte Sesto
SS412
SP164

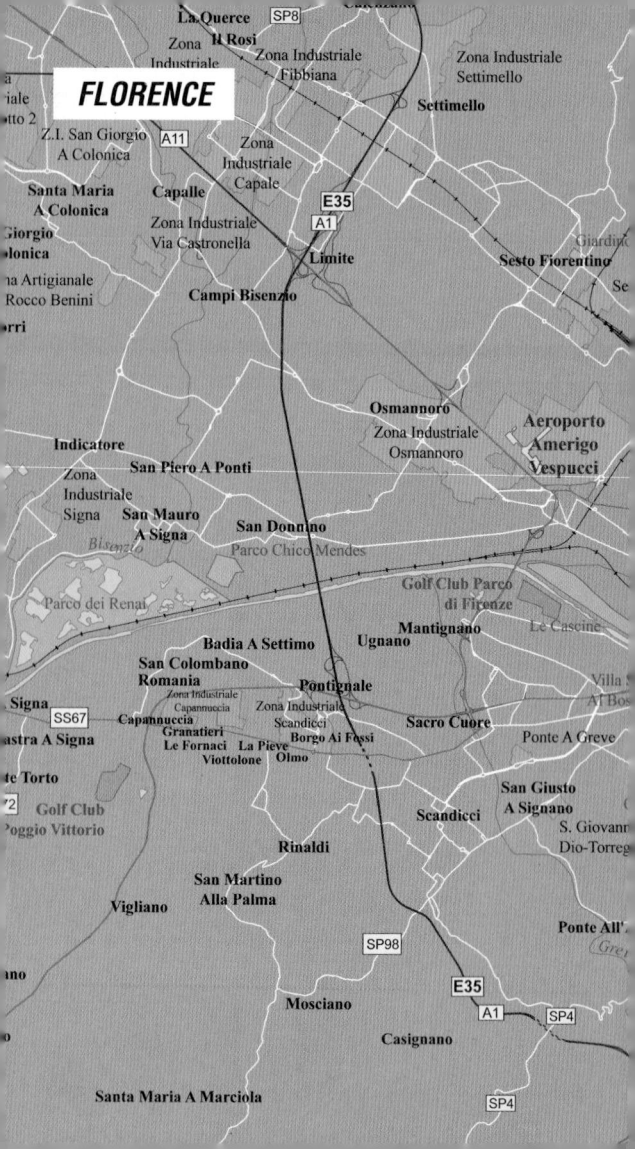
FLORENCE
La Querce
SP8
Il Rosi
Zona Industriale
Zona Industriale Fibbiana
Zona Industriale Settimello
Settimello
Z.I. San Giorgio A Colonica
A11
Zona Industriale Capale
Santa Maria A Colonica
Capalle
E35
A1
Zona Industriale Via Castronella
Limite
Sesto Fiorentino
Campi Bisenzio
Osmannoro
Zona Industriale Osmannoro
Aeroporto Amerigo Vespucci
Indicatore
San Piero A Ponti
Zona Industriale Signa
San Mauro A Signa
San Donnino
Parco Chico Mendes
Golf Club Parco di Firenze
Parco dei Renai
Mantignano
Ugnano
Badia A Settimo
San Colombano Romania
Pontignale
Zona Industriale
Zona Industriale Capannuccia
SS67
Capannuccia
Granatieri
Le Fornaci
La Pieve
Olmo
Viottolone
Scandicci
Borgo Ai Fossi
Sacro Cuore
Ponte A Greve
San Giusto A Signano
Scandicci
Golf Club
Rinaldi
San Martino Alla Palma
Vigliano
SP98
E35
A1
SP4
Mosciano
Casignano
Santa Maria A Marciola
SP4